The Philosophy of Poverty

Pierre-Joseph Proudhon

Originally published in 1847.

Large Print Edition published 2015 by Skyler J. Collins.
Visit: www.skylerjcollins.com
ISBN-13: 978-1514226872
ISBN-10: 1514226871

Contents

Introduction. The hypothesis of a God

Before entering upon the subject-matter of these new memoirs, I must explain an hypothesis which will undoubtedly seem strange, but in the absence of which it is impossible for me to proceed intelligibly: I mean the hypothesis of a God.

To suppose God, it will be said, is to deny him. Why do you not affirm him?

Is it my fault if belief in Divinity has become a suspected opinion; if the bare suspicion of a Supreme Being is already noted as evidence of a weak mind; and if, of all philosophical Utopias, this is the only one which the world no longer tolerates? Is it my fault if hypocrisy and imbecility everywhere hide behind this holy formula?

Let a public teacher suppose the existence, in the universe, of an unknown force governing suns and atoms, and keeping the whole machine in motion. With him this supposition, wholly gratuitous, is perfectly natural; it is received, encouraged: witness attraction — an hypothesis which will never be verified, and which, nevertheless, is the glory of its originator. But when, to explain the course of human events, I suppose, with all imaginable caution, the intervention of a God, I am sure to shock scientific gravity and offend critical ears: to so wonderful an extent has our piety discredited Providence, so many tricks have been played by means of this dogma or fiction by charlatans of every stamp! I have seen the theists of my time, and blasphemy has played over my lips; I have studied the belief of the people, — this people that Brydaine called the best friend of God, — and have shuddered at the negation which was about to escape me. Tormented by conflicting feelings, I appealed to reason; and it is reason which, amid so many dogmatic contradictions, now forces the hypothesis upon me. A priori dogmatism, applying itself to God, has proved fruitless: who knows whither the hypothesis, in its turn, will lead us?

I will explain therefore how, studying in the silence of my heart, and far from every human consideration, the mystery of social revolutions, God, the great unknown, has become for me an hypothesis, — I mean a necessary dialectical tool.

I.

If I follow the God-idea through its successive transformations, I find that this idea is preeminently social: I mean by this that it is much more a collective act of faith than an individual conception. Now, how and under what circumstances is this act of faith produced? This point it is important to determine.

From the moral and intellectual point of view, society, or the collective man, is especially distinguished from the individual by spontaneity of action, — in other words, instinct. While the individual obeys, or imagines he obeys, only those motives of which he is fully conscious, and upon which he can at will decline or consent to act; while, in a word, he thinks himself free, and all the freer when he knows that he is possessed of keener reasoning faculties and larger information, — society is governed by impulses which, at first blush, exhibit no deliberation and design, but which gradually seem to be directed by a superior power, existing outside of society, and pushing it with irresistible might toward an unknown goal. The establishment of monarchies and republics, caste-distinctions, judicial institutions, etc., are so many manifestations of this social spontaneity, to note the effects of which is much easier than to point out its principle and show its cause. The whole effort, even of those who, following Bossuet, Vico, Herder, Hegel, have applied themselves to the philosophy of history, has been hitherto to establish the presence of a providential destiny presiding over all the movements of man. And I observe, in this connection, that society never fails to evoke its genius previous to action: as if it wished the powers above to ordain what its own spontaneity has already resolved on. Lots, oracles, sacrifices, popular acclamation, public prayers, are the commonest forms of these tardy deliberations of society.

This mysterious faculty, wholly intuitive, and, so to speak, super-social, scarcely or not at all perceptible in persons, but which hovers over humanity like an inspiring genius, is the primordial fact of all psychology.

Now, unlike other species of animals, which, like him, are governed at the same time by individual desires and collective impulses, man has the privilege of perceiving and designating to his own mind the instinct or fatum which leads him; we shall see later that he has also the power of foreseeing and even influencing its decrees. And the first act of man, filled and carried away with enthusiasm (of the divine breath), is to adore the invisible Providence on which he feels that he depends, and which he calls GOD, — that is, Life, Being, Spirit, or, simpler still, Me; for all these words, in the ancient tongues, are synonyms and homophones.

"I am Me," God said to Abraham, "and I covenant with Thee." . . . And to Moses: "I am the Being. Thou shalt say unto the children of Israel, 'The Being hath sent me unto you.'" These two words, the Being and Me, have in the original language — the most religious that men have ever spoken — the same characteristic.[1] Elsewhere, when Ie-hovah, acting as law-giver through the instrumentality of Moses, attests his eternity and swears by his own essence, he uses, as a form of oath, I; or else, with redoubled force, I, the Being. Thus the God of the Hebrews is the most personal and wilful of all the gods, and none express better than he the intuition of humanity.

God appeared to man, then, as a me, as a pure and permanent essence, placing himself before him as a monarch before his servant, and expressing himself now through the mouth of poets, legislators, and soothsayers, musa, nomos, numen; now through the popular voice, vox populi vox Dei. This may serve, among other things, to explain the existence of true and false oracles; why individuals secluded from birth do not attain of themselves to the idea of God, while they eagerly grasp it as soon as it is presented to them by the collective mind; why, finally, stationary races, like the Chinese, end by losing it.[2] In the first place, as to oracles, it is clear that all their accuracy depends upon the universal conscience which inspires them; and, as to the idea of God, it is easily seen why isolation and statu quo are alike fatal to it. On the one hand, absence of communication keeps the mind absorbed in animal self-contemplation; on the other, absence of motion, gradually changing social life into mechanical routine, finally eliminates the idea

---

Ie-hovah, and in composition Iah, the Being; Iao, ioupitur, same meaning; ha-iah, Heb., he was; ei, Gr, he is, ei-nai, to be; an-i, Heb., and in conjugation th-i, me; e-go, io, ich, i, m-i, me, t-ibi, te, and all the personal pronouns in which the vowels i, e, ei, oi, denote personality in general, and the consonants, m or n, s or t, serve to indicate the number of the person. For the rest, let who will dispute over these analogies; I have no objections: at this depth, the science of the philologist is but cloud and mystery. The important point to which I wish to call attention is that the phonetic relation of names seems to correspond to the metaphysical relation of ideas.

The Chinese have preserved in their traditions the remembrance of a religion which had ceased to exist among them five or six centuries before our era. (See Pauthier, "China," Paris, Didot.) More surprising still is it that this singular people, in losing its primitive faith, seems to have understood that divinity is simply the collective me of humanity: so that, more than two thousand years ago, China had reached, in its commonly-accepted belief, the latest results of the philosophy of the Occident. "What Heaven sees and understands," it is written in the Shu-king, "is only that which the people see and understand. What the people deem worthy of reward and punishment is that which Heaven wishes to punish and reward. There is an intimate communication between Heaven and the people: let those who govern the people, therefore, be watchful and cautious." Confucius expressed the same idea in another manner: "Gain the affection of the people, and you gain empire. Lose the affection of the people, and you lose empire." There, then, general reason was regarded as queen of the world, a distinction which elsewhere has been bestowed upon revelations. The Tao-te-king is still more explicit. In this work, which is but an outline criticism of pure reason, the philosopher Lao-tse continually identifies, under the name of TAO, universal reason and the infinite being; and all the obscurity of the book of Lao tse consists, in my opinion, of this constant identification of principles which our religious and metaphysical habits have so widely separated.

6

of will and providence. Strange fact! religion, which perishes through progress, perishes also through quiescence.

Notice further that, in attributing to the vague and (so to speak) objectified consciousness of a universal reason the first revelation of Divinity, we assume absolutely nothing concerning even the reality or non-reality of God. In fact, admitting that God is nothing more than collective instinct or universal reason, we have still to learn what this universal reason is in itself. For, as we shall show directly, universal reason is not given in individual reason, in other words, the knowledge of social laws, or the theory of collective ideas, though deduced from the fundamental concepts of pure reason, is nevertheless wholly empirical, and never would have been discovered a priori by means of deduction, induction, or synthesis. Whence it follows that universal reason, which we regard as the origin of these laws; universal reason, which exists, reasons, labors, in a separate sphere and as a reality distinct from pure reason, just as the planetary system, though created according to the laws of mathematics, is a reality distinct from mathematics, whose existence could not have been deduced from mathematics alone: it follows, I say, that universal reason is, in modern languages, exactly what the ancients called God. The name is changed: what do we know of the thing?

Let us now trace the evolution of the Divine idea.

The Supreme Being once posited by a primary mystical judgment, man immediately generalizes the subject by another mysticism, — analogy. God, so to speak, is as yet but a point: directly he shall fill the world.

As, in sensing his social me, man saluted his Author, so, in finding evidence of design and intention in animals, plants, springs, meteors, and the whole universe, he attributes to each special object, and then to the whole, a soul, spirit, or genius presiding over it; pursuing this inductive process of apotheosis from the highest summit of Nature, which is society, down to the humblest forms of life, to inanimate and inorganic matter. From his collective me, taken as the superior pole of creation, to the last atom of matter, man extends, then, the idea of God, — that is, the idea of personality and intelligence, — just as God himself extended heaven, as the book of Genesis tells us; that is, created space and time, the conditions of all things.

Thus, without a God or master-builder, the universe and man would not exist: such is the social profession of faith. But also without man God would not be thought, or — to clear the interval — God would be nothing. If humanity needs an author, God and the gods equally need a revealer; theogony, the history of heaven, hell, and their inhabitants, — those dreams of the human mind, — is the counterpart of the universe, which certain philosophers have called in return the dream of God. And how magnificent this theological creation, the work of society!

The creation of the demiourgos was obliterated; what we call the Omnipotent was conquered; and for centuries the enchanted imagination of mortals was turned away from the spectacle of Nature by the contemplation of Olympian marvels.

Let us descend from this fanciful region: pitiless reason knocks at the door; her terrible questions demand a reply.

"What is God?" she asks; "where is he? what is his extent? what are his wishes? what his powers? what his promises?" — and here, in the light of analysis, all the divinities of heaven, earth, and hell are reduced to an incorporeal, insensible, immovable, incomprehensible, undefinable I-know-not-what; in short, to a negation of all the attributes of existence. In fact, whether man attributes to each object a special spirit or genius, or conceives the universe as governed by a single power, he in either case but SUPPOSES an unconditioned, that is, an impossible, entity, that he may deduce therefrom an explanation of such phenomena as he deems inconceivable on any other hypothesis. The mystery of God and reason! In order to render the object of his idolatry more and more rational, the believer despoils him successively of all the qualities which would make him real; and, after marvellous displays of logic and genius, the attributes of the Being par excellence are found to be the same as those of nihility. This evolution is inevitable and fatal: atheism is at the bottom of all theodicy.

Let us try to understand this progress.

God, creator of all things, is himself no sooner created by the conscience, — in other words, no sooner have we lifted God from the idea of the social me to the idea of the cosmic me, — than immediately our reflection begins to demolish him under the pretext of perfecting him. To perfect the idea of God, to purify the theological dogma, was the second hallucination of the human race.

The spirit of analysis, that untiring Satan who continually questions and denies, must sooner or later look for proof of religious dogmas. Now, whether the philosopher determine the idea of God, or declare it indeterminable; whether he approach it with his reason, or retreat from it, — I say that this idea receives a blow; and, as it is impossible for speculation to halt, the idea of God must at last disappear. Then the atheistic movement is the second act of the theologic drama; and this second act follows from the first, as effect from cause. "The heavens declare the glory of God," says the Psalmist. Let us add, And their testimony dethrones him.

Indeed, in proportion as man observes phenomena, he thinks that he perceives, between Nature and God, intermediaries; such as relations of number, form, and succession; organic laws, evolutions, analogies, — forming an unmistakable series of manifestations which invariably produce or give rise to each other. He even observes that, in the development of this society of which he is a part, private wills and associative deliberations have some influence; and he says to himself that the

Great Spirit does not act upon the world directly and by himself, or arbitrarily and at the dictation of a capricious will, but mediately, by perceptible means or organs, and by virtue of laws. And, retracing in his mind the chain of effects andcauses, he places clear at the extremity, as a balance, God.

A poet has said, —

Par dela tous les cieux, le Dieu des cieux reside.

Thus, at the first step in the theory, the Supreme Being is reduced to the function of a motive power, a mainspring, a corner-stone, or, if a still more trivial comparison may be allowed me, a constitutional sovereign, reigning but not governing, swearing to obey the law and appointing ministers to execute it. But, under the influence of the mirage which fascinates him, the theist sees, in this ridiculous system, only a new proof of the sublimity of his idol; who, in his opinion, uses his creatures as instruments of his power, and causes the wisdom of human beings to redound to his glory.

Soon, not content with limiting the power of the Eternal, man, increasingly deicidal in his tendencies, insists on sharing it.

If I am a spirit, a sentient me giving voice to ideas, continues the theist, I consequently am a part of absolute existence; I am free, creative, immortal, equal with God. Cogito, ergo sum, — I think, therefore I am immortal, that is the corollary, the translation of Ego sum qui sum: philosophy is in accord with the Bible. The existence of God and the immortality of the soul are posited by the conscience in the same judgment: there, man speaks in the name of the universe, to whose bosom he transports his me; here, he speaks in his own name, without perceiving that, in this going and coming, he only repeats himself.

The immortality of the soul, a true division of divinity, which, at the time of its first promulgation, arriving after a long interval, seemed a heresy to those faithful to the old dogma, has been none the less considered the complement of divine majesty, necessarily postulated by eternal goodness and justice. Unless the soul is immortal, God is incomprehensible, say the theists; resembling in this the political theorists who regard sovereign representation and perpetual tenure of office as essential conditions of monarchy. But the inconsistency of the ideas is as glaring as the parity of the doctrines is exact: consequently the dogma of immortality soon became the stumbling-block of philosophical theologians, who, ever since the days of Pythagoras and Orpheus, have been making futile attempts to harmonize divine attributes with human liberty, and reason with faith. A subject of triumph for the impious!. . . But the illusion could not yield so soon: the dogma of immortality, for the very reason that it was a limitation of the uncreated Being, was a step in advance. Now, though the human mind deceives itself by a partial acquisition of the truth, it never retreats, and this perseverance in progress is proof of its infallibility. Of this we shall soon see fresh evidence.

In making himself like God, man made God like himself: this correlation, which for many centuries had been execrated, was the secret spring which determined the new myth. In the days of the patriarchs God made an alliance with man; now, to strengthen the compact, God is to become a man. He will take on our flesh, our form, our passions, our joys, and our sorrows; will be born of woman, and die as we do. Then, after this humiliation of the infinite, man will still pretend that he has elevated the ideal of his God in making, by a logical conversion, him whom he had always called creator, a saviour, a redeemer. Humanity does not yet say, I am God: such a usurpation would shock its piety; it says, God is in me, IMMANUEL, nobiscum Deus. And, at the moment when philosophy with pride, and universal conscience with fright, shouted with unanimous voice, The gods are departing! excedere deos! a period of eighteen centuries of fervent adoration and superhuman faith was inaugurated.

But the fatal end approaches. The royalty which suffers itself to be limited will end by the rule of demagogues; the divinity which is defined dissolves in a pandemonium. Christolatry is the last term of this long evolution of human thought. The angels, saints, and virgins reign in heaven with God, says the catechism; and demons and reprobates live in the hells of eternal punishment. Ultramundane society has its left and its right: it is time for the equation to be completed; for this mystical hierarchy to descend upon earth and appear in its real character.

When Milton represents the first woman admiring herself in a fountain, and lovingly extending her arms toward her own image as if to embrace it, he paints, feature for feature, the human race. — This God whom you worship, O man! this God whom you have made good, just, omnipotent, omniscient, immortal, and holy, is yourself: this ideal of perfection is your image, purified in the shining mirror of your conscience. God, Nature, and man are three aspects of one and the same being; man is God himself arriving at self-consciousness through a thousand evolutions. In Jesus Christ man recognized himself as God; and Christianity is in reality the religion of God-man. There is no other God than he who in the beginning said, ME; there is no other God than THEE.

Such are the last conclusions of philosophy, which dies in unveiling religion's mystery and its own.

II.

It seems, then, that all is ended; it seems that, with the cessation of the worship and mystification of humanity by itself, the theological problem is for ever put aside. The gods have gone: there is nothing left for man but to grow weary and die in his egoism. What frightful solitude extends around me, and forces its way to the bottom of my soul! My exaltation resembles annihilation; and, since I made myself a God, I seem but a shadow. It is possible that I am still a me, but it is very difficult to regard myself as the absolute; and, if I am not the absolute, I am only half of an idea.

Some ironical thinker, I know not who, has said: "A little philosophy leads away from religion, and much philosophy leads back to it." This proposition is humiliatingly true.

Every science develops in three successive periods, which may be called — comparing them with the grand periods of civilization — the religious period, the sophistical period, the scientific period.[3] Thus, alchemy represents the religious period of the science afterwards called chemistry, whose definitive plan is not yet discovered; likewise astrology was the religious period of another science, since established, — astronomy.

Now, after being laughed at for sixty years about the philosopher's stone, chemists, governed by experience, no longer dare to deny the transmutability of bodies; while astronomers are led by the structure of the world to suspect also an organism of the world; that is, something precisely like astrology. Are we not justified in saying, in imitation of the philosopher just quoted, that, if a little chemistry leads away from the philosopher's stone, much chemistry leads back to it; and similarly, that, if a little astronomy makes us laugh at astrologers, much astronomy will make us believe in them?[4]

---

[3] See, among others, Auguste Comte, "Course of Positive Philosophy," and P. J. Proudhon, "Creation of Order in Humanity."

[4] I do not mean to affirm here in a positive manner the transmutability of bodies, or to point it out as a subject for investigation; still less do I pretend to say what ought to be the opinion of savants upon this point. I wish only to call attention to the species of scepticism generated in every uninformed mind by the most general conclusions of chemical philosophy, or, better, by the irreconcilable hypotheses which serve as the basis of its theories. Chemistry is truly the despair of reason: on all sides it mingles with the fanciful; and the more knowledge of it we gain by experience, the more it envelops itself in impenetrable mysteries. This thought was recently suggested to me by reading M. Liebig's "Letters on Chemistry" (Paris, Masgana, 1845, translation of Bertet-Dupiney and Dubreuil Helion).

Thus M. Liebig, after having banished from science hypothetical causes and all the entities admitted by the ancients, — such as the creative power of matter, the horror of a vacuum, the esprit recteur, etc. (p. 22), — admits immediately, as necessary to the comprehension of chemical phenomena, a series of entities no less obscure, — vital force, chemical force, electric force, the force of attraction, etc. (pp. 146, 149). One might call it a realization of the properties of bodies, in imitation of the psychologists' realization of the faculties of the soul under the names liberty, imagination, memory, etc. Why not keep to the elements? Why, if the atoms have weight of their own, as M. Liebig appears to believe, may they not also have electricity and life of their own? Curious thing! the phenomena of matter, like those of mind, become intelligible only by supposing them to be produced by unintelligible forces and governed by contradictory laws: such is the inference to be drawn from every page of M. Liebig's book.

Matter, according to M. Liebig, is essentially inert and entirely destitute of spontaneous activity (p. 148): why, then, do the atoms have weight? Is not the weight inherent in atoms the real, eternal, and spontaneous motion of matter? And that which we chance to regard as rest, — may it not be equilibrium rather? Why, then, suppose now an inertia which definitions contradict, now an external potentiality which nothing proves?

Atoms having weight, M. Liebig infers that they are indivisible (p. 58). What logic! Weight is only force, that is, a thing hidden from the senses, whose phenomena alone are perceptible, — a thing, consequently, to which the idea of division and indivision is inapplicable; and from the presence of this force, from the hypothesis of an indeterminate and immaterial entity, is inferred an indivisible material existence!

For the rest, M. Liebig confesses that it is impossible for the mind to conceive of particles absolutely indivisible; he recognizes, further, that the fact of this indivisibility is not proved; but he adds that science cannot dispense with this hypothesis: so that, by the confession of its teachers, chemistry has for its point of departure a fiction as repugnant to the mind as it is foreign to experience. What irony!

Atoms are unequal in weight, says M. Liebig, because unequal in volume: nevertheless, it is impossible to demonstrate that chemical equivalents express the relative weight of atoms, or, in other words, that what the calculation of atomic equivalents leads us to regard as an atom is not composed of several atoms. This is tantamount to saying that more matter weighs more than less matter; and, since weight is the essence of materiality, we may logically conclude that, weight being universally identical with itself, there is also an identity in matter; that the differences of simple bodies are due solely, either to different methods of atomic association, or to different degrees of molecular condensation, and that, in reality, atoms are transmutable: which M. Liebig does not admit.

"We have," he says, "no reason for believing that one element is convertible into another element" (p. 135). What do you know about it? The reasons for believing in such a conversion can very well exist and at the same time escape your attention; and it is not certain that your intelligence in this respect has risen to the level of your experience. But, admitting the negative argument of M. Liebig, what follows? That, with about fifty-six exceptions, irreducible as yet, all matter is in a condition of perpetual metamorphosis. Now, it is a law of our reason to suppose in Nature unity of substance as well as unity of force and system; moreover, the series of chemical compounds and simple substances themselves leads us irresistibly to this conclusion. Why, then, refuse to follow to the end the road opened by science, and to admit an hypothesis which is the inevitable result of experience itself?

M. Liebig not only denies the transmutability of elements, but rejects the spontaneous formation of germs. Now, if we reject the spontaneous formation of germs, we are forced to admit their eternity; and as, on the other hand, geology proves that the globe has not been inhabited always, we must admit also that, at a given moment, the eternal germs of animals and plants were born, without father or mother, over the whole face of the earth. Thus, the denial of spontaneous generation leads back to the hypothesis of spontaneity: what is there in much-derided metaphysics more contradictory?

Let it not be thought, however, that I deny the value and certainty of chemical theories, or that the atomic theory seems to me absurd, or that I share the Epicurean opinion as to spontaneous generation. Once more, all that I wish to point out is that, from the point of view of principles, chemistry needs to exercise extreme tolerance, since its own existence depends on a certain number of fictions, contrary to reason and experience, and destructive of each other.

I certainly have less inclination to the marvellous than many atheists, but I cannot help thinking that the stories of miracles, prophecies, charms, etc., are but distorted accounts of the extraordinary effects produced by certain latent forces, or, as was formerly said, by occult powers. Our science is still so brutal and unfair; our professors exhibit so much impertinence with so little knowledge; they deny so impudently facts which embarrass them, in order to protect the opinions which they champion, — that I distrust strong minds equally with superstitious ones. Yes, I am convinced of it; our gross rationalism is the inauguration of a period which, thanks to science, will become truly prodigious; the universe, to my eyes, is only a laboratory of magic, from which anything may be expected... This said, I return to my subject.

They would be deceived, then, who should imagine, after my rapid survey of religious progress, that metaphysics has uttered its last word upon the double enigma expressed in these four words, — the existence of God, the immortality of the soul. Here, as elsewhere, the most advanced and best established conclusions, those which seem to have settled for ever the theological question, lead us back to primeval mysticism, and involve the new data of an inevitable philosophy. The criticism of religious opinions makes us smile today both at ourselves and at religions; and yet the resume of this criticism is but a reproduction of the problem. The human race, at the present moment, is on the eve of recognizing and affirming something equivalent to the old notion of Divinity; and this, not by a spontaneous movement as before, but through reflection and by means of irresistible logic. I will try, in a few words, to make myself understood.

If there is a point on which philosophers, in spite of themselves, have finally succeeded in agreeing, it is without doubt the distinction between intelligence and necessity, the subject of thought and its object, the me and the not-me; in ordinary terms, spirit and matter. I know well that all these terms express nothing that is real and true; that each of them designates only a section of the absolute, which alone is true and real; and that, taken separately, they involve, all alike, a contradiction. But it is no less certain also that the absolute is completely inaccessible to us; that we know it only by its opposite extremes, which alone fall within the limits of our experience; and that, if unity only can win our faith, duality is the first condition of science.

Thus, who thinks, and what is thought? What is a soul? what is a body? I defy any one to escape this dualism. It is with essences as with ideas: the former are seen separated in Nature, as the latter in the understanding; and just as the ideas of God and immortality, in spite of their identity, are posited successively and contradictorily in philosophy, so, in spite of their fusion in the absolute, the me and the not-me posit themselves separately and contradictorily in Nature, and we have beings who think, at the same time with others which do not think.

Now, whoever has taken pains to reflect knows today that such a distinction, wholly realized though it be, is the most unintelligible, most contradictory, most absurd thing which reason can possibly meet. Being is no more conceivable without the properties of spirit than without the properties of matter: so that if you deny spirit, because, included in none of the categories of time, space, motion, solidity, etc., it seems deprived of all the attributes which constitute reality, I in my turn will deny matter, which, presenting nothing appreciable but its inertia, nothing intelligible but its forms, manifests itself nowhere as cause (voluntary and free), and disappears from view entirely as substance; and we arrive at pure idealism, that is, nihility. But nihility is inconsistent with the existence of living, reasoning — I know not what to call them — uniting in themselves, in a state of commenced synthesis or imminent dissolution, all the antagonistic attributes of being. We are compelled, then, to end in a dualism whose terms we know perfectly well to be false, but which, being for us the condition of the truth, forces itself irresistibly upon us; we are compelled, in short, to commence, like Descartes and the human race, with the me; that is, with spirit.

But, since religions and philosophies, dissolved by analysis, have disappeared in the theory of the absolute, we know no better than before what spirit is, and in this differ from the ancients only in the wealth of language with which we adorn the darkness that envelops us. With this exception, however; that while, to the ancients, order revealed intelligence outside of the world, to the people of today it seems to reveal it rather within the world. Now, whether we place it within or without, from the moment we affirm it on the ground of order, we must admit it wherever order is manifested, or deny it altogether. There is no more reason for attributing intelligence to the head which produced the "Iliad" than to a mass of matter which crystallizes in octahedrons; and, reciprocally, it is as absurd to refer the system of the world to physical laws, leaving out an ordaining ME, as to attribute the victory of Marengo to strategic combinations, leaving out the first consul. The only distinction that can be made is that, in the latter case, the thinking ME is located in the brain of a Bonaparte, while, in the case of the universe, the ME has no special location, but extends everywhere.

The materialists think that they have easily disposed of their opponents by saying that man, having likened the universe to his body, finishes the comparison by presuming the existence in the universe of a soul similar to that which he supposes to be the principle of his own life and thought; that thus all the arguments in support of the existence of God are reducible to an analogy all the more false because the term of comparison is itself hypothetical.

It is certainly not my intention to defend the old syllogism: Every arrangement implies an ordaining intelligence; there is wonderful order in the world; then the world is the work of an intelligence. This syllogism, discussed so widely since the days of Job and Moses, very far from being a solution, is but the statement of the problem which it assumes to solve. We know perfectly well what order is, but we are absolutely ignorant of the meaning of the words Soul, Spirit, Intelligence: how, then, can we logically reason from the presence of the one to the existence of the other? I reject, then, even when advanced by the most thoroughly informed, the pretended proof of the existence of God drawn from the presence of order in the world; I see in it at most only an equation offered to philosophy. Between the conception of order and the affirmation of spirit there is a deep gulf of metaphysics to be filled up; I am unwilling, I repeat, to take the problem for the demonstration.

But this is not the point which we are now considering. I have tried to show that the human mind was inevitably and irresistibly led to the distinction of being into me and not-me, spirit and matter, soul and body. Now, who does not see that the objection of the materialists proves the very thing it is intended to deny? Man distinguishing within himself a spiritual principle and a material principle, — what is this but Nature herself, proclaiming by turns her double essence, and bearing testimony to her own laws? And notice the inconsistency of materialism: it denies, and has to deny, that man is free; now, the less liberty man has, the more weight is to be attached to his words, and the greater their claim to be regarded as the expression of truth. When I hear this machine say to me, "I am soul and I am body," though such a revelation astonishes and confounds me, it is invested in my eyes with an authority incomparably greater than that of the materialist who, correcting conscience and Nature, undertakes to make them say, "I am matter and only matter, and intelligence is but the material faculty of knowing."

What would become of this assertion, if, assuming in my turn the offensive, I should demonstrate that belief in the existence of bodies, or, in other words, in the reality of a purely corporeal nature, is untenable? Matter, they say, is impenetrable. — Impenetrable by what? I ask. Itself, undoubtedly; for they would not dare to say spirit, since they would therein admit what they wish to set aside. Whereupon I raise this double question: What do you know about it, and what does it signify?

1. Impenetrability, which is pretended to be the definition of matter, is only an hypothesis of careless naturalists, a gross conclusion deduced from a superficial judgment. Experience shows that matter possesses infinite divisibility, infinite expansibility, porosity without assignable limits, and permeability by heat, electricity, and magnetism, together with a power of retaining them indefinitely; affinities, reciprocal influences, and transformations without number: qualities, all of them, hardly compatible with the assumption of an impenetrable aliquid. Elasticity, which, better than any other property of matter, could lead, through the idea of spring or resistance, to that of impenetrability, is subject to the control of a thousand circumstances, and depends entirely on molecular attraction: now, what

is more irreconcilable with impenetrability than this attraction? Finally, there is a science which might be defined with exactness as the science of penetrability of matter: I mean chemistry. In fact, how does what is called chemical composition differ from penetration?[5] . . . In short, we know matter only through its forms; of its substance we know nothing. How, then, is it possible to affirm the reality of an invisible, impalpable, incoercible being, ever changing, ever vanishing, impenetrable to thought alone, to which it exhibits only its disguises? Materialist! I permit you to testify to the reality of your sensations; as to what occasions them, all that you can say involves this reciprocity: something (which you call matter) is the occasion of sensations which are felt by another something (which I call spirit).

2. But what, then, is the source of this supposition that matter is impenetrable, which external observation does not justify and which is not true; and what is its meaning?

Here appears the triumph of dualism. Matter is pronounced impenetrable, not, as the materialists and the vulgar fancy, by the testimony of the senses, but by the conscience. The me, an incomprehensible nature, feeling itself free, distinct, and permanent, and meeting outside of itself another nature equally incomprehensible, but also distinct and permanent in spite of its metamorphoses, declares, on the strength of the sensations and ideas which this essence suggests to it, that the not-me is extended and impenetrable. Impenetrability is a figurative term, an image by which thought, a division of the absolute, pictures to itself material reality, another division of the absolute; but this impenetrability, without which

---

Chemists distinguish between mixture and composition, just as logicians distinguish between the association of ideas and their synthesis. It is true, nevertheless, that, according to the chemists, composition may be after all but a mixture, or rather an aggregation of atoms, no longer fortuitous, but systematic, the atoms forming different compounds by varying their arrangement. But still this is only an hypothesis, wholly gratuitous; an hypothesis which explains nothing, and has not even the merit of being logical. Why does a purely numerical or geometrical difference in the composition and form of atoms give rise to physiological properties so different? If atoms are indivisible and impenetrable, why does not their association, confined to mechanical effects, leave them unchanged in essence? Where is the relation between the cause supposed and the effect obtained?

We must distrust our intellectual vision: it is with chemical theories as with psychological systems. The mind, in order to account for phenomena, works with atoms, which it does not and can never see, as with the me, which it does not perceive: it applies its categories to everything; that is, it distinguishes, individualizes, concretes, numbers, compares, things which, material or immaterial, are thoroughly identical and indistinguishable. Matter, as well as spirit, plays, as we view it, all sorts of parts; and, as there is nothing arbitrary in its metamorphoses, we build upon them these psychologic and atomic theories, true in so far as they faithfully represent, in terms agreed upon, the series of phenomena, but radically false as soon as they pretend to realize their abstractions and are accepted literally.

matter disappears, is, in the last analysis, only a spontaneous judgment of inward sensation, a metaphysical a priori, an unverified hypothesis of spirit.

Thus, whether philosophy, after having overthrown theological dogmatism, spiritualizes matter or materializes thought, idealizes being or realizes ideas; or whether, identifying substance and cause, it everywhere substitutes FORCE, phrases, all, which explain and signify nothing, — it always leads us back to this everlasting dualism, and, in summoning us to believe in ourselves, compels us to believe in God, if not in spirits. It is true that, making spirit a part of Nature, in distinction from the ancients, who separated it, philosophy has been led to this famous conclusion, which sums up nearly all the fruit of its researches: In man spirit knows itself, while everywhere else it seems not to know itself — "That which is awake in man, which dreams in the animal, and sleeps in the stone," said a philosopher.

Philosophy, then, in its last hour, knows no more than at its birth: as if it had appeared in the world only to verify the words of Socrates, it says to us, wrapping itself solemnly around with its funeral pall, "I know only that I know nothing." What do I say? Philosophy knows today that all its judgments rest on two equally false, equally impossible, and yet equally necessary and inevitable hypotheses, — matter and spirit. So that, while in former times religious intolerance and philosophic disputes, spreading darkness everywhere, excused doubt and tempted to libidinous indifference, the triumph of negation on all points no longer permits even this doubt; thought, freed from every barrier, but conquered by its own successes, is forced to affirm what seems to it clearly contradictory and absurd. The savages say that the world is a great fetich watched over by a great manitou. For thirty centuries the poets, legislators, and sages of civilization, handing down from age to age the philosophic lamp, have written nothing more sublime than this profession of faith. And here, at the end of this long conspiracy against God, which has called itself philosophy, emancipated reason concludes with savage reason, The universe is a not-me, objectified by a me.

Humanity, then, inevitably supposes the existence of God: and if, during the long period which closes with our time, it has believed in the reality of its hypothesis; if it has worshipped the inconceivable object; if, after being apprehended in this act of faith, it persists knowingly, but no longer voluntarily, in this opinion of a sovereign being which it knows to be only a personification of its own thought; if it is on the point of again beginning its magic invocations, — we must believe that so astonishing an hallucination conceals some mystery, which deserves to be fathomed.

I say hallucination and mystery, but without intending to deny thereby the superhuman content of the God-idea, and without admitting the necessity of a new symbolism, — I mean a new religion. For if it is indisputable that humanity, in affirming God, — or all that is included in the word me or spirit, — only affirms itself, it is equally undeniable that it affirms itself as something other than its own conception of itself, as all mythologies and theologies show. And since, moreover, this affirmation is incontestable, it depends, without doubt, upon hidden relations, which ought, if possible, to be determined scientifically.

In other words, atheism, sometimes called humanism, true in its critical and negative features, would be, if it stopped at man in his natural condition, if it discarded as an erroneous judgment the first affirmation of humanity, that it is the daughter, emanation, image, reflection, or voice of God, -humanism, I say, if it thus denied its past, would be but one contradiction more. We are forced, then, to undertake the criticism of humanism; that is, to ascertain whether humanity, considered as a whole and throughout all its periods of development, satisfies the Divine idea, after eliminating from the latter the exaggerated and fanciful attributes of God; whether it satisfies the perfection of being; whether it satisfies itself. We are forced, in short, to inquire whether humanity tends toward God, according to the ancient dogma, or is itself becoming God, as modern philosophers claim. Perhaps we shall find in the end that the two systems, despite their seeming opposition, are both true and essentially identical: in that case, the infallibility of human reason, in its collective manifestations as well as its studied speculations, would be decisively confirmed. — In a word, until we have verified to man the hypothesis of God, there is nothing definitive in the atheistic negation.

It is, then, a scientific, that is, an empirical demonstration of the idea of God, that we need: now, such a demonstration has never been attempted. Theology dogmatizing on the authority of its myths, philosophy speculating by the aid of categories, God has existed as a transcendental conception, incognizable by the reason, and the hypothesis always subsists.

It subsists, I say, this hypothesis, more tenacious, more pitiless than ever. We have reached one of those prophetic epochs when society, scornful of the past and doubtful of the future, now distractedly clings to the present, leaving a few solitary thinkers to establish the new faith; now cries to God from the depths of its enjoyments and asks for a sign of salvation, or seeks in the spectacle of its revolutions, as in the entrails of a victim, the secret of its destiny.

Why need I insist further? The hypothesis of God is allowable, for it forces itself upon every man in spite of himself: no one, then, can take exception to it. He who believes can do no less than grant me the supposition that God exists; he who denies is forced to grant it to me also, since he entertained it before me, every negation implying a previous affirmation; as for him who is in doubt, he needs but to reflect a moment to understand that his doubt necessarily supposes an unknown something, which, sooner or later, he will call God.

But if I possess, through the fact of my thought, the right to suppose God, I must abandon the right to affirm him. In other words, if my hypothesis is irresistible, that, for the present, is all that I can pretend. For to affirm is to determine; now, every determination, to be true, must be reached empirically. In fact, whoever says determination, says relation, conditionality, experience. Since, then, the determination of the idea of God must result from an empirical demonstration, we must abstain from everything which, in the search for this great unknown, not being established by experience, goes beyond the hypothesis, under penalty of relapsing into the contradictions of theology, and consequently arousing anew atheistic dissent.

III.

It remains for me to tell why, in a work on political economy, I have felt it necessary to start with the fundamental hypothesis of all philosophy.

And first, I need the hypothesis of God to establish the authority of social science. — When the astronomer, to explain the system of the world, judging solely from appearance, supposes, with the vulgar, the sky arched, the earth flat, the sun much like a football, describing a curve in the air from east to west, he supposes the infallibility of the senses, reserving the right to rectify subsequently, after further observation, the data with which he is obliged to start. Astronomic philosophy, in fact, could not admit a priori that the senses deceive us, and that we do not see what we do see: admitting such a principle, what would become of the certainty of astronomy? But the evidence of the senses being able, in certain cases, to rectify and complete itself, the authority of the senses remains unshaken, and astronomy is possible.

So social philosophy does not admit a priori that humanity can err or be deceived in its actions: if it should, what would become of the authority of the human race, that is, the authority of reason, synonymous at bottom with the sovereignty of the people? But it thinks that human judgments, always true at the time they are pronounced, can successively complete and throw light on each other, in proportion to the acquisition of ideas, in such a way as to maintain continual harmony between universal reason and individual speculation, and indefinitely extend the sphere of certainty: which is always an affirmation of the authority of human judgments.

Now, the first judgment of the reason, the preamble of every political constitution seeking a sanction and a principle, is necessarily this: There is a God; which means that society is governed with design, premeditation, intelligence. This judgment, which excludes chance, is, then, the foundation of the possibility of a social science; and every historical and positive study of social facts, undertaken with a view to amelioration and progress, must suppose, with the people, the existence of God, reserving the right to account for this judgment at a later period.

Thus the history of society is to us but a long determination of the idea of God, a progressive revelation of the destiny of man. And while ancient wisdom made all depend on the arbitrary and fanciful notion of Divinity, oppressing reason and conscience, and arresting progress through fear of an invisible master, the new philosophy, reversing the method, trampling on the authority of God as well as that of man, and accepting no other yoke than that of fact and evidence, makes all converge toward the theological hypothesis, as toward the last of its problems.

Humanitarian atheism is, therefore, the last step in the moral and intellectual enfranchisement of man, consequently the last phase of philosophy, serving as a pathway to the scientific reconstruction and verification of all the demolished dogmas.

I need the hypothesis of God, not only, as I have just said, to give a meaning to history, but also to legitimate the reforms to be effected, in the name of science, in the State.

Whether we consider Divinity as outside of society, whose movements it governs from on high (a wholly gratuitous and probably illusory opinion); or whether we deem it immanent in society and identical with that impersonal and unconscious reason which, acting instinctively, makes civilization advance (although impersonality and ignorance of self are contrary to the idea of intelligence); or whether, finally, all that is accomplished in society results from the relation of its elements (a system whose whole merit consists in changing an active into a passive, in making intelligence necessity, or, which amounts to the same thing, in taking law for cause), — it always follows that the manifestations of social activity, necessarily appearing to us either as indications of the will of the Supreme Being, or as a sort of language typical of general and impersonal reason, or, finally, as landmarks of necessity, are absolute authority for us. Being connected in time as well as in spirit, the facts accomplished determine and legitimate the facts to be accomplished; science and destiny are in accord; everything which happens resulting from reason, and, reciprocally, reason judging only from experience of that which happens, science has a right to participate in government, and that which establishes its competency as a counsellor justifies its intervention as a sovereign.

Science, expressed, recognized, and accepted by the voice of all as divine, is queen of the world. Thus, thanks to the hypothesis of God, all conservative or retrogressive opposition, every dilatory plea offered by theology, tradition, or selfishness, finds itself peremptorily and irrevocably set aside.

I need the hypothesis of God to show the tie which unites civilization with Nature.

In fact, this astonishing hypothesis, by which man is assimilated to the absolute, implying identity of the laws of Nature and the laws of reason, enables us to see in human industry the complement of creative action, unites man with the globe which he inhabits, and, in the cultivation of the domain in which Providence has placed us, which thus becomes in part our work, gives us a conception of the principle and end of all things. If, then, humanity is not God, it is a continuation of God; or, if a different phraseology be preferred, that which humanity does today by design is the same thing that it began by instinct, and which Nature seems to accomplish by necessity. In all these cases, and whichever opinion we may choose, one thing remains certain: the unity of action and law. Intelligent beings, actors in an intelligently-devised fable, we may fearlessly reason from ourselves to the universe and the eternal; and, when we shall have completed the organization of labor, may say with pride, The creation is explained.

Thus philosophy's field of exploration is fixed; tradition is the starting-point of all speculation as to the future; utopia is forever exploded; the study of the me, transferred from the individual conscience to the manifestations of the social will, acquires the character of objectivity of which it has been hitherto deprived; and, history becoming psychology, theology anthropology, the natural sciences metaphysics, the theory of the reason is deduced no longer from the vacuum of the intellect, but from the innumerable forms of a Nature abundantly and directly observable.

I need the hypothesis of God to prove my good-will towards a multitude of sects, whose opinions I do not share, but whose malice I fear: — theists; I know one who, in the cause of God, would be ready to draw sword, and, like Robespierre, use the guillotine until the last atheist should be destroyed, not dreaming that that atheist would be himself; — mystics, whose party, largely made up of students and women marching under the banner of MM. Lamennais, Quinet, Leroux, and others, has taken for a motto, "Like master, like man;" like God, like people; and, to regulate the wages of the workingman, begins by restoring religion; — spiritualists, who, should I overlook the rights of spirit, would accuse me of establishing the worship of matter, against which I protest with all the strength of my soul; — sensualists and materialists, to whom the divine dogma is the symbol of constraint and the principle of enslavement of the passions, outside of which, they say, there is for man neither pleasure, nor virtue, nor genius; — eclectics and sceptics, sellers and publishers of all the old philosophies, but not philosophers themselves, united in one vast brotherhood, with approbation and privilege, against whoever thinks, believes, or affirms without their permission; -conservatives finally, retrogressives, egotists, and hypocrites, preaching the love of God by hatred of their neighbor, attributing to liberty the world's misfortunes since the deluge, and scandalizing reason by their foolishness.

Is it possible, however, that they will attack an hypothesis which, far from blaspheming the revered phantoms of faith, aspires only to exhibit them in broad daylight; which, instead of rejecting traditional dogmas and the prejudices of conscience, asks only to verify them; which, while defending itself against exclusive opinions, takes for an axiom the infallibility of reason, and, thanks to this fruitful principle, will doubtless never decide against any of the antagonistic sects? Is it possible that the religious and political conservatives will charge me with disturbing the order of society, when I start with the hypothesis of a sovereign intelligence, the source of every thought of order; that the semi-Christian democrats will curse me as an enemy of God, and consequently a traitor to the republic, when I am seeking for the meaning and content of the idea of God; and that the tradesmen of the university will impute to me the impiety of demonstrating the non-value of their philosophical products, when I am especially maintaining that philosophy should be studied in its object, — that is, in the manifestations of society and Nature? . . .

I need the hypothesis of God to justify my style.

In my ignorance of everything regarding God, the world, the soul, and destiny; forced to proceed like the materialist, — that is, by observation and experience, — and to conclude in the language of the believer, because there is no other; not knowing whether my formulas, theological in spite of me, would be taken literally or figuratively; in this perpetual contemplation of God, man, and things, obliged to submit to the synonymy of all the terms included in the three categories of thought, speech, and action, but wishing to affirm nothing on either one side or the other, — rigorous logic demanded that I should suppose, no more, no less, this unknown that is called God. We are full of Divinity, *Jovis omnia plena*; our monuments, our traditions, our laws, our ideas, our languages, and our sciences, all are infected by this indelible superstition outside of which we can neither speak nor act, and without which we do not even think.

Finally, I need the hypothesis of God to explain the publication of these new memoirs.

Our society feels itself big with events, and is anxious about the future: how account for these vague presentiments by the sole aid of a universal reason, immanent if you will, and permanent, but impersonal, and therefore dumb, or by the idea of necessity, if it implies that necessity is self-conscious, and consequently has presentiments? There remains then, once more, an agent or nightmare which weighs upon society, and gives it visions.

Now, when society prophesies, it puts questions in the mouths of some, and answers in the mouths of others. And wise, then, he who can listen and understand; for God himself has spoken, quia locutus est Deus.

The Academy of Moral and Political Sciences has proposed the following question: —

"To determine the general facts which govern the relations of profits to wages, and to explain their respective oscillations."

A few years ago the same Academy asked, "What are the causes of misery?" The nineteenth century has, in fact, but one idea, — equality and reform. But the wind bloweth where it listeth: many began to reflect upon the question, no one answered it. The college of aruspices has, therefore, renewed its question, but in more significant terms. It wishes to know whether order prevails in the workshop; whether wages are equitable; whether liberty and privilege compensate each other justly; whether the idea of value, which controls all the facts of exchange, is, in the forms in which the economists have represented it, sufficiently exact; whether credit protects labor; whether circulation is regular; whether the burdens of society weigh equally on all, etc.

And, indeed, insufficiency of income being the immediate cause of misery, it is fitting that we should know why, misfortune and malevolence aside, the workingman's income is insufficient. It is still the same question of inequality of fortunes, which has made such a stir for a century past, and which, by a strange fatality, continually reappears in academic programmes, as if there lay the real difficulty of modern times.

Equality, then, — its principle, its means, its obstacles, its theory, the motives of its postponement, the cause of social and providential iniquities, — these the world has got to learn, in spite of the sneers of incredulity.

I know well that the views of the Academy are not thus profound, and that it equals a council of the Church in its horror of novelties; but the more it turns towards the past, the more it reflects the future, and the more, consequently, must we believe in its inspiration: for the true prophets are those who do not understand their utterances. Listen further.

"What," the Academy has asked, "are the most useful applications of the principle of voluntary and private association that we can make for the alleviation of misery?"

And again: —

"To expound the theory and principles of the contract of insurance, to give its history, and to deduce from its rationale and the facts the developments of which this contract is capable, and the various useful applications possible in the present state of commercial and industrial progress."

Publicists admit that insurance, a rudimentary form of commercial solidarity, is an association in things, *societas in re*; that is, a society whose conditions, founded on purely economical relations, escape man's arbitrary dictation. So that a philosophy of insurance or mutual guarantee of security, which shall be deduced from the general theory of real (*in re*) societies, will contain the formula of universal association, in which no member of the Academy believes. And when, uniting subject and object in the same point of view, the Academy demands, by the side of a theory of association of interests, a theory of voluntary association, it reveals to us the most perfect form of society, and thereby affirms all that is most at variance with its convictions. Liberty, equality, solidarity, association! By what inconceivable blunder has so eminently conservative a body offered to the citizens this new programme of the rights of man? It was in this way that Caiaphas prophesied redemption by disowning Jesus Christ.

Upon the first of these questions, forty-five memoirs were addressed to the Academy within two years, — a proof that the subject was marvellously well suited to the state of the public mind. But among so many competitors no one having been deemed worthy of the prize, the Academy has withdrawn the question; alleging as a reason the incapacity of the competitors, but in reality because, the failure of the contest being the sole object that the Academy had in view, it behooved it to declare, without further delay, that the hopes of the friends of association were groundless.

Thus, then, the gentlemen of the Academy disavow, in their session-chamber, their announcements from the tripod! There is nothing in such a contradiction astonishing to me; and may God preserve me from calling it a crime! The ancients believed that revolutions announced their advent by dreadful signs, and that among other prodigies animals spoke. This was a figure, descriptive of those unexpected ideas and strange words which circulate suddenly among the masses at critical moments, and which seem to be entirely without human antecedent, so far removed are they from the sphere of ordinary judgment. At the time in which we live, such a thing could not fail to occur. After having, by a prophetic instinct and a mechanical spontaneity, *pecudesque locutae*, proclaimed association, the gentlemen of the Academy of Moral and Political Sciences have returned to their ordinary prudence; and with them custom has conquered inspiration. Let us learn, then, how to distinguish heavenly counsel from the interested judgments of men, and hold it for certain that, in the discourse of sages, that is the most trustworthy to which they have given the least reflection.

Nevertheless the Academy, in breaking so rudely with its intuitions, seems to have felt some remorse. In place of a theory of association in which, after reflection, it no longer believes, it asks for a "Critical examination of Pestalozzi's system of instruction and education, considered mainly in its relation to the well-being and morality of the poor classes." Who knows? perchance the relation between profits and wages, association, the organization of labor indeed, are to be found at the bottom of a system of instruction. Is not man's life a perpetual apprenticeship? Are not philosophy and religion humanity's education? To organize instruction, then, would be to organize industry and fix the theory of society: the Academy, in its lucid moments, always returns to that.

"What influence," the Academy again asks, "do progress and a desire for material comfort have upon a nation's morality?"

Taken in its most obvious sense, this new question of the Academy is commonplace, and fit at best to exercise a rhetorisian's skill. But the Academy, which must continue till the end in its ignorance of the revolutionary significance of its oracles, has drawn aside the curtain in its commentary. What, then, so profound has it discovered in this Epicurean thesis?

"The desire for luxury and its enjoyments," it tells us; "the singular love of it felt by the majority; the tendency of hearts and minds to occupy themselves with it exclusively; the agreement of individuals AND THE STATE in making it the motive and the end of all their projects, all their efforts, and all their sacrifices, — engender general or individual feelings which, beneficent or injurious, become principles of action more potent, perhaps, than any which have heretofore governed men."

Never had moralists a more favorable opportunity to assail the sensualism of the century, the venality of consciences, and the corruption instituted by the government: instead of that, what does the Academy of Moral Sciences do? With the most automatic calmness, it establishes a series in which luxury, so long proscribed by the stoics and ascetics, — those masters of holiness, — must appear in its turn as a principle of conduct as legitimate, as pure, and as grand as all those formerly invoked by religion and philosophy. Determine, it tells us, the motives of action (undoubtedly now old and worn-out) of which LUXURY is historically the providential successor, and, from the results of the former, calculate the effects of the latter. Prove, in short, that Aristippus was only in advance of his century, and that his system of morality must have its day, as well as that of Zeno and A Kempis.

We are dealing, then, with a society which no longer wishes to be poor; which mocks at everything that was once dear and sacred to it, — liberty, religion, and glory, — so long as it has not wealth; which, to obtain it, submits to all outrages, and becomes an accomplice in all sorts of cowardly actions: and this burning thirst for pleasure, this irresistible desire to arrive at luxury, — a symptom of a new period in civilization, — is the supreme commandment by virtue of which we are to labor for the abolition of poverty: thus saith the Academy. What becomes, then, of the doctrine of expiation and abstinence, the morality of sacrifice, resignation, and happy moderation? What distrust of the compensation promised in the other life, and what a contradiction of the Gospel! But, above all, what a justification of a government which has adopted as its system the golden key! Why have religious men, Christians, Senecas, given utterance in concert to so many immoral maxims?

The Academy, completing its thought, will reply to us: —

"Show how the progress of criminal justice, in the prosecution and punishment of attacks upon persons and property, follows and marks the ages of civilization from the savage condition up to that of the best-governed nations."

Is it possible that the criminal lawyers in the Academy of Moral Sciences foresaw the conclusion of their premises? The fact whose history is now to be studied, and which the Academy describes by the words "progress of criminal justice," is simply the gradual mitigation which manifests itself, both in the forms of criminal examinations and in the penalties inflicted, in proportion as civilization increases in liberty, light, and wealth. So that, the principle of repressive institutions being the direct opposite of all those on which the welfare of society depends, there is a constant elimination of all parts of the penal system as well as all judicial paraphernalia, and the final inference from this movement is that the guarantee of order lies neither in fear nor punishment; consequently, neither in hell nor religion.

What a subversion of received ideas! What a denial of all that it is the business of the Academy of Moral Sciences to defend! But, if the guarantee of order no longer lies in the fear of a punishment to be suffered, either in this life or in another, where then are to be found the guarantees protective of persons and property? Or rather, without repressive institutions, what becomes of property? And without property, what becomes of the family?

The Academy, which knows nothing of all these things, replies without agitation: —

"Review the various phases of the organization of the family upon the soil of France from ancient times down to our day."

Which means: Determine, by the previous progress of family organization, the conditions of the existence of the family in a state of equality of fortunes, voluntary and free association, universal solidarity, material comfort and luxury, and public order without prisons, courts, police, or hangmen.

There will be astonishment, perhaps, at finding that the Academy of Moral and Political Sciences, after having, like the boldest innovators, called in question all the principles of social order, — religion, family, property, justice, — has not also proposed this problem: What is the best form of government? In fact, government is for society the source of all initiative, every guarantee, every reform. It would be, then, interesting to know whether the government, as constituted by the Charter, is adequate to the practical solution of the Academy's questions.

But it would be a misconception of the oracles to imagine that they proceed by induction and analysis; and precisely because the political problem was a condition or corollary of the demonstrations asked for, the Academy could not offer it for competition. Such a conclusion would have opened its eyes, and, without waiting for the memoirs of the competitors, it would have hastened to suppress its entire programme. The Academy has approached the question from above. It has said: —

The works of God are beautiful in their own essence, justificata in semet ipsa; they are true, in a word, because they are his. The thoughts of man resemble dense vapors pierced by long and narrow flashes. What, then, is the truth in relation to us, and what is the character of certainty?

As if the Academy had said to us: You shall verify the hypothesis of your existence, the hypothesis of the Academy which interrogates you, the hypotheses of time, space, motion, thought, and the laws of thought. Then you may verify the hypothesis of pauperism, the hypothesis of inequality of conditions, the hypothesis of universal association, the hypothesis of happiness, the hypotheses of monarchy and republicanism, the hypothesis of Providence!...

A complete criticism of God and humanity.

I point to the programme of the honorable society: it is not I who have fixed the conditions of my task, it is the Academy of Moral and Political Sciences. Now, how can I satisfy these conditions, if I am not myself endowed with infallibility; in a word, if I am not God or divine? The Academy admits, then, that divinity and humanity are identical, or at least correlative; but the question now is in what consists this correlation: such is the meaning of the problem of certainty, such is the object of social philosophy.

Thus, then, in the name of the society that God inspires, an Academy questions.

In the name of the same society, I am one of the prophets who attempt to answer. The task is an immense one, and I do not promise to accomplish it: I will go as far as God shall give me strength. But, whatever I may say, it does not come from me: the thought which inspires my pen is not personal, and nothing that I write can be attributed to me. I shall give the facts as I have seen them; I shall judge them by what I shall have said; I shall call everything by its strongest name, and no one will take offence. I shall inquire freely, and by the rules of divination which I have learned, into the meaning of the divine purpose which is now expressing itself through the eloquent lips of sages and the inarticulate wailings of the people: and, though I should deny all the prerogatives guaranteed by our Constitution, I shall not be factious. I shall point my finger whither an invisible influence is pushing us; and neither my action nor my words shall be irritating. I shall stir up the cloud, and, though I should cause it to launch the thunderbolt, I should be innocent. In this solemn investigation to which the

Academy invites me, I have more than the right to tell the truth, — I have the right to say what I think: may my thought, my words, and the truth be but one and the same thing!

And you, reader, — for without a reader there is no writer, — you are half of my work. Without you, I am only sounding brass; with the aid of your attention, I will speak marvels. Do you see this passing whirlwind called SOCIETY, from which burst forth, with startling brilliancy, lightnings, thunders, and voices? I wish to cause you to place your finger on the hidden springs which move it; but to that end you must reduce yourself at my command to a state of pure intelligence. The eyes of love and pleasure are powerless to recognize beauty in a skeleton, harmony in naked viscera, life in dark and coagulated blood: consequently the secrets of the social organism are a sealed letter to the man whose brain is beclouded by passion and prejudice. Such sublimities are unattainable except by cold and silent contemplation. Suffer me, then, before revealing to your eyes the leaves of the book of life, to prepare your soul by this sceptical purification which the great teachers of the people — Socrates, Jesus Christ, St. Paul, St. Remi, Bacon, Descartes, Galileo, Kant, etc. — have always claimed of their disciples.

Whoever you may be, clad in the rags of misery or decked in the sumptuous vestments of luxury, I restore you to that state of luminous nudity which neither the fumes of wealth nor the poisons of envious poverty dim. How persuade the rich that the difference of conditions arises from an error in the accounts; and how can the poor, in their beggary, conceive that the proprietor possesses in good faith? To investigate the sufferings of the laborer is to the idler the most intolerable of amusements; just as to do justice to the fortunate is to the miserable the bitterest of draughts.

You occupy a high position: I strip you of it; there you are, free. There is too much optimism beneath this official costume, too much subordination, too much idleness. Science demands an insurrection of thought: now, the thought of an official is his salary.

Your mistress, beautiful, passionate, artistic, is, I like to believe, possessed only by you. That is, your soul, your spirit, your conscience, have passed into the most charming object of luxury that nature and art have produced for the eternal torment of fascinated mortals. I separate you from this divine half of yourself: at the present day it is too much to wish for justice and at the same time to love a woman. To think with grandeur and clearness, man must remove the lining of his nature and hold to his masculine hypostasis. Besides, in the state in which I have put you, your lover would no longer know you: remember the wife of Job.

What is your religion?... Forget your faith, and, through wisdom, become an atheist. — What! you say; an atheist in spite of our hypothesis! — No, but because of our hypothesis. One's thought must have been raised above divine things for a long time to be entitled to suppose a personality beyond man, a life beyond this life. For the rest, have no fears for your salvation. God is not angry with those who are led by reason to deny him, any more than he is anxious for those who are led by faith to worship him; and, in the state of your conscience, the surest course for you is to think nothing about him. Do you not see that it is with religion as with governments, the most perfect of which would be the denial of all? Then let no political or religious fancy hold your soul captive; in this way only can you now keep from being either a dupe or a renegade. Ah! said I in the days of my enthusiastic youth, shall I not hear the tolling for the second vespers of the republic, and our priests, dressed in white tunics, singing after the Doric fashion the returning hymn: Change, ô Dieu, notre servitude, comme le vent du desert en un souffle rafraîchissan!.... But I have despaired of republicans, and no longer know either religion or priests.

I should like also, in order to thoroughly secure your judgment, dear reader, to render your soul insensible to pity, superior to virtue, indifferent to happiness. But that would be too much to expect of a neophyte. Remember only, and never forget, that pity, happiness, and virtue, like country, religion, and love, are masks...

Chapter I. Of the Economic Science.

1. — Opposition between FACT and RIGHT in social economy.

I AFFIRM the REALITY of an economic science.

This proposition, which few economists now dare to question, is the boldest, perhaps, that a philosopher ever maintained; and the inquiries to follow will prove, I hope, that its demonstration will one day be deemed the greatest effort of the human mind.

I affirm, on the other hand, the absolute certainty as well as the progressive nature of economic science, of all the sciences in my opinion the most comprehensive, the purest, the best supported by facts: a new proposition, which alters this science into logic or metaphysics in concreto, and radically changes the basis of ancient philosophy. In other words, economic science is to me the objective form and realization of metaphysics; it is metaphysics in action, metaphysics projected on the vanishing plane of time; and whoever studies the laws of labor and exchange is truly and specially a metaphysician.

After what I have said in the introduction, there is nothing in this which should surprise any one. The labor of man continues the work of God, who, in creating all beings, did but externally realize the eternal laws of reason. Economic science is, then, necessarily and at once a theory of ideas, a natural theology, and a psychology. This general outline alone would have sufficed to explain why, having to treat of economic matters, I was obliged previously to suppose the existence of God, and by what title I, a simple economist, aspire to solve the problem of certainty.

But I hasten to say that I do not regard as a science the incoherent ensemble of theories to which the name political economy has been officially given for almost a hundred years, and which, in spite of the etymology of the name, is after ail but the code, or immemorial routine, of property. These theories offer us only the rudiments, or first section, of economic science; and that is why, like property, they are all contradictory of each other, and half the time inapplicable. The proof of this assertion, which is, in one sense, a denial of political economy as handed down to us by Adam Smith, Ricardo, Malthus, and J. B. Say, and as we have known it for half a century, will be especially developed in this treatise.

The inadequacy of political economy has at all times impressed thoughtful minds, who, too fond of their dreams for practical investigation, and confining themselves to the estimation of apparent results, have constituted from the beginning a party of opposition to the statu quo, and have devoted themselves to persevering, and systematic ridicule of civilization and its customs. Property, on the other hand, the basis of all social institutions, has never lacked zealous defenders, who, proud to be called practical, have exchanged blow for blow with the traducers of political economy, and have labored with a courageous and often skilful hand to strengthen the edifice which general prejudice and individual liberty have erected in concert. The controversy between conservatives and reformers, still pending, finds its counterpart, in the history of philosophy, in the quarrel between realists and nominalists; it is almost useless to add that, on both sides, right and wrong are equal, and that the rivalry, narrowness, and intolerance of opinions have been the sole cause of the misunderstanding.

Thus two powers are contending for the government of the world, and cursing each other with the fervor of two hostile religions: political economy, or tradition; and socialism, or utopia.

What is, then, in more explicit terms, political economy? What is socialism?

Political economy is a collection of the observations thus far made in regard to the phenomena of the production and distribution of wealth; that is, in regard to the most common, most spontaneous, and therefore most genuine, forms of labor and exchange.

The economists have classified these observations as far as they were able; they have described the phenomena, and ascertained their contingencies and relations; they have observed in them, in many cases, a quality of necessity which has given them the name of laws; and this ensemble of information, gathered from the simplest manifestations of society, constitutes political economy.

Political economy is, therefore, the natural history of the most apparent and most universally accredited customs, traditions, practices, and methods of humanity in all that concerns the production and distribution of wealth. By this title, political economy considers itself legitimate in fact and in right: in fact, because the phenomena which it studies are constant, spontaneous, and universal; in right, because these phenomena rest on the authority of the human race, the strongest authority possible. Consequently, political economy calls itself a science; that is, a rational and systematic knowledge of regular and necessary facts.

Socialism, which, like the god Vishnu, ever dying and ever returning to life, has experienced within a score of years its ten-thousandth incarnation in the persons of five or six revelators, — socialism affirms the irregularity of the present constitution of society, and, consequently, of all its previous forms. It asserts, and proves, that the order of civilization is artificial, contradictory, inadequate; that it engenders oppression, misery, and crime; it denounces, not to say calumniates, the whole past of social life, and pushes on with all its might to a reformation of morals and institutions.

Socialism concludes by declaring political economy a false and sophistical hypothesis, devised to enable the few to exploit the many; and applying the maxim A fructibus cognoscetis, it ends with a demonstration of the impotence and emptiness of political economy by the list of human calamities for which it makes it responsible.

But if political economy is false, jurisprudence, which in all countries is the science of law and custom, is false also; since, founded on the distinction of thine and mine, it supposes the legitimacy of the facts described and classified by political economy. The theories of public and international law, with all the varieties of representative government, are also false, since they rest on the principle of individual appropriation and the absolute sovereignty of wills.

All these consequences socialism accepts. To it, political economy, regarded by many as the physiology of wealth, is but the organization of robbery and poverty; just as jurisprudence, honored by legists with the name of written reason, is, in its eyes, but a compilation of the rubrics of legal and official spoliation, — in a word, of property. Considered in their relations, these two pretended sciences, political economy and law, form, in the opinion of socialism, the complete theory of iniquity and discord. Passing then from negation to affirmation, socialism opposes the principle of property with that of association, and makes vigorous efforts to reconstruct social economy from top to bottom; that is, to establish a new code, a new political system, with institutions and morals diametrically opposed to the ancient forms.

Thus the line of demarcation between socialism and political economy is fixed, and the hostility flagrant.

Political economy tends toward the glorification of selfishness; socialism favors the exaltation of communism.

The economists, saving a few violations of their principles, for which they deem it their duty to blame governments, are optimists with regard to accomplished facts; the socialists, with regard to facts to be accomplished.

The first affirm that that which ought to be is; the second, that that which ought to be is not. Consequently, while the first are defenders of religion, authority, and the other principles contemporary with, and conservative of, property, — although their criticism, based solely on reason, deals frequent blows at their own prejudices, — the second reject authority and faith, and appeal exclusively to science, — although a certain religiosity, utterly illiberal, and an unscientific disdain for facts, are always the most obvious characteristics of their doctrines.

For the rest, neither party ever ceases to accuse the other of incapacity and sterility.

The socialists ask their opponents to account for the inequality of conditions, for those commercial debaucheries in which monopoly and competition, in monstrous union, perpetually give birth to luxury and misery; they reproach economic theories, always modeled after the past, with leaving the future hopeless; in short, they point to the regime of property as a horrible hallucination, against which humanity has protested and struggled for four thousand years.

The economists, on their side, defy socialists to produce a system in which property, competition, and political organization can be dispensed with; they prove, with documents in hand, that all reformatory projects have ever been nothing but rhapsodies of fragments borrowed from the very system that socialism sneers at, — plagiarisms, in a word, of political economy, outside of which socialism is incapable of conceiving and formulating an idea.

Every day sees the proofs in this grave suit accumulating, and the question becoming confused.

While society has traveled and stumbled, suffered and thrived, in pursuing the economic routine, the socialists, since Pythagoras, Orpheus, and the unfathomable Hermes, have labored to establish their dogma in opposition to political economy. A few attempts at association in accordance with their views have even been made here and there: but as yet these exceptional undertakings, lost in the ocean of property, have been without result; and, as if destiny had resolved to exhaust the economic hypothesis before attacking the socialistic utopia, the reformatory party is obliged to content itself with pocketing the sarcasms of its adversaries while waiting for its own turn to come.

This, then, is the state of the cause: socialism incessantly denounces the crimes of civilization, verifies daily the powerlessness of political economy to satisfy the harmonic attractions of man, and presents petition after petition; political economy fills its brief with socialistic systems, all of which, one after another, pass away and die, despised by common sense. The persistence of evil nourishes the complaint of the one, while the constant succession of reformatory checks feeds the malicious irony of the other. When will judgment be given? The tribunal is deserted; meanwhile, political economy improves its opportunities, and, without furnishing bail, continues to lord it over the world; possideo quia possideo.

If we descend from the sphere of ideas to the realities of the world, the antagonism will appear still more grave and threatening.

When, in these recent years, socialism, instigated by prolonged convulsions, made its fantastic appearance in our midst, men whom all controversy had found until then indifferent and lukewarm went back in fright to monarchical and religious ideas; democracy, which was charged with being developed at last to its ultimate, was cursed and driven back. This accusation of the conservatives against the democrats was a libel. Democracy is by nature as hostile to the socialistic idea as incapable of filling the place of royalty, against which it is its destiny endlessly to conspire. This soon became evident, and we are witnesses of it daily in the professions of Christian and proprietary faith by democratic publicists, whose abandonment by the people began at that moment.

On the other hand, philosophy proves no less distinct from socialism, no less hostile to it, than politics and religion.

For just as in politics the principle of democracy is the sovereignty of numbers, and that of monarchy the sovereignty of the prince; just as likewise in affairs of conscience religion is nothing but submission to a mystical being, called God, and to the priests who represent him; just as finally in the economic world property — that is, exclusive control by the individual of the instruments of labor — is the point of departure of every theory, — so philosophy, in basing itself upon the a priori assumptions of reason, is inevitably led to attribute to the me alone the generation and autocracy of ideas, and to deny the metaphysical value of experience; that is, universally to substitute, for the objective law, absolutism, despotism.

Now, a doctrine which, springing up suddenly in the heart of society, without antecedents and without ancestors, rejected from every department of conscience and society the arbitrary principle, in order to substitute as sole truth the relation of facts; which broke with tradition, and consented to make use of the past only as a point from which to launch forth into the future, — such a doctrine could not fail to stir up against it the established AUTHORITIES; and we can see today how, in spite of their internal discords, the said AUTHORITIES, which are but one, combine to fight the monster that is ready to swallow them.

To the workingmen who complain of the insufficiency of wages and the uncertainty of labor, political economy opposes the liberty of commerce; to the citizens who are seeking for the conditions of liberty and order, the ideologists respond with representative systems; to the tender souls who, having lost their ancient faith, ask the reason and end of their existence, religion proposes the unfathomable secrets of Providence, and philosophy holds doubt in reserve. Subterfuges always; complete ideas, in which heart and mind find rest, never! Socialism cries that it is time to set sail for the mainland, and to enter port: but, say the antisocialists, there is no port; humanity sails onward in God's care, under the command of priests, philosophers, orators, economists, and our circumnavigation is eternal.

Thus society finds itself, at its origin, divided into two great parties: the one traditional and essentially hierarchical, which, according to the object it is considering, calls itself by turns royalty or democracy, philosophy or religion, in short, property; the other socialism, which, coming to life at every crisis of civilization, proclaims itself preeminently anarchical and atheistic; that is, rebellious against all authority, human and divine.

Now, modern civilization has demonstrated that in a conflict of this nature the truth is found, not in the exclusion of one of the opposites, but wholly and solely in the reconciliation of the two; it is, I say, a fact of science that every antagonism, whether in Nature or in ideas, is resolvable in a more general fact or in a complex formula, which harmonizes the opposing factors by absorbing them, so to speak, in each other. Can we not, then, men of common sense, while awaiting the solution which the future will undoubtedly bring forth, prepare ourselves for this great transition by an analysis of the struggling powers, as well as their positive and negative qualities? Such a work, performed with accuracy and conscientiousness, even though it should not lead us directly to the solution, would have at least the inestimable advantage of revealing to us the conditions of the problem, and thereby putting us on our guard against every form of utopia.

What is there, then, in political economy that is necessary and true; whither does it tend; what are its powers; what are its wishes? It is this which I propose to determine in this work. What is the value of socialism? The same investigation will answer this question also.

For since, after all, socialism and political economy pursue the same end, — namely, liberty, order, and well-being among men, — it is evident that the conditions to be fulfilled — in other words, the difficulties to be overcome — to attain this end, are also the same for both, and that it remains only to examine the methods attempted or proposed by either party. But since, moreover, it has been given thus far to political economy alone to translate its ideas into acts, while socialism has scarcely done more than indulge in perpetual satire, it is no less clear that, in judging the works of economy according to their merit, we at the same time shall reduce to its just value the invective of the socialists: so that our criticism, though apparently special, will lead to absolute and definitive conclusions.

This it is necessary to make clearer by a few examples, before entering fully upon the examination of political economy.

2. — Inadequacy of theories and criticisms.

We will record first an important observation: the contending parties agree in acknowledging a common authority, whose support each claims, -SCIENCE.

Plato, a utopian, organized his ideal republic in the name of science, which, through modesty and euphemism, he called philosophy. Aristotle, a practical man, refuted the Platonic utopia in the name of the same philosophy. Thus the social war has continued since Plato and Aristotle. The modern socialists refer all things to science one and indivisible, but without power to agree either as to its content, its limits, or its method; the economists, on their side, affirm that social science in no wise differs from political economy.

It is our first business, then, to ascertain what a science of society must be.

Science, in general, is the logically arranged and systematic knowledge of that which IS.

Applying this idea to society, we will say: Social science is the logically arranged and systematic knowledge, not of that which society has been, nor of that which it will be, but of that which it IS in its whole life; that is, in the sum total of its successive manifestations: for there alone can it have reason and system. Social science must include human order, not alone in such or such a period of duration, nor in a few of its elements; but in all its principles and in the totality of its existence: as if social evolution, spread throughout time and space, should find itself suddenly gathered and fixed in a picture which, exhibiting the series of the ages and the sequence of phenomena, revealed their connection and unity. Such must be the science of every living and progressive reality; such social science indisputably is.

It may be, then, that political economy, in spite of its individualistic tendency and its exclusive affirmations, is a constituent part of social science, in which the phenomena that it describes are like the starting-points of a vast triangulation and the elements of an organic and complex whole. From this point of view, the progress of humanity, proceeding from the simple to the complex, would be entirely in harmony with the progress of science; and the conflicting and so often desolating facts, which are today the basis and object of political economy, would have to be considered by us as so many special hypotheses, successively realized by humanity in view of a superior hypothesis, whose realization would solve all difficulties, and satisfy socialism without destroying political economy. For, as I said in my introduction, in no case can we admit that humanity, however it expresses itself, is mistaken.

Let us now make this clearer by facts.

The question now most disputed is unquestionably that of the organization of labor.

As John the Baptist preached in the desert, Repent ye so the socialists go about proclaiming everywhere this novelty old as the world, Organize labor, though never able to tell what, in their opinion, this organization should be. However that may be, the economists have seen that this socialistic clamor was damaging their theories: it was, indeed, a rebuke to them for ignoring that which they ought first to recognize, — labor. They have replied, therefore, to the attack of their adversaries, first by maintaining that labor is organized, that there is no other organization of labor than liberty to produce and exchange, either on one's own personal account, or in association with others, — in which case the course to be pursued has been prescribed by the civil and commercial codes. Then, as this argument served only to make them the laughing-stock of their antagonists, they assumed the offensive; and, showing that the socialists understood nothing at all themselves of this organization that they held up as a scarecrow, they ended by saying that it was but a new socialistic chimera, a word without sense, — an absurdity. The latest writings of the economists are full of these pitiless conclusions.

Nevertheless, it is certain that the phrase organization of labor contains as clear and rational a meaning as these that follow: organization of the workshop, organization of the army, organization of police, organization of charity, organization of war. In this respect, the argument of the economists is deplorably irrational. No less certain is it that the organization of labor cannot be a utopia and chimera; for at the moment that labor, the supreme condition of civilization, begins to exist, it follows that it is already submitted to an organization, such as it is, which satisfies the economists, but which the socialists think detestable.

There remains, then, relatively to the proposal to organize labor formulated by socialism, this objection, — that labor is organized. Now, this is utterly untenable, since it is notorious that in labor, supply, demand, division, quantity, proportion, price, and security, nothing, absolutely nothing is regulated; on the contrary, everything is given up to the caprices of free-will; that is, to chance.

As for us, guided by the idea that we have formed of social science, we shall affirm, against the socialists and against the economists, not that labor must he organized, nor that it is organized but that it is being organized.

Labor, we say, is being organized: that is, the process of organization has been going on from the beginning of the world, and will continue till the end. Political economy teaches us the primary elements of this organization; but socialism is right in asserting that, in its present form, the organization is inadequate and transitory; and the whole mission of science is continually to ascertain, in view of the results obtained and the phenomena in course of development, what innovations can be immediately effected.

Socialism and political economy, then, while waging a burlesque war, pursue in reality the same idea, — the organization of labor.

But both are guilty of disloyalty to science and of mutual calumny, when on the one hand political economy, mistaking for science its scraps of theory, denies the possibility of further progress; and when socialism, abandoning tradition, aims at reestablishing society on undiscoverable bases.

Thus socialism is nothing but a profound criticism and continual development of political economy; and, to apply here the celebrated aphorism of the school, Nihil est in intellectu, quod non prius fuerit in sensu, there is nothing in the socialistic hypotheses which is not duplicated in economic practice. On the other hand, political economy is but an impertinent rhapsody, so long as it affirms as absolutely valid the facts collected by Adam Smith and J. B. Say.

Another question, no less disputed than the preceding one, is that of usury, or lending at interest.

Usury, or in other words the price of use, is the emolument, of whatever nature, which the proprietor derives from the loan of his property. Quidquid sorti accrescit usura est, say the theologians. Usury, the foundation of credit, was one of the first of the means which social spontaneity employed in its work of organization, and whose analysis discloses the profound laws of civilization. The ancient philosophers and the Fathers of the Church, who must be regarded here as the representatives of socialism in the early centuries of the Christian era, by a singular fallacy, — which arose however from the paucity of economic knowledge in their day, — allowed farm-rent and condemned interest on money, because, as they believed, money was unproductive. They distinguished consequently between the loan of things which are consumed by use — among which they included money — and the loan of things which, without being consumed, yield a product to the user.

The economists had no difficulty in showing, by generalizing the idea of rent, that in the economy of society the action of capital, or its productivity, was the same whether it was consumed in wages or retained the character of an instrument; that, consequently, it was necessary either to prohibit the rent of land or to allow interest on money, since both were by the same title payment for privilege, indemnity for loan. It required more than fifteen centuries to get this idea accepted, and to reassure the consciences that had been terrified by the anathemas pronounced by Catholicism against usury. But finally the weight of evidence and the general desire favored the usurers: they won the battle against socialism; and from this legitimation of usury society gained some immense and unquestionable advantages. Under these circumstances socialism, which had tried to generalize the law enacted by Moses for the Israelites alone, Non foeneraberis proximo tuo, sed alieno, was beaten by an idea which it had accepted from the economic routine, — namely, farm-rent, — elevated into the theory of the productivity of capital.

But the economists in their turn were less fortunate, when they were afterwards called upon to justify farm-rent in itself, and to establish this theory of the product of capital. It may be said that, on this point, they have lost all the advantage they had at first gained against socialism.

Undoubtedly — and I am the first to recognize it — the rent of land, like that of money and all personal and real property, is a spontaneous and universal fact, which has its source in the depths of our nature, and which soon becomes, by its natural development, one of the most potent means of organization. I shall prove even that interest on capital is but the materialization of the aplorism, All labor should leave an excess. But in the face of this theory, or rather this fiction, of the productivity of capital, arises another thesis no less certain, which in these latter days has struck the ablest economists: it is that all value is born of labor, and is composed essentially of wages; in other words, that no wealth has its origin in privilege, or acquires any value except through work; and that, consequently, labor alone is the source of revenue among men. How, then, reconcile the theory of farm-rent or productivity of capital — a theory confirmed by universal custom, which conservative political economy is forced to accept but cannot justify — with this other theory which shows that value is normally composed of wages, and which inevitably ends, as we shall demonstrate, in an equality in society between net product and raw product?

The socialists have not wasted the opportunity. Starting with the principle that labor is the source of all income, they began to call the holders of capital to account for their farm-rents and emoluments; and, as the economists won the first victory by generalizing under a common expression farm-rent and usury, so the socialists have taken their revenge by causing the seignorial rights of capital to vanish before the still more general principle of labor. Property has been demolished from top to bottom: the economists could only keep silent; but, powerless to arrest itself in this new descent, socialism has slipped clear to the farthest boundaries of communistic utopia, and, for want of a practical solution, society is reduced to a position where it can neither justify its tradition, nor commit itself to experiments in which the least mistake would drive it backward several thousand years.

In such a situation what is the mandate of science?

Certainly not to halt in an arbitrary, inconceivable, and impossible juste milieu; it is to generalize further, and discover a third principle, a fact, a superior law, which shall explain the fiction of capital and the myth of property, and reconcile them with the theory which makes labor the origin of all wealth. This is what socialism, if it wishes to proceed logically, must undertake. In fact, the theory of the real productivity of labor, and that of the fictitious productivity of capital, are both essentially economical: socialism has endeavored only to show the contradiction between them, without regard to experience or logic; for it appears to be as destitute of the one as of the other. Now, in law, the litigant who accepts the authority of a title in one particular must accept it in all; it is not allowable to divide the documents and proofs. Had socialism the right to decline the authority of political economy in relation to usury, when it appealed for support to this same authority in relation to the analysis of value? By no means. All that socialism could demand in such a case was, either that political economy should be directed to reconcile its theories, or that it might be itself intrusted with this difficult task.

The more closely we examine these solemn discussions, the more clearly we see that the whole trouble is due to the fact that one of the parties does not wish to see, while the other refuses to advance.

It is a principle of our law that no one can be deprived of his property except for the sake of general utility, and in consideration of a fair indemnity payable in advance.

This principle is eminently an economic one; for, on the one hand, it assumes the right of eminent domain of the citizen expropriated, whose consent, according to the democratic spirit of the social compact, is necessarily presupposed. On the other hand, the indemnity, or the price of the article taken, is fixed, not by the intrinsic value of the article, but by the general law of commerce, — supply and demand; in a word, by opinion. Expropriation in the name of society may be likened to a contract of convenience, agreed to by each with all; not only then must the price be paid, but the convenience also must be paid for: and it is thus, in reality, that the indemnity is estimated. If the Roman legists had seen this analogy, they undoubtedly would have hesitated less over the question of expropriation for the sake of public utility.

Such, then, is the sanction of the social right of expropriation: indemnity.

Now, practically, not only is the principle of indemnity not applied in all cases where it ought to be, but it is impossible that it should be so applied. Thus, the law which established railways provided indemnity for the lands to be occupied by the rails; it did nothing for the multitude of industries dependent upon the previous method of conveyance, whose losses far exceeded the value of the lands whose owners received compensation. Similarly, when the question of indemnifying the manufacturers of beet-root sugar was under consideration, it occurred to no one that the State ought to indemnify also the large number of laborers and employees who earned their livelihood in the beet-root industry, and who were, perhaps, to be reduced to want. Nevertheless, it is certain, according to the idea of capital and the theory of production, that as the possessor of land, whose means of labor is taken from him by the railroad, has a right to be indemnified, so also the manufacturer, whose capital is rendered unproductive by the same railroad, is entitled to indemnification. Why, then, is he not indemnified? Alas! because to indemnify him is impossible. With such a system of justice and impartiality society would be, as a general thing, unable to act, and would return to the fixedness of Roman justice. There must be victims. The principle of indemnity is consequently abandoned; to one or more classes of citizens the State is inevitably bankrupt.

At this point the socialists appear. They charge that the sole object of political economy is to sacrifice the interests of the masses and create privileges; then, finding in the law of expropriation the rudiment of an agrarian law, they suddenly advocate universal expropriation; that is, production and consumption in common.

But here socialism relapses from criticism into utopia, and its incapacity becomes freshly apparent in its contradictions. If the principle of expropriation for the sake of public utility, carried to its logical conclusion, leads to a complete reorganization of society, before commencing the work the character of this new organization must be understood; now, socialism, I repeat, has no science save a few bits of physiology and political economy. Further, it is necessary in accordance with the principle of indemnity, if not to compensate citizens, at least to guarantee to them the values which they part with; it is necessary, in short, to insure them against loss. Now, outside of the public fortune, the management of which it demands, where will socialism find security for this same fortune?

It is impossible, in sound and honest logic, to escape this circle. Consequently the communists, more open in their dealings than certain other sectarians of flowing and pacific ideas, decide the difficulty; and promise, the power once in their hands, to expropriate all and indemnify and guarantee none. At bottom, that would be neither unjust nor disloyal. Unfortunately, to burn is not to reply, as the interesting

Desmoulins said to Robespierre; and such a discussion ends always in fire and the guillotine. Here, as everywhere, two rights, equally sacred, stand in the presence of each other, the right of the citizen and the right of the State; it is enough to say that there is a superior formula which reconciles the socialistic utopias and the mutilated theories of political economy, and that the problem is to discover it. In this emergency what are the contending parties doing? Nothing. We might say rather that they raise questions only to get an opportunity to redress injuries. What do I say? The questions are not even understood by them; and, while the public is considering the sublime problems of society and human destiny, the professors of social science, orthodox and heretics, do not agree on principles. Witness the question which occasioned these inquiries, and which its authors certainly understand no better than its disparagers, — the relation of profits and wages.

What! an Academy of economists has offered for competition a question the terms of which it does not understand! How, then, could it have conceived the idea?

Well! I know that my statement is astonishing and incredible; but it is true. Like the theologians, who answer metaphysical problems only by myths and allegories, which always reproduce the problems but never solve them, the economists reply to the questions which they ask only by relating how they were led to ask them:

should they conceive that it was possible to go further, they would cease to be economists.

For example, what is profit? That which remains for the manager after he has paid all the expenses. Now, the expenses consist of the labor performed and the materials consumed; or, in fine, wages. What, then, is the wages of a workingman? The least that can be given him; that is, we do not know. What should be the price of the merchandise put upon the market by the manager? The highest that he can obtain; that is, again, we do not know. Political economy prohibits the supposition that the prices of merchandise and labor can be fixed, although it admits that they can be estimated; and that for the reason, say the economists, that estimation is essentially an arbitrary operation, which never can lead to sure and certain conclusions. How, then, shall we find the relation between two unknowns which, according to political economy, cannot be determined? Thus political economy proposes insolvable problems; and yet we shall soon see that it must propose them, and that our century must solve them. That is why I said that the Academy of Moral Sciences, in offering for competition the question of the relation of profits and wages, spoke unconsciously, spoke prophetically.

But it will be said, Is it not true that, if labor is in great demand and laborers are scarce, wages will rise, while profits on the other hand will decrease; that if, in the press of competition, there is an excess of production, there will be a stoppage and forced sales, consequently no profit for the manager and a danger of idleness for the laborer; that then the latter will offer his labor at a reduced price; that, if a machine is invented, it will first extinguish the fires of its rivals; then, a monopoly established, and the laborer made dependent on the employer, profits and wages will be inversely proportional? Cannot all these causes, and others besides, be studied, ascertained, counterbalanced, etc.?

Oh, monographs, histories! — we have been saturated with them since the days of Adam Smith and J. B. Say, and they are scarcely more than variations of these authors' words.

But it is not thus that the question should be understood, although the Academy has given it no other meaning. The relation of profits end wages should be considered in an absolute sense, and not from the inconclusive point of view of the accidents of commerce and the division of interests: two things which must ultimately receive their interpretation. Let me explain myself.

Considering producer and consumer as a single individual, whose recompense is naturally equal to his product; then dividing this product into two parts, one which rewards the producer for his outlay, another which represents his profit, according to the axiom that all labor should leave an excess, -we have to determine the relation of one of these parts to the other. This done, it will be easy to deduce the ratio of the fortunes of these two classes of men, employers and wage-laborers, as well as account for all commercial oscillations. This will be a series of corollaries to add to the demonstration.

Now, that such a relation may exist and be estimated, there must necessarily be a law, internal or external, which governs wages and prices; and since, in the present state of things, wages and prices vary and oscillate continually, we must ask what are the general facts, the causes, which make value vary and oscillate, and within what limits this oscillation takes place.

But this very question is contrary to the accepted principles; for whoever says oscillation necessarily supposes a mean direction toward which value's centre of gravity continually tends; and when the Academy asks that we determine the oscillations of profit and wages, it asks thereby that we determine value. Now that is precisely what the gentlemen of the Academy deny: they are unwilling to admit that, if value is variable, it is for that very reason determinable; that variability is the sign and condition of determinability. They pretend that value, ever varying, can never be determined. This is like maintaining that, given the number of oscillations of a pendulum per second, their amplitude, and the latitude and elevation of the spot where the experiment is performed, the length of the pendulum cannot be determined because the pendulum is in motion. Such is political economy's first article of faith.

As for socialism, it does not appear to have understood the question, or to be concerned about it. Among its many organs, some simply and merely put aside the problem by substituting division for distribution, — that is, by banishing number and measure from the social organism: others relieve themselves of the embarrassment by applying universal suffrage to the wages question. It is needless to say that these platitudes find dupes by thousands and hundreds of thousands.

The condemnation of political economy has been formulated by Malthus in this famous passage: —

A man who is born into a world already occupied, his family unable to support him, and society not requiring his labor, — such a man, I say, has not the least right to claim any nourishment whatever: he is really one too many on the earth. At the great banquet of Nature there is no plate laid for him. Nature commands him to take himself away, and she will not be slow to put her order into execution.[1]

This then is the necessary, the fatal, conclusion of political economy, — a conclusion which I shall demonstrate by evidence hitherto unknown in this field of inquiry, — Death to him who does not possess!

---

[1] The passage quoted may not be given in the exact words used by Malthus, it having reached its present shape through the medium of a French rendering — Translator.

In order better to grasp the thought of Malthus, let us translate it into philosophical propositions by stripping it of its rhetorical gloss: —

"Individual liberty, and property, which is its expression, are economical data; equality and solidarity are not.

"Under this system, each one by himself, each one for himself: labor, like all merchandise, is subject to fluctuation: hence the risks of the proletariat.

"Whoever has neither income nor wages has no right to demand anything of others: his misfortune falls on his own head; in the game of fortune, luck has been against him."

From the point of view of political economy these propositions are irrefutable; and Malthus, who has formulated them with such alarming exactness, is secure against all reproach. From the point of view of the conditions of social science, these same propositions are radically false, and even contradictory.

The error of Malthus, or rather of political economy, does not consist in saying that a man who has nothing to eat must die; or in maintaining that, under the system of individual appropriation, there is no course for him who has neither labor nor income but to withdraw from life by suicide, unless he prefers to be driven from it by starvation: such is, on the one hand, the law of our existence; such is, on the other, the consequence of property; and M. Rossi has taken altogether too much trouble to justify the good sense of Malthus on this point. I suspect, indeed, that M. Rossi, in making so lengthy and loving an apology for Malthus, intended to recommend political economy in the same way that his fellow-countryman Machiavel, in his book entitled "The Prince," recommended despotism to the admiration of the world. In pointing out misery as the necessary condition of industrial and commercial absolutism, M. Rossi seems to say to us: There is your law, your justice, your political economy; there is property.

But Gallic simplicity does not understand artifice; and it would have been better to have said to France, in her immaculate tongue: The error of Malthus, the radical vice of political economy, consists, in general terms, in affirming as a definitive state a transitory condition, — namely, the division of society into patricians and proletaires; and, particularly, in saying that in an organized, and consequently solidaire, society, there may be some who possess, labor, and consume, while others have neither possession, nor labor, nor bread. Finally Malthus, or political economy, reasons erroneously when seeing in the faculty of indefinite reproduction — which the human race enjoys in neither greater nor less degree than all animal and vegetable species — a permanent danger of famine; whereas it is only necessary to show the necessity, and consequently the existence, of a law of equilibrium between population and production.

In short, the theory of Malthus — and herein lies the great merit of this writer, a merit which none of his colleagues has dreamed of attributing to him — is a reductio ad absurdum of all political economy.

As for socialism, that was summed up long since by Plato and Thomas More in a single word, UTOPIA, — that is, no-place, a chimera.

Nevertheless, for the honor of the human mind and that justice may be done to all, this must be said: neither could economic and legislative science have had any other beginning than they did have, nor can society remain in this original position.

Every science must first define its domain, produce and collect its materials: before system, facts; before the age of art, the age of learning. The economic science, subject like every other to the law of time and the conditions of experience, before seeking to ascertain how things ought to take place in society, had to tell us how things do take place; and all these processes which the authors speak of so pompously in their books as laws, principles, and theories, in spite of their incoherence and inconsistency, had to be gathered up with scrupulous diligence, and described with strict impartiality. The fulfilment of this task called for more genius perhaps, certainly for more self-sacrifice, than will be demanded by the future progress of the science.

If, then, social economy is even yet rather an aspiration towards the future than a knowledge of reality, it must be admitted that the elements of this study are all included in political economy; and I believe that I express the general sentiment in saying that this opinion has become that of the vast majority of minds. The present finds few defenders, it is true; but the disgust with utopia is no less universal: and everybody understands that the truth lies in a formula which shall reconcile these two terms: CONSERVATION and MOTION.

Thus, thanks to Adam Smith, J. B. Say, Ricardo, and Malthus, as well as their rash opponents, the mysteries of fortune, atria Ditis, are uncovered; the power of capital, the oppression of the laborer, the machinations of monopoly, illumined at all points, shun the public gaze. Concerning the facts observed and described by the economists, we reason and conjecture: abusive laws, iniquitous customs, respected so long as the obscurity which sustained their life lasted, with difficulty dragged to the daylight, are expiring beneath the general reprobation; it is suspected that the government of society must be learned no longer from an empty ideology, after the fashion of the Contrat social, but, as Montesquieu foresaw, from the relation of things; and already a Left of eminently socialistic tendencies, composed of savants, magistrates, legists, professors, and even capitalists and manufacturers, — all born representatives and defenders of privilege, — and of a million of adepts, is forming in the nation above and outside of parliamentary opinions, and seeking, by an analysis of economic facts, to capture the secrets of the life of societies.

Let us represent political economy, then, as an immense plain, strewn with materials prepared for an edifice. The laborers await the signal, full of ardor, and burning to commence the work: but the architect has disappeared without leaving the plan. The economists have stored their memories with many things: unhappily they have not the shadow of an estimate. They know the origin and history of each piece; what it cost to make it; what wood makes the best joists, and what clay the best bricks; what has been expended in tools and carts; how much the carpenters earned, and how much the stone-cutters: they do not know the destination and the place of anything. The economists cannot deny that they have before them the fragments, scattered pell-mell, of a chef-d'oeuvre, disjecti membra poetae; but it has been impossible for them as yet to recover the general design, and, whenever they have attempted any comparisons, they have met only with incoherence. Driven to despair at last by their fruitless combinations, they have erected as a dogma the architectural incongruity of the science, or, as they say, the inconveniences of its principles; in a word, they have denied the science.[2]

Thus the division of labor, without which production would be almost nothing, is subject to a thousand inconveniences, the worst of which is the demoralization of the laborer; machinery causes, not only cheapness, but obstruction of the market and stoppage of business; competition ends in oppression; taxation, the material bond of society, is generally a scourge dreaded equally with fire and hail; credit is necessarily accompanied by bankruptcy; property is a swarm of abuses; commerce degenerates into a game of chance, in which it is sometimes allowable even to cheat: in short, disorder existing everywhere to an equal extent with order, and no one knowing how the latter is to banish the former, taxis ataxien diokein, the economists have decided that all is for the best, and regard every reformatory proposition as hostile to political economy.

The social edifice, then, has been abandoned; the crowd has burst into the wood-yard; columns, capitals, and plinths, wood, stone, and metal, have been distributed in portions and drawn by lot: and, of all these materials collected for a magnificent temple, property, ignorant and barbarous, has built huts. The work before us, then, is not only to recover the plan of the edifice, but to dislodge the occupants, who maintain that their city is superb, and, at the very mention of

---

"The principle which governs the life of nations is not pure science: it is the total of the complex data which depend on the state of enlightenment, on needs and interests." Thus expressed itself, in December, 1844, one of the clearest minds that France contained, M. Leon Faucher. Explain, if you can, how a man of this stamp was led by his economic convictions to declare that the complex data of society are opposed to pure science.

restoration, appear in battle-array at their gates. Such confusion was not seen of old at Babel: happily we speak French, and are more courageous than the companions of Nimrod.

But enough of allegory: the historical and descriptive method, successfully employed so long as the work was one of examination only, is henceforth useless: after thousands of monographs and tables, we are no further advanced than in the age of Xenophon and Hesiod. The Phenicians, the Greeks, the Italians, labored in their day as we do in ours: they invested their money, paid their laborers, extended their domains, made their expeditions and recoveries, kept their books, speculated, dabbled in stocks, and ruined themselves according to all the rules of economic art; knowing as well as ourselves how to gain monopolies and fleece the consumer and laborer. Of all this accounts are only too numerous; and, though we should rehearse forever our statistics and our figures, we should always have before our eyes only chaos, — chaos constant and uniform.

It is thought, indeed, that from the era of mythology to the present year 57 of our great revolution, the general welfare has improved: Christianity has long been regarded as the chief cause of this amelioration, but now the economists claim all the honor for their own principles. For after all, they say, what has been the influence of Christianity upon society? Thoroughly utopian at its birth, it has been able to maintain and extend itself only by gradually adopting all the economic categories, — labor, capital, farm-rent, usury, traffic, property; in short, by consecrating the Roman law, the highest expression of political economy.

Christianity, a stranger in its theological aspect to the theories of production and consumption, has been to European civilization what the trades-unions and free-masons were not long since to itinerant workmen, — a sort of insurance company and mutual aid society; in this respect, it owes nothing to political economy, and the good which it has done cannot be invoked by the latter in its own support. The effects of charity and self-sacrifice are outside of the domain of economy, which must bring about social happiness through justice and the organization of labor. For the rest, I am ready to admit the beneficial effects of the system of property; but I observe that these effects are entirely balanced by the misery which it is the nature of this system to produce; so that, as an illustrious minister recently confessed before the English Parliament, and as we shall soon show, the increase of misery in the present state of society is parallel and equal to the increase of wealth, — which completely annuls the merits of political economy.

Thus political economy is justified neither by its maxims nor by its works; and, as for socialism, its whole value consists in having established this fact. We are forced, then, to resume the examination of political economy, since it alone contains, at least in part, the materials of social science; and to ascertain whether its theories do not conceal some error, the correction of which would reconcile fact and right, reveal the organic law of humanity, and give the positive conception of order.

Chapter II. Of Value.

1. — Opposition of value in USE and value in EXCHANGE.

Value is the corner-stone of the economic edifice. The divine artist who has intrusted us with the continuation of his work has explained himself on this point to no one; but the few indications given may serve as a basis of conjecture. Value, in fact, presents two faces: one, which the economists call value in use, or intrinsic value; another, value in exchange, or of opinion. The effects which are produced by value under this double aspect, and which are very irregular so long as it is not established, — or, to use a more philosophical expression, so long as it is not constituted, -are changed totally by this constitution.

Now, in what consists the correlation between useful value and value in exchange? What is meant by constituted value, and by what sudden change is this constitution effected? To answer these questions is the object and end of political economy. I beg the reader to give his whole attention to what is to follow, this chapter being the only one in the work which will tax his patience. For my part, I will endeavor to be more and more simple and clear.

Everything which can be of any service to me is of value to me, and the more abundant the useful thing is the richer I am: so far there is no difficulty. Milk and flesh, fruits and grains, wool, sugar, cotton, wine, metals, marble; in fact, land, water, air, fire, and sunlight, — are, relatively to me, values of use, values by nature and function. If all the things which serve to sustain my life were as abundant as certain of them are, light for instance, — in other words, if the quantity of every valuable thing was inexhaustible, — my welfare would be forever assured: I should not have to labor; I should not even think. In such a state, things would always be useful, but it would be no longer true to say that they ARE VALUABLE; for value, as we shall soon see, indicates an essentially social relation; and it is solely through exchange, reverting as it were from society to Nature, that we have acquired the idea of utility. The whole development of civilization originates, then, in the necessity which the human race is under of continually causing the creation of new values; just as the evils of society are primarily caused by the perpetual struggle which we maintain against our own inertia. Take away from man that desire which leads him to think and fits him for a life of contemplation, and the lord of creation stands on a level with the highest of the beasts.

But how does value in use become value in exchange? For it should be noticed that the two kinds of value, although coexisting in thought (since the former becomes apparent only in the presence of the latter), nevertheless maintain a relation of succession: exchangeable value is a sort of reflex of useful value; just as the theologians teach that in the Trinity the Father, contemplating himself through all eternity, begets the Son. This generation of the idea of value has not been noted by the economists with sufficient care: it is important that we should tarry over it.

Since, then, of the objects which I need, a very large number exist in Nature only in moderate quantities, or even not at all, I am forced to assist in the production of that which I lack; and, as I cannot turn my hand to so many things, I propose to other men, my collaborators in various functions, to yield me a portion of their products in exchange for mine. I shall then always have in my possession more of my own special product than I consume; just as my fellows will always have in their possession more of their respective products than they use. This tacit agreement is fulfilled by commerce. Here we may observe that the logical succession of the two kinds of value is even more apparent in history than in theory, men having spent thousands of years in disputing over natural wealth (this being what is called primitive communism) before their industry afforded opportunity for exchange.

Now, the capacity possessed by all products, whether natural or the result of labor, of serving to maintain man, is called distinctively value in use; their capacity of purchasing each other, value in exchange. At bottom this is the same thing, since the second case only adds to the first the idea of substitution, which may seem an idle subtlety; practically, the consequences are surprising, and beneficial or fatal by turns.

Consequently, the distinction established in value is based on facts, and is not at all arbitrary: it is for man, in submitting to this law, to use it to increase his welfare and liberty. Labor, as an author (M. Walras) has beautifully expressed it, is a war declared against the parsimony of Nature; by it wealth and society are simultaneously created. Not only does labor produce incomparably more wealth than Nature gives us, — for instance, it has been remarked that the shoemakers alone in France produce ten times more than the mines of Peru, Brazil, and Mexico combined, — but, labor infinitely extending and multiplying its rights by the changes which it makes in natural values, it gradually comes about that all wealth, in running the gauntlet of labor, falls wholly into the hands of him who creates it, and that nothing, or almost nothing, is left for the possessor of the original material.

Such, then, is the path of economic progress: at first, appropriation of the land and natural values; then, association and distribution through labor until complete equality is attained. Chasms are scattered along our road, the sword is suspended over our heads; but, to avert all dangers, we have reason, and reason is omnipotence.

It results from the relation of useful value to exchangeable value that if, by accident or from malice, exchange should be forbidden to a single producer, or if the utility of his product should suddenly cease, though his storehouses were full, he would possess nothing. The more sacrifices he had made and the more courage he had displayed in producing, the greater would be his misery. If the utility of the product, instead of wholly disappearing, should only diminish, — a thing which may happen in a hundred ways, — the laborer, instead of being struck down and ruined by a sudden catastrophe, would be impoverished only; obliged to give a large quantity of his own value for a small quantity of the values of others, his means of subsistence would be reduced by an amount equal to the deficit in his sale: which would lead by degrees from competency to want. If, finally, the utility of the product should increase, or else if its production should become less costly, the balance of exchange would turn to the advantage of the producer, whose condition would thus be raised from fatiguing mediocrity to idle opulence. This phenomenon of depreciation and enrichment is manifested under a thousand forms and by a thousand combinations; it is the essence of the passional and intriguing game of commerce and industry. And this is the lottery, full of traps, which the economists think ought to last forever, and whose suppression the Academy of Moral and Political Sciences unwittingly demands, when, under the names of profit and wages, it asks us to reconcile value in use and value in exchange; that is, to find the method of rendering all useful values equally exchangeable, and, vice versa, all exchangeable values equally useful.

The economists have very clearly shown the double character of value, but what they have not made equally plain is its contradictory nature. Here begins our criticism.

Utility is the necessary condition of exchange; but take away exchange, and utility vanishes: these two things are indissolubly connected. Where, then, is the contradiction?

Since all of us live only by labor and exchange, and grow richer as production and exchange increase, each of us produces as much useful value as possible, in order to increase by that amount his exchanges, and consequently his enjoyments. Well, the first effect, the inevitable effect, of the multiplication of values is to LOWER them: the more abundant is an article of merchandise, the more it loses in exchange and depreciates commercially. Is it not true that there is a contradiction between the necessity of labor and its results?

I adjure the reader, before rushing ahead for the explanation, to arrest his attention upon the fact.

A peasant who has harvested twenty sacks of wheat, which he with his family proposes to consume, deems himself twice as rich as if he had harvested only ten; likewise a housewife who has spun fifty yards of linen believes that she is twice as rich as if she had spun but twenty-five. Relatively to the household, both are right; looked at in their external relations, they may be utterly mistaken. If the crop of wheat is double throughout the whole country, twenty sacks will sell for less than ten would have sold for if it had been but half as great; so, under similar circumstances, fifty yards of linen will be worth less than twenty-five: so that value decreases as the production of utility increases, and a producer may arrive at poverty by continually enriching himself. And this seems unalterable, inasmuch as there is no way of escape except all the products of industry become infinite in quantity, like air and light, which is absurd. God of my reason! Jean Jacques would have said: it is not the economists who are irrational; it is political economy itself which is false to its definitions. Mentita est iniquitas sibi.

In the preceding examples the useful value exceeds the exchangeable value: in other cases it is less. Then the same phenomenon is produced, but in the opposite direction: the balance is in favor of the producer, while the consumer suffers. This is notably the case in seasons of scarcity, when the high price of provisions is always more or less factitious. There are also professions whose whole art consists in giving to an article of minor usefulness, which could easily be dispensed with, an exaggerated value of opinion: such, in general, are the arts of luxury. Man, through his aesthetic passion, is eager for the trifles the possession of which would highly satisfy his vanity, his innate desire for luxury, and his more noble and more respectable love of the beautiful: upon this the dealers in this class of articles speculate. To tax fancy and elegance is no less odious or absurd than to tax circulation: but such a tax is collected by a few fashionable merchants, whom general infatuation protects, and whose whole merit generally consists in warping taste and generating fickleness. Hence no one complains; and all the maledictions of opinion are reserved for the monopolists who, through genius, succeed in raising by a few cents the price of linen and bread.

It is little to have pointed out this astonishing contrast between useful value and exchangeable value, which the economists have been in the habit of regarding as very simple: it must be shown that this pretended simplicity conceals a profound mystery, which it is our duty to fathom.

I summon, therefore, every serious economist to tell me, otherwise than by transforming or repeating the question, for what reason value decreases in proportion as production augments, and reciprocally what causes this same value to increase in proportion as production diminishes. In technical terms, useful value and exchangeable value, necessary to each other, are inversely proportional to each other; I ask, then, why scarcity, instead of utility, is synonymous with dearness. For — mark it well — the price of merchandise is independent of the amount of labor expended in production; and its greater or less cost does not serve at all to explain the variations in its price. Value is capricious, like liberty: it considers neither utility nor labor; on the contrary, it seems that, in the ordinary course of affairs, and exceptional derangements aside, the most useful objects are those which are sold at the lowest price; in other words, that it is just that the men who perform the most attractive labor should be the best rewarded, while those whose tasks demand the most exertion are paid the least. So that, in following the principle to its ultimate consequences, we reach the most logical of conclusions: that things whose use is necessary and quantity infinite must be gratuitous, while those which are without utility and extremely scarce must bear an inestimable price. But, to complete the embarrassment, these extremes do not occur in practice: on the one hand, no human product can ever become infinite in quantity; on the other, the rarest things must be in some degree useful, else they would not be susceptible of value. Useful value and exchangeable value remain, then, in inevitable attachment, although it is their nature continually to tend towards mutual exclusion.

I shall not fatigue the reader with a refutation of the logomachies which might be offered in explanation of this subject: of the contradiction inherent in the idea of value there is no assignable cause, no possible explanation. The fact of which I speak is one of those called primitive, — that is, one of those which may serve to explain others, but which in themselves, like the bodies called simple, are inexplicable. Such is the dualism of spirit and matter. Spirit and matter are two terms each of which, taken separately, indicates a special aspect of spirit, but corresponds to no reality. So, given man's needs of a great variety of products together with the obligation of procuring them by his labor, the opposition of useful value to exchangeable value necessarily results; and from this opposition a contradiction on the very threshold of political economy. No intelligence, no will, divine or human, can prevent it.

Therefore, instead of searching for a chimerical explanation, let us content ourselves with establishing the necessity of the contradiction. Whatever the abundance of created values and the proportion in which they exchange for each other, in order that we may exchange our products, mine must suit you when you are the buyer, and I must be satisfied with yours when you are the seller. For no one has a right to impose his own merchandise upon another: the sole judge of utility, or in other words the want, is the buyer. Therefore, in the first case, you have the deciding power; in the second, I have it. Take away reciprocal liberty, and exchange is no longer the expression of industrial solidarity: it is robbery. Communism, by the way, will never surmount this difficulty.

But, where there is liberty, production is necessarily undetermined, either in quantity or in quality; so that from the point of view of economic progress, as from that of the relation of consumers, valuation always is an arbitrary matter, and the price of merchandise will ever fluctuate. Suppose for a moment that all producers should sell at a fixed price: there would be some who, producing at less cost and in better quality, would get much, while others would get nothing. In every way equilibrium would be destroyed. Do you wish, in order to prevent business stagnation, to limit production strictly to the necessary amount? That would be a violation of liberty: for, in depriving me of the power of choice, you condemn me to pay the highest price; you destroy competition, the sole guarantee of cheapness, and encourage smuggling. In this way, to avoid commercial absolutism, you would rush into administrative absolutism; to create equality, you would destroy liberty, which is to deny equality itself. Would you group producers in a single workshop (supposing you to possess this secret)? That again does not suffice: it would be necessary also to group consumers in a common household, whereby you would abandon the point. We are not to abolish the idea of value, which is as impossible as to abolish labor, but to determine it; we are not to kill individual liberty, but to socialize it. Now, it is proved that it is the free will of man that gives rise to the opposition between value in use and value in exchange: how reconcile this opposition while free will exists? And how sacrifice the latter without sacrificing man?

Then, from the very fact that I, as a free purchaser, am judge of my own wants, judge of the fitness of the object, judge of the price I wish to pay, and that you on the other hand, as a free producer, control the means of production, and consequently have the power to reduce your expenses, absolutism forces itself forward as an element of value, and causes it to oscillate between utility and opinion.

But this oscillation, clearly pointed out by the economists, is but the effect of a contradiction which, repeating itself on a vast scale, engenders the most unexpected phenomena. Three years of fertility, in certain provinces of Russia, are a public calamity, just as, in our vineyards, three years of abundance are a calamity to the wine-grower I know well that the economists attribute this distress to a lack of markets; wherefore this question of markets is an important one with them. Unfortunately the theory of markets, like that of emigration with which they attempted to meet Malthus, is a begging of the question. The States having the largest market are as subject to over-production as the most isolated countries: where are high and low prices better known than in the stock-exchanges of Paris and London?

From the oscillation of value and the irregular effects resulting therefrom the socialists and economists, each in their own way, have reasoned to opposite, but equally false, conclusions: the former have made it a text for the slander of political economy and its exclusion from social science; the latter, for the denial of all possibility of reconciliation, and the affirmation of the incommensurability of values, and consequently the inequality of fortunes, as an absolute law of commerce.

I say that both parties are equally in error.

1. The contradictory idea of value, so clearly exhibited by the inevitable distinction between useful value and value in exchange does not arise from a false mental perception, or from a vicious terminology, or from any practical error; it lies deep in the nature of things, and forces itself upon the mind as a general form of thought, — that is, as a category. Now, as the idea of value is the point of departure of political economy, it follows that all the elements of the science — I use the word science in anticipation — are contradictory in themselves and opposed to each other: so truly is this the case that on every question the economist finds himself continually placed between an affirmation and a negation alike irrefutable. ANTINOMY, in fine, to use a word sanctioned by modern philosophy, is the essential characteristic of political economy; that is to say, it is at once its death-sentence and its justification.

Antinomy, literally counter-law, means opposition in principle or antagonism in relation, just as contradiction or antilogy indicates opposition or discrepancy in speech. Antinomy, — I ask pardon for entering into these scholastic details, comparatively unfamiliar as yet to most economists, — antinomy is the conception of a law with two faces, the one positive, the other negative. Such, for instance, is the law called attraction, by which the planets revolve around the sun, and which mathematicians have analyzed into centripetal force and centrifugal force. Such also is the problem of the infinite divisibility of matter, which, as Kant has shown, can be denied and affirmed successively by arguments equally plausible and irrefutable.

Antinomy simply expresses a fact, and forces itself imperatively on the mind; contradiction, properly speaking, is an absurdity. This distinction between antinomy (contra-lex) and contradiction (contra-dictio) shows in what sense it can be said that, in a certain class of ideas and facts, the argument of contradiction has not the same value as in mathematics.

In mathematics it is a rule that, a proposition being proved false, its opposite is true, and vice versa. In fact, this is the principal method of mathematical demonstration. In social economy, it is not the same: thus we see, for example, that property being proved by its results to be false, the opposite formula, communism, is none the truer on this account, but is deniable at the same time and by the same title as property. Does it follow, as has been said with such ridiculous emphasis, that every truth, every idea, results from a contradiction, — that is, from a something which is affirmed and denied at the same moment and from the same point of view, — and that it may be necessary to abandon wholly the old-fashioned logic, which regards contradiction as the infallible sign of error? This babble is worthy of sophists who, destitute of faith and honesty, endeavor to perpetuate scepticism in order to maintain their impertinent uselessness. Because antinomy, immediately it is misunderstood, leads inevitably to contradiction, these have been mistaken for each other, especially among the French, who like to judge everything by its effects. But neither contradiction nor antinomy, which analysis discovers at the bottom of every simple idea, is the principle of truth. Contradiction is always synonymous with nullity; as for antinomy, sometimes called by the same name, it is indeed the forerunner of truth, the material of which, so to speak, it supplies; but it is not truth, and, considered in itself, it is the efficient cause of disorder, the characteristic form of delusion and evil.

An antinomy is made up of two terms, necessary to each other, but always opposed, and tending to mutual destruction. I hardly dare to add, as I must, that the first of these terms has received the name thesis, position, and the second the name anti-thesis, counter-position. This method of thought is now so well-known that it will soon figure, I hope, in the text-books of the primary schools. We shall see directly how from the combination of these two zeros unity springs forth, or the idea which dispels the antinomy.

Thus, in value, there is nothing useful that cannot be exchanged, nothing exchangeable if it be not useful: value in use and value in exchange are inseparable. But while, by industrial progress, demand varies and multiplies to an infinite extent, and while manufactures tend in consequence to increase the natural utility of things, and finally to convert all useful value into exchangeable value, production, on the other hand, continually increasing the power of its instruments and always reducing its expenses, tends to restore the venal value of things to their primitive utility: so that value in use and value in exchange are in perpetual struggle.

The effects of this struggle are well-known: the wars of commerce and of the market; obstructions to business; stagnation; prohibition; the massacres of competition; monopoly; reductions of wages; laws fixing maximum prices; the crushing inequality of fortunes; misery, — all these result from the antinomy of value. The proof of this I may be excused from giving here, as it will appear naturally in the chapters to follow.

The socialists, while justly demanding that this antagonism be brought to an end, have erred in mistaking its source, and in seeing in it only a mental oversight, capable of rectification by a legal decree. Hence this lamentable outbreak of sentimentalism, which has rendered socialism so insipid to positive minds, and which, spreading the absurdest delusions, makes so many fresh dupes every day.

My complaint of socialism is not that it has appeared among us without cause, but that it has clung so long and so obstinately to its silliness.

2. But the economists have erred no less gravely in rejecting a priori, and just because of the contradictory, or rather antinomical, nature of value, every idea and hope of reform, never desiring to understand that, for the very reason that society has arrived at its highest point of antagonism, reconciliation and harmony are at hand. This, nevertheless, is what a close study of political economy would have shown to its adepts, had they paid more attention to the lights of modern metaphysics. It is indeed demonstrated, by the most positive evidence known to the human mind, that wherever an antinomy appears there is a promise of a resolution of its terms, and consequently an announcement of a coming change. Now, the idea of value, as developed by J. B. Say among others, satisfies exactly these conditions. But the economists, who have remained for the most part by an inconceivable fatality ignorant of the movement of philosophy, have guarded against the supposition that the essentially contradictory, or, as they say, variable, character of value might be at the same time the authentic sign of its constitutionality, — that is, of its eminently harmonious and determinable nature. However dishonorable it may be to the economists of the various schools, it is certain that their opposition to socialism results solely from this false conception of their own principles; one proof, taken from a thousand, will suffice.

The Academy of Sciences (not that of Moral Sciences, but the other), going outside of its province one day, listened to a paper in which it was proposed to calculate tables of value for all kinds of merchandise upon the basis of the average product per man and per day's labor in each branch of industry. "Le Journal des Economistes" (August, 1845) immediately made this communication, intrusive in its eyes, the text of a protest against the plan of tariff which was its object, and the occasion of a reestablishment of what it called true principles: —

"There is no measure of value, no standard of value," it said in its conclusions; "economic science tells us this, just as mathematical science tells us that there is no perpetual motion or quadrature of the circle, and that these never will be found. Now, if there is no standard of value, if the measure of value is not even a metaphysical illusion, what then is the law which governs exchanges?.... As we have said before, it is, in a general way, supply and demand: that is the last word of science."

Now, how did "Le Journal des Economistes" prove that there is no measure of value? I use the consecrated expression: though I shall show directly that this phrase, measure of value, is somewhat ambiguous, and does not convey the exact meaning which it is intended, and which it ought, to express.

This journal repeated, with accompanying examples, the exposition that we have just given of the variability of value, but without arriving, as we did, at the contradiction. Now, if the estimable editor, one of the most distinguished economists of the school of Say, had had stricter logical habits; if he had been long used, not only to observing facts, but to seeking their explanation in the ideas which produce them, — I do not doubt that he would have expressed himself more cautiously, and that, instead of seeing in the variability of value the last word of science, he would have recognized unaided that it is the first. Seeing that the variability of value proceeds not from things, but from the mind, he would have said that, as human liberty has its law, so value must have its law; consequently, that the hypothesis of a measure of value, this being the common expression, is not at all irrational; quite the contrary, that it is the denial of this measure that is illogical, untenable.

And indeed, what is there in the idea of measuring, and consequently of fixing, value, that is unscientific? All men believe in it; all wish it, search for it, suppose it: every proposition of sale or purchase is at bottom only a comparison between two values, — that is, a determination, more or less accurate if you will, but nevertheless effective. The opinion of the human race on the existing difference between real value and market price may be said to be unanimous. It is for this reason that so many kinds of merchandise are sold at a fixed price; there are some, indeed, which, even in their variations, are always fixed, — bread, for instance. It will not be denied that, if two manufacturers can supply one another by an account current, and at a settled price, with quantities of their respective products, ten, a hundred, a thousand manufacturers can do the same. Now, that would be a solution of the problem of the measure of value. The price of everything would be debated upon, I allow, because debate is still our only method of fixing prices; but yet, as all light is the result of conflict, debate, though it may be a proof of uncertainty, has for its object, setting aside the greater or less amount of good faith that enters into it, the discovery of the relation of values to each other, — that is, their measurement, their law.

Ricardo, in his theory of rent, has given a magnificent example of the commensurability of values. He has shown that arable lands are to each other as the crops which they yield with the same outlay; and here universal practice is in harmony with theory. Now who will say that this positive and sure method of estimating the value of land, and in general of all engaged capital, cannot be applied to products also? . . . .

They say: Political economy is not affected by a priori arguments; it pronounces only upon facts. Now, facts and experience teach us that there is no measure of value and can be none, and prove that, though the conception of such an idea was necessary in the nature of things, its realization is wholly chimerical. Supply and demand is the sole law of exchange.

I will not repeat that experience proves precisely the contrary; that everything, in the economic progress of society, denotes a tendency toward the constitution and establishment of value; that that is the culminating point of political economy — which by this constitution becomes transformed — and the supreme indication of order in society: this general outline, reiterated without proof, would become tiresome. I confine myself for the moment within the limits of the discussion, and say that supply and demand, held up as the sole regulators of value, are nothing more than two ceremonial forms serving to bring useful value and exchangeable value face to face, and to provoke their reconciliation. They are the two electric poles, whose connection must produce the economical phenomenon of affinity called EXCHANGE. Like the poles of a battery, supply and demand are diametrically opposed to each other, and tend continually to mutual annihilation; it is by their antagonism that the price of things is either increased, or reduced to nothing: we wish to know, then, if it is not possible, on every occasion, so to balance or harmonize these two forces that the price of things always may be the expression of their true value, the expression of justice. To say after that that supply and demand is the law of exchange is to say that supply and demand is the law of supply and demand; it is not an explanation of the general practice, but a declaration of its absurdity; and I deny that the general practice is absurd.

I have just quoted Ricardo as having given, in a special instance, a positive rule for the comparison of values: the economists do better still. Every year they gather from tables of statistics the average prices of the various grains. Now, what is the meaning of an average? Every one can see that in a single operation, taken at random from a million, there is no means of knowing which prevailed, supply — that is, useful value — or exchangeable value, — that is, demand. But as every increase in the price of merchandise is followed sooner or later by a proportional reduction; as, in other words, in society the profits of speculation are equal to the losses, — we may regard with good reason the average of prices during a complete period as indicative of the real and legitimate value of products. This average, it is true, is ascertained too late: but who knows that we could not discover it in advance? Is there an economist who dares to deny it?

Nolens volens, then, the measure of value must be sought for: logic commands it, and her conclusions are adverse to economists and socialists alike. The opinion which denies the existence of this measure is irrational, unreasonable. Say as often as you please, on the one hand, that political economy is a science of facts, and that the facts are contrary to the hypothesis of a determination of value, or, on the other, that this troublesome question would not present itself in a system of universal association, which would absorb all antagonism, — I will reply still, to the right and to the left: —

1. That as no fact is produced which has not its cause, so none exists which has not its law; and that, if the law of exchange is not discovered, the fault is, not with the facts, but with the savants.

2. That, as long as man shall labor in order to live, and shall labor freely, justice will be the condition of fraternity and the basis of association; now, without a determination of value, justice is imperfect, impossible.

2. — Constitution of value; definition of wealth.

We know value in its two opposite aspects; we do not know it in its TOTALITY. If we can acquire this new idea, we shall have absolute value; and a table of values, such as was called for in the memoir read to the Academy of Sciences, will be possible.

Let us picture wealth, then, as a mass held by a chemical force in a permanent state of composition, in which new elements, continually entering, combine in different proportions, but according to a certain law: value is the proportional relation (the measure) in which each of these elements forms a part of the whole.

From this two things result: one, that the economists have been wholly deluded when they have looked for the general measure of value in wheat, specie, rent, etc., and also when, after having demonstrated that this standard of measure was neither here nor there, they have concluded that value has neither law nor measure; the other, that the proportion of values may continually vary without ceasing on that account to be subject to a law, whose determination is precisely the solution sought.

This idea of value satisfies, as we shall see, all the conditions: for it includes at once both the positive and fixed element in useful value and the variable element in exchangeable value; in the second place, it puts an end to the contradiction which seemed an insurmountable obstacle in the way of the determination of value; further, we shall show that value thus understood differs entirely from a simple juxtaposition of the two ideas of useful and exchangeable value, and that it is endowed with new properties.

The proportionality of products is not a revelation that we pretend to offer to the world, or a novelty that we bring into science, any more than the division of labor was an unheard-of thing when Adam Smith explained its marvels. The proportionality of products is, as we might prove easily by innumerable quotations, a common idea running through the works on political economy, but to which no one as yet has dreamed of attributing its rightful importance: and this is the task which we undertake today. We feel bound, for the rest, to make this declaration in order to reassure the reader concerning our pretensions to originality, and to satisfy those minds whose timidity leads them to look with little favor upon new ideas.

The economists seem always to have understood by the measure of value only a standard, a sort of original unit, existing by itself, and applicable to all sorts of merchandise, as the yard is applicable to all lengths. Consequently, many have thought that such a standard is furnished by the precious metals. But the theory of money has proved that, far from being the measure of values, specie is only their arithmetic, and a conventional arithmetic at that. Gold and silver are to value what the thermometer is to heat. The thermometer, with its arbitrarily graduated scale, indicates clearly when there is a loss or an increase of heat: but what the laws of heat-equilibrium are; what is its proportion in various bodies; what amount is necessary to cause a rise of ten, fifteen, or twenty degrees in the thermometer, — the thermometer does not tell us; it is not certain even that the degrees of the scale, equal to each other, correspond to equal additions of heat.

The idea that has been entertained hitherto of the measure of value, then, is inexact; the object of our inquiry is not the standard of value, as has been said so often and so foolishly, but the law which regulates the proportions of the various products to the social wealth; for upon the knowledge of this law depends the rise and fall of prices in so far as it is normal and legitimate. In a word, as we understand by the measure of celestial bodies the relation resulting from the comparison of these bodies with each other, so, by the measure of values, we must understand the relation which results from their comparison. Now, I say that this relation has its law, and this comparison its principle.

I suppose, then, a force which combines in certain proportions the elements of wealth, and makes of them a homogeneous whole: if the constituent elements do not exist in the desired proportion, the combination will take place nevertheless; but, instead of absorbing all the material, it will reject a portion as useless. The internal movement by which the combination is produced, and which the affinities of the various substances determine — this movement in society is exchange; exchange considered no longer simply in its elementary form and between man and man, but exchange considered as the fusion of all values produced by private industry in one and the same mass of social wealth. Finally, the proportion in which each element enters into the compound is what we call value; the excess remaining after the combination is non-value, until the addition of a certain quantity of other elements causes further combination and exchange.

We will explain later the function of money.

This determined, it is conceivable that at a given moment the proportions of values constituting the wealth of a country may be determined, or at least empirically approximated, by means of statistics and inventories, in nearly the same way that the chemists have discovered by experience, aided by analysis, the proportions of hydrogen and oxygen necessary to the formation of water. There is nothing objectionable in this method of determining values; it is, after all, only a matter of accounts. But such a work, however interesting it might be, would teach us nothing very useful. On the one hand, indeed, we know that the proportion continually varies; on the other, it is clear that from a statement of the public wealth giving the proportions of values only for the time and place when and where the statistics should be gathered we could not deduce the law of proportionality of wealth. For that, a single operation of this sort would not be sufficient; thousands and millions of similar ones would be necessary, even admitting the method to be worthy of confidence.

Now, here there is a difference between economic science and chemistry. The chemists, who have discovered by experience such beautiful proportions, know no more of their how or why than of the force which governs them. Social economy, on the contrary, to which no a posteriori investigation could reveal directly the law of proportionality of values, can grasp it in the very force which produces it, and which it is time to announce.

This force, which Adam Smith has glorified so eloquently, and which his successors have misconceived (making privilege its equal), — this force is LABOR. Labor differs in quantity and quality with the producer; in this respect it is like all the great principles of Nature and the most general laws, simple in their action and formula, but infinitely modified by a multitude of special causes, and manifesting themselves under an innumerable variety of forms. It is labor, labor alone, that produces all the elements of wealth, and that combines them to their last molecules according to a law of variable, but certain, proportionality. It is labor, in fine, that, as the principle of life, agitates (mens agitat) the material (molem) of wealth, and proportions it.

Society, or the collective man, produces an infinitude of objects, the enjoyment of which constitutes its well-being. This well-being is developed not only in the ratio of the quantity of the products, but also in the ratio of their variety (quality) and proportion. From this fundamental datum it follows that society always, at each instant of its life, must strive for such proportion in its products as will give the greatest amount of well-being, considering the power and means of production. Abundance, variety, and proportion in products are the three factors which constitute WEALTH: wealth, the object of social economy, is subject to the same conditions of existence as beauty, the object of art; virtue, the object of morality; and truth, the object of metaphysics.

But how establish this marvelous proportion, so essential that without it a portion of human labor is lost, — that is, useless, inharmonious, untrue, and consequently synonymous with poverty and annihilation?

Prometheus, according to the fable, is the symbol of human activity. Prometheus steals the fire of heaven, and invents the early arts; Prometheus foresees the future, and aspires to equality with Jupiter; Prometheus is God. Then let us call society Prometheus.

Prometheus devotes, on an average, ten hours a day to labor, seven to rest, and seven to pleasure. In order to gather from his toil the most useful fruit, Prometheus notes the time and trouble that each object of his consumption costs him. Only experience can teach him this, and this experience lasts throughout his life. While laboring and producing, then, Prometheus is subject to an infinitude of disappointments. But, as a final result, the more he labors, the greater is his well-being and the more idealized his luxury; the further he extends his conquests over Nature, the more strongly he fortifies within him the principle of life and intelligence in the exercise of which he alone finds happiness; till finally, the early education of the Laborer completed and order introduced into his occupations, to labor, with him, is no longer to suffer, — it is to live, to enjoy. But the attractiveness of labor does not nullify the rule, since, on the contrary, it is the fruit of it; and those who, under the pretext that labor should be attractive, reason to the denial of justice and to communism, resemble children who, after having gathered some flowers in the garden, should arrange a flower-bed on the staircase.

In society, then, justice is simply the proportionality of values; its guarantee and sanction is the responsibility of the producer.

Prometheus knows that such a product costs an hour's labor, such another a day's, a week's, a year's; he knows at the same time that all these products, arranged according to their cost, form the progression of his wealth. First, then, he will assure his existence by providing himself with the least costly, and consequently most necessary, things; then, as fast as his position becomes secure, he will look forward to articles of luxury, proceeding always, if he is wise, according to the natural position of each article in the scale of prices. Sometimes Prometheus will make a mistake in his calculations, or else, carried away by passion, he will sacrifice an immediate good to a premature enjoyment, and, after having toiled and moiled, he will starve. Thus, the law carries with it its own sanction; its violation is inevitably accompanied by the immediate punishment of the transgressor.

Say, then, was right in saying: "The happiness of this class (the consumers), composed of all the others, constitutes the general well-being, the state of prosperity of a country." Only he should have added that the happiness of the class of producers, which also is composed of all the others, equally constitutes the general well-being, the state of prosperity of a country. So, when he says: "The fortune of each consumer is perpetually at war with all that he buys," he should have added again: "The fortune of each producer is incessantly attacked by all that he sells." In the absence of a clear expression of this reciprocity, most economical phenomena become unintelligible; and I will soon show how, in consequence of this grave omission, most economists in writing their books have talked wildly about the balance of trade.

I have just said that society produces first the least costly, and consequently most necessary, things. Now, is it true that cheapness of products is always a correlative of their necessity, and vice versa; so that these two words, necessity and cheapness, like the following ones, costliness and superfluity, are synonymes?

If each product of labor, taken alone, would suffice for the existence of man, the synonymy in question would not be doubtful; all products having the same qualities, those would be most advantageously produced, and therefore the most necessary, which cost the least. But the parallel between the utility and price of products is not characterized by this theoretical precision: either through the foresight of Nature or from some other cause, the balance between needs and productive power is more than a theory, — it is a fact, of which daily practice, as well as social progress, gives evidence.

Imagine ourselves living in the day after the birth of man at the beginning of civilization: is it not true that the industries originally the simplest, those which required the least preparation and expense, were the following: gathering, pasturage, hunting, and fishing, which were followed long afterwards by agriculture? Since then, these four primitive industries have been perfected, and moreover appropriated: a double circumstance which does not change the meaning of the facts, but, on the contrary, makes it more manifest. In fact, property has always attached itself by preference to objects of the most immediate utility, to made values, if I may so speak; so that the scale of values might be fixed by the progress of appropriation.

In his work on the "Liberty of Labor" M. Dunoyer has positively accepted this principle by distinguishing four great classes of industry, which he arranges according to the order of their development, — that is, from the least labor-cost to the greatest. These are extractive industry, — including all the semi-barbarous functions mentioned above, — commercial industry, manufacturing, industry, agricultural industry. And it is for a profound reason that the learned author placed agriculture last in the list. For, despite its great antiquity, it is certain that this industry has not kept pace with the others, and the succession of human affairs is not decided by their origin, but by their entire development. It may be that agricultural industry was born before the others, and it may be that all were contemporary; but that will be deemed of the latest date which shall be perfected last.

Thus the very nature of things, as well as his own wants, indicates to the laborer the order in which he should effect the production of the values that make up his well-being. Our law of proportionality, then, is at once physical and logical, objective and subjective; it has the highest degree of certainty. Let us pursue the application.

Of all the products of labor, none perhaps has cost longer and more patient efforts than the calendar. Nevertheless, there is none the enjoyment of which can now be procured more cheaply, and which, consequently, by our own definitions, has become more necessary. How, then, shall we explain this change? Why has the calendar, so useless to the early hordes, who only needed the alternation of night and day, as of winter and summer, become at last so indispensable, so unexpensive, so perfect? For, by a marvelous harmony, in social economy all these adjectives are interconvertible. How account, in short, by our law of proportion, for the variability of the value of the calendar?

In order that the labor necessary to the production of the calendar might be performed, might be possible, man had to find means of gaining time from his early occupations and from those which immediately followed them. In other words, these industries had to become more productive, or less costly, than they were at the beginning: which amounts to saying that it was necessary first to solve the problem of the production of the calendar from the extractive industries themselves.

Suppose, then, that suddenly, by a fortunate combination of efforts, by the division of labor, by the use of some machine, by better management of the natural resources, — in short, by his industry, — Prometheus finds a way of producing in one day as much of a certain object as he formerly produced in ten: what will follow? The product will change its position in the table of the elements of wealth; its power of affinity for other products, so to speak, being increased, its relative value will be proportionately diminished, and, instead of being quoted at one hundred, it will thereafter be quoted only at ten. But this value will still and always be none the less accurately determined, and it will still be labor alone which will fix the degree of its importance. Thus value varies, and the law of value is unchangeable: further, if value is susceptible of variation, it is because it is governed by a law whose principle is essentially inconstant, — namely, labor measured by time.

The same reasoning applies to the production of the calendar as to that of all possible values. I do not need to explain how — civilization (that is, the social fact of the increase of life) multiplying our tasks, rendering our moments more and more precious, and obliging us to keep a perpetual and detailed record of our whole life — the calendar has become to all one of the most necessary things. We know, moreover, that this wonderful discovery has given rise, as its natural complement, to one of our most valuable industries, the manufacture of clocks and watches.

At this point there very naturally arises an objection, the only one that can be offered against the theory of the proportionality of values.

Say and the economists who have succeeded him have observed that, labor being itself an object of valuation, a species of merchandise indeed like any other, to take it as the principal and efficient cause of value is to reason in a vicious circle. Therefore, they conclude, it is necessary to fall back on scarcity and opinion.

These economists, if they will allow me to say it, herein have shown themselves wonderfully careless. Labor is said to have value, not as merchandise itself, but in view of the values supposed to be contained in it potentially. The value of labor is a figurative expression, an anticipation of effect from cause.

It is a fiction by the same title as the productivity of capital. Labor produces, capital has value: and when, by a sort of ellipsis, we say the value of labor, we make an enjambement which is not at all contrary to the rules of language, but which theorists ought to guard against mistaking for a reality. Labor, like liberty, love, ambition, genius, is a thing vague and indeterminate in its nature, but qualitatively defined by its object, — that is, it becomes a reality through its product. When, therefore, we say: This man's labor is worth five francs per day, it is as if we should say: The daily product of this man's labor is worth five francs.

Now, the effect of labor is continually to eliminate scarcity and opinion as constitutive elements of value, and, by necessary consequence, to transform natural or indefinite utilities (appropriated or not) into measurable or social utilities: whence it follows that labor is at once a war declared upon the parsimony of Nature and a permanent conspiracy against property.

According to this analysis, value, considered from the point of view of the association which producers, by division of labor and by exchange, naturally form among themselves, is the proportional relation of the products which constitute wealth, and what we call the value of any special product is a formula which expresses, in terms of money, the proportion of this product to the general wealth. — Utility is the basis of value; labor fixes the relation; the price is the expression which, barring the fluctuations that we shall have to consider, indicates this relation.

Such is the centre around which useful and exchangeable value oscillate, the point where they are finally swallowed up and disappear: such is the absolute, unchangeable law which regulates economic disturbances and the freaks of industry and commerce, and governs progress. Every effort of thinking and laboring humanity, every individual and social speculation, as an integrant part of collective wealth, obeys this law. It was the destiny of political economy, by successively positing all its contradictory terms, to make this law known; the object of social economy, which I ask permission for a moment to distinguish from political economy, although at bottom there is no difference between them, will be to spread and apply it universally.

The theory of the measure or proportionality of values is, let it be noticed, the theory of equality itself. Indeed, just as in society, where we have seen that there is a complete identity between producer and consumer, the revenue paid to an idler is like value cast into the flames of Etna, so the laborer who receives excessive wages is like a gleaner to whom should be given a loaf of bread for gathering a stalk of grain: and all that the economists have qualified as unproductive consumption is in reality simply a violation of the law of proportionality.

We shall see in the sequence how, from these simple data, the social genius gradually deduces the still obscure system of organization of labor, distribution of wages, valuation of products, and universal solidarity. For social order is established upon the basis of inexorable justice, not at all upon the paradisical sentiments of fraternity, self-sacrifice, and love, to the exercise of which so many honorable socialists are endeavoring now to stimulate the people. It is in vain that, following Jesus Christ, they preach the necessity, and set the example, of sacrifice; selfishness is stronger, and only the law of severity, economic fatality, is capable of mastering it. Humanitarian enthusiasm may produce shocks favorable to the progress of civilization; but these crises of sentiment, like the oscillations of value, must always result only in a firmer and more absolute establishment of justice. Nature, or Divinity, we distrust in our hearts: she has never believed in the love of man for his fellow; and all that science reveals to us of the ways of Providence in the progress of society — I say it to the shame of the human conscience, but our hypocrisy must be made aware of it — shows a profound misanthropy on the part of God. God helps us, not from motives of goodness, but because order is his essence; God promotes the welfare of the world, not because he deems it worthy, but because the religion of his supreme intelligence lays the obligation upon him: and while the vulgar give him the sweet name Father, it is impossible for the historian, for the political economist, to believe that he either loves or esteems us.

Let us imitate this sublime indifference, this stoical ataraxia, of God; and, since the precept of charity always has failed to promote social welfare, let us look to pure reason for the conditions of harmony and virtue.

Value, conceived as the proportionality of products, otherwise called CONSTITUTED VALUE, necessarily implies in an equal degree utility and venality, indivisibly and harmoniously united. It implies utility, for, without this condition, the product would be destitute of that affinity which renders it exchangeable, and consequently makes it an element of wealth; it implies venality, since, if the product was not acceptable in the market at any hour and at a known price, it would be only a non-value, it would be nothing.

But, in constituted value, all these properties acquire a broader, more regular, truer significance than before. Thus, utility is no longer that inert capacity, so to speak, which things possess of serving for our enjoyments and in our researches; venality is no longer the exaggeration of a blind fancy or an unprincipled opinion; finally, variability has ceased to explain itself by a disingenuous discussion between supply and demand: all that has disappeared to give place to a positive, normal, and, under all possible circumstances, determinable idea. By the constitution of values each product, if it is allowable to establish such an analogy, becomes like the nourishment which, discovered by the alimentary instinct, then prepared by the digestive organs, enters into the general circulation, where it is converted, according to certain proportions, into flesh, bone, liquid, etc., and gives to the body life, strength, and beauty.

Now, what change does the idea of value undergo when we rise from the contradictory notions of useful value and exchangeable value to that of constituted value or absolute value? There is, so to speak, a joining together, a reciprocal penetration, in which the two elementary concepts, grasping each other like the hooked atoms of Epicurus, absorb one another and disappear, leaving in their place a compound possessed, but in a superior degree, of all their positive properties, and divested of all their negative properties. A value really such — like money, first-class business paper, government annuities, shares in a well-established enterprise — can neither be increased without reason nor lost in exchange: it is governed only by the natural law of the addition of special industries and the increase of products. Further, such a value is not the result of a compromise, — that is, of eclecticism, juste-milieu, or mixture; it is the product of a complete fusion, a product entirely new and distinct from its components, just as water, the product of the combination of hydrogen and oxygen, is a separate body, totally distinct from its elements.

The resolution of two antithetical ideas in a third of a superior order is what the school calls synthesis. It alone gives the positive and complete idea, which is obtained, as we have seen, by the successive affirmation or negation — for both amount to the same thing — of two diametrically opposite concepts. Whence we deduce this corollary, of the first importance in practice as well as in theory: wherever, in the spheres of morality, history, or political economy, analysis has established the antinomy of an idea, we may affirm on a priori grounds that this antinomy conceals a higher idea, which sooner or later will make its appearance.

I am sorry to have to insist at so great length on ideas familiar to all young college graduates: but I owed these details to certain economists, who, apropos of my critique of property, have heaped dilemmas on dilemmas to prove that, if I was not a proprietor, I necessarily must be a communist; all because they did not understand thesis, antithesis, and synthesis.

The synthetic idea of value, as the fundamental condition of social order and progress, was dimly seen by Adam Smith, when, to use the words of M. Blanqui, "he showed that labor is the universal and invariable measure of values, and proved that everything has its natural price, toward which it continually gravitates amid the fluctuations of the market, occasioned by accidental circumstances foreign to the venal value of the thing."

But this idea of value was wholly intuitive with Adam Smith, and society does not change its habits upon the strength of intuitions; it decides only upon the authority of facts. The antinomy had to be expressed in a plainer and clearer manner: J. B. Say was its principal interpreter. But, in spite of the imaginative efforts and fearful subtlety of this economist, Smith's definition controls him without his knowledge, and is manifest throughout his arguments.

"To put a value on an article," says Say, "is to declare that it should be estimated equally with some other designated article . . . . . The value of everything is vague and arbitrary until it is RECOGNIZED . . . .." There is, therefore, a method of recognizing the value of things, — that is, of determining it; and, as this recognition or determination results from the comparison of things with each other, there is, further, a common feature, a principle, by means of which we are able to declare that one thing is worth more or less than, or as much as, another.

Say first said: "The measure of value is the value of an other product." Afterwards, having seen that this phrase was but a tautology, he modified it thus: "The measure of value is the quantity of another product," which is quite as unintelligible. Moreover, this writer, generally so clear and decided, embarrasses himself with vain distinctions: "We may appreciate the value of things; we cannot measure it, — that is, compare it with an invariable and known standard, for no such standard exists. We can do nothing but estimate the value of things by comparing them." At other times he distinguishes between real values and relative values: "The former are those whose value changes with the cost of production; the latter are those whose value changes relatively to the value of other kinds of merchandise."

Singular prepossession of a man of genius, who does not see that to compare, to appraise, to appreciate, is to MEASURE; that every measure, being only a comparison, indicates for that very reason a true relation, provided the comparison is accurate; that, consequently, value, or real measure, and value, or relative measure, are perfectly identical; and that the difficulty is reduced, not to the discovery of a standard of measure, since all quantities may serve each other in that capacity, but to the determination of a point of comparison. In geometry the point of comparison is extent, and the unit of measure is now the division of the circle into three hundred and sixty parts, now the circumference of the terrestrial globe, now the average dimension of the human arm, hand, thumb, or foot. In economic science, we have said after Adam Smith, the point of view from which all values are compared is labor; as for the unit of measure, that adopted in France is the FRANC. It is incredible that so many sensible men should struggle for forty years against an idea so simple. But no: The comparison of values is effected without a point of comparison between them, and without a unit of measure, — such is the proposition which the economists of the nineteenth century, rather than accept the revolutionary idea of equality, have resolved to maintain against all comers. What will posterity say?

I shall presently show, by striking examples, that the idea of the measure or proportion of values, theoretically necessary, is constantly realized in every-day life.

3. — Application of the law of proportionality of values.

Every product is a representative of labor.

Every product, therefore, can be exchanged for some other, as universal practice proves.

But abolish labor, and you have left only articles of greater or less usefulness, which, being stamped with no economic character, no human seal, are without a common measure, — that is, are logically unexchangeable.

Gold and silver, like other articles of merchandise, are representatives of value; they have, therefore, been able to serve as common measures and mediums of exchange. But the special function which custom has allotted to the precious metals, — that of serving as a commercial agent, — is purely conventional, and any other article of merchandise, less conveniently perhaps, but just as authentically, could play this part: the economists admit it, and more than one example of it can be cited. What, then, is the reason of this preference generally accorded to the metals for the purpose of money, and how shall we explain this speciality of function, unparalleled in political economy, possessed by specie? For every unique thing incomparable in kind is necessarily very difficult of comprehension, and often even fails of it altogether. Now, is it possible to reconstruct the series from which money seems to have been detached, and, consequently, restore the latter to its true principle?

In dealing with this question the economists, following their usual course, have rushed beyond the limits of their science; they have appealed to physics, to mechanics, to history, etc.; they have talked of all things, but have given no answer.

The precious metals, they have said, by their scarcity, density, and incorruptibility, are fitted to serve as money in, a degree unapproached by other kinds of merchandise. In short, the economists, instead of replying to the economic question put to them, have set themselves to the examination of a question of art. They have laid great stress on the mechanical adaptation of gold and silver for the purpose of money; but not one of them has seen or understood the economic reason which gave to the precious metals the privilege they now enjoy.

Now, the point that no one has noticed is that, of all the various articles of merchandise, gold and silver were the first whose value was determined. In the patriarchal period, gold and silver still were bought and sold in ingots, but already with a visible tendency to superiority and with a marked preference. Gradually sovereigns took possession of them and stamped them with their seal; and from this royal consecration was born money, — that is, the commodity par excellence; that which, notwithstanding all commercial shocks, maintains a determined proportional value, and is accepted in payment for all things.

That which distinguishes specie, in fact, is not the durability of the metal, which is less than that of steel, nor its utility, which is much below that of wheat, iron, coal, and numerous other substances, regarded as almost vile when compared with gold; neither is it its scarcity or density, for in both these respects it might be replaced, either by labor spent upon other materials, or, as at present, by bank notes representing vast amounts of iron or copper. The distinctive feature of gold and silver, I repeat, is the fact that, owing to their metallic properties, the difficulties of their production, and, above all, the intervention of public authority, their value as merchandise was fixed and authenticated at an early date.

I say then that the value of gold and silver, especially of the part that is made into money, although perhaps it has not yet been calculated accurately, is no longer arbitrary; I add that it is no longer susceptible of depreciation, like other values, although it may vary continually nevertheless. All the logic and erudition that has been expended to prove, by the example of gold and silver, that value is essentially indeterminable, is a mass of paralogisms, arising from a false idea of the question, ab ignorantia elenchi.

Philip I, King of France, mixed with the livre tournois of Charlemagne one-third alloy, imagining that, since he held the monopoly of the power of coining money, he could do what every merchant does who holds the monopoly of a product. What was, in fact, this adulteration of money, for which Philip and his successors are so severely blamed? A very sound argument from the standpoint of commercial routine, but wholly false in the view of economic science, — namely, that, supply and demand being the regulators of value, we may, either by causing an artificial scarcity or by monopolizing the manufacture, raise the estimation, and consequently the value, of things, and that this is as true of gold and silver as

71

of wheat, wine, oil, tobacco. Nevertheless, Philip's fraud was no sooner suspected than his money was reduced to its true value, and he lost himself all that he had expected to gain from his subjects. The same thing happened after all similar attempts. What was the reason of this disappointment?

Because, say the economists, the quantity of gold and silver in reality being neither diminished nor increased by the false coinage, the proportion of these metals to other merchandise was not changed, and consequently it was not in the power of the sovereign to make that which was worth but two worth four. For the same reason, if, instead of debasing the coin, it had been in the king's power to double its mass, the exchangeable value of gold and silver would have decreased one-half immediately, always on account of this proportionality and equilibrium. The adulteration of the coin was, then, on the part of the king, a forced loan, or rather, a bankruptcy, a swindle.

Marvelous! the economists explain very clearly, when they choose, the theory of the measure of value; that they may do so, it is necessary only to start them on the subject of money. Why, then, do they not see that money is the written law of commerce, the type of exchange, the first link in that long chain of creations all of which, as merchandise, must receive the sanction of society, and become, if not in fact, at least in right, acceptable as money in settlement of all kinds of transactions?

"Money," M. Augier very truly says, "can serve, either as a means of authenticating contracts already made, or as a good medium of exchange, only so far as its value approaches the ideal of permanence; for in all cases it exchanges or buys only the value which it possesses."[1]

Let us turn this eminently judicious observation into a general formula.

Labor becomes a guarantee of well-being and equality only so far as the product of each individual is in proportion with the mass; for in all cases it exchanges or buys a value equal only to its own.

Is it not strange that the defence of speculative and fraudulent commerce is undertaken boldly, while at the same time the attempt of a royal counterfeiter, who, after all, did but apply to gold and silver the fundamental principle of political economy, the arbitrary instability of values, is frowned down? If the administration should presume to give twelve ounces of tobacco for a pound,[2] the economists would cry robbery; but, if the same administration, using its privilege, should increase the price a few cents a pound, they would regard it as dear, but would discover no violation of principles. What an imbroglio is political economy!

"History of Public Credit."
In France, the sale of tobacco is a government monopoly. — Translator.

There is, then, in the monetization of gold and silver something that the economists have given no account of; namely, the consecration of the law of proportionality, the first act in the constitution of values. Humanity does all things by infinitely small degrees: after comprehending the fact that all products of labor must be submitted to a proportional measure which makes all of them equally exchangeable, it begins by giving this attribute of absolute exchangeability to a special product, which shall become the type and model of all others. In the same way, to lift its members to liberty and equality, it begins by creating kings. The people have a confused idea of this providential progress when, in their dreams of fortune and in their legends, they speak continually of gold and royalty; and the philosophers only do homage to universal reason when, in their so-called moral homilies and their socialistic utopias, they thunder with equal violence against gold and tyranny. Auri sacra fames! Cursed gold! ludicrously shouts some communist. As well say cursed wheat, cursed vines, cursed sheep; for, like gold and silver, every commercial value must reach an exact and accurate determination. The work was begun long since; today it is making visible progress.

Let us pass to other considerations.

It is an axiom generally admitted by the economists that all labor should leave an excess.

I regard this proposition as universally and absolutely true; it is a corollary of the law of proportionality, which may be regarded as an epitome of the whole science of economy. But — I beg pardon of the economists -the principle that all labor should leave an excess has no meaning in their theory, and is not susceptible of demonstration. If supply and demand alone determine value, how can we tell what is an excess and what is a sufficiency? If neither cost, nor market price, nor wages can be mathematically determined, how is it possible to conceive of a surplus, a profit? Commercial routine has given us the idea of profit as well as the word; and, since we are equal politically, we infer that every citizen has an equal right to realize profits in his personal industry. But commercial operations are essentially irregular, and it has been proved beyond question that the profits of commerce are but an arbitrary discount forced from the consumer by the producer, — in short, a displacement, to say the least. This we should soon see, if it was possible to compare the total amount of annual losses with the amount of profits. In the thought of political economy, the principle that all labor should leave an excess is simply the consecration of the constitutional right which all of us gained by the revolution, — the right of robbing one's neighbor.

The law of proportionality of values alone can solve this problem. I will approach the question a little farther back: its gravity warrants me in treating it with the consideration that it merits.

Most philosophers, like most philologists, see in society only a creature of the mind, or rather, an abstract name serving to designate a collection of men. It is a prepossession which all of us received in our infancy with our first lessons in grammar, that collective nouns, the names of genera and species, do not designate realities. There is much to say under this head, but I confine myself to my subject. To the true economist, society is a living being, endowed with an intelligence and an activity of its own, governed by special laws discoverable by observation alone, and whose existence is manifested, not under a material aspect, but by the close concert and mutual interdependence of all its members. Therefore, when a few pages back, adopting the allegorical method, we used a fabulous god as a symbol of society, our language in reality was not in the least metaphorical: we only gave a name to the social being, an organic and synthetic unit. In the eyes of any one who has reflected upon the laws of labor and exchange (I disregard every other consideration), the reality, I had almost said the personality, of the collective man is as certain as the reality and the personality of the individual man. The only difference is that the latter appears to the senses as an organism whose parts are in a state of material coherence, which is not true of society. But intelligence, spontaneity, development, life, all that constitutes in the highest degree the reality of being, is as essential to society as to man: and hence it is that the government of societies is a science, — that is, a study of natural relations, — and not an art, — that is, good pleasure and absolutism. Hence it is, finally, that every society declines the moment it falls into the hands of the ideologists.

The principle that all labor should leave an excess, undemonstrable by political economy, — that is, by proprietary routine, — is one of those which bear strongest testimony to the reality of the collective person: for, as we shall see, this principle is true of individuals only because it emanates from society, which thus confers upon them the benefit of its own laws.

Let us turn to facts. It has been observed that railroad enterprises are a source of wealth to those who control them in a much less degree than to the State. The observation is a true one; and it might have been added that it applies, not only to railroads, but to every industry. But this phenomenon, which is essentially the result of the law of proportionality of values and of the absolute identity of production and consumption, is at variance with the ordinary notion of useful value and exchangeable value.

The average price charged for the transportation of merchandise by the old method is eighteen centimes per ton and kilometer, the merchandise taken and delivered at the warehouses. It has been calculated that, at this price, an ordinary railroad corporation would net a profit of not quite ten per cent., nearly the same as the profit made by the old method. But let us admit that the rapidity of transportation by rail is to that by wheels, all allowances made, as four to one: in society time itself being value, at the same price the railroad would have an advantage over the stage-wagon of four hundred per cent. Nevertheless, this enormous advantage, a very real one so far as society is concerned, is by no means realized in a like proportion by the carrier, who, while he adds four hundred per cent. to the social value, makes personally less than ten per cent. Suppose, in fact, to make the thing still clearer, that the railroad should raise its price to twenty-five centimes, the rate by the old method remaining at eighteen; it would lose immediately all its consignments; shippers, consignees, everybody would return to the stage-wagon, if necessary. The locomotive would be abandoned; a social advantage of four hundred per cent. would be sacrificed to a private loss of thirty-three per cent.

The reason of this is easily seen. The advantage which results from the rapidity of the railroad is wholly social, and each individual participates in it only in a very slight degree (do not forget that we are speaking now only of the transportation of merchandise); while the loss falls directly and personally on the consumer. A special profit of four hundred per cent. in a society composed of say a million of men represents four ten-thousandths for each individual; while a loss to the consumer of thirty-three per cent means a social deficit of thirty-three millions. Private interest and collective interest, seemingly so divergent at first blush, are therefore perfectly identical and equal: and this example may serve to show already how economic science reconciles all interests.

Consequently, in order that society may realize the profit above supposed, it is absolutely necessary that the railroad's prices shall not exceed, or shall exceed but very little, those of the stage-wagon.

But, that this condition may be fulfilled, — in other words, that the railroad may be commercially possible, — the amount of matter transported must be sufficiently great to cover at least the interest on the capital invested and the running expenses of the road. Then a railroad's first condition of existence is a large circulation, which implies a still larger production and a vast amount of exchanges.

But production, circulation, and exchange are not self-creative things; again, the various kinds of labor are not developed in isolation and independently of each other: their progress is necessarily connected, solidary, proportional. There may be antagonism among manufacturers; but, in spite of them, social action is one, convergent, harmonious, — in a word, personal. Further, there is a day appointed for the creation of great instruments of labor: it is the day when general consumption shall be able to maintain their employment, — that is, for all these propositions are interconvertible, the day when ambient labor can feed new machinery. To anticipate the hour appointed by the progress of labor would be to imitate the fool who, going from Lyons to Marseilles, chartered a steamer for himself alone.

These points cleared up, nothing is easier than to explain why labor must leave an excess for each producer.

And first, as regards society: Prometheus, emerging from the womb of Nature, awakens to life in a state of inertia which is very charming, but which would soon become misery and torture if he did not make haste to abandon it for labor. In this original idleness, the product of Prometheus being nothing, his well-being is the same as that of the brute, and may be represented by zero.

Prometheus begins to work: and from his first day's labor, the first of the second creation, the product of Prometheus — that is, his wealth, his well-being — is equal to ten.

The second day Prometheus divides his labor, and his product increases to one hundred.

The third day, and each following day, Prometheus invents machinery, discovers new uses in things, new forces in Nature; the field of his existence extends from the domain of the senses to the sphere of morals and intelligence, and with every step that his industry takes the amount of his product increases, and assures him additional happiness. And since, finally, with him, to consume is to produce, it is clear that each day's consumption, using up only the product of the day before, leaves a surplus product for the day after.

But notice also — and give especial heed to this all-important fact — that the well-being of man is directly proportional to the intensity of labor and the multiplicity of industries: so that the increase of wealth and the increase of labor are correlative and parallel.

To say now that every individual participates in these general conditions of collective development would be to affirm a truth which, by reason of the evidence in its support, would appear silly. Let us point out rather the two general forms of consumption in society.

Society, like the individual, has first its articles of personal consumption, articles which time gradually causes it to feel the need of, and which its mysterious instincts command it to create. Thus in the middle ages there was, with a large number of cities, a decisive moment when the building of city halls and cathedrals became a violent passion, which had to be satisfied at any price; the life of the community depended upon it. Security and strength, public order, centralization, nationality, country, independence, these are the elements which make up the life of society, the totality of its mental faculties; these are the sentiments which must find expression and representation. Such formerly was the object of the temple of Jerusalem, real palladium of the Jewish nation; such was the temple of Jupiter Capitolinus of Rome. Later, after the municipal palace and the temple, — organs, so to speak, of centralization and progress, — came the other works of public utility, — bridges, theatres, schools, hospitals, roads, etc.

The monuments of public utility being used essentially in common, and consequently gratuitously, society is rewarded for its advances by the political and moral advantages resulting from these great works, and which, furnishing security to labor and an ideal to the mind, give fresh impetus to industry and the arts.

But it is different with the articles of domestic consumption, which alone fall within the category of exchange. These can be produced only upon the conditions of mutuality which make consumption possible, — that is, immediate payment with advantage to the producers. These conditions we have developed sufficiently in the theory of proportionality of values, which we might call as well the theory of the gradual reduction of cost.

I have demonstrated theoretically and by facts the principle that all labor should leave an excess; but this principle, as certain as any proposition in arithmetic, is very far from universal realization. While, by the progress of collective industry, each individual day's labor yields a greater and greater product, and while, by necessary consequence, the laborer, receiving the same wages, must grow ever richer, there exist in society classes which thrive and classes which perish; laborers paid twice, thrice, a hundred times over, and laborers continually out of pocket; everywhere, finally, people who enjoy and people who suffer, and, by a monstrous division of the means of industry, individuals who consume and do not produce. The distribution of well-being follows all the movements of value, and reproduces them in misery and luxury on a frightful scale and with terrible energy. But everywhere, too, the progress of wealth — that is, the proportionality of values — is the dominant law; and when the economists combat the complaints of the socialists with the progressive increase of public wealth and the alleviations of the condition of even the most unfortunate classes, they proclaim, without suspecting it, a truth which is the condemnation of their theories.

For I entreat the economists to question themselves for a moment in the silence of their hearts, far from the prejudices which disturb them, and regardless of the employments which occupy them or which they wait for, of the interests which they serve, of the votes which they covet, of the distinctions which tickle their vanity: let them tell me whether, hitherto, they have viewed the principle that all labor should leave an excess in connection with this series of premises and conclusions which we have elaborated, and whether they ever have understood these words to mean anything more than the right to speculate in values by manipulating supply and demand; whether it is not true that they affirm at once, on the one hand the progress of wealth and well-being, and consequently the measure of values, and on the other the arbitrariness of commercial transactions and the incommensurability of values, — the flattest of contradictions? Is it not because of this contradiction that we continually hear repeated in lectures, and read in the works on political economy, this absurd hypothesis: If the price of ALL things was doubled . . . . . ? As if the price of all things was not the proportion of things, and as if we could double a proportion, a relation, a law! Finally, is it not because of the proprietary and abnormal routine upheld by political economy that every one, in commerce, industry, the arts, and the State, on the pretended ground of services rendered to society, tends continually to exaggerate his importance, and solicits rewards, subsidies, large pensions, exorbitant fees: as if the reward of every service was not determined necessarily by the sum of its expenses? Why do not the economists, if they believe, as they appear to, that the labor of each should leave an excess, use all their influence in spreading this truth, so simple and so luminous: Each man's labor can buy only the value which it contains, and this value is proportional to the services of all other laborers?

But here a last consideration presents itself, which I will explain in a few words.

J. B. Say, who of all the economists has insisted the most strenuously upon the absolute indeterminability of value, is also the one who has taken the most pains to refute that idea. He, if I am not mistaken, is the author of the formula: Every product is worth what it costs; or, what amounts to the same thing: Products are bought with products. This aphorism, which leads straight to equality, has been controverted since by other economists; we will examine in turn the affirmative and the negative.

When I say that every product is worth the products which it has cost, I mean that every product is a collective unit which, in a new form, groups a certain number of other products consumed in various quantities. Whence it follows that the products of human industry are, in relation to each other, genera and species, and that they form a series from the simple to the composite, according to the number and proportion of the elements, all equivalent to each other, which constitute each product. It matters little, for the present, that this series, as well as the equivalence of its elements, is expressed in practice more or less exactly by the equilibrium of wages and fortunes; our first business is with the relation of things, the economic law. For here, as ever, the idea first and spontaneously generates the fact, which, recognized then by the thought which has given it birth, gradually rectifies itself and conforms to its principle. Commerce, free and competitive, is but a long operation of redressal, whose object is to define more and more clearly the proportionality of values, until the civil law shall recognize it as a guide in matters concerning the condition of persons. I say, then, that Say's principle, Every product is worth what it costs, indicates a series in human production analogous to the animal and vegetable series, in which the elementary units (day's works) are regarded as equal. So that political economy affirms at its birth, but by a contradiction, what neither Plato, nor Rousseau, nor any ancient or modern publicist has thought possible, -equality of conditions and fortunes.

Prometheus is by turns husbandman, wine-grower, baker, weaver. Whatever trade he works at, laboring only for himself, he buys what he consumes (his products) with one and the same money (his products), whose unit of measurement is necessarily his day's work. It is true that labor itself is liable to vary; Prometheus is not always in the same condition, and from one moment to another his enthusiasm, his fruitfulness, rises and falls. But, like everything that is subject to variation, labor has its average, which justifies us in saying that, on the whole, day's work pays for day's work, neither more nor less. It is quite true that, if we compare the products of a certain period of social life with those of another, the hundred millionth day's work of the human race will show a result incomparably superior to that of the first; but it must be remembered also that the life of the collective being can no more be divided than that of the individual; that, though the days may not resemble each other, they are indissolubly united, and that in the sum total of existence pain and pleasure are common to them. If, then, the tailor, for rendering the value of a day's work, consumes ten times the product of the day's work of the weaver, it is as if the weaver gave ten days of his life for one day of the tailor's. This is exactly what happens when a peasant pays twelve francs to a lawyer for a document which it takes him an hour to prepare; and this inequality, this iniquity in exchanges, is the most potent cause of misery that the socialists have unveiled, — as the economists confess in secret while awaiting a sign from the master that shall permit them to acknowledge it openly.

Every error in commutative justice is an immolation of the laborer, a transfusion of the blood of one man into the body of another. . . . Let no one be frightened; I have no intention of fulminating against property an irritating philippic; especially as I think that, according to my principles, humanity is never mistaken; that, in establishing itself at first upon the right of property, it only laid down one of the principles of its future organization; and that, the pre-ponderance of property once destroyed, it remains only to reduce this famous antithesis to unity. All the objections that can be offered in favor of property I am as well acquainted with as any of my critics, whom I ask as a favor to show their hearts when logic fails them. How can wealth that is not measured by labor be valuable? And if it is labor that creates wealth and legitimates property, how explain the consumption of the idler? Where is the honesty in a system of distribution in which a product is worth, according to the person, now more, now less, than it costs.

Say's ideas led to an agrarian law; therefore, the conservative party hastened to protest against them. "The original source of wealth," M. Rossi had said, "is labor. In proclaiming this great principle, the industrial school has placed in evidence not only an economic principle, but that social fact which, in the hands of a skilful historian, becomes the surest guide in following the human race in its marchings and haltings upon the face of the earth."

Why, after having uttered these profound words in his lectures, has M. Rossi thought it his duty to retract them afterwards in a review, and to compromise gratuitously his dignity as a philosopher and an economist?

"Say that wealth is the result of labor alone; affirm that labor is always the measure of value, the regulator of prices; yet, to escape one way or another the objections which these doctrines call forth on all hands, some incomplete, others absolute, you will be obliged to generalize the idea of labor, and to substitute for analysis an utterly erroneous synthesis."

I regret that a man like M. Rossi should suggest to me so sad a thought; but, while reading the passage that I have just quoted, I could not help saying: Science and truth have lost their influence: the present object of worship is the shop, and, after the shop, the desperate constitutionalism which represents it. To whom, then, does M. Rossi address himself? Is he in favor of labor or something else; analysis or synthesis? Is he in favor of all these things at once? Let him choose, for the conclusion is inevitably against him.

If labor is the source of all wealth, if it is the surest guide in tracing the history of human institutions on the face of the earth, why should equality of distribution, equality as measured by labor, not be a law?

If, on the contrary, there is wealth which is not the product of labor, why is the possession of it a privilege? Where is the legitimacy of monopoly? Explain then, once for all, this theory of the right of unproductive consumption; this jurisprudence of caprice, this religion of idleness, the sacred prerogative of a caste of the elect.

What, now, is the significance of this appeal from analysis to the false judgments of the synthesis? These metaphysical terms are of no use, save to indoctrinate simpletons, who do not suspect that the same proposition can be construed, indifferently and at will, analytically or synthetically. Labor is the principle of value end the source of wealth: an analytic proposition such as M. Rossi likes, since it is the summary of an analysis in which it is demonstrated that the primitive notion of labor is identical with the subsequent notions of product, value, capital, wealth, etc. Nevertheless, we see that M. Rossi rejects the doctrine which results from this analysis. Labor, capital, and land are the sources of wealth: a synthetic proposition, precisely such as M. Rossi does not like. Indeed, wealth is considered here as a general notion, produced in three distinct, but not identical, ways. And yet the doctrine thus formulated is the one that M. Rossi prefers. Now, would it please M. Rossi to have us render his theory of monopoly analytically and ours of labor synthetically? I can give him the satisfaction. . . . But I should blush, with so earnest a man, to prolong such badinage. M. Rossi knows better than any one that analysis and synthesis of themselves prove absolutely nothing, and that the important work, as Bacon said, is to make exact comparisons and complete enumerations.

Since M. Rossi was in the humor for abstractions, why did he not say to the phalanx of economists who listen so respectfully to the least word that falls from his lips:

"Capital is the material of wealth, as gold and silver are the material of money, as wheat is the material of bread, and, tracing the series back to the end, as earth, water, fire, and air are the material of all our products. But it is labor, labor alone, which successively creates each utility given to these materials, and which consequently transforms them into capital and wealth. Capital is the result of labor, — that is, realized intelligence and life, — as animals and plants are realizations of the soul of the universe, and as the chefs d'oeuvre of Homer, Raphael, and Rossini are expressions of their ideas and sentiments. Value is the proportion in which all the realizations of the human soul must balance each other in order to produce a harmonious whole, which, being wealth, gives us well-being, or rather is the token, not the object, of our happiness.

"The proposition, there is no measure of value, is illogical and contradictory, as is shown by the very arguments which have been offered in its support.

"The proposition, labor is the principle of proportionality of values, not only is true, resulting as it does from an irrefutable analysis, but it is the object of progress, the condition and form of social well-being, the beginning and end of political economy. From this proposition and its corollaries, every product is worth what it costs, and products are bought with products, follows the dogma of equality of conditions.

"The idea of value socially constituted, or of proportionality of values, serves to explain further: (a) how a mechanical invention, notwithstanding the privilege which it temporarily creates and the disturbances which it occasions, always produces in the end a general amelioration; (b) how the value of an economical process to its discoverer can never equal the profit which it realizes for society; (c) how, by a series of oscillations between supply and demand, the value of every product constantly seeks a level with cost and with the needs of consumption, and consequently tends to establish itself in a fixed and positive manner; (d) how, collective production continually increasing the amount of consumable things, and the day's work constantly obtaining higher and higher pay, labor must leave an excess for each producer; (e) how the amount of work to be done, instead of being diminished by industrial progress, ever increases in both quantity and quality — that is, in intensity and difficulty — in all branches of industry; (f) how social value continually eliminates fictitious values, — in other words, how industry effects the socialization of capital and property; (g) finally, how the distribution of products, growing in regularity with the strength of the mutual guarantee resulting from the constitution of value, pushes society onward to equality of conditions and fortunes.

"Finally, the theory of the successive constitution of all commercial values implying the infinite progress of labor, wealth, and well-being, the object of society, from the economic point of view, is revealed to us: To produce incessantly, with thee least possible amount of labor for each product, the greatest possible quantity and variety of values, in such a way as to realize, for each individual, the greatest amount of physical, moral, and intellectual well-being, and, for the race, the highest perfection and infinite glory.

Now that we have determined, not without difficulty, the meaning of the question asked by the Academy of Moral Sciences touching the oscillations of profit and wages, it is time to begin the essential part of our work. Wherever labor has not been socialized, — that is, wherever value is not synthetically determined, — there is irregularity and dishonesty in exchange; a war of stratagems and ambuscades; an impediment to production, circulation, and consumption; unproductive labor; insecurity; spoliation; insolidarity; want; luxury: but at the same time an effort of the genius of society to obtain justice, and a constant tendency toward association and order. Political economy is simply the history of this grand struggle. On the one hand, indeed, political economy, in so far as it sanctions and pretends to perpetuate the anomalies of value and the prerogatives of selfishness, is truly the theory of misfortune and the organization of misery; but in so far as it explains the means invented by civilization to abolish poverty, although these means always have been used exclusively in the interest of monopoly, political economy is the preamble of the organization of wealth.

It is important, then, that we should resume the study of economic facts and practices, discover their meaning, and formulate their philosophy. Until this is done, no knowledge of social progress can be acquired, no reform attempted. The error of socialism has consisted hitherto in perpetuating religious reverie by launching forward into a fantastic future instead of seizing the reality which is crushing it; as the wrong of the economists has been in regarding every accomplished fact as an injunction against any proposal of reform.

For my own part, such is not my conception of economic science, the true social science. Instead of offering a priori arguments as solutions of the formidable problems of the organization of labor and the distribution of wealth, I shall interrogate political economy as the depositary of the secret thoughts of humanity; I shall cause it to disclose the facts in the order of their occurrence, and shall relate their testimony without intermingling it with my own. It will be at once a triumphant and a lamentable history, in which the actors will be ideas, the episodes theories, and the dates formulas.

Chapter III. Economic Evolutions. — First Period. — The Division of Labor.

The fundamental idea, the dominant category, of political economy is VALUE.

Value reaches its positive determination by a series of oscillations between supply and demand.

Consequently, value appears successively under three aspects: useful value, exchangeable value, and synthetic, or social, value, which is true value. The first term gives birth to the second in contradiction to it, and the two together, absorbing each other in reciprocal penetration, produce the third: so that the contradiction or antagonism of ideas appears as the point of departure of all economic science, allowing us to say of it, parodying the sentence of Tertullian in relation to the Gospel, Credo quia absurdum: There is, in social economy, a latent truth wherever there is an apparent contradiction, Credo quia contrarium.

From the point of view of political economy, then, social progress consists in a continuous solution of the problem of the constitution of values, or of the proportionality and solidarity of products.

But while in Nature the synthesis of opposites is contemporary with their opposition, in society the antithetic elements seem to appear at long intervals, and to reach solution only after long and tumultuous agitation. Thus there is no example — the idea even is inconceivable — of a valley without a hill, a left without a right, a north pole without a south pole, a stick with but one end, or two ends without a middle, etc. The human body, with its so perfectly antithetic dichotomy, is formed integrally at the very moment of conception; it refuses to be put together and arranged piece by piece, like the garment patterned after it which, later, is to cover it.[1]

In society, on the contrary, as well as in the mind, so far from the idea reaching its complete realization at a single bound, a sort of abyss separates, so to speak, the two antinomical positions, and even when these are recognized at last, we still do not see what the synthesis will be. The primitive concepts must be fertilized, so to speak, by burning controversy and passionate struggle; bloody battles will be the preliminaries of peace. At the present moment, Europe, weary of war and discussion, awaits a reconciling principle; and it is the vague perception of

---

[1] A subtle philologist, M. Paul Ackermann, has shown, using the French language as an illustration, that, since every word in a language has its opposite, or, as the author calls it, its antonym, the entire vocabulary might be arranged in couples, forming a vast dualistic system. (See Dictionary of Antonyms. By PAUL ACKERMAN. Paris: Brockhaus & Avenarius. 1842)

this situation which induces the Academy of Moral and Political Sciences to ask, "What are the general facts which govern the relations of profits to wages and determine their oscillations?" in other words, what are the most salient episodes and the most remarkable phases of the war between labor and capital?

If, then, I demonstrate that political economy, with all its contradictory hypotheses and equivocal conclusions, is nothing but an organization of privilege and misery, I shall have proved thereby that it contains by implication the promise of an organization of labor and equality, since, as has been said, every systematic contradiction is the announcement of a composition; further, I shall have fixed the bases of this composition. Then, indeed, to unfold the system of economical contradictions is to lay the foundations of universal association; to show how the products of collective labor come out of society is to explain how it will be possible to make them return to it; to exhibit the genesis of the problems of production and distribution is to prepare the way for their solution. All these propositions are identical and equally evident.

1. — Antagonistic effects of the principle of division.

All men are equal in the state of primitive communism, equal in their nakedness and ignorance, equal in the indefinite power of their faculties. The economists generally look at only the first of these aspects; they neglect or overlook the second. Nevertheless, according to the profoundest philosophers of modern times, La Rochefoucault, Helvetius, Kant, Fichte, Hegel, Jacotot, intelligence differs in individuals only qualitatively, each having thereby his own specialty or genius; in its essence, — namely, judgment, — it is quantitatively equal in all. Hence it follows that, a little sooner or a little later, according as circumstances shall be more or less favorable, general progress must lead all men from original and negative equality to a positive equivalence of talents and acquirements.

I insist upon this precious datum of psychology, the necessary consequence of which is that the hierarchy of capacities henceforth cannot be allowed as a principle and law of organization: equality alone is our rule, as it is also our ideal. Then, just as the equality of misery must change gradually into equality of well-being, as we have proved by the theory of value, so the equality of minds, negative in the beginning, since it represents only emptiness, must reappear in a positive form at the completion of humanity's education. The intellectual movement proceeds parallelly with the economic movement; they are the expression, the translation, of each other; psychology and social economy are in accord, or rather, they but unroll the same history, each from a different point of view. This appears especially in Smith's great law, the division of labor.

Considered in its essence, the division of labor is the way in which equality of condition and intelligence is realized. Through diversity of function, it gives rise to proportionality of products and equilibrium in exchange, and consequently opens for us the road to wealth; as also, in showing us infinity everywhere in art and Nature, it leads us to idealize our acts, and makes the creative mind — that is, divinity itself, mentem diviniorem — immanent and perceptible in all laborers.

Division of labor, then, is the first phase of economic evolution as well as of intellectual development: our point of departure is true as regards both man and things, and the progress of our exposition is in no wise arbitrary.

But, at this solemn hour of the division of labor, tempestuous winds begin to blow upon humanity. Progress does not improve the condition of all equally and uniformly, although in the end it must include and transfigure every intelligent and industrious being. It commences by taking possession of a small number of privileged persons, who thus compose the elite of nations, while the mass continues, or even buries itself deeper, in barbarism. It is this exception of persons on the part of progress which has perpetuated the belief in the natural and providential inequality of conditions, engendered caste, and given an hierarchical form to all societies. It has not been understood that all inequality, never being more than a negation, carries in itself the proof of its illegitimacy and the announcement of its downfall: much less still has it been imagined that this same inequality proceeds accidentally from a cause the ulterior effect of which must be its entire disappearance.

Thus, the antinomy of value reappearing in the law of division, it is found that the first and most potent instrument of knowledge and wealth which Providence has placed in our hands has become for us an instrument of misery and imbecility. Here is the formula of this new law of antagonism, to which we owe the two oldest maladies of civilization, aristocracy and the proletariat: Labor, in dividing itself according to the law which is peculiar to it, and which is the primary condition of its productivity, ends in the frustration of its own objects, and destroys itself, in other words: Division, in the absence of which there is no progress, no wealth, no equality, subordinates the workingman, and renders intelligence useless, wealth harmful, and equality impossible.

All the economists, since Adam Smith, have pointed out the advantages and the inconveniences of the law of division, but at the same time insisting much more strenuously upon the first than the second, because such a course was more in harmony with their optimistic views, and not one of them ever asking how a law can have inconveniences. This is the way in which J. B. Say summed up the question: —

"A man who during his whole life performs but one operation, certainly acquires the power to execute it better and more readily than another; but at the same time he becomes less capable of any other occupation, whether physical or moral; his other faculties become extinct, and there results a degeneracy in the individual man. That one has made only the eighteenth part of a pin is a sad account to give of one's self: but let no one imagine that it is the workingman who spends his life in handling a file or a hammer that alone degenerates in this way from the dignity of his nature; it is the same with the man whose position leads him to exercise the most subtle faculties of his mind... On the whole, it may be said that the separation of tasks is an advantageous use of human forces; that it increases enormously the products of society; but that it takes something from the capacity of each man taken individually."[2]

What, then, after labor, is the primary cause of the multiplication of wealth and the skill of laborers? Division.

What is the primary cause of intellectual degeneracy and, as we shall show continually, civilized misery? Division.

How does the same principle, rigorously followed to its conclusions, lead to effects diametrically opposite? There is not an economist, either before or since Adam Smith, who has even perceived that here is a problem to be solved. Say goes so far as to recognize that in the division of labor the same cause which produces the good engenders the evil; then, after a few words of pity for the victims of the separation of industries, content with having given an impartial and faithful exhibition of the facts, he leaves the matter there. "You know," he seems to say, "that the more we divide the workmen's tasks, the more we increase the productive power of labor; but at the same time the more does labor, gradually reducing itself to a mechanical operation, stupefy intelligence."

In vain do we express our indignation against a theory which, creating by labor itself an aristocracy of capacities, leads inevitably to political inequality; in vain do we protest in the name of democracy and progress that in the future there will be no nobility, no bourgeoisie no pariahs. The economist replies, with the impassibility of destiny: You are condemned to produce much, and to produce cheaply; otherwise your industry will be always insignificant, your commerce will amount to nothing, and you will drag in the rear of civilization instead of taking the lead. — What! among us, generous men, there are some predestined to brutishness; and the more perfect our industry becomes, the larger will grow the number of our accursed brothers!.... — Alas!.... That is the last word of the economist.

We cannot fail to recognize in the division of labor, as a general fact and as a cause, all the characteristics of a LAW; but as this law governs two orders of phenomena radically opposite and destructive of each other, it must be confessed also

---

"Treatise on Political Economy."

that this law is of a sort unknown in the exact sciences, — that it is, strange to say, a contradictory law, a counter-law an antinomy. Let us add, in anticipation, that such appears to be the identifying feature of social economy, and consequently of philosophy.

Now, without a RECOMPOSITION of labor which shall obviate the inconveniences of division while preserving its useful effects, the contradiction inherent in the principle is irremediable. It is necessary, — following the style of the Jewish priests, plotting the death of Christ, — it is necessary that the poor should perish to secure the proprietor his for tune, expedit unum hominem pro populo mori. I am going to demonstrate the necessity of this decree; after which, if the parcellaire laborer still retains a glimmer of intelligence, he will console himself with the thought that he dies according to the rules of political economy.

Labor, which ought to give scope to the conscience and render it more and more worthy of happiness, leading through parcellaire division to prostration of mind, dwarfs man in his noblest part, minorat capitis, and throws him back into animality. Thenceforth the fallen man labors as a brute, and consequently must be treated as a brute. This sentence of Nature and necessity society will execute.

The first effect of parcellaire labor, after the depravation of the mind, is the lengthening of the hours of labor, which increase in inverse proportion to the amount of intelligence expended. For, the product increasing in quantity and quality at once, if, by any industrial improvement whatever, labor is lightened in one way, it must pay for it in another. But as the length of the working-day cannot exceed from sixteen to eighteen hours, when compensation no longer can be made in time, it will be taken from the price, and wages will decrease. And this decrease will take place, not, as has been foolishly imagined, because value is essentially arbitrary, but because it is essentially determinable. Little matters it that the struggle between supply and demand ends, now to the advantage of the employer, now to the benefit of the employee; such oscillations may vary in amplitude, this depending on well-known accessory circumstances which have been estimated a thousand times. The certain point, and the only one for us to notice now, is that the universal conscience does not set the same price upon the labor of an overseer and the work of a hod-carrier. A reduction in the price of the day's work, then, is necessary: so that the laborer, after having been afflicted in mind by a degrading function, cannot fail to be struck also in his body by the meagreness of his reward. This is the literal application of the words of the Gospel: He that hath not, from him shall be taken even that which he hath.

There is in economic accidents a pitiless reason which laughs at religion and equity as political aphorisms, and which renders man happy or unhappy according as he obeys or escapes the prescriptions of destiny. Certainly this is far from that Christian charity with which so many honorable writers today are inspired, and which, penetrating to the heart of the bourgeoisie, endeavors to temper the rigors of the law by numerous religious institutions. Political economy knows only justice, justice as inflexible and unyielding as the miser's purse; and it is because political economy is the effect of social spontaneity and the expression of the divine will that I have been able to say: God is man's adversary, and Providence a misanthrope. God makes us pay, in weight of blood and measure of tears, for each of our lessons; and to complete the evil, we, in our relations with our fellows, all act like him. Where, then, is this love of the celestial father for his creatures? Where is human fraternity?

Can he do otherwise? say the theists. Man falling, the animal remains: how could the Creator recognize in him his own image? And what plainer than that he treats him then as a beast of burden? But the trial will not last for ever, and sooner or later labor, having been particularized, will be synthetized.

Such is the ordinary argument of all those who seek to justify Providence, but generally succeed only in lending new weapons to atheism. That is to say, then, that God would have envied us, for six thousand years, an idea which would have saved millions of victims, a distribution of labor at once special and synthetic! In return, he has given us, through his servants Moses, Buddha, Zoroaster, Mahomet, etc., those insipid writings, the disgrace of our reason, which have killed more men than they contain letters! Further, if we must believe primitive revelation, social economy was the cursed science, the fruit of the tree reserved for God, which man was forbidden to touch! Why this religious depreciation of labor, if it is true, as economic science already shows, that labor is the father of love and the organ of happiness? Why this jealousy of our advancement? But if, as now sufficiently appears, our progress depends upon ourselves alone, of what use is it to adore this phantom of divinity, and what does he still ask of us through the multitude of inspired persons who pursue us with their sermons? All of you, Christians, protestant and orthodox, neo-revelators, charlatans and dupes, listen to the first verse of the humanitarian hymn upon God's mercy: "In proportion as the principle of division of labor receives complete application, the worker becomes weaker, narrower, and more dependent. Art advances: the artisan recedes!"[3]

Then let us guard against anticipating conclusions and prejudging the latest revelation of experience. At present God seems less favorable than hostile: let us confine ourselves to establishing the fact.

Just as political economy, then, at its point of departure, has made us understand these mysterious and dismal words: In proportion as the production of utility increases, venality decreases; so arrived at its first station, it warns us in a terrible

Tocqueville, "Democracy in America."

88

voice: In proportion as art advances, the artisan recedes. To fix the ideas better, let us cite a few examples.

In all the branches of metal-working, who are the least industrious of the wage-laborers? Precisely those who are called machinists. Since tools have been so admirably perfected, a machinist is simply a man who knows how to handle a file or a plane: as for mechanics, that is the business of engineers and foremen. A country blacksmith often unites in his own person, by the very necessity of his position, the various talents of the locksmith, the edge-tool maker, the gunsmith, the machinist, the wheel-wright, and the horse-doctor: the world of thought would be astonished at the knowledge that is under the hammer of this man, whom the people, always inclined to jest, nickname brule-fer. A workingman of Creuzot, who for ten years has seen the grandest and finest that his profession can offer, on leaving his shop, finds himself unable to render the slightest service or to earn his living. The incapacity of the subject is directly proportional to the perfection of the art; and this is as true of all the trades as of metal-working.

The wages of machinists are maintained as yet at a high rate: sooner or later their pay must decrease, the poor quality of the labor being unable to maintain it.

I have just cited a mechanical art; let us now cite a liberal industry.

Would Gutenburg and his industrious companions, Faust and Schoffer, ever have believed that, by the division of labor, their sublime invention would fall into the domain of ignorance — I had almost said idiocy? There are few men so weak-minded, so unlettered, as the mass of workers who follow the various branches of the typographic industry, — compositors, pressmen, type-founders, book-binders, and paper-makers. The printer, as he existed even in the days of the Estiennes, has become almost an abstraction. The employment of women in type-setting has struck this noble industry to the heart, and consummated its degradation. I have seen a female compositor — and she was one of the best — who did not know how to read, and was acquainted only with the forms of the letters. The whole art has been withdrawn into the hands of foremen and proof-readers, modest men of learning whom the impertinence of authors and patrons still humiliates, and a few workmen who are real artists. The press, in a word, fallen into mere mechanism, is no longer, in its personnel, at the level of civilization: soon there will be left of it but a few souvenirs.

I am told that the printers of Paris are endeavoring by association to rise again from their degradation: may their efforts not be exhausted in vain empiricism or misled into barren utopias!

After private industries, let us look at public administration.

In the public service, the effects of parcellaire labor are no less frightful, no less intense: in all the departments of administration, in proportion as the art develops, most of the employees see their salaries diminish. A letter-carrier receives from four hundred to six hundred francs per annum, of which the administration retains about a tenth for the retiring pension. After thirty years of labor, the pension, or rather the restitution, is three hundred francs per annum, which, when given to an alms-house by the pensioner, entitles him to a bed, soup, and washing. My heart bleeds to say it, but I think, nevertheless, that the administration is generous: what reward would you give to a man whose whole function consists in walking? The legend gives but five sous to the Wandering Jew; the letter-carriers receive twenty or thirty; true, the greater part of them have a family. That part of the service which calls into exercise the intellectual faculties is reserved for the postmasters and clerks: these are better paid; they do the work of men.

Everywhere, then, in public service as well as free industry, things are so ordered that nine-tenths of the laborers serve as beasts of burden for the other tenth: such is the inevitable effect of industrial progress and the indispensable condition of all wealth. It is important to look well at this elementary truth before talking to the people of equality, liberty, democratic institutions, and other utopias, the realization of which involves a previous complete revolution in the relations of laborers.

The most remarkable effect of the division of labor is the decay of literature.

In the Middle Ages and in antiquity the man of letters, a sort of encyclopaedic doctor, a successor of the troubadour and the poet, all-knowing, was almighty. Literature lorded it over society with a high hand; kings sought the favor of authors, or revenged themselves for their contempt by burning them, — them and their books. This, too, was a way of recognizing literary sovereignty.

Today we have manufacturers, lawyers, doctors, bankers, merchants, professors, engineers, librarians, etc.; we have no men of letters. Or rather, whoever has risen to a remarkable height in his profession is thereby and of necessity lettered: literature, like the baccalaureate, has become an elementary part of every profession. The man of letters, reduced to his simplest expression, is the public writer, a sort of writing commissioner in the pay of everybody, whose best-known variety is the journalist.

It was a strange idea that occurred to the Chambers four years ago, -that of making a law on literary property! As if henceforth the idea was not to become more and more the all-important point, the style nothing. Thanks to God, there is an end of parliamentary eloquence as of epic poetry and mythology; the theatre rarely attracts business men and savants; and while the connoisseurs are astonished at the decline of art, the philosophic observer sees only the progress of manly reason, troubled rather than rejoiced at these dainty trifles. The interest in romance is sustained only as long as it resembles reality; history is reducing itself to anthropological exegesis; everywhere, indeed, the art of talking well appears as a subordinate auxiliary of the idea, the fact. The worship of speech, too mazy and slow for impatient minds, is neglected, and its artifices are losing daily their power of seduction. The language of the nineteenth century is made up of facts and figures, and he is the most eloquent among us who, with the fewest words, can say the most things. Whoever cannot speak this language is mercilessly relegated to the ranks of the rhetoricians; he is said to have no ideas.

In a young society the progress of letters necessarily outstrips philosophical and industrial progress, and for a long time serves for the expression of both. But there comes a day when thought leaves language in the rear, and when, consequently, the continued preeminence of literature in a society becomes a sure symptom of decline. Language, in fact, is to every people the collection of its native ideas, the encyclopædia which Providence first reveals to it; it is the field which its reason must cultivate before directly attacking Nature through observation and experience. Now, as soon as a nation, after having exhausted the knowledge contained in its vocabulary, instead of pursuing its education by a superior philosophy, wraps itself in its poetic mantle, and begins to play with its periods and its hemistichs, we may safely say that such a society is lost. Everything in it will become subtle, narrow, and false; it will not have even the advantage of maintaining in its splendor the language of which it is foolishly enamored; instead of going forward in the path of the geniuses of transition, the Tacituses, the Thucydides, the Machiavels, and the Montesquieus, it will be seen to fall, with irresistible force, from the majesty of Cicero to the subtleties of Seneca, the antitheses of St. Augustine, and the puns of St. Bernard.

Let no one, then, be deceived: from the moment that the mind, at first entirely occupied with speech, passes to experience and labor, the man of letters, properly speaking, is simply the puny personification of the least of our faculties; and literature, the refuse of intelligent industry, finds a market only with the idlers whom it amuses and the proletaires whom it fascinates, the jugglers who besiege power and the charlatans who shelter themselves behind it, the hierophants of divine right who blow the trumpet of Sinai, and the fanatical proclaimers of the sovereignty of the people, whose few mouth-pieces, compelled to practise their tribunician eloquence from tombs until they can shower it from the height of rostrums, know no better than to give to the public parodies of Gracchus and Demosthenes.

All the powers of society, then, agree in indefinitely deteriorating the condition of the parcellaire laborer; and experience, universally confirming the theory, proves that this worker is condemned to misfortune from his mother's womb, no political reform, no association of interests, no effort either of public charity or of instruction, having the power to aid him. The various specifics proposed in these latter days, far from being able to cure the evil, would tend rather to inflame it by irritation; and all that has been written on this point has only exhibited in a clear light the vicious circle of political economy.

This we shall demonstrate in a few words.

2. — Impotence of palliatives. — MM. Blanqui, Chevalier, Dunoyer, Rossi, and Passy.

All the remedies proposed for the fatal effects of parcellaire division may be reduced to two, which really are but one, the second being the inversion of the first: to raise the mental and moral condition of the workingman by increasing his comfort and dignity; or else, to prepare the way for his future emancipation and happiness by instruction.

We will examine successively these two systems, one of which is represented by M. Blanqui, the other by M. Chevalier.

M. Blanqui is a friend of association and progress, a writer of democratic tendencies, a professor who has a place in the hearts of the proletariat. In his opening discourse of the year 1845, M. Blanqui proclaimed, as a means of salvation, the association of labor and capital, the participation of the working man in the profits, — that is, a beginning of industrial solidarity. "Our century," he exclaimed, "must witness the birth of the collective producer." M. Blanqui forgets that the collective producer was born long since, as well as the collective consumer, and that the question is no longer a genetic, but a medical, one. Our task is to cause the blood proceeding from the collective digestion, instead of rushing wholly to the head, stomach, and lungs, to descend also into the legs and arms. Besides, I do not know what method M. Blanqui proposes to employ in order to realize his generous thought, — whether it be the establishment of national workshops, or the loaning of capital by the State, or the expropriation of the conductors of business enterprises and the substitution for them of industrial associations, or, finally, whether he will rest content with a recommendation of the savings bank to workingmen, in which case the participation would be put off till doomsday.

However this may be, M. Blanqui's idea amounts simply to an increase of wages resulting from the copartnership, or at least from the interest in the business, which he confers upon the laborers. What, then, is the value to the laborer of a participation in the profits?

A mill with fifteen thousand spindles, employing three hundred hands, does not pay at present an annual dividend of twenty thousand francs. I am informed by a Mulhouse manufacturer that factory stocks in Alsace are generally below par and that this industry has already become a means of getting money by stock-jobbing instead of by labor. To SELL; to sell at the right time; to sell dear, — is the only object in view; to manufacture is only to prepare for a sale. When I assume, then, on an average, a profit of twenty thousand francs to a factory employing three hundred persons, my argument being general, I am twenty thousand francs out of the way. Nevertheless, we will admit the correctness of this amount. Dividing twenty thousand francs, the profit of the mill, by three hundred, the number of persons, and again by three hundred, the number of working days, I find an increase of pay for each person of twenty-two and one-fifth centimes, or for daily expenditure an addition of eighteen centimes, just a morsel of bread. Is it worth while, then, for this, to expropriate mill-owners and endanger the public welfare, by erecting establishments which must be insecure, since, property being divided into infinitely small shares, and being no longer supported by profit, business enterprises would lack ballast, and would be unable to weather commercial gales. And even if no expropriation was involved, what a poor prospect to offer the working class is an increase of eighteen centimes in return for centuries of economy; for no less time than this would be needed to accumulate the requisite capital, supposing that periodical suspensions of business did not periodically consume its savings!

The fact which I have just stated has been pointed out in several ways. M. Passy[4] himself took from the books of a mill in Normandy where the laborers were associated with the owner the wages of several families for a period of ten years, and he found that they averaged from twelve to fourteen hundred francs per year. He then compared the situation of mill-hands paid in proportion to the prices obtained by their employers with that of laborers who receive fixed wages, and found that the difference is almost imperceptible. This result might easily have been foreseen. Economic phenomena obey laws as abstract and immutable as those of numbers: it is only privilege, fraud, and absolutism which disturb the eternal harmony.

M. Blanqui, repentant, as it seems, at having taken this first step toward socialistic ideas, has made haste to retract his words. At the same meeting in which M. Passy demonstrated the inadequacy of cooperative association, he exclaimed: "Does it not seem that labor is a thing susceptible of organization, and that it is in the power of the State to regulate the happiness of humanity as it does the march of an army, and with an entirely mathematical precision? This is an evil tendency, a delusion which the Academy cannot oppose too strongly, because it is not only a chimera, but a dangerous sophism. Let us respect good and honest intentions; but let us not fear to say that to publish a book upon the organization of labor is

---

[4] Meeting of the Academy of Moral and Political Sciences, September, 1845.

to rewrite for the fiftieth time a treatise upon the quadrature of the circle or the philosopher's stone."

Then, carried away by his zeal, M. Blanqui finishes the destruction of his theory of cooperation, which M. Passy already had so rudely shaken, by the following example: "M. Dailly, one of the most enlightened of farmers, has drawn up an account for each piece of land and an account for each product; and he proves that within a period of thirty years the same man has never obtained equal crops from the same piece of land. The products have varied from twenty-six thousand francs to nine thousand or seven thousand francs, sometimes descending as low as three hundred francs. There are also certain products — potatoes, for instance — which fail one time in ten. How, then, with these variations and with revenues so uncertain, can we establish even distribution and uniform wages for laborers? . . ."

It might be answered that the variations in the product of each piece of land simply indicate that it is necessary to associate proprietors with each other after having associated laborers with proprietors, which would establish a more complete solidarity: but this would be a prejudgment on the very thing in question, which M. Blanqui definitively decides, after reflection, to be unattainable, — namely, the organization of labor. Besides, it is evident that solidarity would not add an obolus to the common wealth, and that, consequently, it does not even touch the problem of division.

In short, the profit so much envied, and often a very uncertain matter with employers, falls far short of the difference between actual wages and the wages desired; and M. Blanqui's former plan, miserable in its results and disavowed by its author, would be a scourge to the manufacturing industry. Now, the division of labor being henceforth universally established, the argument is generalized, and leads us to the conclusion that misery is an effect of labor, as well as of idleness.

The answer to this is, and it is a favorite argument with the people: Increase the price of services; double and triple wages.

I confess that if such an increase was possible it would be a complete success, whatever M. Chevalier may have said, who needs to be slightly corrected on this point.

According to M. Chevalier, if the price of any kind of merchandise whatever is increased, other kinds will rise in a like proportion, and no one will benefit thereby.

This argument, which the economists have rehearsed for more than a century, is as false as it is old, and it belonged to M. Chevalier, as an engineer, to rectify the economic tradition. The salary of a head clerk being ten francs per day, and the wages of a workingman four, if the income of each is increased five francs, the ratio of their fortunes, which was formerly as one hundred to forty, will be thereafter as one hundred to sixty. The increase of wages, necessarily taking place by addition and not by proportion, would be, therefore, an excellent method of equalization; and the economists would deserve to have thrown back at them by the socialists the reproach of ignorance which they have bestowed upon them at random.

But I say that such an increase is impossible, and that the supposition is absurd: for, as M. Chevalier has shown very clearly elsewhere, the figure which indicates the price of the day's labor is only an algebraic exponent without effect on the reality: and that which it is necessary first to endeavor to increase, while correcting the inequalities of distribution, is not the monetary expression, but the quantity of products. Till then every rise of wages can have no other effect than that produced by a rise of the price of wheat, wine, meat, sugar, soap, coal, etc., — that is, the effect of a scarcity. For what is wages?

It is the cost price of wheat, wine, meat, coal; it is the integrant price of all things. Let us go farther yet: wages is the proportionality of the elements which compose wealth, and which are consumed every day reproductively by the mass of laborers. Now, to double wages, in the sense in which the people understand the words, is to give to each producer a share greater than his product, which is contradictory: and if the rise pertains only to a few industries, a general disturbance in exchange ensues, — that is, a scarcity. God save me from predictions! but, in spite of my desire for the amelioration of the lot of the working class, I declare that it is impossible for strikes followed by an increase of wages to end otherwise than in a general rise in prices: that is as certain as that two and two make four. It is not by such methods that the workingmen will attain to wealth and — what is a thousand times more precious than wealth — liberty. The workingmen, supported by the favor of an indiscreet press, in demanding an increase of wages, have served monopoly much better than their own real interests: may they recognize, when their situation shall become more painful, the bitter fruit of their inexperience!

Convinced of the uselessness, or rather, of the fatal effects, of an increase of wages, and seeing clearly that the question is wholly organic and not at all commercial, M. Chevalier attacks the problem at the other end. He asks for the working class, first of all, instruction, and proposes extensive reforms in this direction.

Instruction! this is also M. Arago's word to the workingmen; it is the principle of all progress. Instruction! . . . It should be known once for all what may be expected from it in the solution of the problem before us; it should be known, I say, not whether it is desirable that all should receive it, — this no one doubts, — but whether it is possible.

To clearly comprehend the complete significance of M. Chevalier's views, a knowledge of his methods is indispensable.

M. Chevalier, long accustomed to discipline, first by his polytechnic studies, then by his St. Simonian connections, and finally by his position in the University, does not seem to admit that a pupil can have any other inclination than to obey the regulations, a sectarian any other thought than that of his chief, a public functionary any other opinion than that of the government. This may be a conception of order as respectable as any other, and I hear upon this subject no expressions of approval or censure. Has M. Chevalier an idea to offer peculiar to himself? On the principle that all that is not forbidden by law is allowed, he hastens to the front to deliver his opinion, and then abandons it to give his adhesion, if there is occasion, to the opinion of authority. It was thus that M. Chevalier, before settling down in the bosom of the Constitution, joined M. Enfantin: it was thus that he gave his views upon canals, railroads, finance, property, long before the administration had adopted any system in relation to the construction of railways, the changing of the rate of interest on bonds, patents, literary property, etc.

M. Chevalier, then, is not a blind admirer of the University system of instruction, — far from it; and until the appearance of the new order of things, he does not hesitate to say what he thinks. His opinions are of the most radical.

M. Villemain had said in his report: "The object of the higher education is to prepare in advance a choice of men to occupy and serve in all the positions of the administration, the magistracy, the bar and the various liberal professions, including the higher ranks and learned specialties of the army and navy."

"The higher education," thereupon observes M. Chevalier,[5] "is designed also to prepare men some of whom shall be farmers, others manufacturers, these merchants, and those private engineers. Now, in the official programme, all these classes are forgotten. The omission is of considerable importance; for, indeed, industry in its various forms, agriculture, commerce, are neither accessories nor accidents in a State: they are its chief dependence... If the University desires to justify its name, it must provide a course in these things; else an industrial university will be established in opposition to it... We shall have altar against altar, etc..."

And as it is characteristic of a luminous idea to throw light on all questions connected with it, professional instruction furnishes M. Chevalier with a very expeditious method of deciding, incidentally, the quarrel between the clergy and the University on liberty of education.

"It must be admitted that a very great concession is made to the clergy in allowing Latin to serve as the basis of education. The clergy know Latin as well as the University; it is their own tongue. Their tuition, moreover, is cheaper; hence

_____

Journal des Economistes," April, 1843.

they must inevitably draw a large portion of our youth into their small seminaries and their schools of a higher grade . . ."

The conclusion of course follows: change the course of study, and you de-catholicize the realm; and as the clergy know only Latin and the Bible, when they have among them neither masters of art, nor farmers, nor accountants; when, of their forty thousand priests, there are not twenty, perhaps, with the ability to make a plan or forge a nail, — we soon shall see which the fathers of families will choose, industry or the breviary, and whether they do not regard labor as the most beautiful language in which to pray to God.

Thus would end this ridiculous opposition between religious education and profane science, between the spiritual and the temporal, between reason and faith, between altar and throne, old rubrics henceforth meaningless, but with which they still impose upon the good nature of the public, until it takes offence.

M. Chevalier does not insist, however, on this solution: he knows that religion and monarchy are two powers which, though continually quarrelling, cannot exist without each other; and that he may not awaken suspicion, he launches out into another revolutionary idea, — equality.

"France is in a position to furnish the polytechnic school with twenty times as many scholars as enter at present (the average being one hundred and seventy-six, this would amount to three thousand five hundred and twenty). The University has but to say the word . . . If my opinion was of any weight, I should maintain that mathematical capacity is much less special than is commonly supposed. I remember the success with which children, taken at random, so to speak, from the pavements of Paris, follow the teaching of La Martiniere by the method of Captain Tabareau."

If the higher education, reconstructed according to the views of M. Chevalier, was sought after by all young French men instead of by only ninety thousand as commonly, there would be no exaggeration in raising the estimate of the number of minds mathematically inclined from three thousand five hundred and twenty to ten thousand; but, by the same argument, we should have ten thousand artists, philologists, and philosophers; ten thousand doctors, physicians, chemists, and naturalists; ten thousand economists, legists, and administrators; twenty thousand manufacturers, foremen, merchants, and accountants; forty thousand farmers, wine-growers, miners, etc., — in all, one hundred thousand specialists a year, or about one-third of our youth. The rest, having, instead of special adaptations, only mingled adaptations, would be distributed indifferently elsewhere.

It is certain that so powerful an impetus given to intelligence would quicken the progress of equality, and I do not doubt that such is the secret desire of M. Chevalier. But that is precisely what troubles me: capacity is never wanting, any more than population, and the problem is to find employment for the one and bread for the other. In vain does M. Chevalier tell us: "The higher education would give less ground for the complaint that it throws into society crowds of ambitious persons without any means of satisfying their desires, and interested in the overthrow of the State; people without employment and unable to get any, good for nothing and believing themselves fit for anything, especially for the direction of public affairs. Scientific studies do not so inflate the mind. They enlighten and regulate it at once; they fit men for practical life . . ." Such language, I reply, is good to use with patriarchs: a professor of political economy should have more respect for his position and his audience. The government has only one hundred and twenty offices annually at its disposal for one hundred and seventy-six students admitted to the polytechnic school: what, then, would be its embarrassment if the number of admissions was ten thousand, or even, taking M. Chevalier's figures, three thousand five hundred? And, to generalize, the whole number of civil positions is sixty thousand, or three thousand vacancies annually; what dismay would the government be thrown into if, suddenly adopting the reformatory ideas of M. Chevalier, it should find itself besieged by fifty thousand office-seekers! The following objection has often been made to republicans without eliciting a reply: When everybody shall have the electoral privilege, will the deputies do any better, and will the proletariat be further advanced? I ask the same question of M. Chevalier: When each academic year shall bring you one hundred thousand fitted men, what will you do with them?

To provide for these interesting young people, you will go down to the lowest round of the ladder. You will oblige the young man, after fifteen years of lofty study, to begin, no longer as now with the offices of aspirant engineer, sub-lieutenant of artillery, second lieutenant, deputy, comptroller, general guardian, etc., but with the ignoble positions of pioneer, train-soldier, dredger, cabin-boy, fagot-maker, and exciseman. There he will wait, until death, thinning the ranks, enables him to advance a step. Under such circumstances a man, a graduate of the polytechnic school and capable of becoming a Vauban, may die a laborer on a second class road, or a corporal in a regiment

Oh! how much more prudent Catholicism has shown itself, and how far it has surpassed you all, St. Simonians, republicans, university men, economists, in the knowledge of man and society! The priest knows that our life is but a voyage, and that our perfection cannot be realized here below; and he contents himself with outlining on earth an education which must be completed in heaven. The man whom religion has moulded, content to know, do, and obtain what suffices for his earthly destiny, never can become a source of embarrassment to the government: rather would he be a martyr. O beloved religion! is it necessary that a bourgeoisie which stands in such need of you should disown you? . . .

Into what terrible struggles of pride and misery does this mania for universal instruction plunge us! Of what use is professional education, of what good are agricultural and commercial schools, if your students have neither employment nor capital? And what need to cram one's self till the age of twenty with all sorts of knowledge, then to fasten the threads of a mule-jenny or pick coal at the bottom of a pit? What! you have by your own confession only three thousand positions annually to bestow upon fifty thousand possible capacities, and yet you talk of establishing schools! Cling rather to your system of exclusion and privilege, a system as old as the world, the support of dynasties and patriciates, a veritable machine for gelding men in order to secure the pleasures of a caste of Sultans. Set a high price upon your teaching, multiply obstacles, drive away, by lengthy tests, the son of the proletaire whom hunger does not permit to wait, and protect with all your power the ecclesiastical schools, where the students are taught to labor for the other life, to cultivate resignation, to fast, to respect those in high places, to love the king, and to pray to God. For every useless study sooner or later becomes an abandoned study: knowledge is poison to slaves.

Surely M. Chevalier has too much sagacity not to have seen the consequences of his idea. But he has spoken from the bottom of his heart, and we can only applaud his good intentions: men must first be men; after that, he may live who can.

Thus we advance at random, guided by Providence, who never warns us except with a blow: this is the beginning and end of political economy.

Contrary to M. Chevalier, professor of political economy at the College of France, M. Dunoyer, an economist of the Institute, does not wish instruction to be organized. The organization of instruction is a species of organization of labor; therefore, no organization. Instruction, observes M. Dunoyer, is a profession, not a function of the State; like all professions, it ought to be and remain free. It is communism, it is socialism, it is the revolutionary tendency, whose principal agents have been Robespierre, Napoleon, Louis XVIII, and M. Guizot, which have thrown into our midst these fatal ideas of the centralization and absorption of all activity in the State. The press is very free, and the pen of the journalist is an object of merchandise; religion, too, is very free, and every wearer of a gown, be it short or long, who knows how to excite public curiosity, can draw an audience about him. M. Lacordaire has his devotees, M. Leroux his apostles, M. Buchez his convent. Why, then, should not instruction also be free? If the right of the instructed, like that of the buyer, is unquestionable, and that of the instructor, who is only a variety of the seller, is its correlative, it is impossible to infringe upon the liberty of instruction without doing violence to the most precious of liberties, that of the conscience. And then, adds M. Dunoyer, if the State owes instruction to everybody, it will soon be maintained that it owes labor; then lodging; then shelter... Where does that lead to?

The argument of M. Dunoyer is irrefutable: to organize instruction is to give to every citizen a pledge of liberal employment and comfortable wages; the two are as intimately connected as the circulation of the arteries and the veins. But M. Dunoyer's theory implies also that progress belongs only to a certain select portion of humanity, and that barbarism is the eternal lot of nine-tenths of the human race. It is this which constitutes, according to M. Dunoyer, the very essence of society, which manifests itself in three stages, religion, hierarchy, and beggary. So that in this system, which is that of Destutt de Tracy, Montesquieu, and Plato, the antinomy of division, like that of value, is without solution.

It is a source of inexpressible pleasure to me, I confess, to see M. Chevalier, a defender of the centralization of instruction, opposed by M. Dunoyer, a defender of liberty; M. Dunoyer in his turn antagonized by M. Guizot; M. Guizot, the representative of the centralizers, contradicting the Charter, which posits liberty as a principle; the Charter trampled under foot by the University men, who lay sole claim to the privilege of teaching, regardless of the express command of the Gospel to the priests: Go and teach. And above all this tumult of economists, legislators, ministers, academicians, professors, and priests, economic Providence giving the lie to the Gospel, and shouting: Pedagogues! what use am I to make of your instruction?

Who will relieve us of this anxiety? M. Rossi leans toward eclecticism: Too little divided, he says, labor remains unproductive; too much divided, it degrades man. Wisdom lies between these extremes; in medio virtus. Unfortunately this intermediate wisdom is only a small amount of poverty joined with a small amount of wealth, so that the condition is not modified in the least. The proportion of good and evil, instead of being as one hundred to one hundred, becomes as fifty to fifty: in this we may take, once for all, the measure of eclecticism. For the rest, M. Rossi's juste-milieu is in direct opposition to the great economic law: To produce with the least possible expense the greatest possible quantity of values... Now, how can labor fulfil its destiny without an extreme division? Let us look farther, if you please.

"All economic systems and hypotheses," says M. Rossi, "belong to the economist, but the intelligent, free, responsible man is under the control of the moral law... Political economy is only a science which examines the relations of things, and draws conclusions therefrom. It examines the effects of labor; in the application of labor, you should consider the importance of the object in view. When the application of labor is unfavorable to an object higher than the production of wealth, it should not be applied... Suppose that it would increase the national wealth to compel children to labor fifteen hours a day: morality would say that

that is not allowable. Does that prove that political economy is false? No; that proves that you confound things which should be kept separate."

If M. Rossi had a little more of that Gallic simplicity so difficult for foreigners to acquire, he would very summarily have thrown his tongue to the dogs, as Madame de Sevigne said. But a professor must talk, talk, talk, not for the sake of saying anything, but in order to avoid silence. M. Rossi takes three turns around the question, then lies down: that is enough to make certain people believe that he has answered it.

It is surely a sad symptom for a science when, in developing itself according to its own principles, it reaches its object just in time to be contradicted by another; as, for example, when the postulates of political economy are found to be opposed to those of morality, for I suppose that morality is a science as well as political economy. What, then, is human knowledge, if all its affirmations destroy each other, and on what shall we rely? Divided labor is a slave's occupation, but it alone is really productive; undivided labor belongs to the free man, but it does not pay its expenses. On the one hand, political economy tells us to be rich; on the other, morality tells us to be free; and M. Rossi, speaking in the name of both, warns us at the same time that we can be neither free nor rich, for to be but half of either is to be neither. M. Rossi's doctrine, then, far from satisfying this double desire of humanity, is open to the objection that, to avoid exclusiveness, it strips us of everything: it is, under another form, the history of the representative system.

But the antagonism is even more profound than M. Rossi has supposed. For since, according to universal experience (on this point in harmony with theory), wages decrease in proportion to the division of labor, it is clear that, in submitting ourselves to parcellaire slavery, we thereby shall not obtain wealth; we shall only change men into machines: witness the laboring population of the two worlds. And since, on the other hand, without the division of labor, society falls back into barbarism, it is evident also that, by sacrificing wealth, we shall not obtain liberty: witness all the wandering tribes of Asia and Africa. Therefore it is necessary — economic science and morality absolutely command it — for us to solve the problem of division: now, where are the economists? More than thirty years ago, Lemontey, developing a remark of Smith, exposed the demoralizing and homicidal influence of the division of labor. What has been the reply; what investigations have been made; what remedies proposed; has the question even been understood?

Every year the economists report, with an exactness which I would commend more highly if I did not see that it is always fruitless, the commercial condition of the States of Europe. They know how many yards of cloth, pieces of silk, pounds of iron, have been manufactured; what has been the consumption per head of wheat, wine, sugar, meat: it might be said that to them the ultimate of science is to publish inventories, and the object of their labor is to become general comptrollers of nations. Never did such a mass of material offer so fine a field for investigation. What has been found; what new principle has sprung from this mass; what solution of the many problems of long standing has been reached; what new direction have studies taken?

One question, among others, seems to have been prepared for a final judgment, — pauperism. Pauperism, of all the phenomena of the civilized world, is today the best known: we know pretty nearly whence it comes, when and how it arrives, and what it costs; its proportion at various stages of civilization has been calculated, and we have convinced ourselves that all the specifics with which it hitherto has been fought have been impotent. Pauperism has been divided into genera, species, and varieties: it is a complete natural history, one of the most important branches of anthropology. Well I the unquestionable result of all the facts collected, unseen, shunned, covered by the economists with their silence, is that pauperism is constitutional and chronic in society as long as the antagonism between labor and capital continues, and that this antagonism can end only by the absolute negation of political economy. What issue from this labyrinth have the economists discovered?

This last point deserves a moment's attention.

In primitive communism misery, as I have observed in a preceding paragraph, is the universal condition.

Labor is war declared upon this misery.

Labor organizes itself, first by division, next by machinery, then by competition, etc.

Now, the question is whether it is not in the essence of this organization, as given us by political economy, at the same time that it puts an end to the misery of some, to aggravate that of others in a fatal and unavoidable manner. These are the terms in which the question of pauperism must be stated, and for this reason we have undertaken to solve it.

What means, then, this eternal babble of the economists about the improvidence of laborers, their idleness, their want of dignity, their ignorance, their debauchery, their early marriages, etc.? All these vices and excesses are only the cloak of pauperism; but the cause, the original cause which inexorably holds four-fifths of the human race in disgrace, — what is it? Did not Nature make all men equally gross, averse to labor, wanton, and wild? Did not patrician and proletaire spring from the same clay? Then how happens it that, after so many centuries, and in spite of so many miracles of industry, science, and art, comfort and culture have not become the inheritance of all? How happens it that in Paris and London, centres of social wealth, poverty is as hideous as in the days of Caesar and

Agricola? Why, by the side of this refined aristocracy, has the mass remained so uncultivated? It is laid to the vices of the people: but the vices of the upper class appear to be no less; perhaps they are even greater. The original stain affected all alike: how happens it, once more, that the baptism of civilization has not been equally efficacious for all? Does this not show that progress itself is a privilege, and that the man who has neither wagon nor horse is forced to flounder about for ever in the mud? What do I say? The totally destitute man has no desire to improve: he has fallen so low that ambition even is extinguished in his heart.

"Of all the private virtues," observes M. Dunoyer with infinite reason, "the most necessary, that which gives us all the others in succession, is the passion for well-being, is the violent desire to extricate one's self from misery and abjection, is that spirit of emulation and dignity which does not permit men to rest content with an inferior situation. . . But this sentiment, which seems so natural, is unfortunately much less common than is thought. There are few reproaches which the generality of men deserve less than that which ascetic moralists bring against them of being too fond of their comforts: the opposite reproach might be brought against them with infinitely more justice. . . There is even in the nature of men this very remarkable feature, that the less their knowledge and resources, the less desire they have of acquiring these. The most miserable savages and the least enlightened of men are precisely those in whom it is most difficult to arouse wants, those in whom it is hardest to inspire the desire to rise out of their condition; so that man must already have gained a certain degree of comfort by his labor, before he can feel with any keenness that need of improving his condition, of perfecting his existence, which I call the love of well-being."[6]

Thus the misery of the laboring classes arises in general from their lack of heart and mind, or, as M. Passy has said somewhere, from the weakness, the inertia of their moral and intellectual faculties. This inertia is due to the fact that the said laboring classes, still half savage, do not have a sufficiently ardent desire to ameliorate their condition: this M. Dunoyer shows. But as this absence of desire is itself the effect of misery, it follows that misery and apathy are each other's effect and cause, and that the proletariat turns in a circle.

To rise out of this abyss there must be either well-being, — that is, a gradual increase of wages, — or intelligence and courage, — that is, a gradual development of faculties: two things diametrically opposed to the degradation of soul and body which is the natural effect of the division of labor. The misfortune of the proletariat, then, is wholly providential, and to undertake to extinguish it in the present state of political economy would be to produce a revolutionary whirlwind.

---

[6] "The Liberty of Labor," Vol. II, p. 80.

For it is not without a profound reason, rooted in the loftiest considerations of morality, that the universal conscience, expressing itself by turns through the selfishness of the rich and the apathy of the proletariat, denies a reward to the man whose whole function is that of a lever and spring. If, by some impossibility, material well-being could fall to the lot of the parcellaire laborer, we should see something monstrous happen: the laborers employed at disagreeable tasks would become like those Romans, gorged with the wealth of the world, whose brutalized minds became incapable of devising new pleasures. Well-being without education stupefies people and makes them insolent: this was noticed in the most ancient times. Incrassatus est, et recalcitravit, says

Deuteronomy. For the rest, the parcellaire laborer has judged himself: he is content, provided he has bread, a pallet to sleep on, and plenty of liquor on Sunday. Any other condition would be prejudicial to him, and would endanger public order.

At Lyons there is a class of men who, under cover of the monopoly given them by the city government, receive higher pay than college professors or the head-clerks of the government ministers: I mean the porters. The price of loading and unloading at certain wharves in Lyons, according to the schedule of the Rigues or porters' associations, is thirty centimes per hundred kilogrammes. At this rate, it is not seldom that a man earns twelve, fifteen, and even twenty francs a day: he only has to carry forty or fifty sacks from a vessel to a warehouse. It is but a few hours' work. What a favorable condition this would be for the development of intelligence, as well for children as for parents, if, of itself and the leisure which it brings, wealth was a moralizing principle! But this is not the case: the porters of Lyons are today what they always have been, drunken, dissolute, brutal, insolent, selfish, and base. It is a painful thing to say, but I look upon the following declaration as a duty, because it is the truth: one of the first reforms to be effected among the laboring classes will be the reduction of the wages of some at the same time that we raise those of others. Monopoly does not gain in respectability by belonging to the lowest classes of people, especially when it serves to maintain only the grossest individualism. The revolt of the silk-workers met with no sympathy, but rather hostility, from the porters and the river population generally. Nothing that happens off the wharves has any power to move them. Beasts of burden fashioned in advance for despotism, they will not mingle with politics as long as their privilege is maintained. Nevertheless, I ought to say in their defence that, some time ago, the necessities of competition having brought their prices down, more social sentiments began to awaken in these gross natures: a few more reductions seasoned with a little poverty, and the Rigues of Lyons will be chosen as the storming-party when the time comes for assaulting the bastilles.

In short, it is impossible, contradictory, in the present system of society, for the proletariat to secure well-being through education or education through well-being. For, without considering the fact that the proletaire, a human machine, is as unfit for comfort as for education, it is demonstrated, on the one hand, that his wages continually tend to go down rather than up, and, on the other, that the cultivation of his mind, if it were possible, would be useless to him; so that he always inclines towards barbarism and misery. Everything that has been attempted of late years in France and England with a view to the amelioration of the condition of the poor in the matters of the labor of women and children and of primary instruction, unless it was the fruit of some hidden thought of radicalism, has been done contrary to economic ideas and to the prejudice of the established order. Progress, to the mass of laborers, is always the book sealed with the seven seals; and it is not by legislative misconstructions that the relentless enigma will be solved.

For the rest, if the economists, by exclusive attention to their old routine, have finally lost all knowledge of the present state of things, it cannot be said that the socialists have better solved the antinomy which division of labor raised. Quite the contrary, they have stopped with negation; for is it not perpetual negation to oppose, for instance, the uniformity of parcellaire labor with a so-called variety in which each one can change his occupation ten, fifteen, twenty times a day at will?

As if to change ten, fifteen, twenty times a day from one kind of divided labor to another was to make labor synthetic; as if, consequently, twenty fractions of the day's work of a manual laborer could be equal to the day's work of an artist! Even if such industrial vaulting was practicable, — and it may be asserted in advance that it would disappear in the presence of the necessity of making laborers responsible and therefore functions personal, — it would not change at all the physical, moral, and intellectual condition of the laborer; the dissipation would only be a surer guarantee of his incapacity and, consequently, his dependence. This is admitted, moreover, by the organizers, communists, and others. So far are they from pretending to solve the antinomy of division that all of them admit, as an essential condition of organization, the hierarchy of labor, — that is, the classification of laborers into parcellaires and generalizers or organizers, — and in all utopias the distinction of capacities, the basis or everlasting excuse for inequality of goods, is admitted as a pivot. Those reformers whose schemes have nothing to recommend them but logic, and who, after having complained of the simplism, monotony, uniformity, and extreme division of labor, then propose a plurality as a SYNTHESIS, — such inventors, I say, are judged already, and ought to be sent back to school.

But you, critic, the reader undoubtedly will ask, what is your solution? Show us this synthesis which, retaining the responsibility, the personality, in short, the specialty of the laborer, will unite extreme division and the greatest variety in one complex and harmonious whole.

My reply is ready: Interrogate facts, consult humanity: we can choose no better guide. After the oscillations of value, division of labor is the economic fact which influences most perceptibly profits and wages. It is the first stake driven by Providence into the soil of industry, the starting-point of the immense triangulation which finally must determine the right and duty of each and all. Let us, then, follow our guides, without which we can only wander and lose ourselves.

Tu longe seggere, et vestigia semper adora.

Chapter IV. Second Period. — Machinery.

"I HAVE witnessed with profound regret the CONTINUANCE OF DISTRESS in the manufacturing districts of the country."

Words of Queen Victoria on the reassembling of parliament.

If there is anything of a nature to cause sovereigns to reflect, it is that, more or less impassible spectators of human calamities, they are, by the very constitution of society and the nature of their power, absolutely powerless to cure the sufferings of their subjects; they are even prohibited from paying any attention to them. Every question of labor and wages, say with one accord the economic and representative theorists, must remain outside of the attributes of power. From the height of the glorious sphere where religion has placed them, thrones, dominations, principalities, powers, and all the heavenly host view the torment of society, beyond the reach of its stress; but their power does not extend over the winds and floods. Kings can do nothing for the salvation of mortals. And, in truth, these theorists are right: the prince is established to maintain, not to revolutionize; to protect reality, not to bring about utopia. He represents one of the antagonistic principles: hence, if he were to establish harmony, he would eliminate himself, which on his part would be sovereignly unconstitutional and absurd.

But as, in spite of theories, the progress of ideas is incessantly changing the external form of institutions in such a way as to render continually necessary exactly that which the legislator neither desires nor foresees, — so that, for instance, questions of taxation become questions of distribution; those of public utility, questions of national labor and industrial organization; those of finance, operations of credit; and those of international law, questions of customs duties and markets, — it stands as demonstrated that the prince, who, according to theory, should never interfere with things which nevertheless, without theory's foreknowledge, are daily and irresistibly becoming matters of government, is and can be henceforth, like Divinity from which he emanates, whatever may be said, only an hypothesis, a fiction.

And finally, as it is impossible that the prince and the interests which it is his mission to defend should consent to diminish and disappear before emergent principles and new rights posited, it follows that progress, after being accomplished in the mind insensibly, is realized in society by leaps, and that force, in spite of the calumny of which it is the object, is the necessary condition of reforms. Every society in which the power of insurrection is suppressed is a society dead to progress: there is no truth of history better proven.

And what I say of constitutional monarchies is equally true of representative democracies: everywhere the social compact has united power and conspired against life, it being impossible for the legislator either to see that he was working against his own ends or to proceed otherwise.

Monarchs and representatives, pitiable actors in parliamentary comedies, this in the last analysis is what you are: talismans against the future! Every year brings you the grievances of the people; and when you are asked for the remedy, your wisdom covers its face! Is it necessary to support privilege, — that is, that consecration of the right of the strongest which created you and which is changing every day? Promptly, at the slightest nod of your head, a numerous army starts up, runs to arms, and forms in line of battle. And when the people complain that, in spite of their labor and precisely because of their labor, misery devours them, when society asks you for life, you recite acts of mercy! All your energy is expended for conservatism, all your virtue vanishes in aspirations! Like the Pharisee, instead of feeding your father, you pray for him! Ah! I tell you, we possess the secret of your mission: you exist only to prevent us from living. Nolite ergo imperare, get you gone!

As for us, who view the mission of power from quite another standpoint, and who wish the special work of government to be precisely that of exploring the future, searching for progress, and securing for all liberty, equality, health, and wealth, we continue our task of criticism courageously, entirely sure that, when we have laid bare the cause of the evils of society, the principle of its fevers, the motive of its disturbances, we shall not lack the power to apply the remedy.

1. — Of the function of machinery in its relations to liberty.

The introduction of machinery into industry is accomplished in opposition to the law of division, and as if to reestablish the equilibrium profoundly compromised by that law. To truly appreciate the significance of this movement and grasp its spirit, a few general considerations become necessary.

Modern philosophers, after collecting and classifying their annals, have been led by the nature of their labors to deal also with history: then it was that they saw, not without surprise, that the history of philosophy was the same thing at bottom as the philosophy of history; further, that these two branches of speculation, so different in appearance, the history of philosophy and the philosophy of history, were also only the stage representation of the concepts of metaphysics, which is philosophy entire.

Now, dividing the material of universal history among a certain number of frames, such as mathematics, natural history, social economy, etc., it will be found that each of these divisions contains also metaphysics. And it will be the same down to the last subdivision of the totality of history: so that entire philosophy lies at the bottom of every natural or industrial manifestation; that it is no respecter of degrees or qualities; that, to rise to its sublimest conceptions, all prototypes may be employed equally well; and, finally, that, all the postulates of reason meeting in the most modest industry as well as in the most general sciences, to make every artisan a philosopher, — that is, a generalizing and highly synthetic mind, — it would be enough to teach him — what? his profession.

Hitherto, it is true, philosophy, like wealth, has been reserved for certain classes: we have the philosophy of history, the philosophy of law, and some other philosophies also; this is a sort of appropriation which, like many others of equally noble origin, must disappear. But, to consummate this immense equation, it is necessary to begin with the philosophy of labor, after which each laborer will be able to attempt in his turn the philosophy of his trade.

Thus every product of art and industry, every political and religious constitution, like every creature organized or unorganized, being only a realization, a natural or practical application, of philosophy, the identity of the laws of nature and reason, of being and idea, is demonstrated; and when, for our own purpose, we establish the constant conformity of economic phenomena to the pure laws of thought, the equivalence of the real and the ideal in human facts, we only repeat in a particular case this eternal demonstration.

What do we say, in fact?

To determine value, — in other words, to organize within itself the production and distribution of wealth, — society proceeds exactly as the mind does in the generation of concepts. First it posits a primary fact, acts upon a primary hypothesis, the division of labor, a veritable antinomy, the antagonistic results of which are evolved in social economy, just as the consequences might have been deduced in the mind: so that the industrial movement, following in all respects the deduction of ideas, is divided into a double current, one of useful effects, the other of subversive results, all equally necessary and legitimate products of the same law. To harmonically establish this two-faced principle and solve this antinomy, society evokes a second, soon to be followed by a third; and such will be the progress of the social genius until, having exhausted all its contradictions, — supposing, though it is not proved, that there is an end to contradiction in humanity, — it shall cover with one backward leap all its previous positions and in a single formula solve all problems.

In following in our exposition this method of the parallel development of the reality and the idea, we find a double advantage: first, that of escaping the reproach of materialism, so often applied to economists, to whom facts are truth simply because they are facts, and material facts. To us, on the contrary, facts are not matter, — for we do not know what the word matter means, — but visible manifestations of invisible ideas. So viewed, the value of facts is measured by the idea which they represent; and that is why we have rejected as illegitimate and non-conclusive useful value and value in exchange, and later the division of labor itself, although to the economists all these have an absolute authority.

On the other hand, it is as impossible to accuse us of spiritualism, idealism, or mysticism: for, admitting as a point of departure only the external manifestation of the idea, — the idea which we do not know, which does not exist, as long as it is not reflected, like light, which would be nothing if the sun existed by itself in an infinite void, — and brushing aside all a prori reasoning upon theogony and cosmogony, all inquiry into substance, cause, the me and the not-me, we confine ourselves to searching for the laws of being and to following the order of their appearance as far as reason can reach.

Doubtless all knowledge brings up at last against a mystery: such, for instance, as matter and mind, both of which we admit as two unknown essences, upon which all phenomena rest. But this is not to say that mystery is the point of departure of knowledge, or that mysticism is the necessary condition of logic: quite the contrary, the spontaneity of our reason tends to the perpetual rejection of mysticism; it makes an a priori protest against all mystery, because it has no use for mystery except to deny it, and because the negation of mysticism is the only thing for which reason has no need of experience.

In short, human facts are the incarnation of human ideas: therefore, to study the laws of social economy is to constitute the theory of the laws of reason and create philosophy. We may now pursue the course of our investigation.

At the end of the preceding chapter we left the laborer at loggerheads with the law of division: how will this indefatigable OEdipus manage to solve this enigma?

In society the incessant appearance of machinery is the antithesis, the inverse formula, of the division of labor; it is the protest of the industrial genius against parcellaire and homicidal labor. What is a machine, in fact? A method of re-uniting divers particles of labor which division had separated. Every machine may be defined as a summary of several operations, a simplification of powers, a condensation of labor, a reduction of costs. In all these respects machinery is the counterpart of division. Therefore through machinery will come a restoration of the parcellaire laborer, a decrease of toil for the workman, a fall in the price of his product, a movement in the relation of values, progress towards new discoveries, advancement of the general welfare.

As the discovery of a formula gives a new power to the geometer, so the invention of a machine is an abridgment of manual labor which multiplies the power of the producer, from which it may be inferred that the antinomy of the division of labor, if not entirely destroyed, will be balanced and neutralized. No one should fail to read the lectures of M. Chevalier setting forth the innumerable advantages resulting to society from the intervention of machinery; they make a striking picture to which I take pleasure in referring my reader.

Machinery, positing itself in political economy in opposition to the division of labor, represents synthesis opposing itself in the human mind to analysis; and just as in the division of labor and in machinery, as we shall soon see, political economy entire is contained, so with analysis and synthesis goes the possession of logic entire, of philosophy. The man who labors proceeds necessarily and by turns by division and the aid of tools; likewise, he who reasons performs necessarily and by turns the operations of synthesis and analysis, nothing more, absolutely nothing. And labor and reason will never get beyond this: Prometheus, like Neptune, attains in three strides the confines of the world.

From these principles, as simple and as luminous as axioms, immense consequences follow.

As in the operation of the mind analysis and synthesis are essentially inseparable, and as, looking at the matter from another point, theory becomes legitimate only on condition of following experience foot by foot, it follows that labor, uniting analysis and synthesis, theory and experience, in a continuous action, — labor, the external form of logic and consequently a summary of reality and idea, — appears again as a universal method of instruction. Fit fabricando faber: of all systems of education the most absurd is that which separates intelligence from activity, and divides man into two impossible entities, theorizer and automaton. That is why we applaud the just complaints of M. Chevalier, M. Dunoyer, and all those who demand reform in university education; on that also rests the hope of the results that we have promised ourselves from such reform. If education were first of all experimental and practical, reserving speech only to explain, summarize, and coordinate work; if those who cannot learn with imagination and memory were permitted to learn with their eyes and hands, — soon we should witness a multiplication, not only of the forms of labor, but of capacities; everybody, knowing the theory of something, would thereby possess the language of philosophy; on occasion he could, were it only for once in his life, create, modify, perfect, give proof of intelligence and comprehension, produce his master-piece, in a word, show himself a man. The inequality in the acquisitions of memory would not affect the equivalence of faculties, and genius would no longer seem to us other than what it really is, — mental health.

The fine minds of the eighteenth century went into extended disputations about what constitutes genius, wherein it differs from talent, what we should understand by mind, etc. They had transported into the intellectual sphere the same distinctions that, in society, separate persons. To them there were kings and rulers of genius, princes of genius, ministers of genius; and then there were also noble minds and bourgeois minds, city talents and country talents. Clear at the foot of the ladder lay the gross industrial population, souls imperfectly outlined, excluded from the glory of the elect. All rhetorics are still filled with these impertinences, which monarchical interests, literary vanity, and socialistic hypocrisy strain themselves to sanction, for the perpetual slavery of nations and the maintenance of the existing order.

But, if it is demonstrated that all the operations of the mind are reducible to two, analysis and synthesis, which are necessarily inseparable, although distinct; if, by a forced consequence, in spite of the infinite variety of tasks and studies, the mind never does more than begin the same canvas over again, — the man of genius is simply a man with a good constitution, who has worked a great deal, thought a great deal, analyzed, compared, classified, summarized, and concluded a great deal; while the limited being, who stagnates in an endemic routine, instead of developing his faculties, has killed his intelligence through inertia and automatism. It is absurd to distinguish as differing in nature that which really differs only in age, and then to convert into privilege and exclusion the various degrees of a development or the fortunes of a spontaneity which must gradually disappear through labor and education.

The psychological rhetoricians who have classified human souls into dynasties, noble races, bourgeois families, and the proletariat observed nevertheless that genius was not universal, and that it had its specialty; consequently Homer, Plato, Phidias, Archimedes, Caesar, etc., all of whom seemed to them first in their sort, were declared by them equals and sovereigns of distinct realms. How irrational! As if the specialty of genius did not itself reveal the law of the equality of minds! As if, looking at it in another light, the steadiness of success in the product of genius were not a proof that it works according to principles outside of itself, which are the guarantee of the perfection of its work, as long as it follows them with fidelity and certainty! This apotheosis of genius, dreamed of with open eyes by men whose chatter will remain forever barren, would warrant a belief in the innate stupidity of the majority of mortals, if it were not a striking proof of their perfectibility.

Labor, then, after having distinguished capacities and arranged their equilibrium by the division of industries, completes the armament of intelligence, if I may venture to say so, by machinery. According to the testimony of history as well as according to analysis, and notwithstanding the anomalies caused by the antagonism of economic principles, intelligence differs in men, not by power, clearness, or reach, but, in the first place, by specialty, or, in the language of the schools, by qualitative determination, and, in the second place, by exercise and education.

Hence, in the individual as in the collective man, intelligence is much more a faculty which comes, forms, and develops, *quae fit*, than an entity or entelechy which exists, wholly formed, prior to apprenticeship. Reason, by whatever name we call it, — genius, talent, industry, — is at the start a naked and inert potentiality, which gradually grows in size and strength, takes on color and form, and shades itself in an infinite variety of ways. By the importance of its acquirements, by its capital, in a word, the intelligence of one individual differs and will always differ from that of another; but, being a power equal in all at the beginning, social progress must consist in rendering it, by an ever increasing perfection of methods, again equal in all at the end. Otherwise labor would remain a privilege for some and a punishment for others.

But the equilibrium of capacities, the prelude of which we have seen in the division of labor, does not fulfil the entire destiny of machinery, and the views of Providence extend far beyond. With the introduction of machinery into economy, wings are given to LIBERTY.

The machine is the symbol of human liberty, the sign of our domination over nature, the attribute of our power, the expression of our right, the emblem of our personality. Liberty, intelligence, — those constitute the whole of man: for, if we brush aside as mystical and unintelligible all speculation concerning the human being considered from the point of view of substance (mind or matter), we have left only two categories of manifestations, — the first including all that we call sensations, volitions, passions, attractions, instincts, sentiments; the other, all phenomena classed under the heads of attention, perception, memory, imagination, comparison, judgment, reasoning, etc. As for the organic apparatus, very far from being the principle or base of these two orders of faculties, it must be considered as their synthetic and positive realization, their living and harmonious expression. For just as from the long-continued issue by humanity of its antagonistic principles must some day result social organization, so man must be conceived as the result of two series of potentialities.

Thus, after having posited itself as logic, social economy, pursuing its work, posits itself as psychology. The education of intelligence and liberty, — in a word, the welfare of man, — all perfectly synonymous expressions, — such is the common object of political economy and philosophy. To determine the laws of the production and distribution of wealth will be to demonstrate, by an objective and concrete exposition, the laws of reason and liberty; it will be to create philosophy and right a posteriori: whichever way we turn, we are in complete metaphysics.

Let us try, now, with the joint data of psychology and political economy, to define liberty.

If it is allowable to conceive of human reason, in its origin, as a lucid and reflecting atom, capable of some day representing the universe, but at first giving no image at all, we may likewise consider liberty, at the birth of conscience, as a living point, *punctum saliens*, a vague, blind, or, rather, indifferent spontaneity, capable of receiving all possible impressions, dispositions, and inclinations. Liberty is the faculty of acting and of not acting, which, through any choice or determination whatever (I use the word determination here both passively and actively), abandons its indifference and becomes will.

I say, then, that liberty, like intelligence, is naturally an undetermined, unformed faculty, which gets its value and character later from external impressions, — a faculty, therefore, which is negative at the beginning, but which gradually defines and outlines itself by exercise, — I mean, by education.

The etymology of the word liberty, at least as I understand it, will serve still better to explain my thought. The root is lib-et, he pleases (German, lieben, to love); whence have been constructed lib-eri, children, those dear to us, a name reserved for the children of the father of a family; lib-ertas, the condition, character, or inclination of children of a noble race; lib-ido, the passion of a slave, who knows neither God nor law nor country, synonymous with licentia, evil conduct. When spontaneity takes a useful, generous, or beneficent direction, it is called libertas; when, on the contrary, it takes a harmful, vicious, base, or evil direction, it is called libido.

A learned economist, M. Dunoyer, has given a definition of liberty which, by its likeness to our own, will complete the demonstration of its exactness.

I call liberty that power which man acquires of using his forces more easily in proportion as he frees himself from the obstacles which originally hindered the exercise thereof. I say that he is the freer the more thoroughly delivered he is from the causes which prevented him from making use of his forces, the farther from him he has driven these causes, the more he has extended and cleared the sphere of his action . . . Thus it is said that a man has a free mind, that he enjoys great liberty of mind, not only when his intelligence is not disturbed by any external violence, but also when it is neither obscured by intoxication, nor changed by disease, nor kept in impotence by lack of exercise.

M. Dunoyer has here viewed liberty only on its negative side, — that is, as if it were simply synonymous with freedom from obstacles. At that rate liberty would not be a faculty of man; it would be nothing. But immediately M. Dunoyer, though persisting in his incomplete definition, seizes the true side of the matter: then it is that it occurs to him to say that man, in inventing a machine, serves his liberty, not, as we express ourselves, because he determines it, but, in M. Dunoyer's style, because he removes a difficulty from its path.

Thus articulate language is a better instrument than language by sign; therefore one is freer to express his thought and impress it upon the mind of another by speech than by gesture. The written word is a more potent instrument than the spoken word; therefore one is freer to act on the mind of his fellows when he knows how to picture the word to their eyes than when he simply knows how to speak it. The press is an instrument two or three hundred times more potent than the pen; therefore one is two or three hundred times freer to enter into relation with other men when he can spread his ideas by printing than when he can publish them only by writing.

I will not point out all that is inexact and illogical in this fashion of representing liberty. Since Destutt de Tracy, the last representative of the philosophy of Condillac, the philosophical spirit has been obscured among economists of the French school; the fear of ideology has perverted their language, and one perceives, in reading them, that adoration of fact has caused them to lose even the perception of theory. I prefer to establish the fact that M. Dunoyer, and political economy with him, is not mistaken concerning the essence of liberty, a force, energy, or spontaneity indifferent in itself to every action, and consequently equally susceptible of any determination, good or bad, useful or harmful. M. Dunoyer has had so strong a suspicion of the truth that he writes himself:

Instead of considering liberty as a dogma, I shall present it as a result; instead of making it the attribute of man, I shall make it the attribute of civilization; instead of imagining forms of government calculated to establish it, I shall do my best to explain how it is born of every step of our progress.

Then he adds, with no less reason:

It will be noticed how much this method differs from that of those dogmatic philosophers who talk only of rights and duties; of what it is the duty of governments to do and the right of nations to demand, etc. I do not say sententiously: men have a right to be free; I confine myself to asking: how does it happen that they are so?

In accordance with this exposition one may sum up in four lines the work that M. Dunoyer has tried to do: A REVIEW of the obstacles that impede liberty and the means (instruments, methods, ideas, customs, religions, governments, etc.) that favor it. But for its omissions, the work of M. Dunoyer would have been the very philosophy of political economy.

After having raised the problem of liberty, political economy furnishes us, then, with a definition conforming in every point to that given by psychology and suggested by the analogies of language: and thus we see how, little by little, the study of man gets transported from the contemplation of the me to the observation of realities.

Now, just as the determinations of man's reason have received the name of ideas (abstract, supposed a priori ideas, or principles, conceptions, categories; and secondary ideas, or those more especially acquired and empirical), so the determinations of liberty have received the name of volitions, sentiments, habits, customs.

Then, language, figurative in its nature, continuing to furnish the elements of primary psychology, the habit has been formed of assigning to ideas, as the place or capacity where they reside, the intelligence, and to volitions, sentiments, etc., the conscience. All these abstractions have been long taken for realities by the philosophers, not one of whom has seen that all distribution of the faculties of the soul is necessarily a work of caprice, and that their psychology is but an illusion.

However that may be, if we now conceive these two orders of determinations, reason and liberty, as united and blended by organization in a living, reasonable, and free person, we shall understand immediately that they must lend each other mutual assistance and influence each other reciprocally. If, through an error or oversight of the reason, liberty, blind by nature, acquires a false and fatal habit, the reason itself will not be slow to feel the effects; instead of true ideas, conforming to the natural relations of things, it will retain only prejudices, as much more difficult to root out of the intelligence afterwards, as they have become dearer to the conscience through age. In this state of things reason and liberty are impaired; the first is disturbed in its development, the second restricted in its scope, and man is led astray, becomes, that is, wicked and unhappy at once.

Thus, when, in consequence of a contradictory perception and an incomplete experience, reason had pronounced through the lips of the economists that there was no regulating principle of value and that the law of commerce was supply and demand, liberty abandoned itself to the passion of ambition, egoism, and gambling; commerce was thereafter but a wager subjected to certain police regulations; misery developed from the sources of wealth; socialism, itself a slave of routine, could only protest against effects instead of rising against causes; and reason was obliged, by the sight of so many evils, to recognize that it had taken a wrong road.

Man can attain welfare only in proportion as his reason and his liberty not only progress in harmony, but never halt in their development. Now, as the progress of liberty, like that of reason, is indefinite, and as, moreover, these two powers are closely connected and solidary, it must be concluded that liberty is the more perfect the more closely it defines itself in conformity with the laws of reason, which are those of things, and that, if this reason were infinite, liberty itself would become infinite. In other words, the fullness of liberty lies in the fullness of reason: summa lex summa libertas.

These preliminaries were indispensable in order to clearly appreciate the role of machinery and to make plain the series of economic evolutions. And just here I will remind the reader that we are not constructing a history in accordance with the order of events, but in accordance with the succession of ideas. The economic phases or categories are now contemporary, now inverted, in their manifestation; hence the extreme difficulty always felt by the economists in systematizing their ideas; hence the chaos of their works, even those most to be commended in every other respect, such as Adam Smith's, Ricardo's, and J. B. Say's. But economic theories none the less have their logical succession and their series in the mind: it is this order which we flatter ourselves that we have discovered, and which will make this work at once a philosophy and a history.

2. — Machinery's contradiction. — Origin of capital and wages.

From the very fact that machinery diminishes the workman's toil, it abridges and diminishes labor, the supply of which thus grows greater from day to day and the demand less. Little by little, it is true, the reduction in prices causing an increase in consumption, the proportion is restored and the laborer set at work again: but as industrial improvements steadily succeed each other and continually tend to substitute mechanical operations for the labor of man, it follows that there is a constant tendency to cut off a portion of the service and consequently to eliminate laborers from production. Now, it is with the economic order as with the spiritual order: outside of the church there is no salvation; outside of labor there is no subsistence. Society and nature, equally pitiless, are in accord in the execution of this new decree.

"When a new machine, or, in general, any process whatever that expedites matters," says J. B. Say, "replaces any human labor already employed, some of the industrious arms, whose services are usefully supplanted, are left without work. A new machine, therefore, replaces the labor of a portion of the laborers, but does not diminish the amount of production, for, if it did, it would not be adopted; it displaces revenue. But the ultimate advantage is wholly on the side of machinery, for, if abundance of product and lessening of cost lower the venal value, the consumer — that is, everybody — will benefit thereby."

Say's optimism is infidelity to logic and to facts. The question here is not simply one of a small number of accidents which have happened during thirty centuries through the introduction of one, two, or three machines; it is a question of a regular, constant, and general phenomenon. After revenue has been displaced as Say says, by one machine, it is then displaced by another, and again by another, and always by another, as long as any labor remains to be done and any exchanges remain to be effected. That is the light in which the phenomenon must be presented and considered: but thus, it must be admitted, its aspect changes singularly. The displacement of revenue, the suppression of labor and wages, is a chronic, permanent, indelible plague, a sort of cholera which now appears wearing the features of Gutenberg, now assumes those of Arkwright; here is called Jacquard, there James Watt or Marquis de Jouffroy. After carrying on its ravages for a longer or shorter time under one form, the monster takes another, and the economists, who think that he has gone, cry out: "It was nothing!" Tranquil and satisfied, provided they insist with all the weight of their dialectics on the positive side of the question, they close their eyes to its subversive side, notwithstanding which, when they are spoken to of poverty, they again begin their sermons upon the improvidence and drunkenness of laborers.

In 1750, — M. Dunoyer makes the observation, and it may serve as a measure of all lucubrations of the same sort, — "in 1750 the population of the duchy of Lancaster was 300,000 souls. In 1801, thanks to the development of spinning machines, this population was 672,000 souls. In 1831 it was 1,336,000 souls. Instead of the 40,000 workmen whom the cotton industry formerly employed, it now employs, since the invention of machinery, 1,500,000."

M. Dunoyer adds that at the time when the number of workmen employed in this industry increased in so remarkable a manner, the price of labor rose one hundred and fifty per cent. Population, then, having simply followed industrial progress, its increase has been a normal and irreproachable fact, — what do I say? — a happy fact, since it is cited to the honor and glory of the development of machinery. But suddenly M. Dunoyer executes an about-face: this multitude of spinning-machines soon being out of work, wages necessarily declined; the population which the machines had called forth found itself abandoned by the machines, at which M. Dunoyer declares: Abuse of marriage is the cause of poverty.

English commerce, in obedience to the demand of the immense body of its patrons, summons workmen from all directions, and encourages marriage; as long as labor is abundant, marriage is an excellent thing, the effects of which they are fond of quoting in the interest of machinery; but, the patronage fluctuating, as soon as work and wages are not to be had, they denounce the abuse of marriage, and accuse laborers of improvidence. Political economy — that is, proprietary despotism — can never be in the wrong: it must be the proletariat.

The example of printing has been cited many a time, always to sustain the optimistic view. The number of persons supported today by the manufacture of books is perhaps a thousand times larger than was that of the copyists and illuminators prior to Gutenberg's time; therefore, they conclude with a satisfied air, printing has injured nobody. An infinite number of similar facts might be cited, all of them indisputable, but not one of which would advance the question a step. Once more, no one denies that machines have contributed to the general welfare; but I affirm, in regard to this incontestable fact, that the economists fall short of the truth when they advance the absolute statement that the simplification of processes has nowhere resulted in a diminution of the number of hands employed in any industry whatever. What the economists ought to say is that machinery, like the division of labor, in the present system of social economy is at once a source of wealth and a permanent and fatal cause of misery.

In 1836, in a Manchester mill, nine frames, each having three hundred and twenty-four spindles, were tended by four spinners. Afterwards the mules were doubled in length, which gave each of the nine six hundred and eighty spindles and enabled two men to tend them.

There we have the naked fact of the elimination of the workman by the machine. By a simple device three workmen out of four are evicted; what matters it that fifty years later, the population of the globe having doubled and the trade of England having quadrupled, new machines will be constructed and the English manufacturers will reemploy their workmen? Do the economists mean to point to the increase of population as one of the benefits of machinery? Let them renounce, then, the theory of Malthus, and stop declaiming against the excessive fecundity of marriage.

They did not stop there: soon a new mechanical improvement enabled a single worker to do the work that formerly occupied four.

A new three-fourths reduction of manual work: in all, a reduction of human labor by fifteen-sixteenths.

A Bolton manufacturer writes: "The elongation of the mules of our frames permits us to employ but twenty-six spinners where we employed thirty-five in 1837."

Another decimation of laborers: one out of four is a victim.

These facts are taken from the "Revue Economique" of 1842; and there is nobody who cannot point to similar ones. I have witnessed the introduction of printing machines, and I can say that I have seen with my own eyes the evil which printers have suffered thereby. During the fifteen or twenty years that the machines have been in use a portion of the workmen have gone back to composition, others have abandoned their trade, and some have died of misery: thus laborers are continually crowded back in consequence of industrial innovations. Twenty years ago eighty canal-boats furnished the navigation service between Beaucaire and Lyons; a score of steam-packets has displaced them all. Certainly commerce is the gainer; but what has become of the boating-population? Has it been transferred from the boats to the packets? No: it has gone where all superseded industries go, — it has vanished.

For the rest, the following documents, which I take from the same source, will give a more positive idea of the influence of industrial improvements upon the condition of the workers.

The average weekly wages, at Manchester, is ten shillings. Out of four hundred and fifty workers there are not forty who earn twenty shillings.

The author of the article is careful to remark that an Englishman consumes five times as much as a Frenchman; this, then, is as if a French workingman had to live on two francs and a half a week.

"Edinburgh Review," 1835: "To a combination of workmen (who did not want to see their wages reduced) we owe the mule of Sharpe and Roberts of Manchester; and this invention has severely punished the imprudent unionists."

Punished should merit punishment. The invention of Sharpe and Roberts of Manchester was bound to result from the situation; the refusal of the workmen to submit to the reduction asked of them was only its determining occasion. Might not one infer, from the air of vengeance affected by the "Edinburgh Review," that machines have a retroactive effect?

An English manufacturer: "The insubordination of our workmen has given us the idea of dispensing with them. We have made and stimulated every imaginable effort of the mind to replace the service of men by tools more docile, and we have achieved our object. Machinery has delivered capital from the oppression of labor. Wherever we still employ a man, we do so only temporarily, pending the invention for us of some means of accomplishing his work without him."

What a system is that which leads a business man to think with delight that society will soon be able to dispense with men! Machinery has delivered capital from the oppression of labor! That is exactly as if the cabinet should undertake to deliver the treasury from the oppression of the taxpayers. Fool! though the workmen cost you something, they are your customers: what will you do with your products, when, driven away by you, they shall consume them no longer? Thus machinery, after crushing the workmen, is not slow in dealing employers a counter-blow; for, if production excludes consumption, it is soon obliged to stop itself.

During the fourth quarter of 1841 four great failures, happening in an English manufacturing city, threw seventeen hundred and twenty people on the street.

These failures were caused by over-production, — that is, by an inadequate market, or the distress of the people. What a pity that machinery cannot also deliver capital from the oppression of consumers! What a misfortune that machines do not buy the fabrics which they weave! The ideal society will be reached when commerce, agriculture, and manufactures can proceed without a man upon earth!

In a Yorkshire parish for nine months the operatives have been working but two days a week.

Machines!

At Geston two factories valued at sixty thousand pounds sterling have been sold for twenty-six thousand. They produced more than they could sell.

Machines!

120

In 1841 the number of children under thirteen years of age engaged in manufactures diminishes, because children over thirteen take their place.

Machines! The adult workman becomes an apprentice, a child, again: this result was foreseen from the phase of the division of labor, during which we saw the quality of the workman degenerate in the ratio in which industry was perfected.

In his conclusion the journalist makes this reflection: "Since 1836 there has been a retrograde movement in the cotton industry"; — that is, it no longer keeps up its relation with other industries: another result foreseen from the theory of the proportionality of values.

Today workmen's coalitions and strikes seem to have stopped throughout England, and the economists rightly rejoice over this return to order, — let us say even to common sense. But because laborers henceforth — at least I cherish the hope — will not add the misery of their voluntary periods of idleness to the misery which machines force upon them, does it follow that the situation is changed? And if there is no change in the situation, will not the future always be a deplorable copy of the past?

The economists love to rest their minds on pictures of public felicity: it is by this sign principally that they are to be recognized, and that they estimate each other. Nevertheless there are not lacking among them, on the other hand, moody and sickly imaginations, ever ready to offset accounts of growing prosperity with proofs of persistent poverty.

M. Theodore Fix thus summed up the general situation in December, 1844:

The food supply of nations is no longer exposed to those terrible disturbances caused by scarcities and famines, so frequent up to the beginning of the nineteenth century. The variety of agricultural growths and improvements has abolished this double scourge almost absolutely. The total wheat crop in France in 1791 was estimated at about 133,000,000 bushels, which gave, after deducting seed, 2.855 bushels to each inhabitant. In 1840 the same crop was estimated at 198,590,000 bushels, or 2.860 bushels to each individual, the area of cultivated surface being almost the same as before the Revolution. . . The rate of increase of manufactured goods has been at least as high as that of food products; and we are justified in saying that the mass of textile fabrics has more than doubled and perhaps tripled within fifty years. The perfecting of technical processes has led to this result. . .

Since the beginning of the century the average duration of life has increased by two or three years, — an undeniable sign of greater comfort, or, if you will, a diminution of poverty.

Within twenty years the amount of indirect revenue, without any burdensome change in legislation, has risen from $40,000,000 francs to 720,000,000, — a symptom of economic, much more than of fiscal, progress.

On January 1, 1844, the deposit and consignment office owed the savings banks 351,500,000 francs, and Paris figured in this sum for 105,000,000. Nevertheless the development of the institution has taken place almost wholly within twelve years, and it should be noticed that the 351,500,000 francs now due to the savings banks do not constitute the entire mass of economies effected, since at a given time the capital accumulated is disposed of otherwise... In 1843, out of 320,000 workmen and 80,000 house-servants living in the capital, 90,000 workmen have deposited in the savings banks 2,547,000 francs, and 34,000 house-servants 1,268,000 francs.

All these facts are entirely true, and the inference to be drawn from them in favor of machines is of the exactest, — namely, that they have indeed given a powerful impetus to the general welfare. But the facts with which we shall supplement them are no less authentic, and the inference to be drawn from these against machines will be no less accurate, — to wit, that they are a continual cause of pauperism. I appeal to the figures of M. Fix himself.

Out of 320,000 workmen and 80,000 house-servants residing in Paris, there are 230,000 of the former and 46,000 of the latter — a total of 276,000 — who do not deposit in the savings banks. No one would dare pretend that these are 276,000 spendthrifts and ne'er-do-weels who expose themselves to misery voluntarily. Now, as among the very ones who make the savings there are to be found poor and inferior persons for whom the savings bank is but a respite from debauchery and misery, we may conclude that, out of all the individuals living by their labor, nearly three-fourths either are imprudent, lazy, and depraved, since they do not deposit in the savings banks, or are too poor to lay up anything. There is no other alternative. But common sense, to say nothing of charity, permits no wholesale accusation of the laboring class: it is necessary, therefore, to throw the blame back upon our economic system. How is it that M. Fix did not see that his figures accused themselves?

They hope that, in time, all, or almost all, laborers will deposit in the savings banks. Without awaiting the testimony of the future, we may test the foundations of this hope immediately.

According to the testimony of M. Vee, mayor of the fifth arrondissement of Paris, "the number of needy families inscribed upon the registers of the charity bureaus is 30,000, — which is equivalent to 65,000 individuals." The census taken at the beginning of 1846 gave 88,474. And poor families not inscribed, — how many are there of those? As many. Say, then, 180,000 people whose poverty is not doubtful, although not official. And all those who live in straitened circumstances, though keeping up the appearance of comfort, — how many are there of those? Twice as many, — a total of 360,000 persons, in Paris, who are somewhat embarrassed for means.

"They talk of wheat," cries another economist, M. Louis Leclerc, "but are there not immense populations which go without bread? Without leaving our own country, are there not populations which live exclusively on maize, buckwheat, chestnuts?"

M. Leclerc denounces the fact: let us interpret it. If, as there is no doubt, the increase of population is felt principally in the large cities, — that is, at those points where the most wheat is consumed, — it is clear that the average per head may have increased without any improvement in the general condition. There is no such liar as an average.

"They talk," continues the same writer, "of the increase of indirect consumption. Vain would be the attempt to acquit Parisian adulteration: it exists; it has its masters, its adepts, its literature, its didactic and classic treatises... France possessed exquisite wines; what has been done with them? What has become of this splendid wealth? Where are the treasures created since Probus by the national genius? And yet, when one considers the excesses to which wine gives rise wherever it is dear, wherever it does not form a part of the regular life of the people; when in Paris, capital of the kingdom of good wines, one sees the people gorging themselves with I know not what, — stuff that is adulterated, sophisticated, sickening, and sometimes execrable, — and well-to-do persons drinking at home or accepting without a word, in famous restaurants, so-called wines, thick, violet-colored, and insipid, flat, and miserable enough to make the poorest Burgundian peasant shudder, — can one honestly doubt that alcoholic liquids are one of the most imperative needs of our nature?

I quote this passage at length, because it sums up in relation to a special case all that could be said upon the inconveniences of machinery. To the people it is with wine as with fabrics, and generally with all goods and merchandise created for the consumption of the poor. It is always the same deduction: to reduce by some process or other the cost of manufacture, in order, first, to maintain advantageously competition with more fortunate or richer rivals; second, to serve the vast numbers of plundered persons who cannot disregard price simply because the quality is good. Produced in the ordinary ways, wine is too expensive for the mass of consumers; it is in danger of remaining in the cellars of the retailers. The manufacturer of wines gets around the difficulty: unable to introduce machinery into the cultivation of the vine, he finds a means, with the aid of some accompaniments, of placing the precious liquid within the reach of all. Certain savages, in their periods of scarcity, eat earth; the civilized workman drinks water. Malthus was a great genius.

As far as the increase of the average duration of life is concerned, I recognize the fact, but at the same time I declare the observation incorrect. Let us explain that. Suppose a population of ten million souls: if, from whatever cause you will, the average life should increase five years for a million individuals, mortality continuing its ravages at the same rate as before among the nine other millions, it would be found, on distributing this increase among the whole, that on an average six months had been added to the life of each individual. It is with the average length of life, the so-called indicator of average comfort, as with average learning: the level of knowledge does not cease to rise, which by no means alters the fact that there are today in France quite as many barbarians as in the days of Francois I. The charlatans who had railroad speculation in view made a great noise about the importance of the locomotive in the circulation of ideas; and the economists, always on the lookout for civilized stupidities, have not failed to echo this nonsense. As if ideas, in order to spread, needed locomotives! What, then, prevents ideas from circulating from the Institute to the Faubourgs Saint-Antoine and Saint-Marceau, in the narrow and wretched streets of Old Paris and the Temple Quarter, everywhere, in short, where dwells this multitude even more destitute of ideas than of bread? How happens it that between a Parisian and a Parisian, in spite of the omnibus and the letter-carrier, the distance is three times greater today than in the fourteenth century?

The ruinous influence of machinery on social economy and the condition of the laborers is exercised in a thousand ways, all of which are bound together and reciprocally labelled: cessation of labor, reduction of wages, over-production, obstruction of the market, alteration and adulteration of products, failures, displacement of laborers, degeneration of the race, and, finally, diseases and death.

M. Théodore Fix has remarked himself that in the last fifty years the average stature of man, in France, has diminished by a considerable fraction of an inch. This observation is worth his previous one: upon whom does this diminution take effect?

In a report read to the Academy of Moral Sciences on the results of the law of March 22, 1841, M. Leon Faucher expressed himself thus:

Young workmen are pale, weak, short in stature, and slow to think as well as to move. At fourteen or fifteen years they seem no more developed than children of nine or ten years in the normal state. As for their intellectual and moral development, there are some to be found who, at the age of thirteen, have no notion of God, who have never heard of their duties, and whose first school of morality was a prison.

That is what M. Léon Faucher has seen, to the great displeasure of M. Charles Dupin, and this state of things he declares that the law of March 22 is powerless to remedy. And let us not get angry over this impotence of the legislator: the evil arises from a cause as necessary for us as the sun; and in the path upon which we have entered, anger of any kind, like palliatives of any kind, could only make our situation worse. Yes, while science and industry are making such marvellous progress, it is a necessity, unless civilization's centre of gravity should suddenly change, that the intelligence and comfort of the proletariat be diminished; while the lives of the well-to-do classes grow longer and easier, it is inevitable that those of the needy should grow harder and shorter. This is established in the writings of the best — I mean, the most optimistic — thinkers.

According to M. de Morogues, 7,500,000 men in France have only ninety-one francs a year to spend, 25 centimes a day. Cing sous! cing sous! (Five cents! five cents!). There is something prophetic, then, in this odious refrain.

In England (not including Scotland and Ireland) the poor-rate was:

1801.	£4,078,891	for a population of	8,872,980
1818.	£7,870,801	" " " "	11,978,875
1833.	£8,000,000	" " " "	14,000,000

The progress of poverty, then, has been more rapid than that of population; in face of this fact, what becomes of the hypotheses of Malthus? And yet it is indisputable that during the same period the average comfort increased: what, then, do statistics signify?

The death-rate for the first arrondissement of Paris is one to every fifty-two inhabitants, and for the twelfth one to every twenty-six. Now, the latter contains one needy person to every seven inhabitants, while the former has only one to every twenty-eight. That does not prevent the average duration of life, even in Paris, from increasing, as M. Fix has very correctly observed.

At Mulhouse the probabilities of average life are twenty-nine years for children of the well-to-do class and TWO years for those of the workers; in 1812 the average life in the same locality was twenty-five years, nine months, and twelve days, while in 1827 it was not over twenty-one years and nine months. And yet throughout France the average life is longer. What does this mean?

M. Blanqui, unable to explain so much prosperity and so much poverty at once, cries somewhere: "Increased production does not mean additional wealth... Poverty, on the contrary, becomes the wider spread in proportion to the con-centration of industries. There must be some radical vice in a system which guarantees no security either to capital or labor, and which seems to multiply the embarrass-ments of producers at the same time that it forces them to multiply their products."

There is no radical vice here. What astonishes M. Blanqui is simply that of which the Academy to which he belongs has asked a determination, — namely, the oscillations of the economic pendulum, VALUE, beating alternately and in regular time good and evil, until the hour of the universal equation shall strike. If

I may be permitted another comparison, humanity in its march is like a column of soldiers, who, starting in the same step and at the same moment to the measured beating of the drum, gradually lose their distances. The whole body advances, but the distance from head to tail grows ever longer; and it is a necessary effect of the movement that there should be some laggards and stragglers.

But it is necessary to penetrate still farther into the antinomy. Machines promised us an increase of wealth; they have kept their word, but at the same time endowing us with an increase of poverty. They promised us liberty; I am going to prove that they have brought us slavery.

I have stated that the determination of value, and with it the tribulations of society, began with the division of industries, without which there could be no exchange, or wealth, or progress. The period through which we are now passing — that of machinery — is distinguished by a special characteristic, — WAGES.

Wages issued in a direct line from the employment of machinery, — that is, to give my thought the entire generality of expression which it calls for, from the economic fiction by which capital becomes an agent of production. Wages, in short, coming after the division of labor and exchange, is the necessary correlative of the theory of the reduction of costs, in whatever way this reduction may be accomplished. This genealogy is too interesting to be passed by without a few words of explanation.

The first, the simplest, the most powerful of machines is the workshop.

Division simply separates the various parts of labor, leaving each to devote himself to the specialty best suited to his tastes: the workshop groups the laborers according to the relation of each part to the whole. It is the most elementary form of the balance of values, undiscoverable though the economists suppose this to be. Now, through the workshop, production is going to increase, and at the same time the deficit.

Somebody discovered that, by dividing production into its various parts and causing each to be executed by a separate workman, he would obtain a multiplication of power, the product of which would be far superior to the amount of labor given by the same number of workmen when labor is not divided.

Grasping the thread of this idea, he said to himself that, by forming a permanent group of laborers assorted with a view to his special purpose, he would produce more steadily, more abundantly, and at less cost. It is not indispensable, however, that the workmen should be gathered into one place: the existence of the workshop does not depend essentially upon such contact. It results from the relation and proportion of the different tasks and from the common thought directing them. In a word, concentration at one point may offer its advantages, which are not to be neglected; but that is not what constitutes the workshop

This, then, is the proposition which the speculator makes to those whose collaboration he desires: I guarantee you a perpetual market for your products, if you will accept me as purchaser or middle-man. The bargain is so clearly advantageous that the proposition cannot fail of acceptance. The laborer finds in it steady work, a fixed price, and security; the employer, on the other hand, will find a readier sale for his goods, since, producing more advantageously, he can lower the price; in short, his profits will be larger because of the mass of his investments. All, even to the public and the magistrate, will congratulate the employer on having added to the social wealth by his combinations, and will vote him a reward.

But, in the first place, whoever says reduction of expenses says reduction of services, not, it is true, in the new shop, but for the workers at the same trade who are left outside, as well as for many others whose accessory services will be less needed in future. Therefore every establishment of a workshop corresponds to an eviction of workers: this assertion, utterly contradictory though it may appear, is as true of the workshop as of a machine.

The economists admit it: but here they repeat their eternal refrain that, after a lapse of time, the demand for the product having increased in proportion to the reduction of price, labor in turn will come finally to be in greater demand than ever. Undoubtedly, WITH TIME, the equilibrium will be restored; but, I must add again, the equilibrium will be no sooner restored at this point than it will be disturbed at another, because the spirit of invention never stops, any more than labor. Now, what theory could justify these perpetual hecatombs?" When we have reduced the number of toilers," wrote Sismondi, "to a fourth or a fifth of what it is at present, we shall need only a fourth or a fifth as many priests, physicians, etc. When we have cut them off altogether, we shall be in a position to dispense with the human race." And that is what really would happen if, in order to put the labor of each machine in proportion to the needs of consumption, — that is, to restore the balance of values continually destroyed, — it were not necessary to continually create new machines, open other markets, and consequently multiply services and displace other arms. So that on the one hand industry and wealth, on the other population and misery, advance, so to speak, in procession, one always dragging the other after it.

I have shown the contractor, at the birth of industry, negotiating on equal terms with his comrades, who have since become his workmen. It is plain, in fact, that this original equality was bound to disappear through the advantageous position of the master and the dependence of the wage-workers. In vain does the law assure to each the right of enterprise, as well as the faculty to labor alone and sell one's products directly. According to the hypothesis, this last resource is impracticable, since it was the object of the workshop to annihilate isolated labor. And as for the right to take the plough, as they say, and go at speed, it is the same in manufactures as in agriculture; to know how to work is nothing, it is necessary to arrive at the right time; the shop, as well as the land, is to the first comer. When an establishment has had the leisure to develop itself, enlarge its foundations, ballast itself with capital, and assure itself a body of patrons, what can the workman who has only his arms do against a power so superior? Hence it was not by an arbitrary act of sovereign power or by fortuitous and brutal usurpation that the guilds and masterships were established in the Middle Ages: the force of events had created them long before the edicts of kings could have given them legal consecration; and, in spite of the reform of '89, we see them reestablishing themselves under our eyes with an energy a hundred times more formidable. Abandon labor to its own tendencies, and the subjection of three-fourths of the human race is assured.

But this is not all. The machine, or the workshop, after having degraded the laborer by giving him a master, completes his degeneracy by reducing him from the rank of artisan to that of common workman.

Formerly the population on the banks of the Saone and Rhone was largely made up of watermen, thoroughly fitted for the conduct of canal-boats or row-boats. Now that the steam-tug is to be found almost everywhere, most of the boatmen, finding it impossible to get a living at their trade, either pass three-fourths of their life in idleness, or else become stokers.

If not misery, then degradation: such is the last alternative which machinery offers to the workman. For it is with a machine as with a piece of artillery: the captain excepted, those whom it occupies are servants, slaves.

Since the establishment of large factories, a multitude of little industries have disappeared from the domestic hearth: does any one believe that the girls who work for ten and fifteen cents have as much intelligence as their ancestors?

"After the establishment of the railway from Paris to Saint Germain," M. Dunoyer tells us, "there were established between Pecq and a multitude of places in the more or less immediate vicinity such a number of omnibus and stage lines that this establishment, contrary to all expectation, has considerably increased the employment of horses."

Contrary to all expectation! It takes an economist not to expect these things. Multiply machinery, and you increase the amount of arduous and disagreeable labor to be done: this apothegm is as certain as any of those which date from the deluge. Accuse me, if you choose, of ill-will towards the most precious invention of our century, — nothing shall prevent me from saying that the principal result of railways, after the subjection of petty industry, will be the creation of a population of degraded laborers, — signalmen, sweepers, loaders, lumpers, draymen, watchmen, porters, weighers, greasers, cleaners, stokers, firemen, etc. Two thousand miles of railway will give France an additional fifty thousand serfs: it is not for such people, certainly, that M. Chevalier asks professional schools.

Perhaps it will be said that, the mass of transportation having increased in much greater proportion than the number of day-laborers, the difference is to the advantage of the railway, and that, all things considered, there is progress. The observation may even be generalized and the same argument applied to all industries.

But it is precisely out of this generality of the phenomenon that springs the subjection of laborers. Machinery plays the leading role in industry, man is secondary: all the genius displayed by labor tends to the degradation of the proletariat. What a glorious nation will be ours when, among forty millions of inhabitants, it shall count thirty-five millions of drudges, paper-scratchers, and flunkies!

With machinery and the workshop, divine right — that is, the principle of authority — makes its entrance into political economy. Capital, Mastership, Privilege, Monopoly, Loaning, Credit, Property, etc., — such are, in economic language, the various names of I know not what, but which is otherwise called Power, Authority, Sovereignty, Written Law, Revelation, Religion, God in short, cause and principle of all our miseries and all our crimes, and who, the more we try to define him, the more eludes us.

Is it, then, impossible that, in the present condition of society, the workshop with its hierarchical organization, and machinery, instead of serving exclusively the interests of the least numerous, the least industrious, and the wealthiest class, should be employed for the benefit of all?

That is what we are going to examine.

3. — Of preservatives against the disastrous influence of machinery.

Reduction of manual labor is synonymous with lowering of price, and, consequently, with increase of exchange, since, if the consumer pays less, he will buy more.

But reduction of manual labor is synonymous also with restriction of market, since, if the producer earns less, he will buy less. And this is the course that things actually take. The concentration of forces in the workshop and the intervention of capital in production, under the name of machinery, engender at the same time overproduction and destitution; and everybody has witnessed these two scourges, more to be feared than incendiarism and plague, develop in our day on the vastest scale and with devouring intensity. Nevertheless it is impossible for us to retreat: it is necessary to produce, produce always, produce cheaply; otherwise, the existence of society is compromised. The laborer, who, to escape the degradation with which the principle of division threatened him, had created so many marvellous machines, now finds himself either prohibited or subjugated by his own works. Against this alternative what means are proposed?

M. de Sismondi, like all men of patriarchal ideas, would like the division of labor, with machinery and manufactures, to be abandoned, and each family to return to the system of primitive indivision, — that is, to each one by himself, each one for himself, in the most literal meaning of the words. That would be to retrograde; it is impossible.

M. Blanqui returns to the charge with his plan of participation by the workman, and of consolidation of all industries in a joint-stock company for the benefit of the collective laborer. I have shown that this plan would impair public welfare without appreciably improving the condition of the laborers; and M. Blanqui himself seems to share this sentiment. How reconcile, in fact, this participation of the workman in the profits with the rights of inventors, contractors, and capitalists, of whom the first have to reimburse themselves for large outlays, as well as for their long and patient efforts; the second continually endanger the wealth they have acquired, and take upon themselves alone the chances of their enterprises, which are often very hazardous; and the third could sustain no reduction of their dividends without in some way losing their savings? How harmonize, in a word, the equality desirable to establish between laborers and employers with the preponderance which cannot be taken from heads of establishments, from loaners of capital, and from inventors, and which involves so clearly their exclusive appropriation of the profits? To decree by a law the admission of all workmen to a share of the profits would be to pronounce the dissolution of society: all the economists have seen this so clearly that they have finally changed into an exhortation to employers what had first occurred to them as a project. Now, as long as the wage-worker gets no profit save what may be allowed him by the contractor, it is perfectly safe to assume that eternal poverty will be his lot: it is not in the power of the holders of labor to make it otherwise.

For the rest, the idea, otherwise very laudable, of associating workmen with employers tends to this communistic conclusion, evidently false in its premises: The last word of machinery is to make man rich and happy without the necessity of labor on his part. Since, then, natural agencies must do everything for us, machinery ought to belong to the State, and the goal of progress is communism.

I shall examine the communistic theory in its place.

But I believe that I ought to immediately warn the partisans of this utopia that the hope with which they flatter themselves in relation to machinery is only an illusion of the economists, something like perpetual motion, which is always sought and never found, because asked of a power which cannot give it. Machines do not go all alone: to keep them in motion it is necessary to organize an immense service around them; so that in the end, man creating for himself an amount of work proportional to the number of instruments with which he surrounds himself, the principal consideration in the matter of machinery is much less to divide its products than to see that it is fed, — that is, to continually renew the motive power. Now, this motive power is not air, water, steam, electricity; it is labor, — that is, the market.

A railroad suppresses all along its line conveyances, stages, harness-makers, saddlers, wheelwrights, inn-keepers: I take facts as they are just after the establishment of the road. Suppose the State, as a measure of preservation or in obedience to the principle of indemnity, should make the laborers displaced by the railroad its proprietors or operators: the transportation rates, let us suppose, being reduced by twenty-five per cent. (otherwise of what use is the railroad?), the income of all these laborers united will be diminished by a like amount, — which is to say that a fourth of the persons formerly living by conveyances will find themselves literally without resources, in spite of the munificence of the State. To meet their deficit they have but one hope, — that the mass of transportation effected over the line may be increased by twenty-five per cent, or else that they may find employment in other lines of industry, — which seems at first impossible, since, by the hypothesis and in fact, places are everywhere filled, proportion is maintained everywhere, and the supply is sufficient for the demand.

Moreover it is very necessary, if it be desired to increase the mass of transportation, that a fresh impetus be given to labor in other industries. Now, admitting that the laborers displaced by this over-production find employment, and that their distribution among the various kinds of labor proves as easy in practice as in theory, the difficulty is still far from settled. For the number of those engaged in circulation being to the number of those engaged in production as one hundred to one thousand, in order to obtain, with a circulation one-fourth less expensive, — in other words, one-fourth more powerful, — the same revenue as before, it will be necessary to strengthen production also by one-fourth, — that is, to add to the agricultural and industrial army, not twenty-five, — the figure which indicates the proportionality of the carrying industry, — but two hundred and fifty. But, to arrive at this result, it will be necessary to create machines, — what is worse, to create men: which continually brings the question back to the same point. Thus contradiction upon contradiction: now not only is labor, in consequence of machinery, lacking to men, but also men, in consequence of their numerical weakness and the insufficiency of their consumption, are lacking to machinery: so that, pending the establishment of equilibrium, there is at once a lack of work and a lack of arms, a lack of products and a lack of markets. And what we say of the railroad is true of all industries: always the man and the machine pursue each other, the former never attaining rest, the latter never attaining satisfaction.

Whatever the pace of mechanical progress; though machines should be invented a hundred times more marvellous than the mule-jenny, the knitting-machine, or the cylinder press; though forces should be discovered a hundred times more powerful than steam, — very far from freeing humanity, securing its leisure, and making the production of everything gratuitous, these things would have no other effect than to multiply labor, induce an increase of population, make the chains of serfdom heavier, render life more and more expensive, and deepen the abyss which separates the class that commands and enjoys from the class that obeys and suffers.

Suppose now all these difficulties overcome; suppose the laborers made available by the railroad adequate to the increase of service demanded for the support of the locomotive, — compensation being effected without pain, nobody will suffer; on the contrary, the well-being of each will be increased by a fraction of the profit realized by the substitution of the railway for the stage-coach. What then, I shall be asked, prevents these things from taking place with such regularity and precision? And what is easier than for an intelligent government to so manage all industrial transitions?

I have pushed the hypothesis as far as it could go in order to show, on the one hand, the end to which humanity is tending, and, on the other, the difficulties which it must overcome in order to attain it. Surely the providential order is that progress should be effected, in so far as machinery is concerned, in the way that I have just spoken of: but what embarrasses society's march and makes it go from Charybdis to Scylla is precisely the fact that it is not organized. We have reached as yet only the second phase of its evolution, and already we have met upon our road two chasms which seem insuperable, — division of labor and machinery. How save the parcellaire workman, if he is a man of intelligence, from degradation, or, if he is degraded already, lift him to intellectual life? How, in the second place, give birth among laborers to that solidarity of interest without which industrial progress counts its steps by its catastrophes, when these same laborers are radically divided by labor, wages, intelligence, and liberty, — that is, by egoism? How, in short, reconcile what the progress already accomplished has had the effect of rendering irreconcilable? To appeal to communism and fraternity would be to anticipate dates: there is nothing in common, there can exist no fraternity, between such creatures as the division of labor and the service of machinery have made. It is not in that direction — at least for the present — that we must seek a solution.

Well! it will be said, since the evil lies still more in the minds than in the system, let us come back to instruction, let us labor for the education of the people.

In order that instruction may be useful, in order that it may even be received, it is necessary, first of all, that the pupil should be free, just as, before planting a piece of ground, we clear it of thorns and dog-grass. Moreover, the best system of education, even so far as philosophy and morality are concerned, would be that of professional education: once more, how reconcile such education with parcellaire division and the service of machinery? How shall the man who, by the effect of his labor, has become a slave, — that is, a chattel, a thing, — again become a person by the same labor, or in continuing the same exercise? Why is it not seen that these ideas are mutually repellent, and that, if, by some impossibility, the proletaire could reach a certain degree of intelligence, he would make use of it in the first place to revolutionize society and change all civil and industrial relations? And what I say is no vain exaggeration. The working class, in Paris and the large cities, is vastly superior in point of ideas to what it was twenty-five years ago; now, let them tell me if this class is not decidedly, energetically revolutionary! And it will become more and more so in proportion as it shall acquire the ideas of justice and order, in proportion especially as it shall reach an understanding of the mechanism of property.

Language, — I ask permission to recur once more to etymology, — language seems to me to have clearly expressed the moral condition of the laborer, after he has been, if I may so speak, depersonalized by industry. In the Latin the idea of servitude implies that of subordination of man to things; and when later feudal law declared the serf attached to the glebe, it only periphrased the literal meaning of the word servus.[1] Spontaneous reason, oracle of fate itself, had therefore condemned the subaltern workman, before science had established his debasement.

---

[1] In spite of the most approved authorities, I cannot accept the idea that serf, in Latin servus, was so called from servare, to keep, because the slave was a prisoner of war who was kept for labor. Servitude, or at least domesticity, is certainly prior to war, although war may have noticeably strengthened it. Why, moreover, if such was the origin of the idea as well as of the thing, should they not have said, instead of serv-us, serv-atus, in conformity with grammatical deduction? To me the real etymology is revealed in the opposition of serv-are and serv-ire, the primitive theme of which is ser-o in-stro, to join, to press, whence ser-ies, joint, continuity, Ser-a, lock, sertir, insert, etc. All these words imply the idea of a principal thing, to which is joined an accessory, as an object of special usefulness. Thence serv-ire, to be an object of usefulness, a thing secondary to another; serv-are, as we say to press, to put aside, to assign a thing its utility; serv-us, a man at hand, a utility, a chattel, in short, a man of service. The opposite of servus is dem-inus (dom-us, dom-anium, and domare); that is, the head of the household, the master of the house, he who utilizes men, servat, animals, domat, and things, possidet. That consequently prisoners of war should have been reserved for slavery, servati ad servitium, or rather serti ad glebam, is perfectly conceivable; their destiny being known, they have simply taken their name from it.

Such being the case, what can the efforts of philanthropy do for beings whom Providence has rejected?

Labor is the education of our liberty. The ancients had a profound perception of this truth when they distinguished the servile arts from the liberal arts. For, like profession, like ideas; like ideas, like morals. Everything in slavery takes on the character of degradation, — habits, tastes, inclinations, sentiments, pleasures: it involves universal subversion. Occupy one's self with the education of the poor! But that would create the most cruel antagonism in these degenerate souls; that would inspire them with ideas which labor would render intolerable to them, affections incompatible with the brutishness of their condition, pleasures of which the perception is dulled in them. If such a project could succeed, instead of making a man of the laborer, it would make a demon of him. Just study those faces which people the prisons and the galleys, and tell me if most of them do not belong to subjects whom the revelation of the beautiful, of elegance, of wealth, of comfort, of honor, and of science, of all that makes the dignity of man, has found too weak, and so has demoralized and killed.

At least wages should be fixed, say the less audacious; schedules of rates should be prepared in all industries, to be accepted by employers and workmen.

This hypothesis of salvation is cited by M. Fix. And he answers victoriously:

Such schedules have been made in England and elsewhere; their value is known; everywhere they have been violated as soon as accepted, both by employers and by workmen.

The causes of the violation of the schedules are easy to fathom: they are to be found in machinery, in the incessant processes and combinations of industry. A schedule is agreed upon at a given moment: but suddenly there comes a new invention which gives its author the power to lower the price of merchandise. What will the other employers do? They will cease to manufacture and will discharge their workmen, or else they will propose to them a reduction. It is the only course open to them, pending a discovery by them in turn of some process by means of which, without lowering the rate of wages, they will be able to produce more cheaply than their competitors: which will be equivalent again to a suppression of workmen.

M. Léon Faucher seems inclined to favor a system of indemnity. He says:

We readily conceive that, in some interest or other, the State, representing the general desire, should command the sacrifice of an industry.

It is always supposed to command it, from the moment that it grants to each the liberty to produce, and protects and defends this liberty against all encroachment.

But this is an extreme measure, an experiment which is always perilous, and which should be accompanied by all possible consideration for individuals. The State has no right to take from a class of citizens the labor by which they live, before otherwise providing for their subsistence or assuring itself that they will find in some new industry employment for their minds and arms. It is a principle in civilized countries that the government cannot seize a piece of private property, even on grounds of public utility, without first buying out the proprietor by a just indemnity paid in advance. Now, labor seems to us property quite as legitimate, quite as sacred, as a field or a house, and we do not understand why it should be expropriated without any sort of compensation...

As chimerical as we consider the doctrines which represent government as the universal purveyor of labor in society, to the same extent does it seem to us just and necessary that every displacement of labor in the name of public utility should be effected only by means of a compensation or a transition, and that neither individuals nor classes should be sacrificed to State considerations. Power, in well-constituted nations, has always time and money to give for the mitigation of these partial sufferings. And it is precisely because industry does not emanate from it, because it is born and developed under the free and individual initiative of citizens, that the government is bound, when it disturbs its course, to offer it a sort of reparation or indemnity.

There's sense for you: whatever M. Léon Faucher may say, he calls for the organization of labor. For government to see to it that every displacement of labor is effected only by means of a compensation or a transition, and that individuals and classes are never sacrificed to State considerations, — that is, to the progress of industry and the liberty of enterprise, the supreme law of the State, — is without any doubt to constitute itself, in some way that the future shall determine, the purveyor of labor in society and the guardian of wages. And, as we have many times repeated, inasmuch as industrial progress and consequently the work of disarranging and rearranging classes in society is continual, it is not a special transition for each innovation that needs to be discovered, but rather a general principle, an organic law of transition, applicable to all possible cases and producing its effect itself. Is M. Léon Faucher in a position to formulate this law and reconcile the various antagonisms which we have described? No, since he prefers to stop at the idea of an indemnity. Power, he says, in well-organized nations, has always time and money to give for the mitigation of these partial sufferings. I am sorry for M. Faucher's generous intentions, but they seem to me radically impracticable.

Power has no time and money save what it takes from the taxpayers. To indemnify by taxation laborers thrown out of work would be to visit ostracism upon new inventions and establish communism by means of the bayonet; that is no solution of the difficulty. It is useless to insist further on indemnification by the State. Indemnity, applied according to M. Faucher's views, would either end in industrial despotism, in something like the government of Mohammed-Ali, or else would degenerate into a poor-tax, — that is, into a vain hypocrisy. For the good of humanity it were better not to indemnify, and to let labor seek its own eternal constitution.

There are some who say: Let government carry laborers thrown out of work to points where private industry is not established, where individual enterprise cannot reach. We have mountains to plant again with trees, ten or twelve million acres of land to clear, canals to dig, in short, a thousand things of immediate and general utility to undertake.

"We certainly ask our readers' pardon for it," answers M. Fix; "but here again we are obliged to call for the intervention of capital. These surfaces, certain communal lands excepted, are fallow, because, if cultivated, they would yield no net product, and very likely not even the costs of cultivation. These lands are possessed by proprietors who either have or have not the capital necessary to cultivate them. In the former case, the proprietor would very probably content himself, if he cultivated these lands, with a very small profit, and perhaps would forego what is called the rent of the land: but he has found that, in undertaking such cultivation, he would lose his original capital, and his other calculations have shown him that the sale of the products would not cover the costs of cultivation. . . All things considered, therefore, this land will remain fallow, because capital that should be put into it would yield no profit and would be lost. If it were otherwise, all these lands would be immediately put in cultivation; the savings now disposed of in another direction would necessarily gravitate in a certain proportion to the cultivation of land; for capital has no affections: it has interests, and always seeks that employment which is surest and most lucrative."

This argument, very well reasoned, amounts to saying that the time to cultivate its waste lands has not arrived for France, just as the time for railroads has not arrived for the Kaffres and the Hottentots. For, as has been said in the second chapter, society begins by working those sources which yield most easily and surely the most necessary and least expensive products: it is only gradually that it arrives at the utilization of things relatively less productive. Since the human race has been tossing about on the face of its globe, it has struggled with no other task; for it the same care is ever recurrent, — that of assuring its subsistence while going forward in the path of discovery. In order that such clearing of land may not become a ruinous speculation, a cause of misery, in other words, in order that it may be possible, it is necessary, therefore, to multiply still further our capital and machinery, discover new processes, and more thoroughly divide labor. Now, to solicit the government to take such an initiative is to imitate the peasants who, on seeing the approach of a storm, begin to pray to God and to invoke their saint. Governments — today it cannot be too often repeated — are the representatives of Divinity, — I had almost said executors of celestial vengeance: they can do nothing for us. Does the English government, for instance, know any way of giving labor to the unfortunates who take refuge in its workhouses? And if it knew, would it dare? Aid yourself, and Heaven will aid you! This note of popular distrust of Divinity tells us also what we must expect of power, — nothing.

Arrived at the second station of our Calvary, instead of abandoning ourselves to sterile contemplations, let us be more and more attentive to the teachings of destiny. The guarantee of our liberty lies in the progress of our torture.

Chapter V. Third Period. — Competition.

BETWEEN the hundred-headed hydra, division of labor, and the unconquered dragon, machinery, what will become of humanity? A prophet has said it more than two thousand years ago: Satan looks on his victim, and the fires of war are kindled, Aspexit gentes, et dissolvit. To save us from two scourges, famine and pestilence, Providence sends us discord.

Competition represents that philosophical era in which, a semi-understanding of the antinomies of reason having given birth to the art of sophistry, the characteristics of the false and the true were confounded, and in which, instead of doctrines, they had nothing but deceptive mental tilts. Thus the industrial movement faithfully reproduces the metaphysical movement; the history of social economy is to be found entire in the writings of the philosophers. Let us study this interesting phase, whose most striking characteristic is to take away the judgment of those who believe as well as those who protest.

1. — Necessity of competition.

M. Louis Reybaud, novelist by profession, economist on occasion, breveted by the Academy of Moral and Political

Sciences for his anti-reformatory caricatures, and become, with the lapse of time, one of the writers most hostile to social ideas, — M. Louis Reybaud, whatever he may do, is none the less profoundly imbued with these same ideas: the opposition which he thus exhibits is neither in his heart nor in his mind; it is in the facts.

In the first edition of his "Studies of Contemporary Reformers," M. Reybaud, moved by the sight of social sufferings as well as the courage of these founders of schools, who believed that they could reform the world by an explosion of sentimentalism, had formally expressed the opinion that the surviving feature of all their systems was ASSOCIATION. M. Dunoyer, one of M. Reybaud's judges, bore this testimony, the more flattering to M. Reybaud from being slightly ironical in form:

M. Reybaud, who has exposed with so much accuracy and talent, in a book which the French Academy has crowned, the vices of the three principal reformatory systems, holds fast to the principle common to them, which serves as their base, — association. Association in his eyes, he declares, is the greatest problem of modern times. It is called, he says, to solve that of the distribution of the fruits of labor. Though authority can do nothing towards the solution of this problem, association could do everything. M. Reybaud speaks here like a writer of the phalansterian school . . .

M. Reybaud had advanced a little, as one may see. Endowed with too much good sense and good faith not to perceive the precipice, he soon felt that he was straying, and began a retrograde movement. I do not call this about-face a crime on his part: M. Reybaud is one of those men who cannot justly be held responsible for their metaphors. He had spoken before reflecting, he retracted: what more natural! If the socialists must blame any one, let it be M. Dunoyer, who had prompted M. Reybaud's recantation by this singular compliment.

M. Dunoyer was not slow in perceiving that his words had not fallen on closed ears. He relates, for the glory of sound principles, that, "in a second edition of the 'Studies of Reformers,' M. Reybaud has himself tempered the absolute tone of his expressions. He has said, instead of could do everything, could do much."

It was an important modification, as M. Dunoyer brought clearly to his notice, but it still permitted M. Reybaud to write at the same time:

These symptoms are grave; they may be considered as prophecies of a confused organization, in which labor would seek an equilibrium and a regularity which it now lacks . . . At the bottom of all these efforts is hidden a principle, association, which it would be wrong to condemn on the strength of irregular manifestations.

Finally M. Reybaud has loudly declared himself a partisan of competition, which means that he has decidedly abandoned the principle of association. For if by association we are to understand only the forms of partnership fixed by the commercial code, the philosophy of which has been summarized for us by MM. Troplong and Delangle, it is no longer worth while to distinguish between socialists and economists, between one party which seeks association and another which maintains that association exists.

Let no one imagine, because M. Reybaud has happened to say heedlessly yes and no to a question of which he does not seem to have yet formed a clear idea, that I class him among those speculators of socialism, who, after having launched a hoax into the world, begin immediately to make their retreat, under the pretext that, the idea now belonging to the public domain, there is nothing more for them to do but to leave it to make its way. M. Reybaud, in my opinion, belongs rather to the category of dupes, which includes in its bosom so many honest people and people of so much brains. M. Reybaud will remain, then, in my eyes, the *vir probus dicendi peritus*, the conscientious and skilful writer, who may easily be caught napping, but who never expresses anything that he does not see or feel. Moreover, M. Reybaud, once placed on the ground of economic ideas, would find the more difficulty in being consistent with himself because of the clearness of his mind and the accuracy of his reasoning. I am going to make this curious experiment under the reader's eyes.

If I could be understood by M. Reybaud, I would say to him: Take your stand in favor of competition, you will be wrong; take your stand against competition, still you will be wrong: which signifies that you will always be right. After that, if, convinced that you have not erred either in the first edition of your book or in the fourth, you should succeed in formulating your sentiment in an intelligible manner, I will look upon you as an economist of as great genius as Turgot and A. Smith; but I warn you that then you will resemble the latter, of whom you doubtless know little; you will be a believer in equality. Do you accept the wager?

To better prepare M. Reybaud for this sort of reconciliation with himself, let us show him first that this versatility of judgment, for which anybody else in my place would reproach him with insulting bitterness, is a treason, not on the part of the writer, but on the part of the facts of which he has made himself the interpreter.

In March, 1844, M. Reybaud published on oleaginous seeds — a subject which interested the city of Marseilles, his birthplace — an article in which he took vigorous ground in favor of free competition and the oil of sesame. According to the facts gathered by the author, which seem authentic, sesame would yield from forty-five to forty-six per cent of oil, while the poppy and the colza yield only twenty-five to thirty per cent, and the olive simply twenty to twenty-two. Sesame, for this reason, is disliked by the northern manufacturers, who have asked and obtained its prohibition. Nevertheless the English are on the watch, ready to take possession of this valuable branch of commerce. Let them prohibit the seed, says M. Reybaud, the oil will reach us mixed, in soap, or in some other way: we shall have lost the profit of manufacture. Moreover, the interest of our marine service requires the protection of this trade; it is a matter of no less than forty thousand casks of seed, which implies a maritime outfit of three hundred vessels and three thousand sailors.

These facts are conclusive: forty-five per cent. of oil instead of twenty-five; in quality superior to all the oils of France; reduction in the price of an article of prime necessity; a saving to consumers; three hundred ships, three thousand sailors, — such would be the value to us of liberty of commerce. Therefore, long live competition and sesame!

Then, in order to better assure these brilliant results, M. Reybaud, impelled by his patriotism and going straight in pursuit of his idea, observes — very judiciously in our opinion — that the government should abstain henceforth from all treaties of reciprocity in the matter of transportation: he asks that French vessels may carry the imports as well as the exports of French commerce.

"What we call reciprocity," he says, "is a pure fiction, the advantage of which is reaped by whichever of the parties can furnish navigation at the smallest expense. Now, as in France the elements of navigation, such as the purchase of the ships, the wages of the crews, and the costs of outfit, rise to an excessive figure, higher than in any of the other maritime nations, it follows that every reciprocity treaty is equivalent on our part to a treaty of abdication, and that, instead of agreeing to an act of mutual convenience, we resign ourselves, knowingly or involuntarily, to a sacrifice."

And M. Reybaud then points out the disastrous consequences of reciprocity:

France consumes five hundred thousand bales of cotton, and the Americans land them on our wharves; she uses enormous quantities of coal, and the English do the carrying thereof; the Swedes and Norwegians deliver to us themselves their iron and wood; the Dutch, their cheeses; the Russians, their hemp and wheat; the Genoese, their rice; the Spaniards, their oils; the Sicilians, their sulphur; the Greeks and Armenians, all the commodities of the Mediterranean and Black seas."

Evidently such a state of things is intolerable, for it ends in rendering our merchant marine useless. Let us hasten back, then, into our ship yards, from which the cheapness of foreign navigation tends to exclude us. Let us close our doors to foreign vessels, or at least let us burden them with a heavy tax. Therefore, down with competition and rival marines!

Does M. Reybaud begin to understand that his economico-socialistic oscillations are much more innocent than he would have believed? What gratitude he owes me for having quieted his conscience, which perhaps was becoming alarmed!

The reciprocity of which M. Reybaud so bitterly complains is only a form of commercial liberty. Grant full and entire liberty of trade, and our flag is driven from the surface of the seas, as our oils would be from the continent. Therefore we shall pay dearer for our oil, if we insist on making it ourselves; dearer for our colonial products, if we wish to carry them ourselves. To secure cheapness it would be necessary, after having abandoned our oils, to abandon our marine: as well abandon straightway our cloths, our linens, our calicoes, our iron products, and then, as an isolated industry necessarily costs too much, our wines, our grains, our forage! Whichever course you may choose, privilege or liberty, you arrive at the impossible, at the absurd.

Undoubtedly there exists a principle of reconciliation; but, unless it be utterly despotic, it must be derived from a law superior to liberty itself: now, it is this law which no one has yet defined, and which I ask of the economists, if they really are masters of their science. For I cannot consider him a savant who, with the greatest sincerity and all the wit in the world, preaches by turns, fifteen lines apart, liberty and monopoly.

Is it not immediately and intuitively evident that COMPETITION DESTROYS COMPETITION? Is there a theorem in geometry more certain, more peremptory, than that? How then, upon what conditions, in what sense, can a principle which is its own denial enter into science? How can it become an organic law of society? If competition is necessary; if, as the school says, it is a postulate of production, — how does it become so devastating in its effects? And if its most certain effect is to ruin those whom it incites, how does it become useful? For the inconveniences which follow in its train, like the good which it procures, are not accidents arising from the work of man: both follow logically from the principle, and subsist by the same title and face to face.

And, in the first place, competition is as essential to labor as division, since it is division itself returning in another form, or rather, raised to its second power; division, I say, no longer, as in the first period of economic evolution, adequate to collective force, and consequently absorbing the personality of the laborer in the workshop, but giving birth to liberty by making each subdivision of labor a sort of sovereignty in which man stands in all his power and independence. Competition, in a word, is liberty in division and in all the divided parts: beginning with the most comprehensive functions, it tends toward its realization even in the inferior operations of parcellaire labor.

Here the communists raise an objection. It is necessary, they say, in all things, to distinguish between use and abuse. There is a useful, praiseworthy, moral competition, a competition which enlarges the heart and the mind, a noble and generous competition, — it is emulation; and why should not this emulation have for its object the advantage of all? There is another competition, pernicious, immoral, unsocial, a jealous competition which hates and which kills, — it is egoism.

So says communism; so expressed itself, nearly a year ago, in its social profession of faith, the journal, "La Reforme."

Whatever reluctance I may feel to oppose men whose ideas are at bottom my own, I cannot accept such dialectics. "La Reforme," in believing that it could reconcile everything by a distinction more grammatical than real, has made use, without suspecting it, of the golden mean, — that is, of the worst sort of diplomacy. Its argument is exactly the same as that of M. Rossi in regard to the division of labor: it consists in setting competition and morality against each other, in order to limit them by each other, as M. Rossi pretended to arrest and restrict economic inductions by morality, cutting here, lopping there, to suit the need and the occasion. I have refuted M. Rossi by asking him this simple question: How can science be in disagreement with itself, the science of wealth with the science of duty? Likewise I ask the communists: How can a principle whose development is clearly useful be at the same time pernicious?

They say: emulation is not competition. I note, in the first place, that this pretended distinction bears only on the divergent effects of the principle, which leads one to suppose that there were two principles which had been confounded. Emulation is nothing but competition itself; and, since they have thrown themselves into abstractions, I willingly plunge in also. There is no emulation without an object, just as there is no passional initiative without an object; and as the object of every passion is necessarily analogous to the passion itself, — woman to the lover, power to the ambitious, gold to the miser, a crown to the poet, — so the object of industrial emulation is necessarily profit.

No, rejoins the communist, the laborer's object of emulation should be general utility, fraternity, love.

But society itself, since, instead of stopping at the individual man, who is in question at this moment, they wish to attend only to the collective man, — society, I say, labors only with a view to wealth; comfort, happiness, is its only object. Why, then, should that which is true of society not be true of the individual also, since, after all, society is man and entire humanity lives in each man? Why substitute for the immediate object of emulation, which in industry is personal welfare, that far-away and almost metaphysical motive called general welfare, especially when the latter is nothing without the former and can result only from the former?

Communists, in general, build up a strange illusion: fanatics on the subject of power, they expect to secure through a central force, and in the special case in question, through collective wealth, by a sort of reversion, the welfare of the laborer who has created this wealth: as if the individual came into existence after society, instead of society after the individual. For that matter, this is not the only case in which we shall see the socialists unconsciously dominated by the traditions of the regime against which they protest.

But what need of insisting? From the moment that the communist changes the name of things, vera rerum vocabala, he tacitly admits his powerlessness, and puts himself out of the question. That is why my sole reply to him shall be: In denying competition, you abandon the thesis; henceforth you have no place in the discussion. Some other time we will inquire how far man should sacrifice himself in the interest of all: for the moment the question is the solution of the problem of competition, — that is, the reconciliation of the highest satisfaction of egoism with social necessities; spare us your moralities.

Competition is necessary to the constitution of value, — that is, to the very principle of distribution, and consequently to the advent of equality. As long as a product is supplied only by a single manufacturer, its real value remains a mystery, either through the producer's misrepresentation or through his neglect or inability to reduce the cost of production to its extreme limit. Thus the privilege of production is a real loss to society, and publicity of industry, like competition between laborers, a necessity. All the utopias ever imagined or imaginable cannot escape this law.

Certainly I do not care to deny that labor and wages can and should be guaranteed; I even entertain the hope that the time of such guarantee is not far off: but I maintain that a guarantee of wages is impossible without an exact knowledge of value, and that this value can be discovered only by competition, not at all by communistic institutions or by popular decree. For in this there is something more powerful than the will of the legislator and of citizens, — namely, the absolute impossibility that man should do his duty after finding himself relieved of all responsibility to himself: now, responsibility to self, in the matter of labor, necessarily implies competition with others. Ordain that, beginning January 1, 1847, labor and wages are guaranteed to all: immediately an immense relaxation will succeed the extreme tension to which industry is now subjected; real value will fall rapidly below nominal value; metallic money, in spite of its effigy and stamp, will experience the fate of the assignats; the merchant will ask more and give less; and we shall find ourselves in a still lower circle in the hell of misery in which competition is only the third turn.

Even were I to admit, with some socialists, that the attractiveness of labor may some day serve as food for emulation without any hidden thought of profit, of what utility could this utopia be in the phase which we are studying? We are yet only in the third period of economic evolution, in the third age of the constitution of labor, — that is, in a period when it is impossible for labor to be attractive. For the attractiveness of labor can result only from a high degree of physical, moral, and intellectual development of the laborer. Now, this development itself, this education of humanity by industry, is precisely the object of which we are in pursuit through the contradictions of social economy. How, then, could the attractiveness of labor serve us as a principle and lever, when it is still our object and our end?

But, if it is unquestionable that labor, as the highest manifestation of life, intelligence, and liberty, carries with it its own attractiveness, I deny that this attractiveness can ever be wholly separated from the motive of utility, and consequently from a return of egoism; I deny, I say, labor for labor, just as I deny style for style, love for love, art for art. Style for style has produced in these days hasty literature and thoughtless improvisation; love for love leads to unnatural vice, onanism, and prostitution; art for art ends in Chinese knick-knacks, caricature, the worship of the ugly. When man no longer looks to labor for anything but the pleasure of exercise, he soon ceases to labor, he plays. History is full of facts which attest this degradation. The games of Greece, Isthmian, Olympic, Pythian, Nemean, exercises of a society which produced everything by its slaves; the life of the Spartans and the ancient Cretans, their models; the gymnasiums, play-grounds, horse-races, and disorders of the market-place among the Athenians; the occupations which Plato assigns to the warriors in his Republic, and which but represent the tastes of his century; finally, in our feudal society, the tilts and tourneys, — all these inventions, as well as many others which I pass in silence, from the game of chess, invented, it is said, at the siege of Troy by Palamedes, to the cards illustrated for Charles VI. by Gringonneur, are examples of what labor becomes as soon as the serious motive of utility is separated from it. Labor, real labor, that which produces wealth and gives knowledge, has too much need of regularity and perseverance and sacrifice to be long the friend of passion, fugitive in its nature, inconstant, and disorderly; it is something too elevated, too ideal, too philosophical, to become exclusively pleasure and enjoyment, — that is, mysticism and sentiment. The faculty of laboring, which distinguishes man from the brutes, has its source in the profoundest depths of the reason: how could it become in us a simple manifestation of life, a voluptuous act of our feeling?

But if now they fall back upon the hypothesis of a transformation of our nature, unprecedented in history, and of which there has been nothing so far that could have expressed the idea, it is nothing more than a dream, unintelligible even to those who defend it, an inversion of progress, a contradiction given to the most certain laws of economic science; and my only reply is to exclude it from the discussion.

Let us stay in the realm of facts, since facts alone have a meaning and can aid us. The French Revolution was effected for industrial liberty as well as for political liberty: and although France in 1789 had not seen all the consequences of the principle for the realization of which she asked, — let us say it boldly, — she was mistaken neither in her wishes nor in her expectation. Whoever would try to deny it would lose in my eyes the right to criticism: I will never dispute with an adversary who would posit as a principle the spontaneous error of twenty-five millions of men.

At the end of the eighteenth century France, wearied with privileges, desired at any price to shake off the torpor of her corporations, and restore the dignity of the laborer by conferring liberty upon him. Everywhere it was necessary to emancipate labor, stimulate genius, and render the manufacturer responsible by arousing a thousand competitors and loading upon him alone the consequences of his indolence, ignorance, and insincerity. Before '89 France was ripe for the transition; it was Turgot who had the glory of effecting the first passage.

Why then, if competition had not been a principle of social economy, a decree of destiny, a necessity of the human soul, why, instead of abolishing corporations, masterships, and wardenships, did they not think rather of repairing them all? Why, instead of a revolution, did they not content themselves with a reform?

Why this negation, if a modification was sufficient? Especially as this middle party was entirely in the line of conservative ideas, which the bourgeoisie shared. Let communism, let quasi-socialistic democracy, which, in regard to the principle of competition, represent — though they do not suspect it — the system of the golden mean, the counter-revolutionary idea, explain to me this unanimity of the nation, if they can!

Moreover the event confirmed the theory. Beginning with the Turgot ministry, an increase of activity and well-being manifested itself in the nation. The test seemed so decisive that it obtained the approval of all legislatures. Liberty of industry and commerce figure in our constitutions on a level with political liberty. To this liberty, in short, France owes the growth of her wealth during the last sixty years.

After this capital fact, which establishes so triumphantly the necessity of competition, I ask permission to cite three or four others, which, being less general in their nature, will throw into bolder relief the influence of the principle which I defend.

Why is our agriculture so prodigiously backward? How is it that routine and barbarism still hover, in so many localities, over the most important branch of national labor? Among the numerous causes that could be cited, I see, in the front rank, the absence of competition. The peasants fight over strips of ground; they compete with each other before the notary; in the fields, no. And speak to them of emulation, of the public good, and with what amazement you fill them! Let the king, they say (to them the king is synonymous with the State, with the public good, with society), let the king attend to his business, and we will attend to ours! Such is their philosophy and their patriotism. Ah! if the king could excite competition with them! Unfortunately it is impossible. While in manufactures competition follows from liberty and property, in agriculture liberty and property are a direct obstacle to competition. The peasant, rewarded, not according to his labor and intelligence, but according to the quality of the land and the caprice of God, aims, in cultivating, to pay the lowest possible wages and to make the least possible advance outlays. Sure of always finding a market for his goods, he is much more solicitous about reducing his expenses than about improving the soil and the quality of its products. He sows, and Providence does the rest. The only sort of competition known to the agricultural class is that of rents; and it cannot be denied that in France, and for instance in Beauce, it has led to useful results. But as the principle of this competition takes effect only at second hand, so to speak, as it does not emanate directly from the liberty and property of the cultivators, it disappears with the cause that produces it, so that, to insure the decline of agricultural industry in many localities, or at least to arrest its progress, perhaps it would suffice to make the farmers proprietors.

Another branch of collective labor, which of late years has given rise to sharp debates, is that of public works. "To manage the building of a road, M. Dunoyer very well says, "perhaps a pioneer and a postilion would be better than an engineer fresh from the School of Roads and Bridges." There is no one who has not had occasion to verify the correctness of this remark.

On one of our finest rivers, celebrated by the importance of its navigation, a bridge was being built. From the beginning of the work the rivermen had seen that the arches would be much too low to allow the circulation of boats at times when the river was high: they pointed this out to the engineer in charge of the work. Bridges, answered the latter with superb dignity, are made for those who pass over, not for those who pass under. The remark has become a proverb in that vicinity. But, as it is impossible for stupidity to prevail forever, the government has felt the necessity of revising the work of its agent, and as I write the arches of the bridge are being raised. Does any one believe that, if the merchants interested in the course of the navigable way had been charged with the enterprise at their own risk and peril, they would have had to do their work twice? One could fill a book with masterpieces of the same sort achieved by young men learned in roads and bridges, who, scarcely out of school and given life positions, are no longer stimulated by competition.

In proof of the industrial capacity of the State, and consequently of the possibility of abolishing competition altogether, they cite the administration of the tobacco industry. There, they say, is no adulteration, no litigation, no bankruptcy, no misery. The condition of the workmen, adequately paid, instructed, sermonized, moralized, and assured of a retiring pension accumulated by their savings, is incomparably superior to that of the immense majority of workmen engaged in free industry.

All this may be true: for my part, I am ignorant on the subject. I know nothing of what goes on in the administration of the tobacco factories; I have procured no information either from the directors or the workmen, and I have no need of any. How much does the tobacco sold by the administration cost? How much is it worth? You can answer the first of these questions: you only need to call at the first tobacco shop you see. But you can tell me nothing about the second, because you have no standard of comparison and are forbidden to verify by experiment the items of cost of administration, which it is consequently impossible to accept. Therefore the tobacco business, made into a monopoly, necessarily costs society more than it brings in; it is an industry which, instead of subsisting by its own product, lives by subsidies, and which consequently, far from furnishing us a model, is one of the first abuses which reform should strike down.

And when I speak of the reform to be introduced in the production of tobacco, I do not refer simply to the enormous tax which triples or quadruples the value of this product; neither do I refer to the hierarchical organization of its employees, some of whom by their salaries are made aristocrats as expensive as they are useless, while others, hopeless receivers of petty wages, are kept forever in the situation of subalterns. I do not even speak of the privilege of the tobacco shops and the whole world of parasites which they support: I have particularly in view the useful labor, the labor of the workmen. From the very fact that the administration's workman has no competitors and is interested neither in profit nor loss, from the fact that he is not free, in a word, his product is necessarily less, and his service too expensive. This being so, let them say that the government treats its employees well and looks out for their comfort: what wonder? Why do not people see that liberty bears the burdens of privilege, and that, if, by some impossibility, all industries were to be treated like the tobacco industry, the source of subsidies failing, the nation could no longer balance its receipts and its expenses, and the State would become a bankrupt?

Foreign products: I cite the testimony of an educated man, though not a political economist, — M. Liebig.

Formerly France imported from Spain every year soda to the value of twenty or thirty millions of francs; for Spanish soda was the best. All through the war with England the price of soda, and consequently that of soap and glass, constantly rose. French manufacturers therefore had to suffer considerably from this state of things. Then it was that Leblanc discovered the method of extracting soda from common salt. This process was a source of wealth to France; the manufacture of soda acquired extraordinary proportions; but neither Leblanc nor Napoleon enjoyed the profit of the invention. The Restoration, which took advantage of the wrath of the people against the author of the continental blockade, refused to pay the debt of the emperor, whose promises had led to Leblanc's discoveries. . .

A few years ago, the king of Naples having undertaken to convert the Sicilian sulphur trade into a monopoly, England, which consumes an immense quantity of this sulphur, warned the king of Naples that, if the monopoly were maintained, it would be considered a casus belli. While the two governments were exchanging diplomatic notes, fifteen patents were taken out in England for the extraction of sulphuric acid from the limestones, iron pyrites, and other mineral substances in which England abounds. But the affair being arranged with the king of Naples, nothing came of these exploitations: it was simply established, by the attempts which were made, that the extraction of sulphuric acid by the new processes could have been carried on successfully, which perhaps would have annihilated Sicily's sulphur trade.

Had it not been for the war with England, had not the king of Naples had a fancy for monopoly, it would have been a long time before any one in France would have thought of extracting soda from sea salt, or any one in England of getting sulphuric acid from the mountains of lime and pyrites which she contains. Now, that is precisely the effect of competition upon industry. Man rouses from his idleness only when want fills him with anxiety; and the surest way to extinguish his genius is to deliver him from all solicitude and take away from him the hope of profit and of the social distinction which results from it, by creating around him peace everywhere, peace always, and transferring to the State the responsibility of his inertia.

Yes, it must be admitted, in spite of modern quietism, — man's life is a permanent war, war with want, war with nature, war with his fellows, and consequently war with himself. The theory of a peaceful equality, founded on fraternity and sacrifice, is only a counterfeit of the Catholic doctrine of renunciation of the goods and pleasures of this world, the principle of beggary, the panegyric of misery. Man may love his fellow well enough to die for him; he does not love him well enough to work for him.

To the theory of sacrifice, which we have just refuted in fact and in right, the adversaries of competition add another, which is just the opposite of the first: for it is a law of the mind that, when it does not know the truth, which is its point of equilibrium, it oscillates between two contradictions. This new theory of anti-competitive socialism is that of encouragements.

What more social, more progressive in appearance, than encouragement of labor and of industry? There is no democrat who does not consider it one of the finest attributes of power, no utopian theorist who does not place it in the front rank as a means of organizing happiness. Now, government is by nature so incapable of directing labor that every reward bestowed by it is a veritable larceny from the common treasury. M. Reybaud shall furnish us the text of this induction.

"The premiums granted to encourage exportation," observes M. Reybaud somewhere, "are equivalent to the taxes paid for the importation of raw material; the advantage remains absolutely null, and serves to encourage nothing but a vast system of smuggling."

This result is inevitable. Abolish customs duties, and national industry suffers, as we have already seen in the case of sesame; maintain the duties without granting premiums for exportation, and national commerce will be beaten in foreign markets. To obviate this difficulty do you resort to premiums? You but restore with one hand what you have received with the other, and you provoke fraud, the last result, the caput mortuum, of all encouragements of industry. Hence it follows that every encouragement to labor, every reward bestowed upon industry, beyond the natural price of its product, is a gratuitous gift, a bribe taken out of the consumer and offered in his name to a favorite of power, in exchange for zero, for nothing. To encourage industry, then, is synonymous at bottom with encouraging idleness: it is one of the forms of swindling.

In the interest of our navy the government had thought it best to grant to outfitters of transport-ships a premium for every man employed on their vessels. Now, I continue to quote M. Reybaud:

On every vessel that starts for Newfoundland from sixty to seventy men embark. Of this number twelve are sailors: the balance consists of villagers snatched from their work in the fields, who, engaged as day laborers for the preparation of fish, remain strangers to the rigging, and have nothing that is marine about them except their feet and stomach. Nevertheless, these men figure on the rolls of the naval inscription, and there perpetuate a deception. When there is occasion to defend the institution of premiums, these are cited in its favor; they swell the numbers and contribute to success.

Base jugglery! doubtless some innocent reformer will exclaim. Be it so: but let us analyze the fact, and try to disengage the general idea to be found therein.

In principle the only encouragement to labor that science can admit is profit. For, if labor cannot find its reward in its own product, very far from encouraging it, it should be abandoned as soon as possible, and, if this same labor results in a net product, it is absurd to add to this net product a gratuitous gift, and thus overrate the value of the service. Applying this principle, I say then: If the merchant service calls only for ten thousand sailors, it should not be asked to support fifteen thousand; the shortest course for the government is to put five thousand conscripts on State vessels, and send them on their expeditions, like princes. Every encouragement offered to the merchant marine is a direct invitation to fraud, — what do I say? — a proposal to pay wages for an impossible service. Do the handling and discipline of vessels and all the conditions of maritime commerce accommodate themselves to these adjuncts of a useless persononel? What, then, can the ship-owner do in face of a government which offers him a bonus to embark on his vessel people of whom he has no need? If the ministry throws the money of the treasury into the street, am I guilty if I pick it up?

Thus — and it is a point worthy of notice — the theory of encouragements emanates directly from the theory of sacrifice; and, in order to avoid holding man responsible, the opponents of competition, by the fatal contradiction of their ideas, are obliged to make him now a god, now a brute. And then they are astonished that society is not moved by their appeal! Poor children! men will never be better or worse than you see them now and than they always have been. As soon as their individual welfare solicits them, they desert the general welfare: in which I find them, if not honorable, at least worthy of excuse. It is your fault if you now demand of them more than they owe you and now stimulate their greed with rewards which they do not deserve. Man has nothing more precious than himself, and consequently no other law than his responsibility. The theory of self-sacrifice, like that of rewards, is a theory of rogues, subversive of society and morality; and by the very fact that you look either to sacrifice or to privilege for the maintenance of order, you create a new antagonism in society. Instead of causing the birth of harmony from the free activity of persons, you render the individual and the State strangers to each other; in commanding union, you breathe discord.

To sum up, outside of competition there remains but this alternative, — encouragement, which is a mystification, or sacrifice, which is hypocrisy.

Therefore competition, analyzed in its principle, is an inspiration of justice; and yet we shall see that competition, in its results, is unjust.

2. — Subversive effects of competition, and the destruction of liberty thereby.

The kingdom of heaven suffereth violence, says the Gospel, and the violent take it by force. These words are the allegory of society. In society regulated by labor, dignity, wealth, and glory are objects of competition; they are the reward of the strong, and competition may be defined as the regime of force. The old economists did not at first perceive this contradiction: the moderns have been forced to recognize it.

"To elevate a State from the lowest degree of barbarism to the highest degree of opulence," wrote A. Smith, "but three things are necessary, — peace, moderate taxes, and a tolerable administration of justice. All the rest is brought about by the natural course of things."

On which the last translator of Smith, M. Blanqui, lets fall this gloomy comment:

We have seen the natural course of things produce disastrous effects, and create anarchy in production, war for markets, and piracy in competition. The division of labor and the perfecting of machinery, which should realize for the great working family of the human race the conquest of a certain amount of leisure to the advantage of its dignity, have produced at many points nothing but degradation and misery.... When A. Smith wrote, liberty had not yet come with its embarrassments and its abuses, and the Glasgow professor foresaw only its blessings... Smith would have written like M. de Sismondi, if he had been a witness of the sad condition of Ireland and the manufacturing districts of England in the times in which we live.

Now then, litterateurs, statesmen, daily publicists, believers and half-believers, all you who have taken upon yourselves the mission of indoctrinating men, do you hear these words which one would take for a translation from Jeremiah? Will you tell us at last to what end you pretend to be conducting civilization? What advice do you offer to society, to the country, in alarm?

But to whom do I speak? Ministers, journalists, sextons, and pedants! Do such people trouble themselves about the problems of social economy? Have they ever heard of competition?

A citizen of Lyons, a soul hardened to mercantile war, travelled in Tuscany. He observes that from five to six hundred thousand straw hats are made annually in that country, the aggregate value of which amounts to four or five millions of francs. This industry is almost the sole support of the people of the little State. "How is it," he says to himself, "that so easily conducted a branch of agriculture and manufactures has not been transported into Provence and Languedoc, where the climate is the same as in Tuscany?" But, thereupon observes an economist, if the industry of the peasants of Tuscany is taken from them, how will they contrive to live?

The manufacture of black silks had become for Florence a specialty the secret of which she guarded preciously.

A shrewd Lyons manufacturer, the tourist notices with satisfaction, has come to set up an establishment in Florence, and has finally got possession of the peculiar processes of dyeing and weaving. Probably this discovery will diminish Florentine exportation. — A Journey in Italy, by M. FULCHIRON.

Formerly the breeding of the silk-worm was abandoned to the peasants of Tuscany; whom it aided to live.

Agricultural societies have been formed; they have represented that the silk-worm, in the peasant's sleeping-room, did not get sufficient ventilation or sufficient steadiness of temperature, or as good care as it would have if the laborers who breed them made it their sole business. Consequently rich, intelligent, and generous citizens have built, amid the applause of the public, what are called bigattieres (from bigatti, silk-worm). — M. DE SISMONDI.

And then, you ask, will these breeders of silk-worms, these manufacturers of silks and hats, lose their work? Precisely: it will even be proved to them that it is for their interest that they should, since they will be able to buy the same products for less than it costs them to manufacture them. Such is competition.

Competition, with its homicidal instinct, takes away the bread of a whole class of laborers, and sees in it only an improvement, a saving; it steals a secret in a cowardly manner, and glories in it as a discovery; it changes the natural zones of production to the detriment of an entire people, and pretends to have done nothing but utilize the advantages of its climate. Competition overturns all notions of equity and justice; it increases the real cost of production by needlessly multiplying the capital invested, causes by turns the dearness of products and their depreciation, corrupts the public conscience by putting chance in the place of right, and maintains terror and distrust everywhere.

But what! Without this atrocious characteristic, competition would lose its happiest effects; without the arbitrary element in exchange and the panics of the market, labor would not continually build factory against factory, and, not being maintained in such good working order, production would realize none of its marvels. After having caused evil to arise from the very utility of its principle, competition again finds a way to extract good from evil; destruction engenders utility, equilibrium is realized by agitation, and it may be said of competition, as Samson said of the lion which he had slain: De comedente cibus exiit, et de forti dulcedo. Is there anything, in all the spheres of human knowledge, more surprising than political economy?

Let us take care, nevertheless, not to yield to an impulse of irony, which would be on our part only unjust invective. It is characteristic of economic science to find its certainty in its contradictions, and the whole error of the economists consists in not having understood this. Nothing poorer than their criticism, nothing more saddening than their mental confusion, as soon as they touch this question of competition: one would say that they were witnesses forced by torture to confess what their conscience would like to conceal. The reader will take it kindly if I put before his eyes the arguments for laissez-passer, introducing him, so to speak, into the presence of a secret meeting of economists.

M. Dunoyer opens the discussion.

Of all the economists M. Dunoyer has most energetically embraced the positive side of competition, and consequently, as might have been expected, most ineffectually grasped the negative side. M. Dunoyer, with whom nothing can be done when what he calls principles are under discussion, is very far from believing that in matters of political economy yes and no may be true at the same moment and to the same extent; let it be said even to his credit, such a conception is the more repugnant to him because of the frankness and honesty with which he holds his doctrines. What would I not give to gain an entrance into this pure but so obstinate soul for this truth as certain to me as the existence of the sun, — that all the categories of political economy are contradictions! Instead of uselessly exhausting himself in reconciling practice and theory; instead of contenting himself with the ridiculous excuse that everything here below has its advantages and its inconveniences, — M. Dunoyer would seek the synthetic idea which solves all the antinomies, and, instead of the paradoxical conservative which he now is, he would become with us an inexorable and logical revolutionist.

"If competition is a false principle," says M. Dunoyer, "it follows that for two thousand years humanity has been pursuing the wrong road."

No, what you say does not follow, and your prejudicial remark is refuted by the very theory of progress. Humanity posits its principles by turns, and sometimes at long intervals: never does it give them up in substance, although it destroys successively their expressions and formulas. This destruction is called negation; because the general reason, ever progressive, continually denies the completeness and sufficiency of its prior ideas. Thus it is that, competition being one of the periods in the constitution of value, one of the elements of the social synthesis, it is true to say at the same time that it is indestructible in its principle, and that nevertheless in its present form it should be abolished, denied. If, then, there is any one here who is in opposition to history, it is you.

I have several remarks to make upon the accusations of which competition has been the object. The first is that this regime, good or bad, ruinous or fruitful, does not really exist as yet; that it is established nowhere except in a partial and most incomplete manner.

This first observation has no sense. Competition kills competition, as we said at the outset; this aphorism may be taken for a definition. How, then, could competition ever be complete? Moreover, though it should be admitted that competition does not yet exist in its integrity, that would simply prove that competition does not act with all the power of elimination that there is in it; but that will not change at all its contradictory nature. What need have we to wait thirty centuries longer to find out that, the more competition develops, the more it tends to reduce the number of competitors?

The second is that the picture drawn of it is unfaithful; and that sufficient heed is not paid to the extension which the general welfare has undergone, including even that of the laboring classes.

If some socialists fail to recognize the useful side of competition, you on your side make no mention of its pernicious effects. The testimony of your opponents coming to complete your own, competition is shown in the fullest light, and from a double falsehood we get the truth as a result. As for the gravity of the evil, we shall see directly what to think about that.

The third is that the evil experienced by the laboring classes is not referred to its real causes.

If there are other causes of poverty than competition, does that prevent it from contributing its share? Though only one manufacturer a year were ruined by competition, if it were admitted that this ruin is the necessary effect of the principle, competition, as a principle, would have to be rejected.

The fourth is that the principal means proposed for obviating it would be inexpedient in the extreme.

Possibly: but from this I conclude that the inadequacy of the remedies proposed imposes a new duty upon you, — precisely that of seeking the most expedient means of preventing the evil of competition.

The fifth, finally, is that the real remedies, in so far as it is possible to remedy the evil by legislation, would be found precisely in the regime which is accused of having produced it, — that is, in a more and more real regime of liberty and competition.

Well! I am willing. The remedy for competition, in your opinion, is to make competition universal. But, in order that competition may be universal, it is necessary to procure for all the means of competing; it is necessary to destroy or modify the predominance of capital over labor, to change the relations between employer and workman, to solve, in a word, the antinomy of division and that of machinery; it is necessary to ORGANIZE LABOR: can you give this solution?

M. Dunoyer then develops, with a courage worthy of a better cause, his own utopia of universal competition: it is a labyrinth in which the author stumbles and contradicts himself at every step.

"Competition," says M. Dunoyer, "meets a multitude of obstacles."

In fact, it meets so many and such powerful ones that it becomes impossible itself. For how is triumph possible over obstacles inherent in the constitution of society and consequently inseparable from competition itself?

In addition to the public services, there is a certain number of professions the practice of which the government has seen fit to more or less exclusively reserve; there is a larger number of which legislation has given a monopoly to a restricted number of individuals. Those which are abandoned to competition are subjected to formalities and restrictions, to numberless barriers, which keep many from approaching, and in these consequently competition is far from being unlimited. In short, there are few which are not submitted to varied taxes, necessary doubtless, etc.

What does all this mean? M. Dunoyer doubtless does not intend that society shall dispense with government, administration, police, taxes, universities, in a word, with everything that constitutes a society. Then, inasmuch as society necessarily implies exceptions to competition, the hypothesis of universal competition is chimerical, and we are back again under the regime of caprice, — a result foretold in the definition of competition. Is there anything serious in this reasoning of M. Dunoyer?

Formerly the masters of the science began by putting far away from them every preconceived idea, and devoted themselves to tracing facts back to general laws, without ever altering or concealing them. The researches of Adam Smith, considering the time of their appearance, are a marvel of sagacity and lofty reasoning. The economic picture presented by Quesnay, wholly unintelligible as it appears, gives evidence of a profound sentiment of the general synthesis. The introduction to J. B. Say's great treatise dwells exclusively upon the scientific characteristics of political economy, and in every line is to be seen how much the author felt the need of absolute ideas. The economists of the last century certainly did not constitute the science, but they sought this constitution ardently and honestly.

How far we are today from these noble thoughts! No longer do they seek a science; they defend the interests of dynasty and caste. The more powerless routine becomes, the more stubbornly they adhere to it; they make use of the most venerated names to stamp abnormal phenomena with a quality of authenticity which they lack; they tax accusing facts with heresy; they calumniate the tendencies of the century; and nothing irritates an economist so much as to pretend to reason with him.

"The peculiar characteristic of the present time," cries M. Dunoyer, in a tone of keen discontent, "is the agitation of all classes; their anxiety, their inability to ever stop at anything and be contented; the infernal labor performed upon the less fortunate that they may become more and more discontented in proportion to the increased efforts of society to make their lot really less pitiful."

Indeed! Because the socialists goad political economy, they are incarnate devils! Can there be anything more impious, in fact, than to teach the proletaire that he is wronged in his labor and his wages, and that, in the surroundings in which he lives, his poverty is irremediable?

M. Reybaud repeats, with greater emphasis, the wail of his master, M. Dunoyer: one would think them the two seraphim of Isaiah chanting a Sanctus to competition. In June, 1844, at the time when he published the fourth edition of his "Contemporary Reformers," M. Reybaud wrote, in the bitterness of his soul:

To socialists we owe the organization of labor, the right to labor; they are the promoters of the regime of surveillance . . . The legislative chambers on either side of the channel are gradually succumbing to their influence . . . Thus utopia is gaining ground . . .

And M. Reybaud more and more deplores the secret influence of socialism on the best minds, and stigmatizes — see the malice! — the unperceived contagion with which even those who have broken lances against socialism allow themselves to be inoculated. Then he announces, as a last act of his high justice against the wicked, the approaching publication, under the title of "Laws of Labor," of a work in which he will prove (unless some new evolution takes place in his ideas) that the laws of labor have nothing in common, either with the right to labor or with the organization of labor, and that the best of reforms is laissez-faire.

"Moreover," adds M. Reybaud, "the tendency of political economy is no longer to theory, but to practice. The abstract portions of the science seem henceforth fixed. The controversy over definitions is exhausted, or nearly so. The works of the great economists on value, capital, supply and demand, wages, taxes, machinery, farm-rent, increase of population, over-accumulation of products, markets, banks, monopolies, etc., seem to have set the limit of dogmatic researches, and form a body of doctrine beyond which there is little to hope."

Facility of speech, impotence in argument, — such would have been the conclusion of Montesquieu upon this strange panegyric of the founders of social economy. THE SCIENCE IS COMPLETE! M. Reybaud makes oath to it; and what he proclaims with so much authority is repeated at the Academy, in the professors' chairs, in the councils of State, in the legislative halls; it is published in the journals; the king is made to say it in his New Year's addresses; and before the courts the cases of claimants are decided accordingly.

THE SCIENCE IS COMPLETE! What fools we are, then, socialists, to hunt for daylight at noonday, and to protest, with our lanterns in our hands, against the brilliancy of these solar rays!

But, gentlemen, it is with sincere regret and profound distrust of myself that I find myself forced to ask you for further light. If you cannot cure our ills, give us at least kind words, give us evidence, give us resignation.

"It is obvious," says M. Dunoyer, "that wealth is infinitely better distributed in our day than it ever has been."

"The equilibrium of pains and pleasures," promptly continues M. Reybaud, "ever tends to restore itself on earth."

What, then! What do you say? Wealth better distributed, equilibrium restored! Explain yourselves, please, as to this better distribution. Is equality coming, or inequality going? Is solidarity becoming closer, or competition diminishing? I will not quit you until you have answered me, non missura cutem. . . For, whatever the cause of the restoration of equilibrium and of the better distribution which you point out, I embrace it with ardor, and will follow it to its last consequences. Before 1830 — I select the date at random — wealth was not so well distributed: how so? Today, in your opinion, it is better distributed: why? You see what I am coming at: distribution being not yet perfectly equitable and the equilibrium not absolutely perfect, I ask, on the one hand, what obstacle it is that disturbs the equilibrium, and, on the other, by virtue of what principle humanity continually passes from the greater to the less evil and from the good to the better? For, in fact, this secret principle of amelioration can be neither competition, nor machinery, nor division of labor, nor supply and demand: all these principles are but levers which by turns cause value to oscillate, as the Academy of Moral Sciences has very clearly seen. What, then, is the sovereign law of well-being? What is this rule, this measure, this criterion of progress, the violation of which is the perpetual cause of poverty? Speak, and quit your haranguing.

Wealth is better distributed, you say. Show us your proofs.

M. Dunoyer:

According to official documents, taxes are assessed on scarcely less than eleven million separate parcels of landed property. The number of proprietors by whom these taxes are paid is estimated at six millions; so that, assuming four individuals to a family, there must be no less than twenty-four million inhabitants out of thirty-four who participate in the ownership of the soil.

Then, according to the most favorable figures, there must be ten million proletaires in France, or nearly one-third of the population. Now, what have you to say to that? Add to these ten millions half of the twenty-four others, whose property, burdened with mortgages, parcelled out, impoverished, wretched, gives them no support, and still you will not have the number of individuals whose living is precarious.

The number of twenty-four million proprietors perceptibly tends to increase.

I maintain that it perceptibly tends to decrease. Who is the real proprietor, in your opinion, — the nominal holder, assessed, taxed, pawned, mortgaged, or the creditor who collects the rent? Jewish and Swiss money-lenders are today the real proprietors of Alsace; and proof of their excellent judgment is to be found in the fact that they have no thought of acquiring landed estates: they prefer to invest their capital.

To the landed proprietors must be added about fifteen hundred thousand holders of patents and licenses, or, assuming four persons to a family, six million individuals interested as leaders in industrial enterprises.

But, in the first place, a great number of these licensed individuals are landed proprietors, and you count them twice. Further, it may be safely said that, of the whole number of licensed manufacturers and merchants, a fourth at most realize profits, another fourth hold their own, and the rest are constantly running behind in their business. Take, then, half at most of the six million so-called leaders in enterprises, which we will add to the very problematical twelve million landed proprietors, and we shall attain a total of fifteen million Frenchmen in a position, by their education, their industry, their capital, their credit, their property, to engage in competition. For the rest of the nation, or nineteen million souls, competition, like Henri IV.'s pullet in the pot, is a dish which they produce for the class which can pay for it, but which they never touch.

Another difficulty. These nineteen million men, within whose reach competition never comes, are hirelings of the competitors. In the same way formerly the serfs fought for the lords, but without being able themselves to carry a banner or put an army on foot. Now, if competition cannot by itself become the common condition, why should not those for whom it offers nothing but perils, exact guarantees from the barons whom they serve? And if these guarantees can not be denied them, how could they be other than barriers to competition, just as the truce of God, invented by the bishops, was a barrier to feudal wars? By the constitution of society, I said a little while ago, competition is an exceptional matter, a privilege; now I ask how it is possible for this privilege to coexist with equality of rights?

And think you, when I demand for consumers and wage-receivers guarantees against competition, that it is a socialist's dream? Listen to two of your most illustrious confreres, whom you will not accuse of performing an infernal work.

M. Rossi (Volume I, Lecture 16) recognizes in the State the right to regulate labor, when the danger is too great and the guarantees insufficient, which means always. For the legislator must secure public order by principles and laws: he does not wait for unforeseen facts to arise in order that he may drive them back with an arbitrary hand. Elsewhere (Volume II, pp. 73–77) the same professor points out, as consequences of exaggerated competition, the incessant formation of a financial and landed aristocracy and the approaching downfall of small holders, and he raises the cry of alarm. M. Blanqui, on his side, declares that the organization of labor is recognized by economic science as in the order of the day (he has since retracted the statement), urges the participation of workers in the profits and the advent of the collective laborer, and thunders continually against the monopolies, prohibitions, and tyranny of capital. Qui habet aures audiendi audiat! M. Rossi, as a writer on criminal law, decrees against the robberies of competition; M. Blanqui, as examining magistrate, proclaims the guilty parties: it is the counterpart of the duet sung just now by MM. Reybaud and Dunoyer. When the latter cry Hosanna, the former respond, like the Fathers in the Councils, Anathema.

But, it will be said, MM. Blanqui and Rossi mean to strike only the abuses of competition; they have taken care not to proscribe the principle, and in that they are thoroughly in accord with MM. Reybaud and Dunoyer.

I protest against this distinction, in the interest of the fame of the two professors.

In fact, abuse has invaded everything, and the exception has become the rule. When M. Troplong, defending, with all the economists, the liberty of commerce, admitted that the coalition of the cab companies was one of those facts against which the legislator finds himself absolutely powerless, and which seem to contradict the sanest notions of social economy, he still had the consolation of saying to himself that such a fact was wholly exceptional, and that there was reason to believe that it would not become general. Now, this fact has become general: the most conservative jurisconsult has only to put his head out of his window to see that today absolutely everything has been monopolized through competition, — transportation (by land, rail, and water), wheat and flour, wine and brandy, wood, coal, oil, iron, fabrics, salt, chemical products, etc. It is sad for jurisprudence, that twin sister of political economy, to see its grave anticipations contradicted in less than a lustre, but it is sadder still for a great nation to be led by such poor geniuses and to glean the few ideas which sustain its life from the brushwood of their writings.

In theory we have demonstrated that competition, on its useful side, should be universal and carried to its maximum of intensity; but that, viewed on its negative side, it must be everywhere stifled, even to the last vestige. Are the economists in a position to effect this elimination? Have they foreseen the consequences, calculated the difficulties? If the answer should be affirmative, I should have the boldness to propose the following case to them for solution.

A treaty of coalition, or rather of association, — for the courts would be greatly embarrassed to define either term, — has just united in one company all the coal mines in the basin of the Loire. On complaint of the municipalities of Lyons and Saint Etienne, the ministry has appointed a commission charged with examining the character and tendencies of this frightful society. Well, I ask, what can the intervention of power, with the assistance of civil law and political economy, accomplish here?

They cry out against coalition. But can the proprietors of mines be prevented from associating, from reducing their general expenses and costs of exploitation, and from working their mines to better advantage by a more perfect understanding with each other? Shall they be ordered to begin their old war over again, and ruin themselves by increased expenses, waste, over-production, disorder, and decreased prices? All that is absurd.

Shall they be prevented from increasing their prices so as to recover the interest on their capital? Then let them be protected themselves against any demands for increased wages on the part of the workmen; let the law concerning joint-stock companies be reenacted; let the sale of shares be prohibited; and when all these measures shall have been taken, as the capitalist-proprietors of the basin cannot justly be forced to lose capital invested under a different condition of things, let them be indemnified.

Shall a tariff be imposed upon them? That would be a law of maximum. The State would then have to put itself in the place of the exploiters; keep the accounts of their capital, interest, and office expenses; regulate the wages of the miners, the salaries of the engineers and directors, the price of the wood employed in the extraction of the coal, the expenditure for material; and, finally, determine the normal and legitimate rate of profit. All this cannot be done by ministerial decree: a law is necessary. Will the legislator dare, for the sake of a special industry, to change the public law of the French, and put power in the place of property? Then of two things one: either commerce in coals will fall into the hands of the State, or else the State must find some means of reconciling liberty and order in carrying on the mining industry, in which case the socialists will ask that what has been executed at one point be imitated at all points.

The coalition of the Loire mines has posited the social question in terms which permit no more evasion. Either competition, — that is, monopoly and what follows; or exploitation by the State, — that is, dearness of labor and continuous impoverishment; or else, in short, a solution based upon equality, — in other words, the organization of labor, which involves the negation of political economy and the end of property.

But the economists do not proceed with this abrupt logic: they love to bargain with necessity. M. Dupin (session of the Academy of Moral and Political Sciences, June 10, 1843) expresses the opinion that, "though competition may be useful within the nation, it must be prevented between nations."

To prevent or to let alone, — such is the eternal alternative of the economists: beyond it their genius does not go. In vain is it cried out at them that it is not a question of preventing anything or of permitting everything; that what is asked of them, what society expects of them, is a reconciliation: this double idea does not enter their head.

"It is necessary," M. Dunoyer replies to M. Dupin, "to distinguish theory from practice."

My God! everybody knows that M. Dunoyer, inflexible as to principles in his works, is very accommodating as to practice in the Council of State. But let him condescend to once ask himself this question: Why am I obliged to continually distinguish practice from theory? Why do they not harmonize?

M. Blanqui, as a lover of peace and harmony, supports the learned M. Dunoyer, — that is, theory. Nevertheless he thinks, with M. Dupin, — that is, with practice, — that competition is not exempt from reproach. So afraid is M. Blanqui of calumniating and stirring up the fire!

M. Dupin is obstinate in his opinion. He cites, as evils for which competition is responsible, fraud, sale by false weights, the exploitation of children. All doubtless in order to prove that competition within the nation may be useful!

M. Passy, with his usual logic, observes that there will always be dishonest people who, etc. Accuse human nature, he cries, but not competition.

At the very outset M. Passy's logic wanders from the question. Competition is reproached with the inconveniences which result from its nature, not with the frauds of which it is the occasion or pretext. A manufacturer finds a way of replacing a workman who costs him three francs a day by a woman to whom he gives but one franc. This expedient is the only one by which he can meet a falling market and keep his establishment in motion. Soon to the working women he will add children. Then, forced by the necessities of war, he will gradually reduce wages and add to the hours of labor. Where is the guilty party here? This argument may be turned about in a hundred ways and applied to all industries without furnishing any ground for accusing human nature.

M. Passy himself is obliged to admit it when he adds: "As for the compulsory labor of children, the fault is on the parents." Exactly. And the fault of the parents on whom?

"In Ireland," continues this orator, "there is no competition, and yet poverty is extreme."

On this point M. Passy's ordinary logic has been betrayed by an extraordinary lack of memory. In Ireland there is a complete, universal monopoly of the land, and unlimited, desperate competition for farms. Competition-monopoly are the two balls which unhappy Ireland drags, one after each foot.

When the economists are tired of accusing human nature, the greed of parents, and the turbulence of radicals, they find delectation in picturing the felicity of the proletariat. But there again they cannot agree with each other or with themselves; and nothing better depicts the anarchy of competition than the disorder of their ideas.

Today the wife of the workingman dresses in elegant robes which in a previous century great ladies would not have disdained. — M. Chevalier: Lecture 4.

And this is the same M. Chevalier who, according to his own calculation, estimates that the total national income would give thirteen cents a day to each individual. Some economists even reduce this figure to eleven cents. Now, as all that goes to make up the large fortunes must come out of this sum, we may accept the estimate of M. de Morogues that the daily income of half the French people does not exceed five cents each.

"But," continues M. Chevalier, with mystical exaltation, "does not happiness consist in the harmony of desires and enjoyments, in the balance of needs and satisfactions? Does it not consist in a certain condition of soul, the conditions of which it is not the function of political economy to prevent, and which it is not its mission to engender? This is the work of religion and philosophy."

Economist, Horace would say to M: Chevalier, if he were living at the present day, attend simply to my income, and leave me to take care of my soul: Det vitam, det opes; oequum mi animum ipse parabo.

M. Dunoyer again has the floor:

It would be easy, in many cities, on holidays, to confound the working class with the bourgeois class [why are there two classes?], so fine is the dress of the former. No less has been the progress in nourishment. Food is at once more abundant, more substantial, and more varied. Bread is better everywhere. Meat, soup, white bread, have become, in many factory towns, infinitely more common than they used to be. In short, the average duration of life has been raised from thirty-five years to forty.

Farther on M. Dunoyer gives a picture of English fortunes according to Marshall. It appears from this picture that in England two million five hundred thousand families have an income of only two hundred and forty dollars. Now, in England an income of two hundred and forty dollars corresponds to an income of one hundred and forty-six dollars in our country, which, divided between four persons, gives each thirty-six dollars and a half, or ten cents a day. That is not far from the thirteen cents which M. Chevalier allows to each individual in France: the difference in favor of the latter arises from the fact that, the progress of wealth being less advanced in France, poverty is likewise less. What must one think of the economists' luxuriant descriptions or of their figures?

"Pauperism has increased to such an extent in England," confesses M. Blanqui, "that the English government has had to seek a refuge in those frightful work-houses". . .

As a matter of fact, those pretended work-houses, where the work consists in ridiculous and fruitless occupations, are, whatever may be said, simply torture-houses. For to a reasonable being there is no torture like that of turning a mill without grain and without flour, with the sole purpose of avoiding rest, without thereby escaping idleness.

"This organization [the organization of competition]," continues M. Blanqui, "tends to make all the profits of labor pass into the hands of capital. . . It is at Reims, at Mulhouse, at Saint-Quentin, as at Manchester, at Leeds, at Spitalfields, that the existence of the workers is most precarious". . .

Then follows a frightful picture of the misery of the work-ers. Men, women, children, young girls, pass before you, starved, blanched, ragged, wan, and wild. The description ends with this stroke:

The workers in the mechanical industries can no longer supply recruits for the army.

It would seem that these do not derive much benefit from M. Dunoyer's white bread and soup.

M. Villerme regards the licentiousness of young working girls as inevitable. Concubinage is their customary status; they are entirely subsidized by employers, clerks, and students. Although as a general thing marriage is more attractive to the people than to the bourgeoisie, there are many proletaires, Malthusians without knowing it, who fear the family and go with the current. Thus, as workingmen are flesh for cannon, workingwomen are flesh for prostitution: that explains the elegant dressing on Sunday. After all, why should these young women be expected to be more virtuous than their mistresses?

M. Buret, crowned by the Academy:

I affirm that the working class is abandoned body and soul to the good pleasure of industry.

The same writer says elsewhere:

The feeblest efforts of speculation may cause the price of bread to vary a cent a pound and more: which represents $124,100 for thirty-four million men.

I may remark, in passing, that the much-lamented Buret regarded the idea of the existence of monopolists as a popular prejudice. Well, sophist! monopolist or speculator, what matters the name, if you admit the thing?

Such quotations would fill volumes. But the object of this treatise is not to set forth the contradictions of the economists and to wage fruitless war upon persons. Our object is loftier and worthier: it is to unfold the System of Economical Contradictions, which is quite a different matter. Therefore we will end this sad review here; and, before concluding, we will throw a glance at the various means proposed whereby to remedy the inconveniences of competition.

3. — Remedies against competition.

Can competition in labor be abolished?

It would be as well worth while to ask if personality, liberty, individual responsibility can be suppressed.

Competition, in fact, is the expression of collective activity; just as wages, considered in its highest acceptation, is the expression of the merit and demerit, in a word, the responsibility, of the laborer. It is vain to declaim and revolt against these two essential forms of liberty and discipline in labor. Without a theory of wages there is no distribution, no justice; without an organization of competition there is no social guarantee, consequently no solidarity.

The socialists have confounded two essentially distinct things when, contrasting the union of the domestic hearth with industrial competition, they have asked themselves if society could not be constituted precisely like a great family all of whose members would be bound by ties of blood, and not as a sort of coalition in which each is held back by the law of his own interests.

The family is not, if I may venture to so speak, the type, the organic molecule, of society. In the family, as M. de Bonald has very well observed, there exists but one moral being, one mind, one soul, I had almost said, with the Bible, one flesh. The family is the type and the cradle of monarchy and the patriciate: in it resides and is preserved the idea of authority and sovereignty, which is being obliterated more and more in the State. It was on the model of the family that all the ancient and feudal societies were organized, and it is precisely against this old patriarchal constitution that modern democracy protests and revolts.

The constitutive unit of society is the workshop.

Now, the workshop necessarily implies an interest as a body and private interests, a collective person and individuals. Hence a system of relations unknown in the family, among which the opposition of the collective will, represented by the employer, and individual wills, represented by the wage-receivers, figures in the front rank. Then come the relations from shop to shop, from capital to capital, — in other words, competition and association. For competition and association are supported by each other; they do not exist independently; very far from excluding each other, they are not even divergent. Whoever says competition already supposes a common object; competition, then, is not egoism, and the most deplorable error of socialism consists in having regarded it as the subversion of society.

Therefore there can be no question here of destroying competition, as impossible as to destroy liberty; the problem is to find its equilibrium, I would willingly say its police. For every force, every form of spontaneity, whether individual or collective, must receive its determination: in this respect it is the same with competition as with intelligence and liberty. How, then, will competition be harmoniously determined in society?

We have heard the reply of M. Dunoyer, speaking for political economy: Competition must be determined by itself. In other words, according to M. Dunoyer and all the economists, the remedy for the inconveniences of competition is more competition; and, since political economy is the theory of property, of the absolute right of use and abuse, it is clear that political economy has no other answer to make. Now, this is as if it should be pretended that the education of liberty is effected by liberty, the instruction of the mind by the mind, the determination of value by value, all of which propositions are evidently tautological and absurd.

And, in fact, to confine ourselves to the subject under discussion, it is obvious that competition, practised for itself and with no other object than to maintain a vague and discordant independence, can end in nothing, and that its oscillations are eternal. In competition the struggling elements are capital, machinery, processes, talent, and experience, — that is, capital again; victory is assured to the heaviest battalions. If, then, competition is practised only to the advantage of private interests, and if its social effects have been neither determined by science nor reserved by the State, there will be in competition, as in democracy, a continual tendency from civil war to oligarchy, from oligarchy to despotism, and then dissolution and return to civil war, without end and without rest. That is why competition, abandoned to itself, can never arrive at its own constitution: like value, it needs a superior principle to socialize and define it. These facts are henceforth well enough established to warrant us in considering them above criticism, and to excuse us from returning to them. Political economy, so far as the police of competition is concerned, having no means but competition itself, and unable to have any other, is shown to be powerless.

It remains now to inquire what solution socialism contem-plates. A single example will give the measure of its means, and will permit us to come to general conclusions regarding it.

Of all modern socialists M. Louis Blanc, perhaps, by his remarkable talent, has been most successful in calling public attention to his writings. In his "Organization of Labor," after having traced back the problem of association to a single point, competition, he unhesitatingly pronounces in favor of its abolition. From this we may judge to what an extent this writer, generally so cautious, is deceived as to the value of political economy and the range of socialism. On the one hand, M. Blanc, receiving his ideas ready made from I know not what source, giving everything to his century and nothing to history, rejects absolutely, in substance and in form, political economy, and deprives himself of the very materials of organization; on the other, he attributes to tendencies revived from all past epochs, which he takes for new, a reality which they do not possess, and misconceives the nature of socialism, which is exclusively critical. M. Blanc, therefore, has given us the spectacle of a vivid imagination ready to confront an impossibility; he has believed in the divination of genius; but he must have perceived that science does not improvise itself, and that, be one's name Adolphe Boyer, Louis Blanc, or J. J. Rousseau, provided there is nothing in experience, there is nothing in the mind.

M. Blanc begins with this declaration:

We cannot understand those who have imagined I know not what mysterious coupling of two opposite principles. To graft association upon competition is a poor idea: it is to substitute hermaphrodites for eunuchs.

These three lines M. Blanc will always have reason to regret. They prove that, when he published the fourth edition of his book, he was as little advanced in logic as in political economy, and that he reasoned about both as a blind man would reason about colors. Hermaphrodism, in politics, consists precisely in exclusion, because exclusion always restores, in some form or other and in the same degree, the idea excluded; and M. Blanc would be greatly surprised were he to be shown, by his continual mixture in his book of the most contrary principles, — authority and right, property and communism, aristocracy and equality, labor and capital, reward and sacrifice, liberty and dictatorship, free inquiry and religious faith, — that the real hermaphrodite, the double-sexed publicist, is himself. M. Blanc, placed on the borders of democracy and socialism, one degree lower than the Republic, two degrees beneath M. Barrot, three beneath M. Thiers, is also, whatever he may say and whatever he may do, a descendant through four generations from M. Guizot, a doctrinaire.

"Certainly," cries M. Blanc, "we are not of those who anathematize the principle of authority. This principle we have a thousand times had occasion to defend against attacks as dangerous as absurd. We know that, when organized force exists nowhere in a society, despotism exists everywhere."

Thus, according to M. Blanc, the remedy for competition, or rather, the means of abolishing it, consists in the intervention of authority, in the substitution of the State for individual liberty: it is the inverse of the system of the economists.

I should dislike to have M. Blanc, whose social tendencies are well known, accuse me of making impolitic war upon him in refuting him. I do justice to M. Blanc's generous intentions; I love and I read his works, and I am especially thankful to him for the service he has rendered in revealing, in his "History of Ten Years," the hopeless poverty of his party. But no one can consent to seem a dupe or an imbecile: now, putting personality entirely aside, what can there be in common between socialism, that universal protest, and the hotch-potch of old prejudices which make up M. Blanc's republic? M. Blanc is never tired of appealing to authority, and socialism loudly declares itself anarchistic; M. Blanc places power above society, and socialism tends to subordinate it to society; M. Blanc makes social life descend from above, and socialism maintains that it springs up and grows from below; M. Blanc runs after politics, and socialism is in quest of science. No more hypocrisy, let me say to M. Blanc: you desire neither Catholicism nor monarchy nor nobility, but you must have a God, a religion, a dictatorship, a censorship, a hierarchy, distinctions, and ranks. For my part, I deny your God, your authority, your sovereignty, your judicial State, and all your representative mystifications; I want neither Robespierre's censer nor Marat's rod; and, rather than submit to your androgynous democracy, I would support the status quo. For sixteen years your party has resisted progress and blocked opinion; for sixteen years it has shown its despotic origin by following in the wake of power at the extremity of the left centre: it is time for it to abdicate or undergo a metamorphosis. Implacable theorists of authority, what then do you propose which the government upon which you make war cannot accomplish in a fashion more tolerable than yours?

M. Blanc's SYSTEM may be summarized in three points:

1. To give power a great force of initiative, — that is, in plain English, to make absolutism omnipotent in order to realize a utopia.

2. To establish public workshops, and supply them with capital, at the State's expense.

3. To extinguish private industry by the competition of national industry.

And that is all.

Has M. Blanc touched the problem of value, which involves in itself alone all others? He does not even suspect its existence. Has he given a theory of distribution? No. Has he solved the antinomy of the division of labor, perpetual cause of the workingman's ignorance, immorality, and poverty? No. Has he caused the contradiction of machinery and wages to disappear, and reconciled the rights of association with those of liberty? On the contrary, M. Blanc consecrates this contradiction. Under the despotic protection of the State, he admits in principle the inequality of ranks and wages, adding thereto, as compensation, the ballot. Are not workingmen who vote their regulations and elect their leaders free? It may very likely happen that these voting workingmen will admit no command or difference of pay among them: then, as nothing will have been provided for the satisfaction of industrial capacities, while maintaining political equality, dissolution will penetrate into the workshop, and, in the absence of police intervention, each will return to his own affairs. These fears seem to M. Blanc neither serious nor well-founded: he awaits the test calmly, very sure that society will not go out of his way to contradict him.

And such complex and intricate questions as those of taxation, credit, international trade, property, heredity, — has M. Blanc fathomed them? Has he solved the problem of population? No, no, no, a thousand times no: when M. Blanc cannot solve a difficulty, he eliminates it. Regarding population, he says:

As only poverty is prolific, and as the social workshop will cause poverty to disappear, there is no reason for giving it any thought.

In vain does M. de Sismondi, supported by universal ex-perience, cry out to him:

We have no confidence in those who exercise delegated powers. We believe that any corporation will do its business worse than those who are animated by individual interest; that on the part of the directors there will be negligence, display, waste, favoritism, fear of compromise, all the faults, in short, to be noticed in the administration of the public wealth as contrasted with private wealth. We believe, further, that in an assembly of stockholders will be found only carelessness, caprice, negligence, and that a mercantile enterprise would be constantly compromised and soon ruined, if it were dependent upon a deliberative commercial assembly.

M. Blanc hears nothing; he drowns all other sounds with his own sonorous phrases; private interest he replaces by devotion to the public welfare; for competition he substitutes emulation and rewards. After having posited industrial hierarchy as a principle, it being a necessary consequence of his faith in God, authority, and genius, he abandons himself to mystic powers, idols of his heart and his imagination.

Thus M. Blanc begins by a coup d'État, or rather, according to his original expression, by an application of the force of initiative which he gives to power; and he levies an extraordinary tax upon the rich in order to supply the proletariat with capital. M. Blanc's logic is very simple, — it is that of the Republic: power can accomplish what the people want, and what the people want is right. A singular fashion of reforming society, this of repressing its most spontaneous tendencies, denying its most authentic manifestations, and, instead of generalizing comfort by the regular development of traditions, displacing labor and income! But, in truth, what is the good of these disguises? Why so much beating about the bush? Was it not simpler to adopt the agrarian law straightway? Could not power, by virtue of its force of initiative, at once declare all capital and tools the property of the State, save an indemnity to be granted to the present holders as a transitional measure? By means of this peremptory, but frank and sincere, policy, the economic field would have been cleared away; it would not have cost utopia more, and M. Blanc could then have proceeded at his ease, and without any hindrance, to the organization of society.

But what do I say? organize! The whole organic work of M. Blanc consists in this great act of expropriation, or substitution, if you prefer: industry once displaced and republicanized and the great monopoly established, M. Blanc does not doubt that production will go on exactly as one would wish; he does not conceive it possible that any one can raise even a single difficulty in the way of what he calls his system. And, in fact, what objection can be offered to a conception so radically null, so intangible as that of M. Blanc? The most curious part of his book is in the select collection which he has made of objections proposed by certain incredulous persons, which he answers, as may be imagined, triumphantly. These critics had not seen that, in discussing M. Blanc's system, they were arguing about the dimensions, weight, and form of a mathematical point. Now, as it has happened, the controversy maintained by M. Blanc has taught him more than his own meditations had done; and one can see that, if the objections had continued, he would have ended by discovering what he thought he had invented, — the organization of labor.

But, in fine, has the aim, however narrow, which M. Blanc pursued, — namely, the abolition of competition and the guarantee of success to an enterprise patronized and backed by the State, — been attained? On this subject I will quote the reflections of a talented economist, M. Joseph Garnier, to whose words I will permit myself to add a few comments.

The government, according to M. Blanc, would choose moral workmen, and would give them good wages.

So M. Blanc must have men made expressly for him: he does not flatter himself that he can act on any sort of temperaments. As for wages, M. Blanc promises that they shall be good; that is easier than to define their measure.

M. Blanc admits by his hypothesis that these workshops would yield a net product, and, further, would compete so successfully with private industry that the latter would change into national workshops.

How could that be, if the cost of the national workshops is higher than that of the free workshops? I have shown in the third chapter that three hundred workmen in a mill do not produce for their employer, among them all, a regular net income of twenty thousand francs, and that these twenty thousand francs, distributed among the three hundred laborers, would add but eighteen centimes a day to their income. Now, this is true of all industries. How will the national workshop, which owes its workmen good wages, make up this deficit? By emulation, says M. Blanc.

M. Blanc points with extreme complacency to the Leclaire establishment, a society of house-painters doing a very successful business, which he regards as a living demonstration of his system. M. Blanc might have added to this example a multitude of similar societies, which would prove quite as much as the Leclaire establishment, — that is, no more. The Leclaire establishment is a collective monopoly, supported by the great society which envelops it. Now, the question is whether entire society can become a monopoly, in M. Blanc's sense and patterned after the Leclaire establishment: I deny it positively. But a fact touching more closely the question before us, and which M. Blanc has not taken into consideration, is that it follows from the distribution accounts furnished by the Leclaire establishment that, the wages paid being much above the general average, the first thing to do in a reorganization of society would be to start up competition with the Leclaire establishment, either among its own workmen or outside.

Wages would be regulated by the government. The members of the social workshop would dispose of them as they liked, and the indisputable excellence of life in common would not be long in causing association in labor to give birth to voluntary association in pleasure.

Is M. Blanc a communist, yes or no? Let him declare himself once for all, instead of holding off; and if communism does not make him more intelligible, we shall at least know what he wants.

In reading the supplement in which M. Blanc has seen fit to combat the objections which some journals have raised, we see more clearly the incompleteness of his conception, daughter of at least three fathers, — Saint-Simonism, Fourierism, and communism, — with the aid of politics and a little, a very little, political economy.

According to his explanations, the State would be only the regulator, legislator, protector of industry, not the universal manufacturer or producer. But as he exclusively protects the social workshops to destroy private industry, he necessarily brings up in monopoly and falls back into the Saint-Simonian theory in spite of himself, at least so far as production is concerned.

M. Blanc cannot deny it: his system is directed against private industry; and with him power, by its force of initiative, tends to extinguish all individual initiative, to proscribe free labor. The coupling of contraries is odious to M. Blanc: accordingly we see that, after having sacrificed competition to association, he sacrifices to it liberty also. I am waiting for him to abolish the family.

Nevertheless hierarchy would result from the elective principle, as in Fourierism, as in constitutional politics. But these social workshops again, regulated by law, — will they be anything but corporations? What is the bond of corporations? The law. Who will make the law? The government. You suppose that it will be good? Well, experience has shown that it has never been a success in regulating the innumerable accidents of industry. You tell us that it will fix the rate of profits, the rate of wages; you hope that it will do it in such a way that laborers and capital will take refuge in the social workshop. But you do not tell us how equilibrium will be established between these workshops which will have a tendency to life in common, to the phalanstery; you do not tell us how these workshops will avoid competition within and without; how they will provide for the excess of population in relation to capital; how the manufacturing social workshops will differ from those of the fields; and many other things besides. I know well that you will answer: By the specific virtue of the law! And if your government, your State, knows not how to make it? Do you not see that you are sliding down a declivity, and that you are obliged to grasp at something similar to the existing law? It is easy to see by reading you that you are especially devoted to the invention of a power susceptible of application to your system; but I declare, after reading you carefully, that in my opinion you have as yet no clear and precise idea of what you need. What you lack, as well as all of us, is the true conception of liberty and equality, which you would not like to disown, and which you are obliged to sacrifice, whatever precautions you may take.

Unacquainted with the nature and functions of power, you have not dared to stop for a single explanation; you have not given the slightest example.

Suppose we admit that the workshops succeed as producers; there will also be commercial workshops to put products in circulation and effect exchanges. And who then will regulate the price? Again the law? In truth, I tell you, you will need a new appearance on Mount Sinai; otherwise you will never get out of your difficulties, you, your Council of State, your chamber of representatives, or your areopagus of senators.

The correctness of these reflections cannot be questioned. M. Blanc, with his organization by the State, is obliged always to end where he should have begun (so beginning, he would have been saved the trouble of writing his book), — that is, in the study of economic science. As his critic very well says: "M. Blanc has made the grave mistake of using political strategy in dealing with questions which are not amenable to such treatment"; he has tried to summon the government to a fulfillment of its obligations, and he has succeeded only in demonstrating more clearly than ever the incompatibility of socialism with haranguing and parliamentary democracy. His pamphlet, all enamelled with eloquent pages, does honor to his literary capacity: as for the philosophical value of the book, it would be absolutely the same if the author had confined himself to writing on each page, in large letters, this single phrase: I PROTEST.

To sum up:

Competition, as an economic position or phase, considered in its origin, is the necessary result of the intervention of machinery, of the establishment of the workshop, and of the theory of reduction of general costs; considered in its own significance and in its tendency, it is the mode by which collective activity manifests and exercises itself, the expression of social spontaneity, the emblem of democracy and equality, the most energetic instrument for the constitution of value, the support of association. As the essay of individual forces, it is the guarantee of their liberty, the first moment of their harmony, the form of responsibility which unites them all and makes them solidary.

But competition abandoned to itself and deprived of the direction of a superior and efficacious principle is only a vague movement, an endless oscillation of industrial power, eternally tossed about between those two equally disastrous extremes, — on the one hand, corporations and patronage, to which we have seen the workshop give birth, and, on the other, monopoly, which will be discussed in the following chapter.

Socialism, while protesting, and with reason, against this anarchical competition, has as yet proposed nothing satisfactory for its regulation, as is proved by the fact that we meet everywhere, in the utopias which have seen the light, the determination or socialization of value abandoned to arbitrary control, and all reforms ending, now in hierarchical corporation, now in State monopoly, or the tyranny of communism.

Chapter VI. Fourth Period. — Monopoly

MONOPOLY, the exclusive commerce, exploitation, or enjoyment of a thing.

Monopoly is the natural opposite of competition. This simple observation suffices, as we have remarked, to overthrow the utopias based upon the idea of abolishing competition, as if its contrary were association and fraternity. Competition is the vital force which animates the collective being: to destroy it, if such a supposition were possible, would be to kill society.

But, the moment we admit competition as a necessity, it implies the idea of monopoly, since monopoly is, as it were, the seat of each competing individuality. Accordingly the economists have demonstrated — and M. Rossi has formally admitted it — that monopoly is the form of social possession, outside of which there is no labor, no product, no exchange, no wealth. Every landed possession is a monopoly; every industrial utopia tends to establish itself as a monopoly; and the same must be said of other functions not included in these two categories.

Monopoly in itself, then, does not carry the idea of injustice; in fact, there is something in it which, pertaining to society as well as to man, legitimates it: that is the positive side of the principle which we are about to examine.

But monopoly, like competition, becomes anti-social and disastrous: how does this happen? By abuse, reply the economists. And it is to defining and repressing the abuses of monopoly that the magistrates apply themselves; it is in denouncing them that the new school of economists glories.

We shall show that the so-called abuses of monopoly are only the effects of the development, in a negative sense, of legal monopoly; that they cannot be separated from their principle without ruining this principle; consequently, that they are inaccessible to the law, and that all repression in this direction is arbitrary and unjust. So that monopoly, the constitutive principle of society and the condition of wealth, is at the same time and in the same degree a principle of spoliation and pauperism; that, the more good it is made to produce, the more evil is received from it; that without it progress comes to a standstill, and that with it labor becomes stationary and civilization disappears.

1. — Necessity of monopoly.

Thus monopoly is the inevitable end of competition, which engenders it by a continual denial of itself: this generation of monopoly is already its justification. For, since competition is inherent in society as motion is in living beings, monopoly which comes in its train, which is its object and its end, and without which competition would not have been accepted, — monopoly is and will remain legitimate as long as competition, as long as mechanical processes and industrial combinations, as long, in fact, as the division of labor and the constitution of values shall be necessities and laws.

Therefore by the single fact of its logical generation monopoly is justified. Nevertheless this justification would seem of little force and would end only in a more energetic rejection of competition than ever, if monopoly could not in turn posit itself by itself and as a principle.

In the preceding chapters we have seen that division of labor is the specification of the workman considered especially as intelligence; that the creation of machinery and the organization of the workshop express his liberty; and that, by competition, man, or intelligent liberty, enters into action. Now, monopoly is the expression of victorious liberty, the prize of the struggle, the glorification of genius; it is the strongest stimulant of all the steps in progress taken since the beginning of the world: so true is this that, as we said just now, society, which cannot exist with it, would not have been formed without it.

Where, then, does monopoly get this singular virtue, which the etymology of the word and the vulgar aspect of the thing would never lead us to suspect?

Monopoly is at bottom simply the autocracy of man over himself: it is the dictatorial right accorded by nature to every producer of using his faculties as he pleases, of giving free play to his thought in whatever direction it prefers, of speculating, in such specialty as he may please to choose, with all the power of his resources, of disposing sovereignly of the instruments which he has created and of the capital accumulated by his economy for any enterprise the risks of which he may see fit to accept on the express condition of enjoying alone the fruits of his discovery and the profits of his venture.

This right belongs so thoroughly to the essence of liberty that to deny it is to mutilate man in his body, in his soul, and in the exercise of his faculties, and society, which progresses only by the free initiative of individuals, soon lacking explorers, finds itself arrested in its onward march.

It is time to give body to all these ideas by the testimony of facts.

I know a commune where from time immemorial there had been no roads either for the clearing of lands or for communication with the outside world. During three-fourths of the year all importation or exportation of goods was prevented; a barrier of mud and marsh served as a protection at once against any invasion from without and any excursion of the inhabitants of the holy and sacred community. Six horses, in the finest weather, scarcely sufficed to move a load that any jade could easily have taken over a good road. The mayor resolved, in spite of the council, to build a road through the town. For a long time he was derided, cursed, execrated. They had got along well enough without a road up to the time of his administration: why need he spend the money of the commune and waste the time of farmers in road-duty, cartage, and compulsory service? It was to satisfy his pride that Monsieur the Mayor desired, at the expense of the poor farmers, to open such a fine avenue for his city friends who would come to visit him! In spite of everything the road was made and the peasants applauded! What a difference! they said: it used to take eight horses to carry thirty sacks to market, and we were gone three days; now we start in the morning with two horses, and are back at night. But in all these remarks nothing further was heard of the mayor. The event having justified him, they spoke of him no more: most of them, in fact, as I found out, felt a spite against him.

This mayor acted after the manner of Aristides. Suppose that, wearied by the absurd clamor, he had from the beginning proposed to his constituents to build the road at his expense, provided they would pay him toll for fifty years, each, however, remaining free to travel through the fields, as in the past: in what respect would this transaction have been fraudulent?

That is the history of society and monopolists.

Everybody is not in a position to make a present to his fellow-citizens of a road or a machine: generally the inventor, after exhausting his health and substance, expects reward. Deny then, while still scoffing at them, to Arkwright, Watt, and Jacquard the privilege of their discoveries; they will shut themselves up in order to work, and possibly will carry their secret to the grave. Deny to the settler possession of the soil which he clears, and no one will clear it.

But, they say, is that true right, social right, fraternal right? That which is excusable on emerging from primitive communism, an effect of necessity, is only a temporary expedient which must disappear in face of a fuller understanding of the rights and duties of man and society.

I recoil from no hypothesis: let us see, let us investigate. It is already a great point that the opponents confess that, during the first period of civilization, things could not have gone otherwise. It remains to ascertain whether the institutions of this period are really, as has been said, only temporary, or whether they are the result of laws immanent in society and eternal. Now, the thesis which I maintain at this moment is the more difficult because in direct opposition to the general tendency, and because I must directly overturn it myself by its contradiction.

I pray, then, that I may be told how it is possible to make appeal to the principles of sociability, fraternity, and solidarity, when society itself rejects every solidary and fraternal transaction? At the beginning of each industry, at the first gleam of a discovery, the man who invents is isolated; society abandons him and remains in the background. To put it better, this man, relatively to the idea which he has conceived and the realization of which he pursues, becomes in himself alone entire society. He has no longer any associates, no longer any collaborators, no longer any sureties; everybody shuns him: on him alone falls the responsibility; to him alone, then, the advantages of the speculation.

But, it is insisted, this is blindness on the part of society, an abandonment of its most sacred rights and interests, of the welfare of future generations; and the speculator, better informed or more fortunate, cannot fairly profit by the monopoly which universal ignorance gives into his hands.

I maintain that this conduct on the part of society is, as far as the present is concerned, an act of high prudence; and, as for the future, I shall prove that it does not lose thereby. I have already shown in the second chapter, by the solution of the antinomy of value, that the advantage of every useful discovery is incomparably less to the inventor, whatever he may do, than to society; I have carried the demonstration of this point even to mathematical accuracy. Later I shall show further that, in addition to the profit assured it by every discovery, society exercises over the privileges which it concedes, whether temporarily or perpetually, claims of several kinds, which largely palliate the excess of certain private fortunes, and the effect of which is a prompt restoration of equilibrium. But let us not anticipate.

I observe, then, that social life manifests itself in a double fashion, — preservation and development.

Development is effected by the free play of individual energies; the mass is by its nature barren, passive, and hostile to everything new. It is, if I may venture to use the comparison, the womb, sterile by itself, but to which come to deposit themselves the germs created by private activity, which, in hermaphroditic society, really performs the function of the male organ.

But society preserves itself only so far as it avoids solidarity with private speculations and leaves every innovation absolutely to the risk and peril of individuals. It would take but a few pages to contain the list of useful inventions. The enterprises that have been carried to a successful issue may be numbered; no figure would express the multitude of false ideas and imprudent ventures which every day are hatched in human brains. There is not an inventor, not a workman, who, for one sane and correct conception, has not given birth to thousands of chimeras; not an intelligence which, for one spark of reason, does not emit whirlwinds of smoke. If it were possible to divide all the products of the human reason into two parts, putting on one side those that are useful, and on the other those on which strength, thought, capital, and time have been spent in error, we should be startled by the discovery that the excess of the latter over the former is perhaps a billion per cent. What would become of society, if it had to discharge these liabilities and settle all these bankruptcies? What, in turn, would become of the responsibility and dignity of the laborer, if, secured by the social guarantee, he could, without personal risk, abandon himself to all the caprices of a delirious imagination and trifle at every moment with the existence of humanity?

Wherefore I conclude that what has been practised from the beginning will be practised to the end, and that, on this point, as on every other, if our aim is reconciliation, it is absurd to think that anything that exists can be abolished. For, the world of ideas being infinite, like nature, and men, today as ever, being subject to speculation, — that is, to error, — individuals have a constant stimulus to speculate and society a constant reason to be suspicious and cautious, wherefore monopoly never lacks material.

To avoid this dilemma what is proposed? Compensation? In the first place, compensation is impossible: all values being monopolized, where would society get the means to indemnify the monopolists? What would be its mortgage? On the other hand, compensation would be utterly useless: after all the monopolies had been compensated, it would remain to organize industry. Where is the system? Upon what is opinion settled? What problems have been solved? If the organization is to be of the hierarchical type, we reenter the system of monopoly; if of the democratic, we return to the point of departure, for the compensated industries will fall into the public domain, — that is, into competition, — and gradually will become monopolies again; if, finally, of the communistic, we shall simply have passed from one impossibility to another, for, as we shall demonstrate at the proper time, communism, like competition and monopoly, is antinomical, impossible.

In order not to involve the social wealth in an unlimited and consequently disastrous solidarity, will they content themselves with imposing rules upon the spirit of invention and enterprise? Will they establish a censorship to distinguish between men of genius and fools? That is to suppose that society knows in advance precisely that which is to be discovered. To submit the projects of schemers to an advance examination is an a priori prohibition of all movement. For, once more, relatively to the end which he has in view, there is a moment when each manufacturer represents in his own person society itself, sees better and farther than all other men combined, and frequently without being able to explain himself or make himself understood. When Copernicus, Kepler, and Galileo, Newton's predecessors, came to the point of saying to Christian society, then represented by the Church: "The Bible is mistaken; the earth revolves, and the sun is stationary," they were right against society, which, on the strength of its senses and traditions, contradicted them. Could society then have accepted solidarity with the Copernican system? So little could it do it that this system openly denied its faith, and that, pending the accord of reason and revelation, Galileo, one of the responsible inventors, underwent torture in proof of the new idea. We are more tolerant, I presume; but this very toleration proves that, while according greater liberty to genius, we do not mean to be less discreet than our ancestors. Patents rain, but without governmental guarantee. Property titles are placed in the keeping of citizens, but neither the property list nor the charter guarantee their value: it is for labor to make them valuable. And as for the scientific and other missions which the government sometimes takes a notion to entrust to penniless explorers, they are so much extra robbery and corruption.

In fact, society can guarantee to no one the capital necessary for the testing of an idea by experiment; in right, it cannot claim the results of an enterprise to which it has not subscribed: therefore monopoly is indestructible. For the rest, solidarity would be of no service: for, as each can claim for his whims the solidarity of all and would have the same right to obtain the government's signature in blank, we should soon arrive at the universal reign of caprice, — that is, purely and simply at the statu quo.

Some socialists, very unhappily inspired — I say it with all the force of my conscience — by evangelical abstractions, believe that they have solved the difficulty by these fine maxims: "Inequality of capacities proves the inequality of duties"; "You have received more from nature, give more to your brothers," and other high-sounding and touching phrases, which never fail of their effect on empty heads, but which nevertheless are as simple as anything that it is possible to imagine. The practical formula deduced from these marvellous adages is that each laborer owes all his time to society, and that society should give back to him in exchange all that is necessary to the satisfaction of his wants in proportion to the resources at its disposal.

May my communistic friends forgive me! I should be less severe upon their ideas if I were not irreversibly convinced, in my reason and in my heart, that communism, republicanism, and all the social, political, and religious utopias which disdain facts and criticism, are the greatest obstacle which progress has now to conquer. Why will they never understand that fraternity can be established only by justice; that justice alone, the condition, means, and law of liberty and fraternity, must be the object of our study; and that its determination and formula must be pursued without relaxation, even to the minutest details? Why do writers familiar with economic language forget that superiority of talents is synonymous with superiority of wants, and that, instead of expecting more from vigorous than from ordinary personalities, society should constantly look out that they do not receive more than they render, when it is already so hard for the mass of mankind to render all that it receives? Turn which way you will, you must always come back to the cash book, to the account of receipts and expenditures, the sole guarantee against large consumers as well as against small producers. The workman continually lives in advance of his production; his tendency is always to get credit contract debts and go into bankruptcy; it is perpetually necessary to remind him of Say's aphorism: Products are bought only with products.

To suppose that the laborer of great capacity will content himself, in favor of the weak, with half his wages, furnish his services gratuitously, and produce, as the people say, for the king of Prussia — that is, for that abstraction called society, the sovereign, or my brothers, — is to base society on a sentiment, I do not say beyond the reach of man, but one which, erected systematically into a principle, is only a false virtue, a dangerous hypocrisy. Charity is recommended to us as a reparation of the infirmities which afflict our fellows by accident, and, viewing it in this light, I can see that charity may be organized; I can see that, growing out of solidarity itself, it may become simply justice. But charity taken as an instrument of equality and the law of equilibrium would be the dissolution of society. Equality among men is produced by the rigorous and inflexible law of labor, the proportionality of values, the sincerity of exchanges, and the equivalence of functions, — in short, by the mathematical solution of all antagonisms.

That is why charity, the prime virtue of the Christian, the legitimate hope of the socialist, the object of all the efforts of the economist, is a social vice the moment it is made a principle of constitution and a law; that is why certain economists have been able to say that legal charity had caused more evil in society than proprietary usurpation. Man, like the society of which he is a part, has a perpetual account current with himself; all that he consumes he must produce. Such is the general rule, which no one can escape without being, ipso facto struck with dishonor or suspected of fraud. Singular idea, truly, — that of decreeing, under pretext of fraternity, the relative inferiority of the majority of men! After this beautiful declaration nothing will be left but to draw its consequences; and soon, thanks to fraternity, aristocracy will be restored.

Double the normal wages of the workman, and you invite him to idleness, humiliate his dignity, and demoralize his conscience; take away from him the legitimate price of his efforts, and you either excite his anger or exalt his pride. In either case you damage his fraternal feelings. On the contrary, make enjoyment conditional upon labor, the only way provided by nature to associate men and make them good and happy, and you go back under the law of economic distribution, products are bought with products. Communism, as I have often complained, is the very denial of society in its foundation, which is the progressive equivalence of functions and capacities. The communists, toward whom all socialism tends, do not believe in equality by nature and education; they supply it by sovereign decrees which they cannot carry out, whatever they may do. Instead of seeking justice in the harmony of facts, they take it from their feelings, calling justice everything that seems to them to be love of one's neighbor, and incessantly confounding matters of reason with those of sentiment.

Why then continually interject fraternity, charity, sacrifice, and God into the discussion of economic questions? May it not be that the utopists find it easier to expatiate upon these grand words than to seriously study social manifestations?

Fraternity! Brothers as much as you please, provided I am the big brother and you the little; provided society, our common mother, honors my primogeniture and my services by doubling my portion. You will provide for my wants, you say, in proportion to your resources. I intend, on the contrary, that such provision shall be in proportion to my labor; if not, I cease to labor.

Charity! I deny charity; it is mysticism. In vain do you talk to me of fraternity and love: I remain convinced that you love me but little, and I feel very sure that I do not love you. Your friendship is but a feint, and, if you love me, it is from self-interest. I ask all that my products cost me, and only what they cost me: why do you refuse me?

Sacrifice! I deny sacrifice; it is mysticism. Talk to me of debt and credit, the only criterion in my eyes of the just and the unjust, of good and evil in society. To each according to his works, first; and if, on occasion, I am impelled to aid you, I will do it with a good grace; but I will not be constrained. To constrain me to sacrifice is to assassinate me.

God! I know no God; mysticism again. Begin by striking this word from your remarks, if you wish me to listen to you; for three thousand years of experience have taught me that whoever talks to me of God has designs on my liberty or on my purse. How much do you owe me? How much do I owe you? That is my religion and my God.

Monopoly owes its existence both to nature and to man: it has its source at once in the profoundest depths of our conscience and in the external fact of our individualization. Just as in our body and our mind everything has its specialty and property, so our labor presents itself with a proper and specific character, which constitutes its quality and value. And as labor cannot manifest itself without material or an object for its exercise, the person necessarily attracting the thing, monopoly is established from subject to object as infallibly as duration is constituted from past to future. Bees, ants, and other animals living in society seem endowed individually only with automatism; with them soul and instinct are almost exclusively collective. That is why, among such animals, there can be no room for privilege and monopoly; why, even in their most volitional operations, they neither consult nor deliberate. But, humanity being individualized in its plurality, man becomes inevitably a monopolist, since, if not a monopolist, he is nothing; and the social problem is to find out, not how to abolish, but how to reconcile, all monopolies.

The most remarkable and the most immediate effects of monopoly are:

1. In the political order, the classification of humanity into families, tribes, cities, nations, States: this is the elementary division of humanity into groups and sub-groups of laborers, distinguished by race, language, customs, and climate. It was by monopoly that the human race took possession of the globe, as it will be by association that it will become complete sovereign thereof.

Political and civil law, as conceived by all legislators with-out exception and as formulated by jurists, born of this patriotic and national organization of societies, forms, in the series of social contradictions, a first and vast branch, the study of which by itself alone would demand four times more time than we can give it in discussing the question of industrial economy propounded by the Academy.

2. In the economic order, monopoly contributes to the increase of comfort, in the first place by adding to the general wealth through the perfecting of methods, and then by CAPITALIZING, — that is, by consolidating the conquests of labor obtained by division, machinery, and competition. From this effect of monopoly has resulted the economic fiction by which the capitalist is considered a producer and capital an agent of production; then, as a consequence of this fiction, the theory of net product and gross product.

On this point we have a few considerations to present. First let us quote J. B. Say:

The value produced is the gross product: after the costs of production have been deducted, this value is the net product.

Considering a nation as a whole, it has no net product; for, as products have no value beyond the costs of production, when these costs are cut off, the entire value of the product is cut off. National production, annual production, should always therefore be understood as gross production.

The annual revenue is the gross revenue.

The term net production is applicable only when considering the interests of one producer in opposition to those of other producers. The manager of an enterprise gets his profit from the value produced after deducting the value consumed. But what to him is value consumed, such as the purchase of a productive service, is so much income to the performer of the service. — Treatise on Political Economy: Analytical Table.

These definitions are irreproachable. Unhappily J. B. Say did not see their full bearing, and could not have foreseen that one day his immediate successor at the College of France would attack them. M. Rossi has pretended to refute the proposition of J. B. Say that to a nation net product is the same thing as gross product by this consideration, — that nations, no more than individuals of enterprise, can produce without advances, and that, if J. B. Say's formula were true, it would follow that the axiom, Ex nihilo nihil fit, is not true

Now, that is precisely what happens. Humanity, in imitation of God, produces everything from nothing, de nihilo hilum just as it is itself a product of nothing, just as its thought comes out of the void; and M. Rossi would not have made such a mistake, if, like the physiocrats, he had not confounded the products of the industrial kingdom with those of the animal, vegetable, and mineral kingdoms. Political economy begins with labor; it is developed by labor; and all that does not come from labor, falling into the domain of pure utility, — that is, into the category of things submitted to man's action, but not yet rendered exchangeable by labor, — remains radically foreign to political economy. Monopoly itself, wholly established as it is by a pure act of collective will, does not change these relations at all, since, according to history, and according to the written law, and according to economic theory, monopoly exists, or is reputed to exist, only after labor's appearance.

Say's doctrine, therefore, is unassailable. Relatively to the man of enterprise, whose specialty always supposes other manufacturers cooperating with him, profit is what remains of the value produced after deducting the values consumed, among which must be included the salary of the man of enterprise, — in other words, his wages. Relatively to society, which contains all possible specialties, net product is identical with gross product.

But there is a point the explanation of which I have vainly sought in Say and in the other economists, — to wit, how the reality and legitimacy of net product is established. For it is plain that, in order to cause the disappearance of net product, it would suffice to increase the wages of the workmen and the price of the values consumed, the selling-price remaining the same. So that, there being nothing seemingly to distinguish net product from a sum withheld in paying wages or, what amounts to the same thing, from an assessment laid upon the consumer in advance, net product has every appearance of an extortion effected by force and without the least show of right.

This difficulty has been solved in advance in our theory of the proportionality of values.

According to this theory, every exploiter of a machine, of an idea, or of capital should be considered as a man who increases with equal outlay the amount of a certain kind of products, and consequently increases the social wealth by economizing time. The principle of the legitimacy of the net product lies, then, in the processes previously in use: if the new device succeeds, there will be a surplus of values, and consequently a profit, -that is, net product; if the enterprise rests on a false basis, there will be a deficit in the gross product, and in the long run failure and bankruptcy. Even in the case — and it is the most frequent — where there is no innovation on the part of the man of enterprise, the rule of net product remains applicable, for the success of an industry depends upon the way in which it is carried on. Now, it being in accordance with the nature of monopoly that the risk and peril of every enterprise should be taken by the initiator, it follows that the net product belongs to him by the most sacred title recognized among men, — labor and intelligence.

It is useless to recall the fact that the net product is often exaggerated, either by fraudulently secured reductions of wages or in some other way. These are abuses which proceed, not from the principle, but from human cupidity, and which remain outside the domain of the theory. For the rest, I have shown, in discussing the constitution of value (Chapter II, section 2): 1, how the net product can never exceed the difference resulting from inequality of the means of production; 2, how the profit which society reaps from each new invention is incomparably greater than that of its originator. As these points have been exhausted once for all, I will not go over them again; I will simply remark that, by industrial progress, the net product of the ingenious tends steadily to decrease, while, on the other hand, their comfort increases, as the concentric layers which make up the trunk of a tree become thinner as the tree grows and as they are farther removed from the centre.

By the side of net product, the natural reward of the laborer, I have pointed out as one of the happiest effects of monopoly the capitalization of values, from which is born another sort of profit, — namely, interest, or the hire of capital. As for rent, although it is often confounded with interest, and although, in ordinary language, it is included with profit and interest under the common expression REVENUE, it is a different thing from interest; it is a consequence, not of monopoly, but of property; it depends on a special theory., of which we will speak in its place.

What, then, is this reality, known to all peoples, and never-theless still so badly defined, which is called interest or the price of a loan, and which gives rise to the fiction of the productivity of capital?

Everybody knows that a contractor, when he calculates his costs of production, generally divides them into three classes: 1, the values consumed and services paid for; 2, his personal salary; 3, recovery of his capital with interest. From this last class of costs is born the distinction between contractor and capitalist, although these two titles always express but one faculty, monopoly.

Thus an industrial enterprise which yields only interest on capital and nothing for net product, is an insignificant enterprise, which results only in a transformation of values without adding anything to wealth, — an enterprise, in short, which has no further reason for existence and is immediately abandoned. Why is it, then, that this interest on capital is not regarded as a sufficient supplement of net product? Why is it not itself the net product?

Here again the philosophy of the economists is wanting. To defend usury they have pretended that capital was productive, and they have changed a metaphor into a reality. The anti-proprietary socialists have had no difficulty in overturning their sophistry; and through this controversy the theory of capital has fallen into such disfavor that today, in the minds of the people, capitalist and idler are synonymous terms. Certainly it is not my intention to retract what I myself have maintained after so many others, or to rehabilitate a class of citizens which so strangely misconceives its duties: but the interests of science and of the proletariat itself oblige me to complete my first assertions and maintain true principles.

1. All production is effected with a view to consumption, — that is, to enjoyment. In society the correlative terms production and consumption, like net product and gross product, designate identically the same thing. If, then, after the laborer has realized a net product, instead of using it to increase his comfort, he should confine himself to his wages and steadily apply his surplus to new production, as so many people do who earn only to buy, production would increase indefinitely, while comfort and, reasoning from the standpoint of society, population would remain unchanged. Now, interest on capital which has been invested in an industrial enterprise and which has been gradually formed by the accumulation of net product, is a sort of compromise between the necessity of increasing production, on the one hand, and, on the other, that of increasing comfort; it is a method of reproducing and consuming the net product at the same time. That is why certain industrial societies pay their stockholders a dividend even before the enterprise has yielded anything. Life is short, success comes slowly; on the one hand labor commands, on the other man wishes to enjoy. To meet all these exigencies the net product shall be devoted to production, but meantime (inter-ea, inter-esse) — that is, while waiting for the new product — the capitalist shall enjoy.

Thus, as the amount of net product marks the progress of wealth, interest on capital, without which net product would be useless and would not even exist, marks the progress of comfort. Whatever the form of government which may be established among men; whether they live in monopoly or in communism; whether each laborer keeps his account by credit and debit, or has his labor and pleasure parcelled out to him by the community, — the law which we have just disengaged will always be fulfilled. Our interest accounts do nothing else than bear witness to it.

2. Values created by net product are classed as savings and capitalized in the most highly exchangeable form, the form which is freest and least susceptible of depreciation, — in a word, the form of specie, the only constituted value. Now, if capital leaves this state of freedom and engages itself, — that is, takes the form of machines, buildings, etc., — it will still be susceptible of exchange, but much more exposed than before to the oscillations of supply and demand. Once engaged, it cannot be disenaged without difficulty; and the sole resource of its owner will be exploitation. Exploitation alone is capable of maintaining engaged capital at its

nominal value; it may increase it, it may diminish it. Capital thus transformed is as if it had been risked in a maritime enterprise: the interest is the insurance premium paid on the capital. And this premium will be greater or less according to the scarcity or abundance of capital.

Later a distinction will also be established between the insurance premium and interest on capital, and new facts will result from this subdivision: thus the history of humanity is simply a perpetual distinction of the mind's concepts.

3. Not only does interest on capital cause the laborer to enjoy the fruit of his toil and insure his savings, but — and this is the most marvellous effect of interest — while rewarding the producer, it obliges him to labor incessantly and never stop.

If a contractor is his own capitalist, it may happen that he will content himself with a profit equal to the interest on his investment: but in that case it is certain that his industry is no longer making progress and consequently is suffering. This we see when the capitalist is distinct from the contractor: for then, after the interest is paid, the manufacturer's profit is absolutely nothing; his industry becomes a perpetual peril to him, from which it is important that he should free himself as soon as possible. For as society's comfort must develop in an indefinite progression, so the law of the producer is that he should continually realize a surplus: otherwise his existence is precarious, monotonous, fatiguing. The interest due to the capitalist by the producer therefore is like the lash of the planter cracking over the head of the sleeping slave; it is the voice of progress crying: "On, on! Toil, toil!" Man's destiny pushes him to happiness: that is why it denies him rest.

4. Finally, interest on money is the condition of capital's circulation and the chief agent of industrial solidarity. This aspect has been seized by all the economists, and we shall give it special treatment when we come to deal with credit.

I have proved, and better, I imagine, than it has ever been proved before:

That monopoly is necessary, since it is the antagonism of competition;

That it is essential to society, since without it society would never have emerged from the primeval forests and without it would rapidly go backwards;

Finally, that it is the crown of the producer, when, whether by net product or by interest on the capital which he devotes to production, it brings to the monopolist that increase of comfort which his foresight and his efforts deserve.

Shall we, then, with the economists, glorify monopoly, and consecrate it to the benefit of well-secured conservatives? I am willing, provided they in turn will admit my claims in what is to follow, as I have admitted theirs in what has preceded.

2. — The disasters in labor and the perversion of ideas caused by monopoly.

Like competition, monopoly implies a contradiction in its name and its definition. In fact, since consumption and production are identical things in society, and since selling is synonymous with buying, whoever says privilege of sale or exploitation necessarily says privilege of consumption and purchase: which ends in the denial of both. Hence a prohibition of consumption as well as of production laid by monopoly upon the wage-receivers. Competition was civil war, monopoly is the massacre of the prisoners.

These various propositions are supported by all sorts of evidence, — physical, algebraic, and metaphysical. What I shall add will be only the amplified exposition: their simple announcement demonstrates them.

Every society considered in its economic relations naturally divides itself into capitalists and laborers, employers and wage-receivers, distributed upon a scale whose degrees mark the income of each, whether this income be composed of wages, profit, interest, rent, or dividends.

From this hierarchical distribution of persons and incomes it follows that Say's principle just referred to: In a nation the net product is equal to the gross product, is no longer true, since, in consequence of monopoly, the selling price is much higher than the cost price. Now, as it is the cost price nevertheless which must pay the selling price, since a nation really has no market but itself, it follows that exchange, and consequently circulation and life, are impossible.

In France, twenty millions of laborers, engaged in all the branches of science, art, and industry, produce everything which is useful to man. Their aggregate annual wages amount, it is estimated, to twenty thousand millions; but, in consequence of the profit (net product and interest) accruing to monopolists, twenty-five thousand millions must be paid for their products. Now, as the nation has no other buyers than its wage-receivers and wage-payers, and as the latter do not pay for the former, and as the selling-price of merchandise is the same for all, it is clear that, to make circulation possible, the laborer would have to pay five for that for which he has received but four. — What is Property: Chapter IV.[1]

This, then, is the reason why wealth and poverty are correlative, inseparable, not only in idea, but in fact; this is the reason why they exist concurrently; this

---

A comparison of this passage, as given here, with the English translation of "What is Property" will show a marked variation in the language. This is explained by the fact that the author, in reproducing the passage, modified it considerably. The same is true of another quotation from the same work which will be found a few pages farther on. — Translator.

is what justifies the pretension of the wage-receiver that the rich man possesses no more than the poor man, except that of which the latter has been defrauded. After the monopolist has drawn up his account of cost, profit, and interest, the wage-paid consumer draws up his; and he finds that, though promised wages stated in the contract as one hundred, he has really been given but seventy-five. Monopoly, therefore, puts the wage-receivers into bankruptcy, and it is strictly true that it lives upon the spoils.

Six years ago I brought out this frightful contradiction: why has it not been thundered through the press? Why have no teachers of renown warned public opinion? Why have not those who demand political rights for the workingman proclaimed that he is robbed? Why have the economists kept silent? Why?

Our revolutionary democracy is so noisy only because it fears revolutions: but, by ignoring the danger which it dares not look in the face, it succeeds only in increasing it. "We resemble," says M. Blanqui, "firemen who increase the quantity of steam at the same time that they place weights on the safety-valve." Victims of monopoly, console yourselves! If your tormentors will not listen, it is because Providence has resolved to strike them: Non audierunt, says the Bible, quia Deus volebat occidere eos.

Sale being unable to fulfil the conditions of monopoly, merchandise accumulates; labor has produced in a year what its wages will not allow it to consume in less than fifteen months: hence it must remain idle one-fourth of the year. But, if it remains idle, it earns nothing: how will it ever buy? And if the monopolist cannot get rid of his products, how will his enterprise endure? Logical impossibility multiplies around the workshop; the facts which translate it are everywhere.

"The hosiers of England," says Eugene Buret, "had come to the point where they did not eat oftener than every other day. This state of things lasted eighteen months." And he cites a multitude of similar cases.

But the distressing feature in the spectacle of monopoly's effects is the sight of the unfortunate workingmen blaming each other for their misery and imagining that by uniting and supporting each other they will prevent the reduction of wages.

"The Irish," says an observer, "have given a disastrous lesson to the working classes of Great Britain. . . . They have taught our laborers the fatal secret of confining their needs to the maintenance of animal life alone, and of contenting themselves, like savages, with the minimum of the means of subsistence sufficient to prolong life. . . . Instructed by this fatal example, yielding partly to necessity, the working classes have lost that laudable pride which led them to furnish their houses properly and to multiply about them the decent conveniences which contribute to happiness."

I have never read anything more afflicting and more stupid. And what would you have these workingmen do? The Irish came: should they have been massacred? Wages were reduced: should death have been accepted in their stead? Necessity commanded, as you say yourselves. Then followed the interminable hours, disease, deformity, degradation, debasement, and all the signs of industrial slavery: all these calamities are born of monopoly and its sad predecessors, — competition, machinery, and the division of labor: and you blame the Irish!

At other times the workingmen blame their luck, and exhort themselves to patience: this is the counterpart of the thanks which they address to Providence, when labor is abundant and wages are sufficient.

I find in an article published by M. Leon Faucher, in the "Journal des Economistes" (September, 1845), that the English workingmen lost some time ago the habit of combining, which is surely a progressive step on which they are only to be congratulated, but that this improvement in the morale of the workingmen is due especially to their economic instruction.

"It is not upon the manufacturers," cried a spinner at the meeting in Bolton, "that wages depend. In periods of depression the employers, so to speak, are only the lash with which necessity is armed; and whether they will or no, they have to strike. The regulative principle is the relation of supply to demand; and the employers have not this power . . . Let us act prudently, then; let us learn to be resigned to bad luck and to make the most of good luck: by seconding the progress of our industry, we shall be useful not only to ourselves, but to the entire country." [Applause.]

Very good: well-trained, model workmen, these! What men these spinners must be that they should submit without complaint to the lash of necessity, because the regulative principle of wages is supply and demand! M. Leon Faucher adds with a charming simplicity:

English workingmen are fearless reasoners. Give them a false principle, and they will push it mathematically to absurdity, without stopping or getting frightened, as if they were marching to the triumph of the truth.

For my part, I hope that, in spite of all the efforts of economic propagandism, French workingmen will never become reasoners of such power. Supply and demand, as well as the lash of necessity, has no longer any hold upon their minds. This was the one misery that England lacked: it will not cross the channel.

By the combined effect of division, machinery, net product, and interest, monopoly extends its conquests in an increasing progression; its developments embrace agriculture as well as commerce and industry, and all sorts of products. Everybody knows the phrase of Pliny upon the landed monopoly which determined the fall of Italy, latifundia perdidere Italiam. It is this same monopoly which still impoverishes and renders uninhabitable the Roman Campagna and which forms the vicious circle in which England moves convulsively; it is this monopoly which, established by violence after a war of races, produces all the evils of Ireland, and causes so many trials to O'Connell, powerless, with all his eloquence, to lead his repealers through this labyrinth. Grand sentiments and rhetoric are the worst remedy for social evils: it would be easier for O'Connell to transport Ireland and the Irish from the North Sea to the Australian Ocean than to overthrow with the breath of his harangues the monopoly which holds them in its grasp. General communions and sermons will do no more: if the religious sentiment still alone maintains the morale of the Irish people, it is high time that a little of that profane science, so much disdained by the Church, should come to the aid of the lambs which its crook no longer protects.

The invasion of commerce and industry by monopoly is too well known to make it necessary that I should gather proofs: moreover, of what use is it to argue so much when results speak so loudly? E. Buret's description of the misery of the working-classes has something fantastic about it, which oppresses and frightens you. There are scenes in which the imagination refuses to believe, in spite of certificates and official reports. Couples all naked, hidden in the back of an unfurnished alcove, with their naked children; entire populations which no longer go to church on Sunday, because they are naked; bodies kept a week before they are buried, because the deceased has left neither a shroud in which to lay him out nor the wherewithal to pay for the coffin and the undertaker (and the bishop enjoys an income of from four to five hundred thousand francs); families heaped up over sewers, living in rooms occupied by pigs, and beginning to rot while yet alive, or dwelling in holes, like Albinoes; octogenarians sleeping naked on bare boards; and the virgin and the prostitute expiring in the same nudity: everywhere despair, consumption, hunger, hunger!.. And this people, which expiates the crimes of its masters, does not rebel! No, by the flames of Nemesis! when a people has no vengeance left, there is no longer any Providence for it.

Exterminations en masse by monopoly have not yet found their poets. Our rhymers, strangers to the things of this world, without bowels for the proletaire, continue to breathe to the moon their melancholy delights. What a subject for meditations, nevertheless, is the miseries engendered by monopoly!

It is Walter Scott who says:

Formerly, though many years since, each villager had his cow and his pig, and his yard around his house. Where a single farmer cultivates today, thirty small farmers lived formerly; so that for one individual, himself alone richer, it is true, than the thirty farmers of old times, there are now twenty-nine wretched day-laborers, without employment for their minds and arms, and whose number is too large by half. The only useful function which they fulfil is to pay, when they can, a rent of sixty shillings a year for the huts in which they dwell.[2]

A modern ballad, quoted by E. Buret, sings the solitude of monopoly:

Le rouet est silencieux dans la vallee:
C'en est fait des sentiments de famille.
Sur un peu de fumee le vieil aieul
Etend ses mains pales; et le foyer vide
Est aussi desole que son coeur.[3]

The reports made to parliament rival the novelist and the poet:

The inhabitants of Glensheil, in the neighborhood of the valley of Dundee, were formerly distinguished from all their neighbors by the superiority of their physical qualities. The men were of high stature, robust, active, and courageous; the women comely and graceful. Both sexes possessed an extraordinary taste for poetry and music. Now, alas! a long experience of poverty, prolonged privation of sufficient food and suitable clothing, have profoundly deteriorated this race, once so remarkably fine.

This is a notable instance of the inevitable degradation pointed out by us in the two chapters on division of labor and machinery. And our litterateurs busy themselves with the pretty things of the past, as if the present were not adequate to their genius! The first among them to venture on these infernal paths has created a scandal in the coterie! Cowardly parasites, vile venders of prose and verse, all worthy of the wages of Marsyas! Oh! if your punishment were to last as long as my contempt, you would be forced to believe in the eternity of hell.

Monopoly, which just now seemed to us so well founded in justice, is the more unjust because it not only makes wages illusory, but deceives the workman in the very valuation of his wages by assuming in relation to him a false title, a false capacity.

M. de Sismondi, in his "Studies of Social Economy," observes somewhere that, when a banker delivers to a merchant bank-notes in exchange for his values, far from giving credit to the merchant, he receives it, on the contrary, from him.

"This credit," adds M. de Sismondi, "is in truth so short that the merchant scarcely takes the trouble to inquire whether the banker is worthy, especially as the former asks credit instead of granting it."

This extract from Scott, as well as that from a parliamentary report cited a few paragraphs later, is here translated from the French, and presumably differs in form somewhat, therefore, from the original English. — Translator.

The spinning-wheel is silent in the valley: family feelings are at an end. Over a little smoke the aged grandsire spreads his pale hands; and the empty hearth is as desolate as his heart. — Translator.

So, according to M. de Sismondi, in the issue of bank paper, the functions of the merchant and the banker are inverted: the first is the creditor, and the second is the credited.

Something similar takes place between the monopolist and wage-receiver.

In fact, the workers, like the merchant at the bank, ask to have their labor discounted; in right, the contractor ought to furnish them bonds and security. I will explain myself.

In any exploitation, no matter of what sort, the contractor cannot legitimately claim, in addition to his own personal labor, anything but the IDEA: as for the EXECUTION, the result of the cooperation of numerous laborers, that is an effect of collective power, with which the authors, as free in their action as the chief, can produce nothing which should go to him gratuitously. Now, the question is to ascertain whether the amount of individual wages paid by the contractor is equivalent to the collective effect of which I speak: for, were it otherwise, Say's axiom, Every product is worth what it costs, would be violated.

"The capitalist," they say, "has paid the laborers their daily wages at a rate agreed upon; consequently he owes them nothing." To be accurate, it must be said that he has paid as many times one day's wage as he has employed laborers, — which is not at all the same thing. For he has paid nothing for that immense power which results from the union of laborers and the convergence and harmony of their efforts; that saving of expense, secured by their formation into a workshop; that multiplication of product, foreseen, it is true, by the capitalist, but realized by free forces. Two hundred grenadiers, working under the direction of an engineer, stood the obelisk upon its base in a few hours; do you think that one man could have accomplished the same task in two hundred days? Nevertheless, on the books of the capitalist, the amount of wages is the same in both cases, because he allots to himself the benefit of the collective power. Now, of two things one: either this is usurpation on his part, or it is error. -What is Property: Chapter III.

To properly exploit the mule-jenny, engineers, builders, clerks, brigades of workingmen and workingwomen of all sorts, have been needed. In the name of their liberty, of their security, of their future, and of the future of their children, these workmen, on engaging to work in the mill, had to make reserves; where are the letters of credit which they have delivered to the employers? Where are the guarantees which they have received? What! millions of men have sold their arms and parted with their liberty without knowing the import of the contract; they have engaged themselves upon the promise of continuous work and adequate reward; they have executed with their hands what the thought of the employers had conceived; they have become, by this collaboration, associates in the enterprise: and when monopoly, unable or unwilling to make further exchanges, suspends its manufacture and leaves these millions of laborers without bread, they are told to be resigned! By the new processes they have lost nine days of their labor out of ten; and for reward they are pointed to the lash of necessity flourished over them! Then, if they refuse to work for lower wages, they are shown that they punish themselves. If they accept the rate offered them, they lose that noble pride, that taste for decent conveniences which constitute the happiness and dignity of the workingman and entitle him to the sympathies of the rich. If they combine to secure an increase of wages, they are thrown into prison! Whereas they ought to prosecute their exploiters in the courts, on them the courts will avenge the violations of liberty of commerce! Victims of monopoly, they will suffer the penalty due to the monopolists! O justice of men, stupid courtesan, how long, under your goddess's tinsel, will you drink the blood of the slaughtered proletaire?

Monopoly has invaded everything, — land, labor, and the instruments of labor, products and the distribution of pro ducts. Political economy itself has not been able to avoid admitting it.

"You almost always find across your path," says M. Rossi, "some monopoly. There is scarcely a product that can be regarded as the pure and simple result of labor; accordingly the economic law which proportions price to cost of production is never completely realized. It is a formula which is profoundly modified by the intervention of one or another of the monopolies to which the instruments of production are subordinated. — Course in Political Economy: Volume I., page 143.

M. Rossi holds too high an office to give his language all the precision and exactness which science requires when monopoly is in question. What he so complacently calls a modification of economic formulas is but a long and odious violation of the fundamental laws of labor and exchange. It is in consequence of monopoly that in society, net product being figured over and above gross product, the collective laborer must repurchase his own product at a price higher than that which this product costs him, — which is contradictory and impossible; that the natural balance between production and consumption is destroyed; that the laborer is deceived not only in his settlements, but also as to the amount of his wages; that in his case progress in comfort is changed into an incessant progress in misery: it is by monopoly, in short, that all notions of commutative justice are perverted, and that social economy, instead of the positive science that it is, becomes a veritable utopia.

This disguise of political economy under the influence of monopoly is a fact so remarkable in the history of social ideas that we must not neglect to cite a few instances.

Thus, from the standpoint of monopoly, value is no longer that synthetic conception which serves to express the relation of a special object of utility to the sum total of wealth: monopoly estimating things, not in their relation to society, but in their relation to itself, value loses its social character, and is nothing but a vague, arbitrary, egoistic, and essentially variable thing. Starting with this principle, the monopolist extends the term product to cover all sorts of servitude, and applies the idea of capital to all the frivolous and shameful industries which his passions and vices exploit. The charms of a courtesan, says Say, are so much capital, of which the product follows the general law of values, — namely, supply and demand. Most of the works on political economy are full of such applications. But as prostitution and the state of dependence from which it emanates are condemned by morality, M. Rossi will bid us observe the further fact that political economy, after having modified its formula in consequence of the intervention of monopoly, will have to submit to a new corrective, although its conclusions are in themselves irreproachable. For, he says, political economy has nothing in common with morality: it is for us to accept it, to modify or correct its formulas, whenever our welfare, that of society, and the interests of morality call for it. How many things there are between political economy and truth!

Likewise, the theory of net product, so highly social, progressive, and conservative, has been individualized, if I may say so, by monopoly, and the principle which ought to secure society's welfare causes its ruin. The monopolist, always striving for the greatest possible net product, no longer acts as a member of society and in the interest of society; he acts with a view to his exclusive interest, whether this interest be contrary to the social interest or not. This change of perspective is the cause to which M. de Sismondi attributes the depopulation of the Roman Campagna. From the comparative researches which he has made regarding the product of the agro romano when in a state of cultivation and its product when left as pasture-land, he has found that the gross product would be twelve times larger in the former case than in the latter; but, as cultivation demands relatively a greater number of hands, he has discovered also that in the former case the net product would be less. This calculation, which did not escape the proprietors, sufficed to confirm them in the habit of leaving their lands uncultivated, and hence the Roman Campagna is uninhabited.

"All parts of the Roman States," adds M. de Sismondi, "present the same contrast between the memories of their prosperity in the Middle Ages and their present desolation. The town of Ceres, made famous by Renzo da Ceri, who defended by turns Marseilles against Charles V. and Geneva against the Duke of Savoy, is nothing but a solitude. In all the fiefs of the Orsinis and the Colonnes not a soul. From the forests which surround the pretty Lake of Vico the human race has disappeared; and the soldiers with whom the formidable prefect of Vico made Rome tremble so often in the fourteenth century have left no descendants. Castro and Ronciglione are desolated." — Studies in Political Economy.

In fact, society seeks the greatest possible gross product, and consequently the greatest possible population, because with it gross product and net product are identical. Monopoly, on the contrary, aims steadily at the greatest net product, even though able to obtain it only at the price of the extermination of the human race.

Under this same influence of monopoly, interest on capital, perverted in its idea, has become in turn a principle of death to society. As we have explained it, interest on capital is, on the one hand, the form under which the laborer enjoys his net product, while utilizing it in new creations; on the other, this interest is the material bond of solidarity between producers, viewed from the standpoint of the increase of wealth. Under the first aspect, the aggregate interest paid can never exceed the amount of the capital itself; under the second, interest allows, in addition to reimbursement, a premium as a reward of service rendered. In no case does it imply perpetuity.

But monopoly, confounding the idea of capital, which is attributable only to the creations of human industry, with that of the exploitable material which nature has given us, and which belongs to all, and favored moreover in its usurpation by the anarchical condition of a society in which possession can exist only on condition of being exclusive, sovereign, and perpetual, — monopoly has imagined and laid it down as a principle that capital, like land, animals, and plants, had in itself an activity of its own, which relieved the capitalist of the necessity of contributing anything else to exchange and of taking any part in the labors of the workshop. From this false idea of monopoly has come the Greek name of usury, tokos, as much as to say the child or the increase of capital, which caused Aristotle to perpetrate this witticism: coins beget no children. But the metaphor of the usurers has prevailed over the joke of the Stagyrite; usury, like rent, of which it is an imitation, has been declared a perpetual right; and only very lately, by a half-return to the principle, has it reproduced the idea of redemption.

Such is the meaning of the enigma which has caused so many scandals among theologians and legists, and regarding which the Christian Church has blundered twice, — first, in condemning every sort of interest, and, second, in taking the side of the economists and thus contradicting its old maxims. Usury, or the right of increase, is at once the expression and the condemnation of monopoly; it is the spoliation of labor by organized and legalized capital; of all the economic subversions it is that which most loudly accuses the old society, and whose scandalous persistence would justify an unceremonious and uncompensated dispossession of the entire capitalistic class.

Finally, monopoly, by a sort of instinct of self-preservation, has perverted even the idea of association, as something that might infringe upon it, or, to speak more accurately, has not permitted its birth.

Who could hope today to define what association among men should be? The law distinguishes two species and four varieties of civil societies, and as many commercial societies, from the simple partnership to the joint-stock company. I have read the most respectable commentaries that have been written upon all these forms of association, and I declare that I have found in them but one application of the routine practices of monopoly between two or more partners who unite their capital and their efforts against everything that produces and consumes, that invents and exchanges, that lives and dies. The sine qua non of all these societies is capital, whose presence alone constitutes them and gives them a basis; their object is monopoly, — that is, the exclusion of all other laborers and capitalists, and consequently the negation of social universality so far as persons are concerned.

Thus, according to the definition of the statute, a commercial society which should lay down as a principle the right of any stranger to become a member upon his simple request, and to straightway enjoy the rights and prerogatives of associates and even managers, would no longer be a society; the courts would officially pronounce its dissolution, its nonexistence. So, again, articles of association in which the contracting parties should stipulate no contribution of capital, but, while reserving to each the express right to compete with all, should confine themselves to a reciprocal guarantee of labor and wages, saying nothing of the branch of exploitation, or of capital, or of interest, or of profit and loss, — such articles would seem contradictory in their tenor, as destitute of purpose as of reason, and would be annulled by the judge on the complaint of the first rebellious associate. Covenants thus drawn up could give rise to no judicial action; people calling themselves the associates of everybody would be considered associates of nobody; treatises contemplating guarantee and competition between associates at the same time, without any mention of social capital and without any designation of purpose, would pass for a work of transcendental charlatanism, whose author could readily be sent to a madhouse, provided the magistrates would consent to regard him as only a lunatic.

And yet it is proved, by the most authentic testimony which history and social economy furnish, that humanity has been thrown naked and without capital upon the earth which it cultivates; consequently that it has created and is daily creating all the wealth that exists; that monopoly is only a relative view serving to designate the grade of the laborer, with certain conditions of enjoyment; and that all progress consists, while indefinitely multiplying products, in determining their proportionality, — that is, in organizing labor and comfort by division, machinery, the workshop, education, and competition. On the other hand, it is evident that all the tendencies of humanity, both in its politics and in its civil laws, are towards universalization, — that is, towards a complete transformation of the idea of society as determined by our statutes.

Whence I conclude that articles of association which should regulate, no longer the contribution of the associates, — since each associate, according to the economic theory, is supposed to possess absolutely nothing upon his entrance into society, — but the conditions of labor and exchange, and which should allow access to all who might present themselves, — I conclude, I say, that such articles of association would contain nothing that was not rational and scientific, since they would be the very expression of progress, the organic formula of labor, and since they would reveal, so to speak, humanity to itself by giving it the rudiment of its constitution.

Now, who, among the jurisconsults and economists, has ever approached even within a thousand leagues of this magnificent and yet so simple idea?

"I do not think," says M. Troplong, "that the spirit of association is called to greater destinies than those which it has accomplished in the past and up to the present time . . . ; and I confess that I have made no attempt to realize such hopes, which I believe exaggerated . . . There are well-defined limits which association should not overstep. No! association is not called upon in France to govern everything. The spontaneous impulse of the individual mind is also a living force in our nation and a cause of its originality . . .

"The idea of association is not new . . . Even among the Romans we see the commercial society appear with all its paraphernalia of monopolies, corners, collusions, combinations, piracy, and venality . . . The joint-stock company realizes the civil, commercial, and maritime law of the Middle Ages: at that epoch it was the most active instrument of labor organized in society . . . From the middle of the fourteenth century we see societies form by stock subscriptions; and up to the time of Law's discomfiture, we see their number continually increase . . . What! we marvel at the mines, factories, patents, and newspapers owned by stock companies! But two centuries ago such companies owned islands, kingdoms, almost an entire hemisphere. We proclaim it a miracle that hundreds of stock subscribers should group themselves around an enterprise; but as long ago as the fourteenth century the entire city of Florence was in similar silent partnership with a few merchants, who pushed the genius of enterprise as far as possible. Then, if our speculations are bad, if we have been rash, imprudent, or credulous, we torment the legislator with our cavilling complaints; we call upon him for prohibitions and nullifications. In our mania for regulating everything, even that which is already codified; for enchaining everything by texts reviewed, corrected, and added to; for administering everything, even the chances and reverses of commerce, — we cry out, in the midst of so many existing laws: 'There is still something to do!'"

M. Troplong believes in Providence, but surely he is not its man. He will not discover the formula of association clamored for today by minds disgusted with all the protocols of combination and rapine of which M. Troplong unrolls the picture in his commentary. M. Troplong gets impatient, and rightly, with those who wish to enchain everything in texts of laws; and he himself pretends to enchain the future in a series of fifty articles, in which the wisest mind could not discover a spark of economic science or a shadow of philosophy. In our mania, he cries, for regulating everything, EVEN THAT WHICH IS ALREADY CODIFIED!... I know nothing more delicious than this stroke, which paints at once the jurisconsult and the economist. After the Code Napoleon, take away the ladder!...

"Fortunately," M. Troplong continues, "all the projects of change so noisily brought to light in 1837 and 1838 are forgotten today. The conflict of propositions and the anarchy of reformatory opinions have led to negative results. At the same time that the reaction against speculators was effected, the common sense of the public did justice to the numerous official plans of organization, much inferior in wisdom to the existing law, much less in harmony with the usages of commerce, much less liberal, after 1830, than the conceptions of the imperial Council of State! Now order is restored in everything, and the commercial code has preserved its integrity, its excellent integrity. When commerce needs it, it finds, by the side of partnership, temporary partnership, and the joint-stock company, the free silent partnership, tempered only by the prudence of the silent partners and by the provisions of the penal code regarding swindling." — Troplong: Civil and Commercial Societies: Preface.

What a philosophy is that which rejoices in the miscarriage of reformatory endeavors, and which counts its triumphs by the negative results of the spirit of inquiry! We cannot now enter upon a more fundamental criticism of the civil and commercial societies, which have furnished M. Troplong material for two volumes. We will reserve this subject for the time when, the theory of economic contradictions being finished, we shall have found in their general equation the programme of association, which we shall then publish in contrast with the practice and conceptions of our predecessors.

A word only as to silent partnership.

One might think at first blush that this form of joint-stock company, by its expansive power and by the facility for change which it offers, could be generalized in such a way as to take in an entire nation in all its commercial and industrial relations. But the most superficial examination of the constitution of this society demonstrates very quickly that the sort of enlargement of which it is susceptible, in the matter of the number of stockholders, has nothing in common with the extension of the social bond.

In the first place, like all other commercial societies, it is necessarily limited to a single branch of exploitation: in this respect it is exclusive of all industries foreign to that peculiarly its own. If it were otherwise, it would have changed its nature; it would be a new form of society, whose statutes would regulate, no longer the profits especially, but the distribution of labor and the conditions of exchange; it would be exactly such an association as M. Troplong denies and as the jurisprudence of monopoly excludes.

As for the personal composition of the company, it naturally divides itself into two categories, — the managers and the stockholders. The managers, very few in number, are chosen from the promoters, organizers, and patrons of the enterprise: in truth, they are the only associates. The stockholders, compared with this little government, which administers the society with full power, are a people of taxpayers who, strangers to each other, without influence and without responsibility, have nothing to do with the affair beyond their investments. They are lenders at a premium, not associates.

One can see from this how all the industries of the kingdom could be carried on by such companies, and each citizen, thanks to the facility for multiplying his shares, be interested in all or most of these companies without thereby improving his condition: it might happen even that it would be more and more compromised. For, once more, the stockholder is the beast of burden, the exploitable material of the company: not for him is this society formed. In order that association may be real, he who participates in it must do so, not as a gambler, but as an active factor; he must have a deliberative voice in the council; his name must be expressed or implied in the title of the society; everything regarding him, in short, should be regulated in accordance with equality. But these conditions are precisely those of the organization of labor, which is not taken into consideration by the code; they form the ULTERIOR object of political economy, and consequently are not to be taken for granted, but to be created, and, as such, are radically incompatible with monopoly.[4]

Socialism, in spite of its high-sounding name, has so far been no more fortunate than monopoly in the definition of society: we may even assert that, in all its plans of organization, it has steadily shown itself in this respect a plagiarist of political economy. M. Blanc, whom I have already quoted in discussing competition, and whom we have seen by turns as a partisan of the hierarchical principle, an officious defender of inequality, preaching communism, denying with a stroke

---

Possibly these paragraphs will not be clear to all without the explanation that the form of association discussed in them, called in French the commandite, is a joint-stock company to which the shareholders simply lend their capital, without acquiring a share in the management or incurring responsibility for the results thereof. — Translator.

of the pen the law of contradiction because he cannot conceive it, aiming above all at power as the final sanction of his system, — M. Blanc offers us again the curious example of a socialist copying political economy without suspecting it, and turning continually in the vicious circle of proprietary routine. M. Blanc really denies the sway of capital; he even denies that capital is equal to labor in production, in which he is in accord with healthy economic theories. But he can not or does not know how to dispense with capital; he takes capital for his point of departure; he appeals to the State for its silent partnership: that is, he gets down on his knees before the capitalists and recognizes the sovereignty of monopoly. Hence the singular contortions of his dialectics. I beg the reader's pardon for these eternal personalities: but since socialism, as well as political economy, is personified in a certain number of writers, I cannot do otherwise than quote its authors.

"Has or has not capital," said "La Phalange," "in so far as it is a faculty in production, the legitimacy of the other productive faculties? If it is illegitimate, its pretensions to a share of the product are illegitimate; it must be excluded; it has no interest to receive: if, on the contrary, it is legitimate, it cannot be legitimately excluded from participation in the profits, in the increase which it has helped to create."

The question could not be stated more clearly. M. Blanc holds, on the contrary, that it is stated in a very confused manner, which means that it embarrasses him greatly, and that he is much worried to find its meaning.

In the first place, he supposes that he is asked "whether it is equitable to allow the capitalist a share of the profits of production equal to the laborer's." To which M. Blanc answers unhesitatingly that that would be unjust. Then follows an outburst of eloquence to establish this injustice.

Now, the phalansterian does not ask whether the share of the capitalist should or should not be equal to the laborer's; he wishes to know simply whether he is to have a share. And to this M. Blanc makes no reply.

Is it meant, continues M. Blanc, that capital is indispensable to production, like labor itself? Here M. Blanc distinguishes: he grants that capital is indispensable, as labor is, but not to the extent that labor is.

Once again, the phalansterian does not dispute as to quantity, but as to right.

Is it meant — it is still M. Blanc who interrogates — that all capitalists are not idlers? M. Blanc, generous to capitalists who work, asks why so large a share should be given to those who do not work? A flow of eloquence as to the impersonal services of the capitalist and the personal services of the laborer, terminated by an appeal to Providence.

For the third time, you are asked whether the participation of capital in profits is legitimate, since you admit that it is indispensable in production.

At last M. Blanc, who has understood all the time, decides to reply that, if he allows interest to capital, he does so only as a transitional measure and to ease the descent of the capitalists. For the rest, his project leading inevitably to the absorption of private capital in association, it would be folly and an abandonment of principle to do more. M. Blanc, if he had studied his subject, would have needed to say but a single phrase: "I deny capital."

Thus M. Blanc, — and under his name I include the whole of socialism, — after having, by a first contradiction of the title of his book, "ORGANIZATION OF LABOR," declared that capital was indispensable in production, and consequently that it should be organized and participate in profits like labor, by a second contradiction rejects capital from organization and refuses to recognize it: by a third contradiction he who laughs at decorations and titles of nobility distributes civic crowns, rewards, and distinctions to such litterateurs inventors, and artists as shall have deserved well of the country; he allows them salaries according to their grades and dignities; all of which is the restoration of capital as really, though not with the same mathematical precision, as interest and net product: by a fourth contradiction M. Blanc establishes this new aristocracy on the principle of equality, — that is, he pretends to vote masterships to equal and free associates, privileges of idleness to laborers, spoliation in short to the despoiled: by a fifth contradiction he rests this equalitarian aristocracy on the basis of a power endowed with great force, — that is, on despotism, another form of monopoly: by a sixth contradiction, after having, by his encouragements to labor and the arts, tried to proportion reward to service, like monopoly, and wages to capacity, like monopoly, he sets himself to eulogize life in common, labor and consumption in common, which does not prevent him from wishing to withdraw from the effects of common indifference, by means of national encouragements taken out of the common product, the grave and serious writers whom common readers do not care for: by a seventh contradiction . . . but let us stop at seven, for we should not have finished at seventy-seven.

It is said that M. Blanc, who is now preparing a history of the French Revolution, has begun to seriously study political economy. The first fruit of this study will be, I do not doubt, a repudiation of his pamphlet on "Organization of Labor," and consequently a change in all his ideas of authority and government. At this price the "History of the French Revolution," by M. Blanc, will be a truly useful and original work.

All the socialistic sects, without exception, are possessed by the same prejudice; all, unconsciously, inspired by the economic contradiction, have to confess their powerlessness in presence of the necessity of capital; all are waiting, for the realization of their ideas, to hold power and money in their hands. The utopias of socialism in the matter of association make more prominent than ever the truth which we announced at the beginning: There is nothing in socialism which is not found in political economy; and this perpetual plagiarism is the irrevocable condemnation of both. Nowhere is to be seen the dawn of that mother-idea, which springs with so much eclat from the generation of the economic categories, — that the superior formula of association has nothing to do with capital, a matter for individual accounts, but must bear solely upon equilibrium of production, the conditions of exchange, the gradual reduction of cost, the one and only source of the increase of wealth. Instead of determining the relations of industry to industry, of laborer to laborer, of province to province, and of people to people, the socialists dream only of providing themselves with capital, always conceiving the problem of the solidarity of laborers as if it were a question of founding some new institution of monopoly. The world, humanity, capital, industry, business machinery, exist; it is a matter now simply of finding their philosophy, — in other words, of organizing them: and the socialists are in search of capital! Always outside of reality, is it astonishing that they miss it?

Thus M. Blanc asks for State aid and the establishment of national workshops; thus Fourier asked for six million francs, and his followers are still engaged today in collecting that sum; thus the communists place their hope in a revolution which shall give them authority and the treasury, and exhaust themselves in waiting for useless subscriptions. Capital and power, secondary organs in society, are always the gods whom socialism adores: if capital and power did not exist, it would invent them. Through its anxieties about power and capital, socialism has completely overlooked the meaning of its own protests: much more, it has not seen that, in involving itself, as it has done, in the economic routine, it has deprived itself of the very right to protest. It accuses society of antagonism, and through the same antago-nism it goes in pursuit of reform. It asks capital for the poor laborers, as if the misery of laborers did not come from the competition of capitalists as well as from the factitious opposition of labor and capital; as if the question were not today precisely what it was before the creation of capital, — that is, still and always a question of equilibrium; as if, in short, — let us repeat it incessantly, let us repeat it to satiety, — the question were henceforth of something other than a synthesis of all the principles brought to light by civilization, and as if, provided this synthesis, the idea which leads the world, were known, there would be any need of the intervention of capital and the State to make them evident.

Socialism, in deserting criticism to devote itself to decla-mation and utopia and in mingling with political and religious intrigues, has betrayed its mission and misunderstood the character of the century. The revolution of 1830 demoralized us; socialism is making us effeminate. Like political economy, whose contradictions it simply sifts again, socialism is powerless to satisfy the movement of minds: it is henceforth, in those whom it subjugates, only a new prejudice to destroy, and, in those who propagate it, a charlatanism to unmask, the more dangerous because almost always sincere.

Chapter VII. Fifth Period. — Police, Or Taxation.

In positing its principles humanity, as if in obedience to a sovereign order, never goes backward. Like the traveller who by oblique windings rises from the depth of the valley to the mountain-top, it follows intrepidly its zigzag road, and marches to its goal with confident step, without repentance and without pause. Arriving at the angle of monopoly, the social genius casts backward a melancholy glance, and, in a moment of profound reflection, says to itself:

"Monopoly has stripped the poor hireling of everything, — bread, clothing, home, education, liberty, and security. I will lay a tax upon the monopolist; at this price I will save him his privilege.

"Land and mines, woods and waters, the original domain of man, are forbidden to the proletaire. I will intervene in their exploitation, I will have my share of the products, and land monopoly shall be respected.

"Industry has fallen into feudalism, but I am the suzerain. The lords shall pay me tribute, and they shall keep the profit of their capital.

"Commerce levies usurious profits on the consumer. I will strew its road with toll-gates, I will stamp its checks and indorse its invoices, and it shall pass.

"Capital has overcome labor by intelligence. I will open schools, and the laborer, made intelligent himself, shall become a capitalist in his turn.

"Products lack circulation, and social life is cramped. I will build roads, bridges, canals, marts, theatres, and temples, and thus furnish at one stroke work, wealth, and a market.

"The rich man lives in plenty, while the workman weeps in famine. I will establish taxes on bread, wine, meat, salt, and honey, on articles of necessity and on objects of value, and these shall supply alms for my poor.

"And I will set guards over the waters, the woods, the fields, the mines, and the roads; I will send collectors to gather the taxes and teachers to instruct the children; I will have an army to put down refractory subjects, courts to judge them, prisons to punish them, and priests to curse them. All these offices shall be given to the proletariat and paid by the monopolists.

"Such is my certain and efficacious will."

We have to prove that society could neither think better nor act worse: this will be the subject of a review which, I hope, will throw new light upon the social problem.

Every measure of general police, every administrative and commercial regulation, like every law of taxation, is at bottom but one of the innumerable articles of this ancient bargain, ever violated and ever renewed, between the patriciate and the proletariat. That the parties or their representatives knew nothing of it, or even that they frequently viewed their political constitutions from another standpoint, is of little consequence to us: not to the man, legislator, or prince do we look for the meaning of his acts, but to the acts themselves.

1. — Synthetic idea of the tax. — Point of departure and development of this idea.

In order to render that which is to follow more intelligible, I will explain, inverting, as it were, the method which we have followed hitherto, the superior theory of the tax; then I will give its genesis; finally I will show the contradiction and results. The synthetic idea of the tax, as well as its original conception, would furnish material for the most extensive developments. I shall confine myself to a simple announcement of the propositions, with a summary indication of the proofs.

The tax, in its essence and positive destiny, is the form of distribution among that species of functionaries which Adam Smith has designated by the word unproductive, although he admits as much as any one the utility and even the necessity of their labor in society. By this adjective, unproductive, Adam Smith, whose genius dimly foresaw everything and left us to do everything, meant that the product of these laborers is negative, which is a very different thing from null, and that consequently distribution so far as they are concerned follows a method other than exchange.

Let us consider, in fact, what takes place, from the point of view of distribution, in the four great divisions of collective labor, — extraction,[1] manufactures, commerce, agriculture. Each producer brings to market a real product whose quantity can be measured, whose quality can be estimated, whose price can be debated, and, finally, whose value can be discounted, either in other services or merchandise, or else in money. In all these industries distribution, therefore, is nothing but the mutual exchange of products according to the law of proportionality of values.

Nothing like this takes place with the functionaries called public. These obtain their right to subsistence, not by the production of real utilities, but by the very state of unproductivity in which, by no fault of their own, they are kept. For them the law of proportionality is inverted: while social wealth is formed and increased in the direct ratio of the quantity, variety, and proportion of the effective

---

Hunting, fishing, mining, — in short, the gathering of all natural products. — Translator.

products furnished by the four great industrial categories, the development of this same wealth, the perfecting of social order, suppose, on the contrary, so far as the personnel of police is concerned, a progressive and indefinite reduction. State functionaries, therefore, are very truly unproductive. On this point J. B. Say agreed with A. Smith, and all that he has written on this subject in correction of his master, and which has been stupidly included among his titles to glory, arises entirely, it is easy to see, from a misunderstanding. In a word, the wages of the government's employees constitute a social deficit; they must be carried to the account of losses, which it must be the object of industrial organization to continually diminish: in this view what other adjective could be used to describe the men of power than that of Adam Smith?

Here, then, is a category of services which, furnishing no real products, cannot be rewarded in the ordinary way; services which do not fall under the law of exchange, which cannot become the object of private speculation, competition, joint-stock association, or any sort of commerce, but which, theoretically regarded as performed gratuitously by all, but entrusted, by virtue of the law of division of labor, to a small number of special men who devote themselves exclusively to them, must consequently be paid for. History confirms this general datum. The human mind, which tries all solutions of every problem, has tried accordingly to submit public functions to exchange; for a long time French magistrates, like notaries, etc., lived solely by their fees. But experience has proved that this method of distribution applied to unproductive laborers was too expensive and subject to too many disadvantages, and it became necessary to abandon it.

The organization of the unproductive services contributes to the general welfare in several ways: first, by relieving producers of public cares, in which all must participate, and to which, consequently, all are more or less slaves; secondly, by establishing in society an artificial centralization, the image and prelude of the future solidarity of industries; and, finally, by furnishing a first attempt at balance and discipline.

So we admit, with J. B. Say, the usefulness of magistrates and the other agents of public authority; but we hold that this usefulness is wholly negative, and we insist, therefore, on describing these functionaries by the adjective unproductive which A. Smith applied to them, not to bring them into discredit, but because they really cannot be classed in the category of producers. "Taxation," very well says an economist of Say's school, M. J. Garnier, — "taxation is a privation which we should try to reduce to the furthest point of compatibility with the needs of society." If the writer whom I quote has reflected upon the meaning of his words, he has seen that the word privation which he uses is synonymous with non-production, and that consequently those for whose benefit taxes are collected are very truly unproductive laborers.

I insist upon this definition, which seems to me the less questionable from the fact that, however much they may dispute over the word, all agree upon the thing, because it contains the germ of the greatest revolution yet to be accomplished in the world, — I mean the subordination of the unproductive functions to the productive functions, in a word, the effective submission, always asked and never obtained, of authority to the citizens.

It is a consequence of the development of the economical contradictions that order in society first shows itself inverted; that that which should be above is placed below, that which should be in relief seems sunken, and that which should receive the light is thrown into the shadow. Thus power, which, in its essence, is, like capital, the auxiliary and subordinate of labor, becomes, through the antagonism of society, the spy, judge, and tyrant of the productive functions; power, whose original inferiority lays upon it the duty of obedience, is prince and sovereign.

In all ages the laboring classes have pursued against the office-holding class the solution of this antinomy, of which economic science alone can give the key. The oscillations — that is, the political agitations which result from this struggle of labor against power — now lead to a depression of the central force, which compromises the very existence of society; now, exaggerating this same force beyond measure, give birth to despotism. Then, the privileges of command, the infinite joy which it gives to ambition and pride, making the unproductive functions an object of universal lust, a new leaven of discord penetrates society, which, divided already in one direction into capitalists and wage-workers, and in another into producers and non-producers, is again divided as regards power into monarchists and democrats. The conflicts between royalty and the republic would furnish us most marvellous and interesting material for our episodes. The confines of this work do not permit us so long an excursion; and after having pointed out this new branch in the vast network of human aberrations, we shall confine ourselves exclusively, in dealing with taxation, to the economic question.

Such, then, in succinctest statement, is the synthetic theory of the tax, — that is, if I may venture to use the familiar comparison, of this fifth wheel of the coach of humanity, which makes so much noise, and which, in governmental parlance, is styled the State. The State, the police, or their means of existence, the tax, is, I repeat, the official name of the class designated in political economy as nonproducers, — in short, as the domestics of society.

But public reason does not attain at a single bound this simple idea, which for centuries had to remain in the state of a transcendental conception. Before civilization can mount to such a height, it must pass through frightful tempests and innumerable revolutions, in each of which, one might say, it renews its strength in a bath of blood. And when at last production, represented by capital, seems on the point of thoroughly subordinating the unproductive organ, the State, then society rises in indignation, labor weeps at the prospect of its immediate freedom, democracy shudders at the abasement of power, justice cries out as if scandalized, and all the oracles of the departing gods exclaim with terror that the abomination of desolation is in the holy places and that the end of the world has come. So true is it that humanity never desires what it seeks, and that the slightest progress cannot be realized without spreading panic among the peoples.

What, then, in this evolution, is the point of departure of society, and by what circuitous route does it reach political reform, — that is, economy in its expenditures, equality in the assessment of its taxes, and the subordination of power to industry? That is what we are about to state in a few words, reserving developments for the sequel.

The original idea of the tax is that of REDEMPTION.

As, by the law of Moses, each first-born was supposed to belong to Jehovah, and had to be redeemed by an offering, so the tax everywhere presents itself in the form of a tithe or royal prerogative by which the proprietor annually redeems from the sovereign the profit of exploitation which he is supposed to hold only by his pleasure. This theory of the tax, moreover, is but one of the special articles of what is called the social contract.

Ancients and moderns all agree, in terms more or less explicit, in regarding the juridical status of societies as a reaction of weakness against strength. This idea is uppermost in all the works of Plato, notably in the "Gorgias," where he maintains, with more subtlety than logic, the cause of the laws against that of violence, — that is, legislative absolutism against aristocratic and military absolutism. In this knotty dispute, in which the weight of evidence is equal on both sides, Plato simply expresses the sentiment of entire antiquity. Long before him, Moses, in making a distribution of lands, declaring patrimony inalienable, and ordering a general and uncompensated cancellation of all mortgages every fiftieth year, had opposed a barrier to the invasions of force. The whole Bible is a hymn to JUSTICE, — that is, in the Hebrew style, to charity, to kindness to the weak on the part of the strong, to voluntary renunciation of the privilege of power. Solon, beginning his legislative mission by a general abolition of debts, and creating rights and reserves, — that is, barriers to prevent their return, — was no less reactionary. Lycurgus went farther; he forbade individual possession, and tried to absorb the man in the State, annihilating liberty the better to preserve equilibrium. Hobbes, deriving, and with great reason, legislation from the state of war, arrived by another road at the establishment of equality upon an exception, — despotism. His book, so much calumniated, is only a development of this famous antithesis. The charter of 1830, consecrating the insurrection made in '89 by the plebeians against the nobility, and decreeing the abstract equality of persons before the law, in spite of the real inequality of powers and talents which is the veritable basis of the social system now in force, is also but a protest of society in favor of the poor against the rich, of the small against the great. All the laws of the human race regarding sale, purchase, hire, property, loans, mortgages, prescription, inheritance, donation, wills, wives' dowries, minority, guardianship, etc., etc., are real barriers erected by judicial absolutism against the absolutism of force. Respect for contracts, fidelity to promises, the religion of the oath, are fictions, osselets,[2] as the famous Lysander aptly said, with which society deceives the strong and brings them under the yoke.

The tax belongs to that great family of preventive, coercive, repressive, and vindictive institutions which A. Smith designated by the generic term police, and which is, as I have said, in its original conception, only the reaction of weakness against strength. This follows, independently of abundant historical testimony which we will put aside to confine ourselves exclusively to economic proof, from the distinction naturally arising between taxes.

All taxes are divisible into two great categories: (1) taxes of assessment, or of privilege: these are the oldest taxes; (2) taxes of consumption, or of quotité,[3] whose tendency is, by absorbing the former, to make public burdens weigh equally upon all.

The first sort of taxes — including in France the tax on land, the tax on doors and windows, the poll-tax, the tax on personal property, the tax on tenants, license-fees, the tax on transfers of property, the tax on officials' fees, road-taxes, and brevets — is the share which the sovereign reserves for himself out of all the monopolies which he concedes or tolerates; it is, as we have said, the indemnity of the poor, the permit granted to property. Such was the form and spirit of the tax in all the old monarchies: feudalism was its beau ideal. Under that regime the tax was only a tribute paid by the holder to the universal proprietor or sleeping-partner (commanditaire), the king.

When later, by the development of public right, royalty, the patriarchal form of sovereignty, begins to get impregnated by the democratic spirit, the tax becomes a quota which each voter owes to the COMMONWEALTH, and which, instead of falling into the hand of the prince, is received into the State treasury. In this evolution the principle of the tax remains intact; as yet there is no transformation of the institution; the real sovereign simply succeeds the figurative sovereign. Whether the tax enters into the peculium of the prince or serves to liquidate

---

Little bones taken from the joints of animals and serving as playthings for children. — Translator.
A tax whose total product is not fixed in advance, but depends upon the quantity of things or persons upon whom it happens to fall. — Translator.

a common debt, it is in either case only a claim of society against privilege; otherwise, it is impossible to say why the tax is levied in the ratio of fortunes.

Let all contribute to the public expenses: nothing more just. But why should the rich pay more than the poor? That is just, they say, because they possess more. I confess that such justice is beyond my comprehension... One of two things is true: either the proportional tax guarantees a privilege to the larger tax-payers, or else it is a wrong. Because, if property is a natural right, as the Declaration of '93 declares, all that belongs to me by virtue of this right is as sacred as my person; it is my blood, my life, myself: whoever touches it offends the apple of my eye. My income of one hundred thousand francs is as inviolable a the grisette's daily wage of seventy-five centimes; her attic is no more sacred than my suite of apartments. The tax is not levied in proportion to physical strength, size, or skill: no more should it be levied in proportion to property. — What is Property: Chapter II.

These observations are the more just because the principle which it was their purpose to oppose to that of proportional assessment has had its period of application. The proportional tax is much later in history than liege-homage, which consisted in a simple officious demonstration without real payment.

The second sort of taxes includes in general all those designated, by a sort of antiphrasis, by the term indirect, such as taxes on liquor, salt, and tobacco, customs duties, and, in short, all the taxes which DIRECTLY affect the only thing which should be taxed, — product. The principle of this tax, whose name is an actual misnomer, is unquestionably better founded in theory and more equitable in tendency than the preceding: accordingly, in spite of the opinion of the mass, always deceived as to that which serves it as well as to that which is prejudicial to it, I do not hesitate to say that this tax is the only normal one, barring its assessment and collection, with which it is not my purpose now to deal.

For, if it is true, as we have just explained, that the real nature of the tax is to pay, according to a particular form of wages, for certain services which elude the usual form of exchange, it follows that all producers, enjoying these services equally as far as personal use is concerned, should contribute to their payment in equal portions. The share for each, therefore, would be a fraction of his exchangeable product, or, in other words, an amount taken from the values delivered by him for purposes of consumption. But, under the monopoly system, and with collection upon land, the treasury strikes the product before it has entered into exchange, even before it is produced, — a circumstance which results in throwing back the amount of the tax into the cost of production, and consequently puts the burden upon the consumer and lifts it from monopoly.

Whatever the significance of the tax of assessment or the tax of quotité, one thing is sure, and this is the thing which it is especially important for us to know, — namely, that, in making the tax proportional, it was the intention of the sovereign to make citizens contribute to the public expenses, no longer, according to the old feudal principle, by means of a poll-tax, which would involve the idea of an assessment figured in the ratio of the number of persons taxed, and not in the ratio of their possessions, but so much per franc of capital, which supposes that capital has its source in an authority superior to the capitalists. Everybody, spontaneously and with one accord, considers such an assessment just; everybody, therefore, spontaneously and with one accord, looks upon the tax as a resumption on the part of society, a sort of redemption exacted from monopoly. This is especially striking in England, where, by a special law, the proprietors of the soil and the manufacturers pay, in proportion to their incomes, a tax of forty million dollars, which is called the poor-rate.

In short, the practical and avowed object of the tax is to effect upon the rich, for the benefit of the people, a proportional resumption of their capital.

Now, analysis and the facts demonstrate:

That the tax of assessment, the tax upon monopoly, instead of being paid by those who possess, is paid almost entirely by those who do not possess;

That the tax of quotité, separating the producer from the consumer, falls solely upon the latter, thereby taking from the capitalist no more than he would have to pay if fortunes were absolutely equal;

Finally, that the army, the courts, the police, the schools, the hospitals, the almshouses, the houses of refuge and correction, public functions, religion itself, all that society creates for the protection, emancipation, and relief of the proletaire, paid for in the first place and sustained by the proletaire, is then turned against the proletaire or wasted as far as he is concerned; so that the proletariat, which at first labored only for the class that devours it, — that of the capitalists, — must labor also for the class that flogs it, — that of the nonproducers.

These facts are henceforth so well known, and the economists — I owe them this justice — have shown them so clearly, that I shall abstain from correcting their demonstrations, which, for the rest, are no longer contradicted by anybody. What I propose to bring to light, and what the economists do not seem to have sufficiently understood, is that the condition in which the laborer is placed by this new phase of social economy is susceptible of no amelioration; that, unless industrial organization, and therefore political reform, should bring about an equality of fortunes, evil is inherent in police institutions as in the idea of charity which gave them birth; in short, that the STATE, whatever form it affects, aristocratic or theocratic, monarchical or republican, until it shall have become the obedient and submissive organ of a society of equals, will be for the people an inevitable hell, — I had almost said a deserved damnation.

2. — Antinomy of the tax.

I sometimes hear the champions of the statu quo maintain that for the present we enjoy liberty enough, and that, in spite of the declamation against the existing order, we are below the level of our institutions. So far at least as taxation is concerned, I am quite of the opinion of these optimists.

According to the theory that we have just seen, the tax is the reaction of society against monopoly. Upon this point opinions are unanimous: citizens and legislators, economists, journalists, and ballad-writers, rendering, each in their own tongue, the social thought, vie with each other in proclaiming that the tax should fall upon the rich, strike the superfluous and articles of luxury, and leave those of prime necessity free. In short, they have made the tax a sort of privilege for the privileged: a bad idea, since it involved a recognition of the legitimacy of privilege, which in no case, whatever shape it may take, is good for anything. The people had to be punished for this egoistic inconsistency: Providence did not fail in its duty.

From the moment, then, of the conception of the tax as a counter-claim, it had to be fixed proportionally to means, whether it struck capital or affected income more especially. Now, I will point out that the levying of the tax at so much a franc being precisely that which should be adopted in a country where all fortunes were equal, saving the differences in the cost of assessment and collection, the treasury is the most liberal feature of our society, and that on this point our morals are really behind our institutions. But as with the wicked the best things cannot fail to be detestable, we shall see the equalitarian tax crush the people precisely because the people are not up to it.

I will suppose that the gross income in France, for each family of four persons, is 1,000 francs: this is a little above the estimate of M. Chevalier, who places it at only 63 centimes a day for each individual, or 919 francs 80 centimes for each household. The tax being today more than a thousand millions, or about an eighth of the total income, each family, earning 1,000 francs a year, is taxed 125 francs.

Accordingly, an income of 2,000 francs pays 250 francs; an income of 3,000 francs, 375; an income of 4,000 francs, 500, etc. The proportion is strict and mathematically irreproachable; the treasury, by arithmetic, is sure of losing nothing.

But on the side of the taxpayers the affair totally changes its aspect. The tax, which, in the intention of the legislator, was to have been proportioned to fortune, is, on the contrary, progressive in the ratio of poverty, so that, the poorer the citizen is, the more he pays. This I shall try to make plain by a few figures.

According to the proportional tax, there is due to the treasury:

for an income of	1,000	2,000	3,000	4,000	5,000	6,000 francs, etc.
a tax of	125	250	375	500	625	750

According to this series, then, the tax seems to increase proportionally to income.

But when it is remembered that each annual income is made up of 365 units, each of which represents the daily income of the taxpayer, the tax will no longer be found proportional; it will be found equal. In fact, if the State levies a tax of 125 francs on an income of 1,000 francs, it is as if it took from the taxed family 45 days' subsistence; likewise the assessments of 250, 375, 500, 625, and 750 francs, corresponding to incomes of 2,000, 3,000, 4,000, 5,000, and 6,000 francs, constitute in each case a tax of 45 days' pay upon each of those who enjoy these incomes.

I say now that this equality of taxation is a monstrous inequality, and that it is a strange illusion to imagine that, because the daily income is larger, the tax of which it is the base is higher. Let us change our point of view from that of personal to that of collective income.

As an effect of monopoly social wealth abandoning the laboring class to go to the capitalistic class, the object of taxation has been to moderate this displacement and react against usurpation by enforcing a proportional replevin upon each privileged person. But proportional to what? To the excess which the privileged person has received undoubtedly, and not to the fraction of the social capital which his income represents. Now, the object of taxation is missed and the law turned into derision when the treasury, instead of taking its eighth where this eighth exists, asks it precisely of those to whom it should be restored. A final calculation will make this evident.

Setting the daily income of each person in France at 68 centimes, the father of a family who, whether as wages or as income from his capital, receives 1,000 francs a year receives four shares of the national income; he who receives 2,000 francs has eight shares; he who receives 4,000 francs has sixteen, etc. Hence it follows that the workman who, on an income of 1,000 francs, pays 125 francs into the treasury renders to public order half a share, or an eighth of his income and his family's subsistence; whereas the capitalist who, on an income of 6,000 francs, pays only 750 francs realizes a profit of 17 shares out of the collective income, or, in other words, gains by the tax 425 per cent.

Let us reproduce the same truth in another form.

The voters of France number about 200,000. I do not know the total amount of taxes paid by these 200,000 voters, but I do not believe that I am very far from the truth in supposing an average of 300 francs each, or a total of 60,000,000 for the 200,000 voters, to which we will add twenty-five per cent. to represent their share of indirect taxes, making in all 75,000,000, or 75 francs for each person (supposing the family of each voter to consist of five persons), which the electoral class pays to the State. The appropriations, according to the "Annuaire Economique" for 1845, being 1,106,000,000, there remains 1,031,000,000, which makes the tax paid by each non-voting citizen 31 francs 30 centimes, — two-fifths of the tax paid by the wealthy class. Now, for this proportion to be equitable, the average welfare of the non-voting class would have to be two-fifths of the average welfare of the voting class: but such is not the truth, as it falls short of this by more than three-fourths.

But this disproportion will seem still more shocking when it is remembered that the calculation which we have just made concerning the electoral class is altogether wrong, altogether in favor of the voters.

In fact, the only taxes which are levied for the enjoyment of the right of suffrage are: (1) the land tax; (2) the tax on polls and personal property; (3) the tax on doors and windows; (4) license-fees. Now, with the exception of the tax on polls and personal property, which varies little, the three other taxes are thrown back on the consumers; and it is the same with all the indirect taxes, for which the holders of capital are reimbursed by the consumers, with the exception, however, of the taxes on property transfers, which fall directly on the proprietor and amount in all to 150,000,000. Now, if we estimate that in this last amount the property of voters figures as one-sixth, which is placing it high, the portion of direct taxes (409,000,000) being 12 francs for each person, and that of indirect taxes (547,000,000) 16 francs, the average tax paid by each voter having a household of five will reach a total of 265 francs, while that paid by the laborer, who has only his arms to support himself, his wife, and two children, will be 112 francs. In more general terms, the average tax upon each person belonging to the upper classes will be 53 francs; upon each belonging to the lower, 28. Whereupon I renew my question: Is the welfare of those below the voting standard half as great as that of those above it?

It is with the tax as with periodical publications, which really cost more the less frequently they appear. A daily journal costs forty francs, a weekly ten francs, a monthly four. Supposing other things to be equal, the subscription prices of these journals are to each other as the numbers forty, seventy, and one hundred and twenty, the price rising with the infrequency of publication. Now, this exactly represents the increase of the tax: it is a subscription paid by each citizen in exchange for the right to labor and to live. He who uses this right in the smallest proportion pays much; he who uses it a little more pays less; he who uses it a great deal pays little.

The economists are generally in agreement about all this. They have attacked the proportional tax, not only in its principle, but in its application; they have

213

pointed out its anomalies, almost all of which arise from the fact that the relation of capital to income, or of cultivated surface to rent, is never fixed.

Given a levy of one-tenth on the income from lands, and lands of different qualities producing, the first eight francs' worth of grain, the second six francs' worth, the third five francs' worth, the tax will call for one-eighth of the income from the most fertile land, one-sixth from that a little less fertile, and, finally, one-fifth from that less fertile still.[4] Will not the tax thus established be just the reverse of what it should be? Instead of land, we may suppose other instruments of production, and compare capitals of the same value, or amounts of labor of the same order, applied to branches of industry differing in productivity: the conclusion will be the same. There is injustice in requiring the same poll-tax of ten francs from the laborer who earns one thousand francs and from the artist or physician who has an income of sixty thousand. — J. Garnier: Principles of Political Economy.

These reflections are very sound, although they apply only to collection or assessment, and do not touch the principle of the tax itself. For, in supposing the assessment to be made upon income instead of upon capital, the fact always remains that the tax, which should be proportional to fortunes, is borne by the consumer.

The economists have taken a resolve; they have squarely recognized the iniquity of the proportional tax.

"The tax," says Say, "can never be levied upon the necessary." This author, it is true, does not tell us what we are to understand by the necessary, but we can supply the omission. The necessary is what each individual gets out of the total product of the country, after deducting what must be taken for taxes. Thus, making the estimate in round numbers, the production of France being eight thousand millions and the tax one thousand millions, the necessary in the case of each individual amounts to fifty-six and a half centimes a day. Whatever is in excess of this income is alone susceptible of being taxed, according to J. B. Say; whatever falls short of it must be regarded by the treasury as inviolable.

The same author expresses this idea in other words when he says: "The proportional tax is not equitable." Adam Smith had already said before him: "It is not unreasonable that the rich man should contribute to the public expenses, not

---

This sentence, as it stands, is unintelligible, and probably is not correctly quoted by Proudhon. At any rate, one of Garnier's works contains a similar passage, which begins thus: "Given a levy of one on the area of the land, and lands of different qualities producing, the first eight, the second six, the third five, the tax will call for one-eighth," etc. This is perfectly clear, and the circumstances supposed are aptly illustrative of Proudhon's point. I should unhesitatingly pronounce it the correct version, except for the fact that Proudhon, in the succeeding paragraph, interprets Garnier as supposing income to be assessed instead of capital. — Translator.

only in proportion to his income, but something more." "I will go further," adds Say; "I will not fear to say that the progressive tax is the only equitable tax." And M. J. Garnier, the latest abridger of the economists, says: "Reforms should tend to establish a progressional equality, if I may use the phrase, much more just, much more equitable, than the pretended equality of taxation, which is only a monstrous inequality."

So, according to general opinion and the testimony of the economists, two things are acknowledged: one, that in its principle the tax is a reaction against monopoly and directed against the rich; the other, that in practice this same tax is false to its object; that, in striking the poor by preference, it commits an injustice; and that the constant effort of the legislator must be to distribute its burden in a more equitable fashion.

I needed to establish this double fact solidly before passing to other considerations: now commences my criticism.

The economists, with that simplicity of honest folk which they have inherited from their elders and which even today is all that stands to their credit, have taken no pains to see that the progressional theory of the tax, which they point out to governments as the ne plus ultra of a wise and liberal administration, was contradictory in its terms and pregnant with a legion of impossibilities. They have attributed the oppression of the treasury by turns to the barbarism of the time, the ignorance of princes, the prejudices of caste, the avarice of collectors, everything, in short, which, in their opinion, preventing the progression of the tax, stood in the way of the sincere practice of equality in the distribution of public burdens; they have not for a moment suspected that what they asked under the name of progressive taxation was the overturn of all economic ideas.

Thus they have not seen, for instance, that the tax was progressive from the very fact that it was proportional, the only difference being that the progression was in the wrong direction, the percentage being, as we have said, not directly, but inversely proportional to fortunes. If the economists had had a clear idea of this overturn, invariable in all countries where taxation exists, so singular a phenomenon would not have failed to draw their attention; they would have sought its causes, and would have ended by discovering that what they took for an accident of civilization, an effect of the inextricable difficulties of human government, was the product of the contradiction inherent in all political economy.

The progressive tax, whether applied to capital or to income, is the very negation of monopoly, of that monopoly which is met everywhere, according to M. Rossi, across the path of social economy; which is the true stimulant of industry, the hope of economy, the preserver and parent of all wealth; of which we have been able to say, in short, that society cannot exist without it, but that, except for it, there would be no society. Let the tax become suddenly what it unquestionably must sometime be, — namely, the proportional (or progressional, which is the same thing) contribution of each producer to the public expenses, and straightway rent and profit are confiscated everywhere for the benefit of the State; labor is stripped of the fruits of its toil; each individual being reduced to the proper allowance of fifty-six and a half centimes, poverty becomes general; the compact formed between labor and capital is dissolved, and society, deprived of its rudder, drifts back to its original state.

It will be said, perhaps, that it is easy to prevent the absolute annihilation of the profits of capital by stopping the progression at any moment.

Eclecticism, the golden mean, compromise with heaven or with morality: is it always to be the same philosophy, then? True science is repugnant to such arrangements. All invested capital must return to the producer in the form of interest; all labor must leave a surplus, all wages be equal to product. Under the protection of these laws society continually realizes, by the greatest variety of production, the highest possible degree of welfare. These laws are absolute; to violate them is to wound, to mutilate society. Capital, accordingly, which, after all, is nothing but accumulated labor, is inviolable. But, on the other hand, the tendency to equality is no less imperative; it is manifested at each economic phase with increasing energy and an invincible authority. Therefore you must satisfy labor and justice at once; you must give to the former guarantees more and more real, and secure the latter without concession or ambiguity.

Instead of that, you know nothing but the continual substitution of the good pleasure of the prince for your theories, the arrest of the course of economic law by arbitrary power, and, under the pretext of equity, the deception of the wage worker and the monopolist alike! Your liberty is but a half-liberty, your justice but a half-justice, and all your wisdom consists in those middle terms whose iniquity is always twofold, since they justify the pretensions of neither one party nor the other! No, such cannot be the science which you have promised us, and which, by unveiling for us the secrets of the production and consumption of wealth, must unequivocally solve the social antinomies. Your semi-liberal doctrine is the code of despotism, and shows that you are powerless to advance as well as ashamed to retreat.

If society, pledged by its economic antecedents, can never retrace its steps; if, until the arrival of the universal equation, monopoly must be maintained in its possession, — no change is possible in the laying of taxes: only there is a contradiction here, which, like every other, must be pushed till exhausted. Have, then, the courage of your opinions, — respect for wealth, and no pity for the poor, whom the God of monopoly has condemned. The less the hireling has wherewith to live, the more he must pay: qui minus habet, etiam quod habet auferetur ab eo. This is necessary, this is inevitable; in it lies the safety of society.

Let us try, nevertheless, to reverse the progression of the tax, and so arrange it that the capitalist, instead of the laborer, will pay the larger share.

I observe, in the first place, that with the usual method of collection, such a reversal is impracticable.

In fact, if the tax falls on exploitable capital, this tax, in its entirety, is included among the costs of production, and then of two things one: either the product, in spite of the increase in its selling value, will be bought by the consumer, and consequently the producer will be relieved of the tax; or else this same product will be thought too dear, and in that case the tax, as J. B. Say has very well said, acts like a tithe levied on seed, -it prevents production. Thus it is that too high a tax on the transfer of titles arrests the circulation of real property, and renders estates less productive by keeping them from changing hands.

If, on the contrary, the tax falls on product, it is nothing but a tax of quotité, which each pays in the ratio of his consumption, while the capitalist, whom it is purposed to strike, escapes.

Moreover, the supposition of a progressive tax based either on product or on capital is perfectly absurd. How can we imagine the same product paying a duty of ten per cent at the store of one dealer and a duty of but five at another's? How are estates already encumbered with mortgages and which change owners every day, how is a capital formed by joint investment or by the fortune of a single individual, to be distinguished upon the official register, and taxed, not in the ratio of their value or rent, but in the ratio of the fortune or presumed profits of the proprietor?

There remains, then, a last resource, — to tax the net income of each tax-payer, whatever his method of getting it. For instance, an income of one thousand francs would pay ten per cent.; an income of two thousand francs, twenty per cent.; an income of three thousand francs, thirty per cent., etc. We will set aside the thousand difficulties and annoyances that must be met in ascertaining these incomes, and suppose the operation as easy as you like. Well! that is exactly the system which I charge with hypocrisy, contradiction, and injustice.

I say in the first place that this system is hypocritical, because, instead of taking from the rich that entire portion of their income in excess of the average national product per family, which is inadmissible, it does not, as is imagined, reverse the order of progression in the direction of wealth; at most it changes the rate of progression. Thus the present progression of the tax, for fortunes yielding incomes of a thousand francs and UNDER, being as that of the numbers 10, 11, 12, 13, etc., and, for fortunes yielding incomes of a thousand francs and OVER, as that of the numbers 10, 9, 8, 7, 6, etc., — the tax always increasing with poverty and decreasing with wealth, — if we should confine ourselves to lifting the indirect tax which falls especially on the poorer class and imposing a corresponding tax upon the incomes of the richer class, the progression thereafter, it is true, would be, for the first, only as that of the numbers 10, 10.25, 10.50, 10.75, 11, 11.25, etc., and, for the second, as 10, 9.75, 9.50, 9.25, 9, 8.75, etc. But this progression, although less rapid on both sides, would still take the same direction nevertheless, would still be a reversal of justice; and it is for this reason that the so-called progressive tax, capable at most of giving the philanthropist something to babble about, is of no scientific value. It changes nothing in fiscal jurisprudence; as the proverb says, it is always the poor man who carries the pouch, always the rich man who is the object of the solicitude of power.

I add that this system is contradictory.

In fact, one cannot both give and keep, say the jurisconsults. Instead, then, of consecrating monopolies from which the holders are to derive no privilege save that of straightway losing, with the income, all the enjoyment thereof, why not decree the agrarian law at once? Why provide in the constitution that each shall freely enjoy the fruit of his labor and industry, when, by the fact or the tendency of the tax, this permission is granted only to the extent of a dividend of fifty-six and a half centimes a day, — a thing, it is true, which the law could not have foreseen, but which would necessarily result from progression? The legislator, in confirming us in our monopolies, intended to favor production, to feed the sacred fire of industry: now, what interest shall we have to produce, if, though not yet associated, we are not to produce for ourselves alone? After we have been declared free, how can we be made subject to conditions of sale, hire, and exchange which annul our liberty?

A man possesses government securities which bring him an income of twenty thousand francs. The tax, under the new system of progression, will take fifty per cent. of this from him. At this rate it is more advantageous to him to withdraw his capital and consume the principal instead of the income. Then let him be repaid. What! repaid! The State cannot be obliged to repay; and, if it consents to redeem, it will do so in proportion to the net income. Therefore a bond for twenty thousand francs will be worth not more than ten thousand to the bondholder, because of the tax, if he wishes to get it redeemed by the State: unless he divides it into twenty lots, in which case it will return him double the amount. Likewise an estate which rents for fifty thousand francs, the tax taking two-thirds of the income, will lose two-thirds of its value. But let the proprietor divide this estate into a hundred lots and sell it at auction, and then, the terror of the treasury no longer deterring purchasers, he can get back his entire capital. So that, with the progressive tax, real estate no longer follows the law of supply and demand and is not valued according to the real income which it yields, but according to the condition of the owner. The consequence will be that large capitals will depreciate in value, and mediocrity be brought to the front; land-owners will hasten to sell, because it will be better for them to consume their property than to get an insufficient rent from it; capitalists will recall their investments, or will invest only at usurious rates; all exploitation on a large scale will be prohibited, every visible fortune proceeded against, and all accumulation of capital in excess of the figure of the necessary proscribed. Wealth, driven back, will retire within itself and never emerge except by stealth; and labor, like a man attached to a corpse, will embrace misery in an endless union. Does it not well become the economists who devise such reforms to laugh at the reformers?

After having demonstrated the contradiction and delusion of the progressive tax, must I prove its injustice also? The progressive tax, as understood by the economists and, in their wake, by certain radicals, is impracticable, I said just now, if it falls on capital and product: consequently I have supposed it to fall on incomes. But who does not see that this purely theoretical distinction between capital, product, and income falls so far as the treasury is concerned, and that the same impossibilities which we have pointed out reappear here with all their fatal character?

A manufacturer discovers a process by means of which, saving twenty per cent of his cost of production, he secures an income of twenty-five thousand francs. The treasury calls on him for fifteen thousand. He is obliged, therefore, to raise his prices, since, by the fact of the tax, his process, instead of saving twenty per cent, saves only eight per cent. Is not this as if the treasury prevented cheapness? Thus, in trying to reach the rich, the progressive tax always reaches the consumer; and it is impossible for it not to reach him without suppressing production altogether: what a mistake!

It is a law of social economy that all invested capital must return continually to the capitalist in the form of interest. With the progressive tax this law is radically violated, since, by the effect of progression, interest on capital is so reduced that industries are established only at a loss of a part or the whole of the capital. To make it otherwise, interest on capital would have to increase progressively in the same ratio as the tax itself, which is absurd. Therefore the progressive tax stops the creation of capital; furthermore it hinders its circulation. Whoever, in fact, should want to buy a plant for any enterprise or a piece of land for cultivation would have to consider, under the system of progressive taxation, not the real value of such plant or land, but rather the tax which it would bring upon him; so that, if the real income were four per cent., and, by the effect of the tax or the condition of the buyer, must go down to three, the purchase could not be effected. After having run counter to all interests and thrown the market into confusion by its categories, the progressive tax arrests the development of wealth and reduces venal value below real value; it contracts, it petrifies society. What tyranny! What derision!

The progressive tax resolves itself, then, whatever may be done, into a denial of justice, prohibition of production, confiscation. It is unlimited and unbridled absolutism, given to power over everything which, by labor, by economy, by improvements, contributes to public wealth.

But what is the use of wandering about in chimerical hypotheses when the truth is at hand. It is not the fault of the proportional principle if the tax falls with such shocking inequality upon the various classes of society; the fault is in our prejudices and our morals. The tax, as far as is possible in human operations, proceeds with equity, precision. Social economy commands it to apply to product; it applies to product. If product escapes it, it strikes capital: what more natural! The tax, in advance of civilization, supposes the equality of laborers and capitalists: the inflexible expression of necessity, it seems to invite us to make ourselves equals by education and labor, and, by balancing our functions and associating our interests, to put ourselves in accord with it. The tax refuses to distinguish between one man and another: and we blame its mathematical severity for the differences in our fortunes! We ask equality itself to comply with our injustice! Was I not right in saying at the outset that, relatively to the tax, we are behind our institutions?

Accordingly we always see the legislator stopping, in his fiscal laws, before the subversive consequences of the progressive tax, and consecrating the necessity, the immutability of the proportional tax. For equality in well-being cannot result from the violation of capital: the antinomy must be methodically solved, under penalty, for society, of falling back into chaos. Eternal justice does not accommodate itself to all the whims of men: like a woman, whom one may outrage, but whom one does not marry without a solemn alienation of one's self, it demands on our part, with the abandonment of our egoism, the recognition of all its rights, which are those of science.

The tax, whose final purpose, as we have shown, is the reward of the non-producers, but whose original idea was a restoration of the laborer, — the tax, under the system of monopoly, reduces itself therefore to a pure and simple protest, a sort of extra-judicial act, the whole effect of which is to aggravate the situation of the wage-worker by disturbing the monopolist in his possession. As for the idea of changing the proportional tax into a progressive tax, or, to speak more accurately, of reversing the order in which the tax progresses, that is a blunder the entire responsibility for which belongs to the economists.

But henceforth menace hovers over privilege. With the power of modifying the proportionality of the tax, government has under its hand an expeditious and sure means of dispossessing the holders of capital when it will; and it is a frightful thing to see everywhere that great institution, the basis of society, the object of so many controversies, of so many laws, of so many cajoleries, and of so many crimes, PROPERTY, suspended at the end of a thread over the yawning mouth of the proletariat.

3. — Disastrous and inevitable consequences of the tax. (Provisions, sumptuary laws, rural and industrial police, patents, trade-marks, etc.)

M. Chevalier addressed to himself, in July, 1843, on the subject of the tax, the following questions:

(1) Is it asked of all or by preference of a part of the nation? (2) Does the tax resemble a levy on polls, or is it exactly proportioned to the fortunes of the tax-payers? (3) Is agriculture more or less burdened than manufactures or commerce? (4) Is real estate more or less spared than personal property? (5) Is he who produces more favored than he who consumes? (6) Have our taxation laws the character of sumptuary laws?

To these various questions M. Chevalier makes the reply which I am about to quote, and which sums up all of the most philosophical considerations upon the subject which I have met:

(a) The tax affects the universality, applies to the mass, takes the nation as a whole; nevertheless, as the poor are the most numerous, it taxes them willingly, certain of collecting more. (b) By the nature of things the tax sometimes takes the form of a levy on polls, as in the case of the salt tax. (c, d, e) The treasury addresses itself to labor as well as to consumption, because in France everybody labors, to real more than to personal property, and to agriculture more than to manufactures. (f) By the same reasoning, our laws partake little of the character of sumptuary laws.

What, professor! is that all that science has taught you? The tax applies to the mass, you say; it takes the nation as a whole. Alas! we know it only too well; but it is this which is iniquitous, and which we ask you to explain. The government, when engaged in the assessment and distribution of the tax, could not have believed, did not believe, that all fortunes were equal; consequently it could not have wished, did not wish, the sums paid to be equal. Why, then, is the practice of the government always the opposite of its theory? Your opinion, if you please, on this difficult matter? Explain; justify or condemn the exchequer; take whatever course you will, provided you take some course and say something. Remember that your readers are men, and that they cannot excuse in a doctor, speaking ex cathedra, such propositions as this: as the poor are the most numerous, it taxes them willingly, certain of collecting more. No, Monsieur: numbers do

221

not regulate the tax; the tax knows perfectly well that millions of poor added to millions of poor do not make one voter. You render the treasury odious by making it absurd, and I maintain that it is neither the one nor the other. The poor man pays more than the rich because Providence, to whom misery is odious like vice, has so ordered things that the miserable must always be the most ground down. The iniquity of the tax is the celestial scourge which drives us towards equality. God! if a professor of political economy, who was formerly an apostle, could but understand this revelation!

By the nature of things, says M. Chevalier, the tax sometimes takes the form of a levy on polls. Well, in what case is it just that the tax should take the form of a levy on polls? Is it always, or never? What is the principle of the tax? What is its object? Speak, answer.

And what instruction, pray, can we derive from the remark, scarcely worthy of quotation, that the treasury addresses itself to labor as well as to consumption, to real more than to personal property, to agriculture more than to manufactures? Of what consequence to science is this interminable recital of crude facts, if your analysis never extracts a single idea from them?

All the deductions made from consumption by taxation, rent, interest on capital, etc., enter into the general expense account and figure in the selling price, so that nearly always the consumer pays the tax: that we know. And as the goods most consumed are also those which yield the most revenue, it necessarily follows that the poorest people are the most heavily burdened: this consequence, like the first, is inevitable. Once more, then, of what importance to us are your fiscal distinctions? Whatever the classification of taxable material, as it is impossible to tax capital beyond its income, the capitalist will be always favored, while the proletaire will suffer iniquity, oppression. The trouble is not in the distribution of taxes; it is in the distribution of goods. M. Chevalier cannot be ignorant of this: why, then, does not M. Chevalier, whose word would carry more weight than that of a writer suspected of not loving the existing order, say as much?

From 1806 to 1811 (this observation, as well as the following, is M. Chevalier's) the annual consumption of wine in Paris was one hundred and forty quarts for each individual; now it is not more than eighty-three. Abolish the tax of seven or eight cents a quart collected from the retailer, and the consumption of wine will soon rise from eighty-three quarts to one hundred and seventy-five; and the wine industry, which does not know what to do with its products, will have a market. Thanks to the duties laid upon the importation of cattle, the consumption of meat by the people has diminished in a ratio similar to that of the falling-off in the consumption of wine; and the economists have recognized with fright that the French workman does less work than the English workman, because he is not as well fed.

Out of sympathy for the laboring classes M. Chevalier would like our manufacturers to feel the goad of foreign competition a little. A reduction of the tax on woollens to the extent of twenty cents on each pair of pantaloons would leave six million dollars in the pockets of the consumers, — half enough to pay the salt tax. Four cents less in the price of a shirt would effect a saving probably sufficient to keep a force of twenty thousand men under arms.

In the last fifteen years the consumption of sugar has risen from one hundred and sixteen million pounds to two hundred and sixty million, which gives at present an average of seven pounds and three-quarters for each individual. This progress demonstrates that sugar must be classed henceforth with bread, wine, meat, wool, cotton, wood, and coal, among the articles of prime necessity. To the poor man sugar is a whole medicine-chest: would it be too much to raise the average individual consumption of this article from seven pounds and three-quarters to fifteen pounds? Abolish the tax, which is about four dollars and a half on a hundred pounds, and your consumption will double.

Thus the tax on provisions agitates and tortures the poor proletaire in a thousand ways: the high price of salt hinders the production of cattle; the duties on meat diminish also the rations of the laborer. To satisfy at once the tax and the need of fermented beverages which the laboring class feels, they serve him with mixtures unknown to the chemist as well as to the brewer and the wine-grower. What further need have we of the dietary prescriptions of the Church? Thanks to the tax, the whole year is Lent to the laborer, and his Easter dinner is not as good as Monseigneur's Good Friday lunch. It is high time to abolish everywhere the tax on consumption, which weakens and starves the people: this is the conclusion of the economists as well as of the radicals.

But if the proletaire does not fast to feed Caesar, what will Caesar eat? And if the poor man does not cut his cloak to cover Caesar's nudity, what will Caesar wear?

That is the question, the inevitable question, the question to be solved.

M. Chevalier, then, having asked himself as his sixth question whether our taxation laws have the character of sumptuary laws, has answered: No, our taxation laws have not the character of sumptuary laws. M. Chevalier might have added — and it would have been both new and true — that that is the best thing about our taxation laws. But M. Chevalier, who, whatever he may do, always retains some of the old leaven of radicalism, has preferred to declaim against luxury, whereby he could not compromise himself with any party. "If in Paris," he cries, "the tax collected from meat should be laid upon private carriages, saddle-horses and carriage-horses, servants, and dogs, it would be a perfectly equitable operation."

Does M. Chevalier, then, sit in the College of France to expound the politics of Masaniello? I have seen the dogs at Basle wearing the treasury badge upon their necks as a sign that they had been taxed, and I looked upon the tax on dogs, in a country where taxation is almost nothing, as rather a moral lesson and a hygienic precaution than a source of revenue. In 1844 the dog tax of forty-two cents a head gave a revenue of $12,600 in the entire province of Brabant, containing 667,000 inhabitants. From this it may be estimated that the same tax, producing in all France $600,000, would lighten the taxes of quotité less than two cents a year for each individual. Certainly I am far from pretending that $600,000 is a sum to be disdained, especially with a prodigal ministry; and I regret that the Chamber should have rejected the dog tax, which would always have served to endow half a dozen highnesses. But I remember that a tax of this nature is levied much less in the interest of the treasury than as a promoter of order; that consequently it is proper to look upon it, from the fiscal point of view, as of no importance; and that it will even have to be abolished as an annoyance when the mass of the people, having become a little more humanized, shall feel a disgust for the companionship of beasts. Two cents a year, what a relief for poverty!

But M. Chevalier has other resources in reserve, — horses, carriages, servants, articles of luxury, luxury at last! How much is contained in that one word, LUXURY!

Let us cut short this phantasmagoria by a simple calculation; reflections will be in order later. In 1842 the duties collected on imports amounted to $25,800,000. In this sum of $25,800,000, sixty-one articles in common use figure for $24,800,000, and one hundred and seventy-seven, used only by those who enjoy a high degree of luxury, for ten thousand dollars. In the first class sugar yielded a revenue of $8,600,000, coffee $2,400,000, cotton $2,200,000, woollens $2,000,000, oils $1,600,000, coal $800,000, linens and hemp $600,000, — making a total of $18,200,000 on seven articles. The amount of revenue, then, is lower in proportion as the article of merchandise from which it is derived is less generally used, more rarely consumed, and found accompanying a more refined degree of luxury. And yet articles of luxury are subject to much the highest taxes. Therefore, even though, to obtain an appreciable reduction upon articles of primary necessity, the duties upon articles of luxury should be made a hundred times higher, the only result would be the suppression of a branch of commerce by a prohibitory tax. Now, the economists all favor the abolition of custom-houses; doubtless they do not wish them replaced by city toll-gates? Let us generalize this example: salt brings the treasury $11,400,000, tobacco $16,800,000. Let them show me, figures in hand, by what taxes upon articles of luxury, after having abolished the taxes on salt and tobacco, this deficit will be made up.

You wish to strike articles of luxury; you take civilization at the wrong end. I maintain, for my part, that articles of luxury should be free. In economic language what are luxuries? Those products which bear the smallest ratio to the total wealth, those which come last in the industrial series and whose creation supposes the preexistence of all the others. From this point of view all the products of human labor have been, and in turn have ceased to be, articles of luxury, since we mean by luxury nothing but a relation of succession, whether chronological or commercial, in the elements of wealth. Luxury, in a word, is synonymous with progress; it is, at each instant of social life, the expression of the maximum of comfort realized by labor and at which it is the right and destiny of all to arrive. Now, just as the tax respects for a time the newly-built house and the newly-cleared field, so it should freely welcome new products and precious articles, the latter because their scarcity should be continually combatted, the former because every invention deserves encouragement. What! under a pretext of luxury would you like to establish new classes of citizens? And do you take seriously the city of Salente and the prosopopoeia of Fabricius?

Since the subject leads us to it, let us talk of morality. Doubtless you will not deny the truth so often dwelt upon by the Senecas of all ages, — that luxury corrupts and weakens morals: which means that it humanizes, elevates, and ennobles habits, and that the first and most effective education for the people, the stimulant of the ideal in most men, is luxury. The Graces were naked, according to the ancients; where has it ever been said that they were needy? It is the taste for luxury which in our day, in the absence of religious principles, sustains the social movement and reveals to the lower classes their dignity. The Academy of Moral and Political Sciences clearly understood this when it chose luxury as the subject of one of its essays, and I applaud its wisdom from the bottom of my heart. Luxury, in fact, is already more than a right in our society, it is a necessity; and he is truly to be pitied who never allows himself a little luxury. And it is when universal effort tends to popularize articles of luxury more and more that you would confine the enjoyment of the people to articles which you are pleased to describe as articles of necessity! It is when ranks approach and blend into each other through the generalization of luxury that you would dig the line of demarcation deeper and increase the height of your steps! The workman sweats and sacrifices and grinds in order to buy a set of jewelry for his sweetheart, a necklace for his granddaughter, or a watch for his son; and you would deprive him of this happiness, unless he pays your tax, — that is, your fine.

But have you reflected that to tax articles of luxury is to prohibit the luxurious arts? Do you think that the silk-workers, whose average wages does not reach forty cents; the milliners at ten cents; the jewellers, goldsmiths, and clockmakers, with their interminable periods of idleness; servants at forty dollars, — do you think that they earn too much?

Are you sure that the tax on luxuries would not be paid by the worker in the luxurious arts, as the tax on beverages is paid by the consumer of beverages? Do you even know whether higher prices for articles of luxury would not be an obstacle to the cheapness of necessary objects, and whether, in trying to favor the most numerous class, you would not render the general condition worse? A fine speculation, in truth! Four dollars to be returned to the laborer on his wine and sugar, and eight to be taken from him in the cost of his pleasures! He shall gain fifteen cents on the leather in his boots, and, to take his family into the country four times a year, he shall pay one dollar and twenty cents more for carriage-hire! A small bourgeois spends one hundred and twenty dollars for a housekeeper, laundress, linen-tender, and errand-boys; but if, by a wiser economy which works for the interest of all, he takes a domestic, the exchequer, in the interest of articles of subsistence, will punish this plan of economy! What an absurd thing is the philanthropy of the economists, when closely scrutinized!

Nevertheless I wish to satisfy your whim; and, since you absolutely must have sumptuary laws, I undertake to give you the receipt. And I guarantee that in my system collection shall be easy: no comptrollers, assessors, tasters, assayers, inspectors, receivers; no watching, no office expenses; not the smallest annoyance or the slightest indiscretion; no constraint whatever. Let it be decreed by a law that no one in future shall receive two salaries at the same time, and that the highest fees, in any situation, shall not exceed twelve hundred dollars in Paris and eight hundred in the departments. What! you lower your eyes! Confess, then, that your sumptuary laws are but hypocrisy.

To relieve the people some would apply commercial practices to taxation. If, for instance, they say, the price of salt were reduced one-half, if letter-postage were lightened in the same proportion, consumption would not fail to increase, the revenue would be more than doubled, the treasury would gain, and so would the consumer.

Let us suppose the event to confirm this anticipation. Then I say: If letter-postage should be reduced three-fourths, and if salt should be given away, would the treasury still gain? Certainly not. What, then, is the significance of what is called the postal reform? That for every kind of product there is a natural rate, ABOVE which profit becomes usurious and tends to decrease consumption, but BELOW which the producer suffers loss. This singularly resembles the determination of value which the economists reject, and in relation to which we said: There is a secret force that fixes the extreme limits between which value oscillates, of which there is a mean term that expresses true value.

Surely no one wishes the postal service to be carried on at a loss; the opinion, therefore, is that this service should be performed at cost. This is so rudimentary in its simplicity that one is astonished that it should have been necessary to resort to a laborious investigation of the results of reducing letter-postage in England; to pile up frightful figures and probabilities beyond the limit of vision, to put the mind to torture, all to find out whether a reduction in France would lead to a surplus or a deficit, and finally to be unable to agree upon anything! What! there was not a man to be found in the Chamber with sense enough to say: There is no need of an ambassador's report or examples from England; letter-postage should be gradually reduced until receipts reach the level of expenditures.[5] What, then, has become of our old Gallic wit?

But, it will be said, if the tax should furnish salt, tobacco, letter-carriage, sugar, wines, meat, etc., at cost, consumption would undoubtedly increase, and the improvement would be enormous; but then how would the State meet its expenses? The amount of indirect taxes is nearly one hundred and twenty million dollars; upon what would you have the State levy this sum? If the treasury makes nothing out of the postal service, it will have to increase the tax on salt; if the tax on salt be lifted also, it will have to throw the burden back upon drinks; there would be no end to this litany. Therefore the supply of products at cost, whether by the State or by private industry, is impossible.

Therefore, I will reply in turn, relief of the unfortunate classes by the State is impossible, as sumptuary laws are impossible, as the progressive tax is impossible; and all your irrelevancies regarding the tax are lawyer's quibbles. You have not even the hope that the increase of population, by dividing the assessments, may lighten the burden of each; because with population misery increases, and with misery the work and the personnel of the State are augmented.

The various fiscal laws voted by the Chamber of Deputies during the session of 1845–46 are so many examples of the absolute incapacity of power, whatever it may be and however it may go to work, to procure the comfort of the people. From the very fact that it is power, — that is, the representative of divine right and of property, the organ of force, — it is necessarily sterile, and all its acts are stamped in the corner with a fatal deception.

I referred just now to the reform in the postage rates, which reduces the price of letter-carriage about one-third. Surely, if motives only are in question, I have no reason to reproach the government which has effected this useful reduction; much

---

[5] Thank heaven! the minister has settled the question, and I tender him my very sincere compliments. By the proposed tariff letter-postage will be reduced to 2 cents for distances under 12 1/2 miles; 4 cents, for distances between 12 1/2 and 25 miles; 6 cents, between 25 and 75 miles; 8 cents, between 75 and 225 miles; 10 cents, for longer distances.]

less still will I seek to diminish its merit by miserable criticisms upon matters of detail, the vile pasturage of the daily press. A tax, considerably burdensome, is reduced thirty per cent.; its distribution is made more equitable and more regular; I see only the fact, and I applaud the minister who has accomplished it. But that is not the question.

In the first place, the advantage which the government gives us by changing the tax on letters leaves the proportional — that is, the unjust — character of this tax intact: that scarcely requires demonstration. The inequality of burdens, so far as the postal tax is concerned, stands as before, the advantage of the reduction going principally, not to the poorest, but to the richest. A certain business house which paid six hundred dollars for letter-postage will pay hereafter only four hundred; it will add, then, a net profit of two hundred dollars to the ten thousand which its business brings it, and it will owe this to the munificence of the treasury. On the other hand, the peasant, the laborer, who shall write twice a year to his son in the army, and shall receive a like number of replies, will have saved ten cents. Is it not true that the postal reform acts in direct opposition to the equitable distribution of the tax? that if, according to M. Chevalier's wish, the government had desired to strike the rich and spare the poor, the tax on letters was the last that it would have needed to reduce? Does it not seem that the treasury, false to the spirit of its institution, has only been awaiting the pretext of a reduction inappreciable by poverty in order to seize the opportunity to make a present to wealth?

That is what the critics of the bill should have said, and that is what none of them saw. It is true that then the criticism, instead of applying to the minister, struck power in its essence, and with power property, which was not the design of the opponents. Truth today has all opinions against it.

And now could it have been otherwise? No, since, if they kept the old tax, they injured all without relieving any; and, if they reduced it, they could not make different rates for classes of citizens without violating the first article of the Charter, which says: "All Frenchmen are equal before the law," — that is, before the tax. Now, the tax on letters is necessarily personal; therefore it is a capitation-tax; therefore, that which is equity in this respect being iniquity from another standpoint, an equilibrium of burdens is impossible.

At the same time another reform was effected by the care of the government, — that of the tax on cattle. Formerly the duties on cattle, whether on importation from foreign countries, or from the country into the cities, were collected at so much a head; henceforth they will be collected according to weight. This useful reform, which has been clamored for so long, is due in part to the influence of the economists, who, on this occasion as on many others which I cannot recall, have shown the most honorable zeal, and have left the idle declamations of socialism very far in the rear. But here again the good resulting from the law for the amelioration of the condition of the poor is wholly illusory. They have equalized, regulated, the collection from beasts; they have not distributed it equitably among men. The rich man, who consumes twelve hundred pounds of meat a year, will feel the effects of the new condition laid upon the butchers; the immense majority of the people, who never eat meat, will not notice it. And I renew my question of a moment ago: Could the government, the Chamber, do otherwise than as it has done? No, once more; for you cannot say to the butcher: You shall sell your meat to the rich man for twenty cents a pound and to the poor man for five cents. It would be rather the contrary that you would obtain from the butcher.

So with salt. The government has reduced four-fifths the tax on salt used in agriculture, on condition of its undergoing a transformation. A certain journalist, having no better objection to raise, has made thereupon a complaint in which he grieves over the lot of those poor peasants who are more maltreated by the law than their cattle. For the third time I ask: Could it be otherwise? Of two things one: either the reduction will be absolute, and then the tax on salt must be replaced by a tax on something else; now I defy entire French journalism to invent a tax which will bear two minutes' examination; or else the reduction will be partial, whether by maintaining a portion of the duties on salt in all its uses, or by abolishing entirely the duties on salt used in certain ways. In the first case, the reduction is insufficient for agriculture and the poor; in the second, the capitation-tax still exists, in its enormous disproportion. Whatever may be done, it is the poor man, always the poor man, who is struck, since, in spite of all theories, the tax can never be laid except in the ratio of the capital possessed or consumed, and since, if the treasury should try to proceed otherwise, it would arrest progress, prohibit wealth, and kill capital.

The democrats, who reproach us with sacrificing the revolutionary interest (what is the revolutionary interest?) to the socialistic interest, ought really to tell us how, without making the State the sole proprietor and without decreeing the community of goods and gains, they mean, by any system of taxation whatever, to relieve the people and restore to labor what capital takes from it. In vain do I rack my brains; on all questions I see power placed in the falsest situation, and the opinion of journals straying into limitless absurdity.

In 1842 M. Arago was in favor of the administration of railways by corporations, and the majority in France thought with him. In 1846 he has announced a change in his opinion; and, apart from the speculators in railways, it may be said again that the majority of citizens have changed as M. Arago has. What is to be believed and what is to be done amid this see-sawing of the savants and of France?

State administration, it would seem, ought to better assure the interests of the country; but it is slow, expensive, and unintelligent. Twenty-five years of mistakes, miscalculations, improvidence, hundreds of millions thrown away, in the great work of canalizing the country, have proved it to the most incredulous. We have even seen engineers, members of the administration, loudly proclaiming the incapacity of the State in the matter of public works as well as of industry.

Administration by corporations is irreproachable, it is true, from the standpoint of the interest of the stockholders; but with these the general interest is sacrificed, the door opened to speculation, and the exploitation of the public by monopoly organized.

The ideal system would be one uniting the advantages of both methods without presenting any of their shortcomings. Now, the means of realizing these contradictory characteristics? the means of breathing zeal, economy, penetration into these irremovable officers who have nothing to gain or to lose? the means of rendering the interests of the public as dear to a corporation as its own, of making these interests veritably its own, and still keeping it distinct from the State and having consequently its private interests? Who is there, in the official world, that conceives the necessity and therefore the possibility of such a reconciliation? much more, then, who possesses its secret?

In such an emergency the government, as usual, has chosen the course of eclecticism; it has taken a part of the administration for itself and left the rest to the corporations; that is, instead of reconciling the contraries, it has placed them exactly in conflict. And the press, which in all things is precisely on a par with power in the matter of wit, — the press, dividing itself into three fractions, has decided, one for the ministerial compromise, another for the exclusion of the State, and the third for the exclusion of the corporations. So that today no more than before do the public or M. Arago, in spite of their somersault, know what they want.

What a herd is the French nation in this nineteenth century, with its three powers, its press, its scientific bodies, its literature, its instruction! A hundred thousand men, in our country, have their eyes constantly open upon everything that interests national progress and the country's honor. Now, propound to these hundred thousand men the simplest question of public order, and you may be assured that all will rush pell-mell into the same absurdity.

Is it better that the promotion of officials should be governed by merit or by length of service?

Certainly there is no one who would not like to see this double method of estimating capacities blended into one. What a society it would be in which the rights of talent would be always in harmony with those of age! But, they say, such perfection is utopian, for it is contradictory in its statement. And instead of seeing that it is precisely the contradiction which makes the thing possible, they begin to dispute over the respective value of the two opposed systems, which, each leading to the absurd, equally give rise to intolerable abuses.

Who shall be the judge of merit? asks one: the government. Now, the government recognizes merit only in its creatures. Therefore no promotion by choice, none of that immoral system which destroys the independence and the dignity of the office-holder.

But, says another, length of service is undoubtedly very respectable. It is a pity that it has the disadvantage of rendering stagnant things which are essentially voluntary and free, — labor and thought; of creating obstacles to power even among its agents, and of bestowing upon chance, often upon incapacity, the reward of genius and audacity.

Finally they compromise: to the government is accorded the power of appointing arbitrarily to a certain number of offices pretended men of merit, who are supposed to have no need of experience, while the rest, apparently deemed incapable, are promoted in turn. And the press, that ambling old nag of all presumptuous mediocrities, which generally lives only by the gratuitous compositions of young people as destitute of talent as of acquired knowledge, hastens to begin again its attacks upon power, accusing it, — not without reason too, — here of favoritism, there of routine.

Who could hope ever to do anything to the satisfaction of the press? After having declaimed and gesticulated against the enormous size of the budget, here it is clamoring for increased salaries for an army of officials, who, to tell the truth, really have not the wherewithal to live. Now it is the teachers, of high and low grade, who make their complaints heard through its columns; now it is the country clergy, so insufficiently paid that they have been forced to maintain their fees, a fertile source of scandal and abuse. Then it is the whole administrative nation, which is neither lodged, nor clothed, nor warmed, nor fed: it is a million men with their families, nearly an eighth of the population, whose poverty brings shame upon France and for whom one hundred million dollars should at once be added to the budget. Note that in this immense personnel there is not one man too many; on the contrary, if the population grows, it will increase proportionally. Are you in a position to tax the nation to the extent of four hundred million dollars? Can you take, out of an average income of $184 for four persons, $47.25 -more than one-fourth — to pay, together with the other expenses of the State, the salaries of the non-productive laborers? And if you cannot, if you can neither pay your expenses nor reduce them, what do you want? of what do you complain?

Let the people know it, then, once for all: all the hopes of reduction and equity in taxation, with which they are lulled by turns by the harangues of power and the diatribes of party leaders, are so many mystifications; the tax cannot be reduced, nor can its assessment be more equitable, under the monopoly system. On the contrary, the lower the condition of the citizen becomes, the heavier becomes his tax; that is inevitable, irresistible, in spite of the avowed design of the legislator and the repeated efforts of the treasury. Whoever cannot become or remain rich, whoever has entered the cavern of misfortune, must make up his mind to pay in proportion to his poverty: Lasciate ogni speranza, voi ch' entrate.

Taxation, then, police, — henceforth we shall not separate these two ideas, — is a new source of pauperism; taxation aggravates the subversive effects of the preceding antinomies, — division of labor, machinery, competition, monopoly. It attacks the laborer in his liberty and in his conscience, in his body and in his soul, by parasitism, vexations, the frauds which it prompts, and the punishments which follow them.

Under Louis XIV. the smuggling of salt alone caused annually thirty-seven hundred domiciliary seizures, two thousand arrests of men, eighteen hundred of women, sixty-six hundred of children, eleven hundred seizures of horses, fifty confiscations of carriages, and three hundred condemnations to the galleys. And this, observes the historian, was the result of one tax alone, — the salt-tax. What, then, was the total number of unfortunates imprisoned, tortured, expropriated, on account of the tax?

In England, out of every four families, one is unproductive, and that is the family which enjoys an abundance. What an advantage it would be for the working-class, you think, if this leprosy of parasitism should be removed! Undoubtedly, in theory, you are right; in practice, the suppression of parasitism would be a calamity. Though one-fourth of the population of England is unproductive, another fourth of the same population is at work for it: now, what would these laborers do, if they should suddenly lose the market for their products? An absurd supposition, you say. Yes, an absurd supposition, but a very real supposition, and one which you must admit precisely because it is absurd. In France a standing army of five hundred thousand men, forty thousand priests, twenty thousand doctors, eighty thousand lawyers, and I know not how many hundred thousand other nonproducers of every sort, constitute an immense market for our agriculture and our manufactures. Let this market suddenly close, and manufactures will stop, commerce will go into bankruptcy, and agriculture will be smothered beneath its products.

But how is it conceivable that a nation should find its market clogged because of having got rid of its useless mouths? Ask rather why an engine, whose consumption has been figured at six hundred pounds of coal an hour, loses its power if it is given only three hundred. But again, might not these non-producers be made producers, since we cannot get rid of them? Eh! child: tell me, then, how you will do without police, and monopoly, and competition, and all the contradictions, in short, of which your order of things is made up. Listen.

In 1844, at the time of the troubles in Rive-de-Gier, M. Anselme Petetin published in the "Revue Independante" two articles, full of reason and sincerity, concerning the anarchy prevailing in the conduct of the coal mines in the basin of the Loire. M. Petetin pointed out the necessity of uniting the mines and centralizing their administration. The facts which he laid before the public were not unknown to power; has power troubled itself about the union of the mines and the organization of that industry? Not at all. Power has followed the principle of free competition; it has let alone and looked on.

Since that time the mining companies have combined, not without causing some anxiety to consumers, who have seen in this combination a plot to raise the price of fuel. Will power, which has received numerous complaints upon this subject, intervene to restore competition and prevent monopoly? It cannot do it; the right of combination is identical in law with the right of association; monopoly is the basis of our society, as competition is its conquest; and, provided there is no riot, power will let alone and look on. What other course could it pursue? Can it prohibit a legally established commercial association? Can it oblige neighbors to destroy each other? Can it forbid them to reduce their expenses? Can it establish a maximum? If power should do any one of these things, it would overturn the established order. Power, therefore, can take no initiative: it is instituted to defend and protect monopoly and competition at once, within the limitations of patents, licenses, land taxes, and other bonds which it has placed upon property. Apart from these limitations power has no sort of right to act in the name of society. The social right is not defined; moreover, it would be a denial of monopoly and competition. How, then, could power take up the defence of that which the law did not foresee or define, of that which is the opposite of the rights recognized by the legislator?

Consequently, when the miner, whom we must consider in the events of Rive-de-Gier as the real representative of society against the mine-owners, saw fit to resist the scheme of the monopolists by defending his wages and opposing combination to combination, power shot the miner down. And the political brawlers accused authority, saying it was partial, ferocious, sold to monopoly, etc. For my part, I declare that this way of viewing the acts of authority seems to me scarcely philosophical, and I reject it with all my energies. It is possible that they might have killed fewer people, possible also that they might have killed more: the fact to be noticed here is not the number of dead and wounded, but the repression of the workers. Those who have criticised authority would have done as it did, barring perhaps the impatience of its bayonets and the accuracy of its aim: they would have repressed, I say; they would not have been able to do anything else. And the reason, which it would be vain to try to brush aside, is that competition is legal, joint-stock association is legal, supply and demand are legal, and all the consequences which flow directly from competition, joint-stock association, and free commerce are legal, whereas workingmen's strikes are ILLEGAL. And it is not only the penal code which says this, but the economic system, the necessity of the established order. As long as labor is not sovereign, it must be a slave; society is possible only on this condition. That each worker individually should have the free disposition of his person and his arms may be tolerated;[6] but that the workers should undertake, by combinations, to do violence to monopoly society cannot permit. Crush monopoly, and you abolish competition, and you disorganize the workshop, and you sow dissolution everywhere. Authority, in shooting down the miners, found itself in the position of Brutus placed between his paternal love and his consular duties: he had to sacrifice either his children or the republic. The alternative was horrible, I admit; but such is the spirit and letter of the social compact, such is the tenor of the charter, such is the order of Providence.

Thus the police function, instituted for the defence of the proletariat, is directed entirely against the proletariat. The proletaire is driven from the forests, from the rivers, from the mountains; even the cross-roads are forbidden him; soon he will know no road save that which leads to prison.

The advance in agriculture has made the advantage of artificial meadows and the necessity of abolishing common land generally felt. Everywhere communal lands are being cleared, let, enclosed; new advances, new wealth. But the poor day-laborer, whose only patrimony is the communal land and who supports a cow and several sheep in summer by letting them feed along the roads, through the underbrush, and over the stripped fields, will lose his sole and last resource. The landed proprietor, the purchaser or farmer of the communal lands, will alone thereafter sell, with his wheat and vegetables, milk and cheese. Instead of weakening an old monopoly, they create a new one. Even the road-laborers reserve for themselves the edges of the roads as a meadow belonging to them, and drive off all non-administrative cattle. What follows? That the day-laborer, before abandoning his cow, lets it feed in contravention of the law, becomes a marauder, commits a thousand depredations, and is punished by fine and imprisonment: of what use to him are police and agricultural progress? Last year the mayor of Mulhouse, to prevent grape-stealing, forbade every individual not an owner of

---

The new law regarding service-books has confined the independence of workers within narrower limits. The democratic press has again thundered its indignation this subject against those in power, as if they had been guilty of anything more than the application of the principles of authority and property, which are those of democracy. What the Chambers have done in regard to service-books was inevitable, and should have been expected. It is as impossible for a society founded on the proprietary principle not to end in class distinctions as for a democracy to avoid despotism, for a religion to be reasonable, for fanaticism to show tolerance. This is the law of contradiction: how long will it take us to understand it?

vines to travel by day or night over roads running by or through vineyards, — a charitable precaution, since it prevented even desires and regrets. But if the public highway is nothing but an accessory of private property; if the communal lands are converted into private property; if the public domain, in short, assimilated to private property, is guarded, exploited, leased, and sold like private property, — what remains for the proletaire? Of what advantage is it to him that society has left the state of war to enter the regime of police?

Industry, as well as land, has its privileges, — privileges consecrated by the law, as always, under conditions and reservations, but, as always also, to the great disadvantage of the consumer. The question is interesting; we will say a few words upon it.

I quote M. Renouard.

"Privileges," says M. Renouard, "were a corrective of regulation."

I ask M. Renouard's permission to translate his thought by reversing his phrase: Regulation was a corrective of privilege. For whoever says regulation says limitation: now, how conceive of limiting privilege before it existed? I can conceive a sovereign submitting privileges to regulations; but I cannot at all understand why he should create privileges expressly to weaken the effect of regulations. There is nothing to prompt such a concession; it would be an effect without a cause. In logic as well as in history, everything is appropriated and monopolized when laws and regulations arrive: in this respect civil legislation is like penal legislation. The first results from possession and appropriation, the second from the appearance of crimes and offences. M. Renouard, preoccupied with the idea of servitude inherent in all regulation, has considered privilege as a compensation for this servitude; and it was this which led him to say that privileges are a corrective of regulation. But what M. Renouard adds proves that he meant the opposite:

The fundamental principle of our legislation, that of granting temporary monopoly as a condition of a contract between society and the laborer, has always prevailed, etc.

What is, in reality, this grant of a monopoly? A simple acknowledgment, a declaration. Society, wishing to favor a new industry and enjoy the advantages which it promises, bargains with the inventor, as it has bargained with the farmer; it guarantees him the monopoly of his industry for a time; but it does not create the monopoly. The monopoly exists by the very fact of the invention; and the acknowledgment of the monopoly is what constitutes society.

This ambiguity cleared up, I pass to the contradictions of the law.

All industrial nations have adopted the establishment of a temporary monopoly as a condition of a contract between society and the inventor . . . . I do not take readily to the belief that all legislators of all countries have committed robbery.

M. Renouard, if ever he reads this work, will do me the justice to admit that, in quoting him, I do not criticise his thought; he himself has perceived the contradictions of the patent law. All that I pretend is to connect this contradiction with the general system.

Why, in the first place, a temporary monopoly in manufacture, while land monopoly is perpetual? The Egyptians were more logical; with them these two monopolies were alike hereditary, perpetual, inviolable. I know the considerations which have prevailed against the perpetuity of literary property, and I admit them all; but these considerations apply equally well to property in land; moreover, they leave intact all the arguments brought forward against them. What, then, is the secret of all these variations of the legislator? For the rest, I do not need to say that, in pointing out this inconsistency, it is not my purpose either to slander or to satirize; I admit that the course of the legislator is determined, not by his will, but by necessity.

But the most flagrant contradiction is that which results from the enacting section of the law. Title IV, article 30, 3, reads: "If the patent relates to principles, methods, systems, discoveries, theoretical or purely scientific conceptions, without indicating their industrial applications, the patent is void."

Now, what is a principle, a method, a theoretical conception, a system? It is the especial fruit of genius, it is invention in its purity, it is the idea, it is everything. The application is the gross fact, nothing. Thus the law excludes from the benefit of the patent the very thing which deserves it, — namely, the idea; on the contrary, it grants a patent to the application, — that is, to the material fact, to a pattern of the idea, as Plato would have said. Therefore it is wrongly called a patent for invention; it should be called a patent for first occupancy.

In our day, if a man had invented arithmetic, algebra, or the decimal system, he would have obtained no patent; but Bareme would have had a right of property in his Computations. Pascal, for his theory of the weight of the atmosphere, would not have been patented; instead of him, a glazier would have obtained the privilege of the barometer. I quote M. Arago:

After two thousand years it occurred to one of our fellow-countrymen that the screw of Archimedes, which is used to raise water, might be employed in forcing down gases; it suffices, without making any change, to turn it from right to left, instead of turning it, as when raising water, from left to right. Large volumes of gas, charged with foreign substances, are thus forced into water to a great depth; the gas is purified in rising again. I maintain that there was an invention; that the person who saw a way to make the screw of Archimedes a blowing machine was entitled to a patent.

What is more extraordinary is that Archimedes himself would thus be obliged to buy the right to use his screw; and M. Arago considers that just.

It is useless to multiply these examples: what the law meant to monopolize is, as I said just now, not the idea, but the fact; not the invention, but the occupancy. As if the idea were not the category which includes all the facts that express it; as if a method, a system, were not a generalization of experiences, and consequently that which properly constitutes the fruit of genius, — invention! Here legislation is more than anti-economic, it borders on the silly. Therefore I am entitled to ask the legislator why, in spite of free competition, which is nothing but the right to apply a theory, a principle, a method, a non-appropriable system, he forbids in certain cases this same competition, this right to apply a principle?" It is no longer possible," says M. Renouard, with strong reason, "to stifle competitors by combining in corporations and guilds; the loss is supplied by patents." Why has the legislator given hands to this conspiracy of monopolies, to this interdict upon theories belonging to all?

But what is the use of continually questioning one who can say nothing? The legislator did not know in what spirit he was acting when he made this strange application of the right of property, which, to be exact, we ought to call the right of priority. Let him explain himself, then, at least, regarding the clauses of the contract made by him, in our name, with the monopolists.

I pass in silence the part relating to dates and other administrative and fiscal formalities, and come to this article:

The patent does not guarantee the invention.

Doubtless society, or the prince who represents it, cannot and should not guarantee the invention, since, in granting a monopoly for fourteen years, society becomes the purchaser of the privilege, and consequently it is for the patentee to furnish the guarantee. How, then, can legislators proudly say to their constituents: "We have negotiated in your name with an inventor; he pledges himself to give you the enjoyment of his discovery on condition of having the exclusive exploitation for fourteen years. But we do not guarantee the invention"? On what, then, have you relied, legislators? How did you fail to see that, without a guarantee of the invention, you conceded a privilege, not for a real discovery, but for a possible discovery, and that thus the field of industry was given up by you before the plough was found? Certainly, your duty bade you to be prudent; but who gave you a commission to be dupes?

Thus the patent for invention is not even the fixing of a date; it is an abandonment in anticipation. It is as if the law should say: "I assure the land to the first occupant, but without guaranteeing its quality, its location, or even its existence; not even knowing whether I ought to give it up or that it falls within the domain of appropriation!" A pretty use of the legislative power!

I know that the law had excellent reasons for abstaining; but I maintain that it also had good reasons for intervening. Proof:

"It cannot be concealed," says M. Renouard, "it cannot be prevented; patents are and will be instruments of quackery as well as a legitimate reward of labor and genius. . . It is for the good sense of the public to do justice to juggleries."

As well say it is for the good sense of the public to distinguish true remedies from false, pure wine from adulterated; or, it is for the good sense of the public to distinguish in a buttonhole the decoration awarded to merit from that prostituted to mediocrity and intrigue. Why, then, do you call yourselves the State, Power, Authority, Police, if the work of Police must be performed by the good sense of the public?

As the proverb says, he who owns land must defend it; likewise, he who holds a privilege is liable to attack.

Well! how will you judge the counterfeit, if you have no guarantee? In vain will they offer you the plea: in right first occupancy, in fact similarity. Where reality depends upon quality, not to demand a guarantee is to grant no right over anything, is to take away the means of comparing processes and identifying the counterfeit. In the matter of industrial processes success depends upon such trifles! Now, these trifles are the whole.

I infer from all this that the law regarding patents for inventions, indispensable so far as its motives are concerned, is impossible — that is, illogical, arbitrary, disastrous — in its economy. Under the control of certain necessities the legislator has thought best, in the general interest, to grant a privilege for a definite thing; and he finds that he has given a signature-in-blank to monopoly, that he has abandoned the chances which the public had of making the discovery or some other similar to it, that he has sacrificed the rights of competitors without compensation, and abandoned the good faith of defenceless consumers to the greed of quacks. Then, in order that nothing might be lacking to the absurdity of the contract, he has said to those whom he ought to guarantee: "Guarantee yourselves!"

I do not believe, any more than M. Renouard, that the legislators of all ages and all countries have wilfully committed robbery in sanctioning the various monopolies which are pivotal in public economy. But M. Renouard might well also agree with me that the legislators of all ages and all countries have never understood at all their own decrees. A deaf and blind man once learned to ring the village bells and wind the village clock. It was fortunate for him, in performing his bell-ringer's functions, that neither the noise of the bells nor the height of the bell-tower made him dizzy. The legislators of all ages and all countries, for whom I profess, with M. Renouard, the profoundest respect, resemble that blind and deaf man; they are the Jacks-in-the-clock-house of all human follies.

What a feather it would be in my cap if I should succeed in making these automata reflect! if I could make them understand that their work is a Penelope's web, which they are condemned to unravel at one end as fast as they weave at the other!

Thus, while applauding the creation of patents, on other points they demand the abolition of privileges, and always with the same pride, the same satisfaction. M. Horace Say wishes trade in meat to be free. Among other reasons he puts forward this strictly mathematical argument:

The butcher who wants to retire from business seeks a purchaser for his investment; he figures in the account his tools, his merchandise, his reputation, and his custom; but under the present system, he adds to these the value of the bare title, — that is, the right to share in a monopoly. Now, this supplementary capital which the purchasing butcher gives for the title bears interest; it is not a new creation; this interest must enter into the price of his meat. Hence the limitation of the number of butchers' stalls has a tendency to raise the price of meat rather than lower it.

I do not fear to affirm incidentally that what I have just said about the sale of a butcher's stall applies to every charge whatever having a salable title.

M. Horace Say's reasons for the abolition of the butcher's privilege are unanswerable; moreover, they apply to printers, notaries, attorneys, process-servers, clerks of courts, auctioneers, brokers, dealers in stocks, druggists, and others, as well as to butchers. But they do not destroy the reasons which have led to the adoption of these monopolies, and which are generally deduced from the need of security, authenticity, and regularity in business, as well as from the interests of commerce and the public health. The object, you say, is not attained. My God! I know it: leave the butcher's trade to competition, and you will eat carrion; establish a monopoly in the butcher's trade, and you will eat carrion. That is the only fruit you can hope for from your monopoly and patent legislation.

Abuses! cry the protective economists. Establish over commerce a supervisory police, make trade-marks obligatory, punish the adulteration of products, etc.

In the path upon which civilization has entered, whichever way we turn, we always end, then, either in the despotism of monopoly, and consequently the oppression of consumers, or else in the annihilation of privilege by the action of the police, which is to go backwards in economy and dissolve society by destroying liberty. Marvellous thing! in this system of free industry, abuses, like lice, being generated by their own remedies, if the legislator should try to suppress all offences, be on the watch against all frauds, and secure persons, property, and the public welfare against any attack, going from reform to reform, he would finally so multiply the non-productive functions that the entire nation would be engaged in them, and that at last there would be nobody left to produce. Everybody would be a policeman; the industrial class would become a myth. Then, perhaps, order would reign in monopoly.

"The principle of the law yet to be made concerning trade-marks," says M. Renouard, "is that these marks cannot and should not be transformed into guarantees of quality."

This is a consequence of the patent law, which, as we have seen, does not guarantee the invention. Adopt M. Renouard's principle; after that of what use will marks be? Of what importance is it to me to read on the cork of a bottle, instead of twelve-cent wine or fifteen-cent wine, WINE-DRINKERS' COMPANY or the name of any other concern you will? What I care for is not the name of the merchant, but the quality and fair price of the merchandise.

The name of the manufacturer is supposed, it is true, to serve as a concise sign of good or bad manufacture, of superior or inferior quality. Then why not frankly take part with those who ask, besides the mark of origin, a mark significant of something? Such a reservation is incomprehensible. The two sorts of marks have the same purpose; the second is only a statement or paraphrase of the first, a condensation of the merchant's prospectus; why, once more, if the origin signifies something, should not the mark define this significance?

M. Wolowski has very clearly developed this argument in his opening lecture of 1843–44, the substance of which lies entirely in the following analogy:

Just as the government has succeeded in determining a standard of quantity, it may, it should also fix a standard of quality; one of these standards is the necessary complement of the other. The monetary unit, the system of weights and measures, have not infringed upon industrial liberty; no more would it be damaged by a system of trade-marks.

M. Wolowski then supports himself on the authority of the princes of the science, A. Smith and J. B. Say, — a precaution always useful with hearers who bow to authority much more than to reason.

I declare, for my part, that I thoroughly share M. Wolowski's idea, and for the reason that I find it profoundly revolutionary. The trade-mark, being, according to M. Wolowski's expression, nothing but a standard of qualities, is equivalent in my eyes to a general scheduling of prices. For, whether a particular administration marks in the name of the State and guarantees the quality of the merchandise, as is the case with gold and silver, or whether the matter of marking is left to the manufacturer, from the moment that the mark must give the intrinsic composition of the merchandise (these are M. Wolowski's own words) and guarantee the consumer against all surprise, it necessarily resolves itself into a fixed price. It is not the same thing as price; two similar products, but differing in origin and quality, may be of equal value, as a bottle of Burgundy may be worth a bottle of Bordeaux; but the mark, being significant, leads to an exact knowledge of the price, since it gives the analysis. To calculate the price of an article of merchandise is to decompose it into its constituent parts; now, that is exactly what the trade-mark must do, if designed to signify anything. Therefore we are on the road, as I have said, to a general scheduling of prices.

But a general scheduling of prices is nothing but a determination of all values, and here again political economy comes into conflict with its own principles and tendencies. Unfortunately, to realize M. Wolowski's reform, it is necessary to begin by solving all the previous contradictions and enter a higher sphere of association; and it is this absence of solution which has brought down upon M. Wolowski's system the condemnation of most of his fellow-economists.

In fact, the system of trade-marks is inapplicable in the existing order, because this system, contrary to the interests of the manufacturers and repugnant to their habits, could be sustained only by the energetic will of power. Suppose for a moment that the administration be charged with affixing the marks; its agents will have to interpose continually in the work of manufacture, as it interposes in the liquor business and the manufacture of beer; further, these agents, whose functions seem already so intrusive and annoying, deal only with taxable quantities, not with exchangeable qualities. These fiscal supervisors and inspectors will have to carry their investigation into all details in order to repress and prevent fraud; and what fraud? The legislator will have defined it either incorrectly or not at all; it is at this point that the task becomes appalling.

There is no fraud in selling wine of the poorest quality, but there is fraud in passing off one quality for another; then you are obliged to differentiate the qualities of wines, and consequently to guarantee them. Is it fraudulent to mix wines? Chaptal, in his treatise on the art of making wine, advises this as eminently useful; on the other hand, experience proves that certain wines, in some way antagonistic to each other or incompatible, produce by their mixture a disagreeable and unhealthy drink. Then you are obliged to say what wines can be usefully mixed, and what cannot. Is it fraudulent to aromatize, alcoholize, and water wines? Chaptal recommends this also; and everybody knows that this drugging produces sometimes advantageous results, sometimes pernicious and detestable effects. What substances will you proscribe? In what cases? In what proportion? Will you prohibit chicory in coffee, glucose in beer, water, cider, and three-six alcohol in wine?

The Chamber of Deputies, in the rude attempt at a law which it was pleased to make this year regarding the adulteration of wines, stopped in the very middle of its work, overcome by the inextricable difficulties of the question. It succeeded in declaring that the introduction of water into wine, and of alcohol above the proportion of eighteen per cent., was fraudulent, and in putting this fraud into the category of offences. It was on the ground of ideology; there one never meets an obstacle. But everybody has seen in this redoubling of severity the interest of the treasury much more than that of the consumer; the Chamber did not dare to create a whole army of wine-tasters, inspectors, etc., to watch for fraud and identify it, and thus load the budget with a few extra millions; in prohibiting watering and alcoholization, the only means left to the merchant-manufacturers of putting wine within the reach of all and realizing profits, it did not succeed in increasing the market by a decrease in production. The chamber, in a word, in prosecuting the adulteration of wines, has simply set back the limits of fraud. To make its work accomplish its purpose it would first have to show how the liquor trade is possible without adulteration, and how the people can buy unadulterated wine, — which is beyond the competency and escapes the capacity of the Chamber.

If you wish the consumer to be guaranteed, both as to value and as to healthfulness, you are forced to know and to determine all that constitutes good and honest production, to be continually at the heels of the manufacturer, and to guide him at every step. He no longer manufactures; you, the State, are the real manufacturer.

Thus you find yourself in a trap. Either you hamper the liberty of commerce by interfering in production in a thousand ways, or you declare yourself sole producer and sole merchant.

In the first case, through annoying everybody, you will finally cause everybody to rebel; and sooner or later, the State getting itself expelled, trade-marks will be abolished. In the second you substitute everywhere the action of power for individual initiative, which is contrary to the principles of political economy and the constitution of society. Do you take a middle course? It is favor, nepotism, hypocrisy, the worst of systems.

Suppose, now, that the marking be left to the manufacturer. I say that then the marks, even if made obligatory, will gradually lose their significance, and at last become only proofs of origin. He knows but little of commerce who imagines that a merchant, a head of a manufacturing enterprise, making use of processes that are not patentable, will betray the secret of his industry, of his profits, of his existence. The significance will then be a delusion; it is not in the power of the police to make it otherwise. The Roman emperors, to discover the Christians who dissembled their religion, obliged everybody to sacrifice to the idols. They made apostates and martyrs; and the number of Christians only increased. Likewise significant marks, useful to some houses, will engender innumerable frauds and repressions; that is all that can be expected of them. To induce the manufacturer to frankly indicate the intrinsic composition — that is, the industrial and commercial value — of his merchandise, it is necessary to free him from the perils of competition and satisfy his monopolistic instincts: can you do it? It is necessary, further, to interest the consumer in the repression of fraud, which, so long as the producer is not utterly disinterested, is at once impossible and contradictory. Impossible: place on the one hand a depraved consumer, China; on the other a desperate merchant, England; between them a venomous drug causing excitement and intoxication; and, in spite of all the police in the world, you will have trade in opium. Contradictory: in society the consumer and the producer are but one, — that is, both are interested in the production of that which it is injurious to them to consume; and as, in the case of each, consumption follows production and sale, all will combine to guard the first interest, leaving it to each to guard himself against the second.

The thought which prompted trade-marks is of the same character as that which formerly inspired the maximum laws. Here again is one of the innumerable cross-roads of political economy.

It is indisputable that maximum laws, though made and supported by their authors entirely as a relief from famine, have invariably resulted in an aggravation of famine. Accordingly it is not injustice or malice with which the economists charge these abhorred laws, but stupidity, inexpediency. But what a contradiction in the theory with which they oppose them!

To relieve famine it is necessary to call up provisions, or, to put it better, to bring them to light; so far there is nothing to reproach. To secure a supply of provisions it is necessary to attract the holders by profits, excite their competition, and assure them complete liberty in the market: does not this process strike you as the absurdest homoeopathy? How is it that the more easily I can be taxed the sooner I shall be provided? Let alone, they say, let pass; let competition and monopoly act, especially in times of famine, and even though famine is the effect of competition and monopoly. What logic! but, above all, what morality!

But why, then, should there not be a tariff for farmers as well as for bakers? Why not a registration of the sowing, of the harvest, of the vintage, of the pasturage, and of the cattle, as well as a stamp for newspapers, circulars, and orders, or an administration for brewers and wine-merchants? Under the monopoly system this would be, I admit, an increase of torments; but with our tendencies to unfairness in trade and the disposition of power to continually increase its personnel and its budget, a law of inquisition regarding crops is becoming daily more indispensable.

Besides, it would be difficult to say which, free trade or the maximum, causes the more evil in times of famine.

But, whichever course you choose, — and you cannot avoid the alternative, — the deception is sure and the disaster immense. With the maximum goods seek concealment; the terror increasing from the very effect of the law, the price of provisions rises and rises; soon circulation stops, and the catastrophe follows, as prompt and pitiless as a band of plunderers. With competition the progress of the scourge is slower, but no less fatal: how many deaths from exhaustion or hunger before the high prices attract food to the market! how many victims of extortion after it has arrived! It is the story of the king to whom God, in punishment for his pride, offered the alternative of three days' pestilence, three months' famine, or three years' war. David chose the shortest; the economists prefer the longest. Man is so miserable that he would rather end by consumption than by apoplexy; it seems to him that he does not die as much. This is the reason why the disadvantages of the maximum and the benefits of free trade have been so much exaggerated.

For the rest, if France during the last twenty-five years has experienced no general famine, the cause is not in the liberty of commerce, which knows very well, when it wishes, how to produce scarcity in the midst of plenty and how to make famine prevail in the bosom of abundance; it is in the improvement in the methods of communication, which, shortening distances, soon restore the equilibrium disturbed for a moment by local penury. A striking example of that sad truth that in society the general welfare is never the effect of a conspiracy of individual wills!

The farther we delve into this system of illusory compromises between monopoly and society, — that is, as we have explained in 1 of this chapter, between capital and labor, between the patriciate and the proletariat, -the more we discover that it is all foreseen, regulated, and executed in accordance with this infernal maxim, with which Hobbes and Machiavel, those theorists of despotism, were unacquainted: EVERYTHING BY THE PEOPLE AND AGAINST THE PEOPLE. While labor produces, capital, under the mask of a false fecundity, enjoys and abuses; the legislator, in offering his mediation, thought to recall the privileged class to fraternal feelings and surround the laborer with guarantees; and now he finds, by the fatal contradiction of interests, that each of these guarantees is an instrument of torture. It would require a hundred volumes, the life of ten men, and a heart of iron, to relate from this standpoint the crimes of the State towards the poor and the infinite variety of its tortures. A summary glance at the principal classes of police will be enough to enable us to estimate its spirit and economy.

After having sown trouble in all minds by a confusion of civil, commercial, and administrative laws, made the idea of justice more obscure by multiplying contradictions, and rendered necessary a whole class of interpreters for the explanation of this system, it has been found necessary also to organize the repression of crimes and provide for their punishment. Criminal justice, that particularly rich order of the great family of non-producers, whose maintenance costs France annually more than six million dollars, has become to society a principle of existence as necessary as bread is to the life of man; but with this difference, — that man lives by the product of his hands, while society devours its members and feeds on its own flesh.

It is calculated by some economists that there is,

In London..	1 criminal to every	89 inhabitants.
In Liverpool..	1 " "	45 "
In Newcastle..	1 " "	27 "

But these figures lack accuracy, and, utterly frightful as they seem, do not express the real degree of social perversion due to the police. We have to determine here not only the number of recognized criminals, but the number of offences. The work of the criminal courts is only a special mechanism which serves to place in relief the moral destruction of humanity under the monopoly system; but this official exhibition is far from including the whole extent of the evil. Here are other figures which will lead us to a more certain approximation.

The police courts of Paris disposed,

In 1835 . . . of	106,467 cases.
In 1836 . . . "	128,489 "
In 1837 . . . "	140,247 "

Supposing this rate of increase to have continued up to 1846, and to this total of misdemeanors adding the cases of the criminal courts, the simple matters that go no further than the police, and all the offences unknown or left unpunished, — offences far surpassing in number, so the magistrates say, those which justice reaches, — we shall arrive at the conclusion that in one year, in the city of Paris, there are more infractions of the law committed than there are inhabitants. And as it is necessary to deduct from the presumable authors of these infractions children of seven years and under, who are outside the limits of guilt, the figures will show that every adult citizen is guilty, three or four times a year, of violating the established order.

Thus the proprietary system is maintained at Paris only by the annual consummation of one or two millions of offences! Now, though all these offences should be the work of a single man, the argument would still hold good: this man would be the scapegoat loaded with the sins of Israel: of what consequence is the number of the guilty, provided justice has its contingent?

Violence, perjury, robbery, cheating, contempt of persons and society, are so much a part of the essence of monopoly; they flow from it so naturally, with such perfect regularity, and in accordance with laws so certain, — that it is possible to submit their perpetration to calculation, and, given the number of a population, the condition of its industry, and the stage of its enlightenment, to rigorously deduce therefrom the statistics of its morality. The economists do not know yet what the principle of value is; but they know, within a few decimals, the proportionality of crime. So many thousand souls, so many malefactors, so many condemnations: about that there can be no mistake. It is one of the most beautiful applications of the theory of chances, and the most advanced branch of economic science. If socialism had invented this accusing theory, the whole world would have cried calumny.

Yet, after all, what is there in it that should surprise us? As misery is a necessary result of the contradictions of society, a result which it is possible to determine mathematically from the rate of interest, the rate of wages, and the prevailing market-prices, so crimes and misdemeanors are another effect of this same antagonism, susceptible, like its cause, of estimation by figures. The materialists have drawn the silliest inferences from this subordination of liberty to the laws of numbers: as if man were not under the influence of all that surrounds him, and as if, since all that surrounds him is governed by inexorable laws, he must not experience, in his freest manifestations, the reaction of those laws!

The same character of necessity which we have just pointed out in the establishment and sustenance of criminal justice is found, but under a more metaphysical aspect, in its morality.

In the opinion of all moralists, the penalty should be such as to secure the reformation of the offender, and consequently free from everything that might cause his degradation. Far be it from me to combat this blessed tendency of minds and disparage attempts which would have been the glory of the greatest men of antiquity. Philanthropy, in spite of the ridicule which sometimes attaches to its name, will remain, in the eyes of posterity, the most honorable characteristic of our time: the abolition of the death penalty, which is merely postponed; the abolition of the stigma; the studies regarding the effects of the cellular system; the establishment of workshops in the prisons; and a multitude of other reforms which I cannot even name, — give evidence of real progress in our ideas and in our morals. What the author of Christianity, in an impulse of sublime love, related of his mystical kingdom, where the repentant sinner was to be glorified above the just and the innocent man, — that utopia of Christian charity has become the aspiration of our sceptical society; and when one thinks of the unanimity of feeling which prevails in respect to it, he asks himself with surprise who then prevents this aspiration from being realized.

Alas! it is because reason is still stronger than love, and logic more tenacious than crime; it is because here as everywhere in our civilization there reigns an insoluble contradiction. Let us not wander into fantastic worlds; let us embrace, in all its frightful nudity, the real one.

Le crime fait la honte, et non pas l'echafaud,[7]

says the proverb. By the simple fact that man is punished, provided he deserved to be, he is degraded: the penalty renders him infamous, not by virtue of the definition of the code, but by reason of the fault which caused the punishment. Of what importance, then, is the materiality of the punishment? of what importance all your penitentiary systems? What you do is to satisfy your feelings, but is powerless to rehabilitate the unfortunate whom your justice strikes. The guilty man, once branded by chastisement, is incapable of reconciliation; his stain is indelible, and his damnation eternal. If it were possible for it to be otherwise, the penalty would cease to be proportional to the offence; it would be no more than a fiction, it would be nothing. He whom misery has led to larceny, if he suffers himself to fall into the hands of justice, remains forever the enemy of God and men; better for him that he had never been born; it was Jesus Christ who said it: Bonum erat ei, si natus non fuisset homo ille. And what Jesus Christ declared, Christians and infidels do not dispute: the irreparability of shame is, of all the revelations of the Gospel, the only one which the proprietary world has understood. Thus, separated from nature by monopoly, cut off from humanity by poverty, the mother of crime and its punishment, what refuge remains for the plebeian whom labor cannot support, and who is not strong enough to take?

To conduct this offensive and defensive war against the proletariat a public force was indispensable: the executive power grew out of the necessities of civil legislation, administration, and justice. And there again the most beautiful hopes have changed into bitter disappointments.

As legislator, as burgomaster, and as judge, the prince has set himself up as a representative of divine authority. A defender of the poor, the widow, and the orphan, he has promised to cause liberty and equality to prevail around the throne, to come to the aid of labor, and to listen to the voice of the people. And the people have thrown themselves lovingly into the arms of power; and, when experience has made them feel that power was against them, instead of blaming the institution, they have fallen to accusing the prince, ever unwilling to understand that, the prince being by nature and destination the chief of non-producers and greatest of monopolists, it was impossible for him, in spite of himself, to take up the cause of the people.

All criticism, whether of the form or the acts of government, ends in this essential contradiction. And when the self-styled theorists of the sovereignty of the people pretend that the remedy for the tyranny of power consists in causing it to emanate from popular suffrage, they simply turn, like the squirrel, in their cage. For, from the moment that the essential conditions of power — that is, authority,

---

[7] The crime makes the shame, and not the scaffold. — Translator.

247

property, hierarchy — are preserved, the suffrage of the people is nothing but the consent of the people to their oppression, — which is the silliest charlatanism.

In the system of authority, whatever its origin, monarchical or democratic, power is the noble organ of society; by it society lives and moves; all initiative emanates from it; order and perfection are wholly its work. According to the definitions of economic science, on the contrary, — definitions which harmonize with the reality of things, — power is the series of non-producers which social organization must tend to indefinitely reduce. How, then, with the principle of authority so dear to democrats, shall the aspiration of political economy, an aspiration which is also that of the people, be realized? How shall the government, which by the hypothesis is everything, become an obedient servant, a subordinate organ? Why should the prince have received power simply to weaken it, and why should he labor, with a view to order, for his own elimination? Why should he not try rather to fortify himself, to add to his courtiers, to continually obtain new subsidies, and finally to free himself from dependence on the people, the inevitable goal of all power originating in the people?

It is said that the people, naming its legislators and through them making its will known to power, will always be in a position to arrest its invasions; that thus the people will fill at once the role of prince and that of sovereign. Such, in a word, is the utopia of democrats, the eternal mystification with which they abuse the proletariat.

But will the people make laws against power; against the principle of authority and hierarchy, which is the principle upon which society is based; against liberty and property? According to our hypothesis, this is more than impossible, it is contradictory. Then property, monopoly, competition, industrial privileges, the inequality of fortunes, the preponderance of capital, hierarchical and crushing centralization, administrative oppression, legal absolutism, will be preserved; and, as it is impossible for a government not to act in the direction of its principle, capital will remain as before the god of society, and the people, still exploited, still degraded, will have gained by their attempt at sovereignty only a demonstration of their powerlessness.

In vain do the partisans of power, all those dynastico-republican doctrinaires who are alike in everything but tactics, flatter themselves that, once in control of affairs, they will inaugurate reform everywhere. Reform what?

Reform the constitution? It is impossible. Though the entire nation should enter the constitutional convention, it would not leave it until it had either voted its servitude under another form, or decreed its dissolution.

Reconstruct the code, the work of the emperor, the pure substance of Roman law and custom? It is impossible. What have you to put in the place of your proprietary routine, outside of which you see and understand nothing? in the place of your laws of monopoly, the limits of whose circle your imagination is powerless to overstep? More than half a century ago royalty and democracy, those two sibyls which the ancient world has bequeathed to us, undertook, by a constitutional compromise, to harmonize their oracles; since the wisdom of the prince has placed itself in unison with the voice of the people, what revelation has resulted? what principle of order has been discovered? what issue from the labyrinth of privilege pointed out? Before prince and people had signed this strange compromise, in what were their ideas not similar? and now that each is trying to break the contract, in what do they differ?

Diminish public burdens, assess taxes on a more equitable basis? It is impossible: to the treasury as to the army the man of the people will always furnish more than his contingent.

Regulate monopoly, bridle competition? It is impossible; you would kill production.

Open new markets? It is impossible.[8]

Organize credit? It is impossible.[9]

Attack heredity? It is impossible.[10]

Create national workshops, assure a minimum to unemployed workmen, and assign to employees a share of the profits? It is impossible. It is in the nature of government to be able to deal with labor only to enchain laborers, as it deals with products only to levy its tithe.

Repair, by a system of indemnities, the disastrous effects of machinery? It is impossible.

Combat by regulations the degrading influence of parcellaire division? It is impossible.

Cause the people to enjoy the benefits of education? It is impossible.

Establish a tariff of prices and wages, and fix the value of things by sovereign authority? It is impossible, it is impossible.

Of all the reforms which society in its distress solicits not one is within the competence of power; not one can be realized by it, because the essence of power is repugnant to them all, and it is not given to man to unite what God has divided.

At least, the partisans of governmental initiative will say, you will admit that, in the accomplishment of the revolution promised by the development of antinomies, power would be a potent auxiliary. Why, then, do you oppose a reform which, putting power in the hands of the people, would second your views so well? Social

---

8   See volume II, chapter IX.
9   Ibid., chapter X.
10 Ibid., chapter XI.

reform is the object; political reform is the instrument: why, if you wish the end, do you reject the means?

Such is today the reasoning of the entire democratic press, which I forgive with all my heart for having at last, by this quasi-socialistic confession of faith, itself proclaimed the emptiness of its theories. It is in the name of science, then, that democracy calls for a political reform as a preliminary to social reform. But science protests against this subterfuge as an insult; science repudiates any alliance with politics, and, very far from expecting from it the slightest aid, must begin with politics its work of exclusion.

How little affinity there is between the human mind and truth! When I see the democracy, socialistic but yesterday, continually asking for capital in order to combat capital's influence; for wealth, in order to cure poverty; for the abandonment of liberty, in order to organize liberty; for the reformation of government, in order to reform society, — when I see it, I say, taking upon itself the responsibility of society, provided social questions be set aside or solved, it seems to me as if I were listening to a fortune-teller who, before answering the questions of those who consult her, begins by inquiring into their age, their condition, their family, and all the accidents of their life. Eh! miserable sorceress, if you know the future, you know who I am and what I want; why do you ask me to tell you?

Likewise I will answer the democrats: If you know the use that you should make of power, and if you know how power should be organized, you possess economic science. Now, if you possess economic science, if you have the key of its contradictions, if you are in a position to organize labor, if you have studied the laws of exchange, you have no need of the capital of the nation or of public force. From this day forth you are more potent than money, stronger than power. For, since the laborers are with you, you are by that fact alone masters of production; you hold commerce, manufactures, and agriculture enchained; you have the entire social capital at your disposition; you have full control of taxation; you block the wheels of power, and you trample monopoly under foot. What other initiative, what greater authority, do you ask? What prevents you from applying your theories?

Surely not political economy, although generally followed and accredited: for, everything in political economy having a true side and a false side, your only problem is to combine the economic elements in such a way that their total shall no longer present a contradiction.

Nor is it the civil law: for that law, sanctioning economic routine solely because of its advantages and in spite of its disadvantages, is susceptible, like political economy itself, of being bent to all the exigencies of an exact synthesis, and consequently is as favorable to you as possible.

Finally, it is not power, which, the last expression of antagonism and created only to defend the law, could stand in your way only by forswearing itself.

Once more, then, what stops you?

If you possess social science, you know that the problem of association consists in organizing, not only the non-producers, — in that direction, thank heaven! little remains to be done, — but also the producers, and by this organization subjecting capital and subordinating power. Such is the war that you have to sustain: a war of labor against capital; a war of liberty against authority; a war of the producer against the non-producer; a war of equality against privilege. What you ask, to conduct the war to a successful conclusion, is precisely that which you must combat. Now, to combat and reduce power, to put it in its proper place in society, it is of no use to change the holders of power or introduce some variation into its workings: an agricultural and industrial combination must be found by means of which power, today the ruler of society, shall become its slave. Have you the secret of that combination?

But what do I say? That is precisely the thing to which you do not consent. As you cannot conceive of society without hierarchy, you have made yourselves the apostles of authority; worshippers of power, you think only of strengthening it and muzzling liberty; your favorite maxim is that the welfare of the people must be achieved in spite of the people; instead of proceeding to social reform by the extermination of power and politics, you insist on a reconstruction of power and politics. Then, by a series of contradictions which prove your sincerity, but the illusory character of which is well known to the real friends of power, the aristocrats and monarchists, your competitors, you promise us, in the name of power, economy in expenditures, an equitable assessment of taxes, protection to labor, gratuitous education, universal suffrage, and all the utopias repugnant to authority and property. Consequently power in your hands has never been anything but ruinous, and that is why you have never been able to retain it; that is why, on the Eighteenth of Brumaire,[11] four men were sufficient to take it away from you, and why today the bourgeoisie, which is as fond of power as you are and which wants a strong power, will not restore it to you.

Thus power, the instrument of collective might, created in society to serve as a mediator between labor and privilege, finds itself inevitably enchained to capital and directed against the proletariat. No political reform can solve this contradiction, since, by the confession of the politicians themselves, such a reform would end only in increasing the energy and extending the sphere of power, and since power would know no way of touching the prerogatives of monopoly without overturning the hierarchy and dissolving society. The problem before

---

[11] Date of the Napoleonic coup d'Etat, according to the revolutionary calendar.

the laboring classes, then, consists, not in capturing, but in subduing both power and monopoly, — that is, in generating from the bowels of the people, from the depths of labor, a greater authority, a more potent fact, which shall envelop capital and the State and subjugate them. Every proposition of reform which does not satisfy this condition is simply one scourge more, a rod doing sentry duty, *virgem vigilantem*, as a prophet said, which threatens the proletariat.

The crown of this system is religion. There is no occasion for me to deal here with the philosophic value of religious opinions, relate their history, or seek their interpretation. I confine myself to a consideration of the economic origin of religion, the secret bond which connects it with police, the place which it occupies in the series of social manifestations.

Man, despairing of finding the equilibrium of his powers, leaps, as it were, outside of himself and seeks in infinity that sovereign harmony the realization of which is to him the highest degree of reason, power, and happiness. Unable to harmonize with himself, he kneels before God and prays. He prays, and his prayer, a hymn sung to God, is a blasphemy against society.

It is from God, man says to himself, that authority and power come to me: then, let us obey God and the prince. *Obedite Deo et principibus.* It is from God that law and justice come to me. *Per me reges regnant et potentes decernunt justitiam.* Let us respect the commands of the legislator and the magistrate. It is God who controls the prosperity of labor, who makes and unmakes fortunes: may his will be done! *Dominus dedit, Dominus abstulit, sit nomen Domini benedictum.* It is God who punishes me when misery devours me, and when I am persecuted for righteousness's sake: let us receive with respect the scourges which his mercy employs for our purification. *Humiliamini igitur sub potenti manu Dei.* This life, which God has given me, is but an ordeal which leads me to salvation: let us shun pleasure; let us love and invite pain; let us find our pleasure in doing penance. The sadness which comes from injustice is a favor from on high; blessed are they that mourn! *Beati qui lugent!* . . . *Haec est enim gratia, si quis sustinet tristitias, patiens injuste.*

A century ago a missionary, preaching before an audience made up of financiers and grandees, did justice to this odious morality. "What have I done?" he cried, with tears. "I have saddened the poor, the best friends of my God! I have preached the rigors of penance to unfortunates who want for bread! It is here, where my eyes fall only on the powerful and on the rich, on the oppressors of suffering humanity, that I must launch the word of God in all the force of its thunder!"

Let us admit, nevertheless, that the theory of resignation has served society by preventing revolt. Religion, consecrating by divine right the inviolability of power and of privilege, has given humanity the strength to continue its journey and exhaust its contradictions. Without this bandage thrown over the eyes of the people society would have been a thousand times dissolved. Some one had to suffer that it might be cured; and religion, the comforter of the afflicted, decided that it should be the poor man. It is this suffering which has led us to our present position; civilization, which owes all its marvels to the laborer, owes also to his voluntary sacrifice its future and its existence. Oblatus est quia ipse voluit, et livore ejus sanati sumus.

O people of laborers! disinherited, harassed, proscribed people! people whom they imprison, judge, and kill! despised people, branded people! Do you not know that there is an end, even to patience, even to devotion? Will you not cease to lend an ear to those orators of mysticism who tell you to pray and to wait, preaching salvation now through religion, now through power, and whose vehement and sonorous words captivate you? Your destiny is an enigma which neither physical force, nor courage of soul, nor the illuminations of enthusiasm, nor the exaltation of any sentiment, can solve. Those who tell you to the contrary deceive you, and all their discourses serve only to postpone the hour of your deliverance, now ready to strike. What are enthusiasm and sentiment, what is vain poesy, when confronted with necessity? To overcome necessity there is nothing but necessity itself, the last reason of nature, the pure essence of matter and spirit.

Thus the contradiction of value, born of the necessity of free will, must be overcome by the proportionality of value, another necessity produced by the union of liberty and intelligence. But, in order that this victory of intelligent and free labor might produce all its consequences, it was necessary that society should pass through a long succession of torments.

It was a necessity that labor, in order to increase its power, should be divided; and a necessity, in consequence of this division, that the laborer should be degraded and impoverished.

It was a necessity that this original division should be reconstructed by scientific instruments and combinations; and a necessity, in consequence of this reconstruction, that the subordinated laborer should lose, together with his legitimate wages, even the exercise of the industry which supported him.

It was a necessity that competition then should step in to emancipate liberty on the point of perishing; and a necessity that this deliverance should end in a vast elimination of laborers.

It was a necessity that the producer, ennobled by his art, as formerly the warrior was by arms, should bear aloft his banner, in order that the valor of man might be honored in labor as in war; and a necessity that of privilege should straightway be born the proletariat.

It was a necessity that society should then take under its protection the conquered plebeian, a beggar without a roof; and a necessity that this protection should be converted into a new series of tortures.

We shall meet on our way still other necessities, all of which will disappear, like the others, before greater necessities, until shall come at last the general equation, the supreme necessity, the triumphant fact, which must establish the kingdom of labor forever.

But this solution cannot result either from surprise or from a vain compromise. It is as impossible to associate labor and capital as to produce without labor and without capital; as impossible to establish equality by power as to suppress power and equality and make a society without people and without police.

There is a necessity, I repeat, of a MAJOR FORCE to invert the actual formulas of society; a necessity that the LABOR of the people, not their valor nor their votes, should, by a scientific, legitimate, immortal, insurmountable combination, subject capital to the people and deliver to them power.

Chapter VIII. Of the Responsibility of Man and Of God, Under the Law of Contradiction, Or a Solution of the Problem of Providence.

THE ancients blamed human nature for the presence of evil in the world.

Christian theology has only embroidered this theme in its own fashion; and, as that theology sums up the whole religious period extending from the origin of society to our own time, it may be said that the dogma of original sin, having in its favor the assent of the human race, acquires by that very fact the highest degree of probability.

So, according to all the testimony of ancient wisdom, each people defending its own institutions as excellent and glorifying them, it is not to religions, or to governments, or to traditional customs accredited by the respect of generations, that the cause of evil must be traced, but rather to a primitive perversion, to a sort of congenital malice in the will of man. As to the question how a being could have perverted and corrupted itself originally, the ancients avoided that difficulty by fables: Eve's apple and Pandora's box have remained celebrated among their symbolic solutions.

Not only, then, had antiquity posited in its myths the question of the origin of evil; it had solved it by another myth, in unhesitatingly affirming the criminality ab ovo of our race.

Modern philosophers have erected against the Christian dogma a dogma no less obscure, — that of the depravity of society. Man is born good, cries Rousseau, in his peremptory style; but society — that is, the forms and institutions of society — depraves him. In such terms was formulated the paradox, or, better, the protest, of the philosopher of Geneva.

Now, it is evident that this idea is only the ancient hypothesis turned about. The ancients accused the individual man; Rousseau accuses the collective man: at bottom, it is always the same proposition, an absurd proposition.

Nevertheless, in spite of the fundamental identity of the principle, Rousseau's formula, precisely because it was an opposition, was a step forward; consequently it was welcomed with enthusiasm, and it became the signal of a reaction full of contradictions and absurdities. Singular thing! it is to the anathema launched by the author of "Emile" against society that modern socialism is to be traced.

For the last seventy or eighty years the principle of social perversion has been exploited and popularized by various sectarians, who, while copying Rousseau, reject with all their might the anti-social philosophy of that writer, without perceiving that, by the very fact that they aspire to reform society, they are as unsocial or unsociable as he. It is a curious spectacle to see these pseudo-innovators, condemning after Jean Jacques monarchy, democracy, property, communism, thine and mine, monopoly, wages, police, taxation, luxury, commerce, money, in a word, all that constitutes society and without which society is inconceivable, and then accusing this same Jean Jacques of misanthropy and paralogism, because, after having seen the emptiness of all utopias, at the same time that he pointed out the antagonism of civilization, he sternly concluded against society, though recognizing that without society there is no humanity.

I advise those who, on the strength of what slanderers and plagiarists say, imagine that Rousseau embraced his theory only from a vain love of eccentricity, to read "Emile" and the "Social Contract" once more. That admirable dialectician was led to deny society from the standpoint of justice, although he was forced to admit it as necessary; just as we, who believe in an indefinite progress, do not cease to deny, as normal and definitive, the existing state of society. Only, whereas Rousseau, by a political combination and an educational system of his own, tried to bring man nearer to what he called nature, and what seemed to him the ideal society, we, instructed in a profounder school, say that the task of society is to continually solve its antinomies, — a matter of which Rousseau could have had no idea. Thus, apart from the now abandoned system of the "Social Contract," and so far as criticism alone is concerned, socialism, whatever it may say, is still in the same position as Rousseau, forced to reform society incessantly, — that is, to perpetually deny it.

Rousseau, in short, simply declared in a summary and definitive manner what the socialists repeat in detail and at every moment of progress, — namely, that social order is imperfect, always lacking something. Rousseau's error does not, can not lie in this negation of society: it consists, as we shall show, in his failure to follow his argument to the end and deny at once society, man, and God.

However that may be, the theory of man's innocence, corresponding to that of the depravity of society, has at last got the upper hand. The immense majority of socialists — Saint-Simon, Owen, Fourier, and their disciples; communists, democrats, progressives of all sorts — have solemnly repudiated the Christian myth of the fall to substitute there for the system of an aberration on the part of society. And, as most of these sectarians, in spite of their flagrant impiety, were still too religious, too pious, to finish the work of Jean Jacques and trace back to God the responsibility for evil, they have found a way of deducing from the hypothesis of God the dogma of the native goodness of man, and have begun to fulminate against society in the finest fashion.

The theoretical and practical consequences of this reaction were that, evil — that is, the effect of internal and external struggle — being abnormal and transitory, penal and repressive institutions are likewise transitory; that in man there is no native vice, but that his environment has depraved his inclinations; that civilization has been mistaken as to its own tendencies; that constraint is immoral, that our passions are holy; that enjoyment is holy and should be sought after like virtue itself, because God, who caused us to desire it, is holy. And, the women coming to the aid of the eloquence of the philosophers, a deluge of anti-restrictive protests has fallen, quasi de vulva erumpens, to make use of a comparison from the Holy Scriptures, upon the wonder-stricken public.

The writings of this school are recognizable by their evangelical style, their melancholy theism, and, above all, their enigmatical dialectics.

"They blame human nature," says M. Louis Blanc, "for almost all our evils; the blame should be laid upon the vicious character of social institutions. Look around you: how many talents misplaced, and CONSEQUENTLY depraved! How many activities have become turbulent for want of having found their legitimate and natural object! They force our passions to traverse an impure medium; is it at all surprising that they become altered? Place a healthy man in a pestilent atmosphere, and he will inhale death . . . Civilization has taken a wrong road, . . . and to say that it could not have been otherwise is to lose the right to talk of equity, of morality, of progress; it is to lose the right to talk of God. Providence disappears to give place to the grossest fatalism."

The name of God recurs forty times, and always to no purpose, in M. Blanc's "Organization of Labor," which I quote from preference, because in my view it represents advanced democratic opinion better than any other work, and because I like to do it honor by refuting it.

Thus, while socialism, aided by extreme democracy, deifies man by denying the dogma of the fall, and consequently dethrones God, henceforth useless to the perfection of his creature, this same socialism, through mental cowardice, falls back upon the affirmation of Providence, and that at the very moment when it denies the providential authority of history.

And as nothing stands such chance of success among men as contradiction, the idea of a religion of pleasure, renewed from Epicurus during an eclipse of public reason, has been taken as an inspiration of the national genius; it is this that distinguishes the new theists from the Catholics, against whom the former have inveighed so loudly during the last two years only out of rivalry in fanaticism. It is the fashion today to speak of God on all occasions and to declaim against the pope; to invoke Providence and to scoff at the Church. Thank God! we are not atheists, said "La Reforme" one day; all the more, it might have added by way of increasing its absurdity, we are not Christians. The word has gone forth to every one who holds a pen to bamboozle the people, and the first article of the new faith is that an infinitely good God has created man as good as himself; which does not prevent man, under the eye of God, from becoming wicked in a detestable society.

Nevertheless it is plain, in spite of these semblances of religion, we might even say these desires for it, that the quarrel between socialism and Christian tradition, between man and society, must end by a denial of Divinity. Social reason is not distinguishable by us from absolute Reason, which is no other than God himself, and to deny society in its past phases is to deny Providence, is to deny God.

Thus, then, we are placed between two negations, two contradictory affirmations: one which, by the voice of entire antiquity, setting aside as out of the question society and God which it represents, finds in man alone the principle of evil; another which, protesting in the name of free, intelligent, and progressive man, throws back upon social infirmity and, by a necessary consequence, upon the creative and inspiring genius of society all the disturbances of the universe.

Now, as the anomalies of social order and the oppression of individual liberties arise principally from the play of economic contradictions, we have to inquire, in view of the data which we have brought to light:

1. Whether fate, whose circle surrounds us, exercises a control over our liberty so imperious and compulsory that infractions of the law, committed under the dominion of antinomies, cease to be imputable to us? And, if not, whence arises this culpability peculiar to man?

2. Whether the hypothetical being, utterly good, omnipotent, omniscient, to whom faith attributes the supreme direction of human agitations, has not himself failed society at the moment of danger? And, if so, to explain this insufficiency of Divinity.

In short, we are to find out whether man is God, whether God himself is God, or whether, to attain the fullness of intelligence and liberty, we must search for a superior cause.

1. — The culpability of man. — Exposition of the myth of the fall.

As long as man lives under the law of egoism, he accuses himself; as soon as he rises to the conception of a social law, he accuses society. In both cases humanity accuses humanity; and so far the clearest result of this double accusation is the strange faculty, which we have not yet pointed out, and which religion attributes to God as well as to man, of REPENTANCE.

Of what, then, does humanity repent? For what does God, who repents as well as ourselves, desire to punish us? Poenituit Deum quod hominem fecisset in terra, et tactus dolore cordis intrinsecus, delebo, inquit, hominem...

If I demonstrate that the offences charged upon humanity are not the consequence of its economic embarrassments, although the latter result from the constitution of its ideas; that man does evil gratuitously and when not under compulsion, just as he honors himself by acts of heroism which justice does not exact, — it will follow that man, at the tribunal of his conscience, may be allowed to plead certain extenuating circumstances, but can never be entirely discharged of his guilt; that the struggle is in his heart as well as in his mind; that he deserves now praise, now blame, which is a confession, in either case, of his inharmonious state; finally, that the essence of his soul is a perpetual compromise between opposing attractions, his morality a system of seesaw, in a word, — and this word tells the whole story, — eclecticism.

My proof shall be soon made.

There exists a law, older than our liberty, promulgated from the beginning of the world, completed by Jesus Christ, preached and certified by apostles, martyrs, confessors, and virgins, graven on the heart of man, and superior to all metaphysics: it is LOVE. Love thy neighbor as thyself, Jesus Christ tells us, after Moses. That is the whole of it. Love thy neighbor as thyself, and society will be perfect; love thy neighbor as thyself, and all distinctions of prince and shepherd, of rich and poor, of learned and ignorant, disappear, all clashing of human interests ceases. Love thy neighbor as thyself, and happiness with industry, without care for the future, shall fill thy days. To fulfil this law and make himself happy man needs only to follow the inclination of his heart and listen to the voice of his sympathies. He resists; he does more: not content wtih {sic} preferring himself to his neighbor, he labors constantly to destroy his neighbor; after having betrayed love through egoism, he overturns it by injustice.

Man, I say, faithless to the law of charity, has, of himself and without any necessity, made the contradictions of society so many instruments of harm; through his egoism civilization has become a war of surprises and ambushes; he lies, he steals, he murders, when not compelled to do so, without provocation, without excuse. In short, he does evil with all the characteristics of a nature deliberately maleficent, and all the more wicked because, when it so wishes, it knows how to do good gratuitously also and is capable of self-sacrifice; wherefore it has been said of it, with as much reason as depth: Homo homini lupus, vel deus.

Not to unduly extend the subject, and especially in order to avoid prejudging the questions that I shall have to consider, I limit myself to the economic facts already analyzed.

With the fact that the division of labor is by nature, pending the attainment of a synthetic organization, an irresistible cause of physical, moral, and mental inequality among men neither society nor conscience have anything to do. That is a fact of necessity, of which the rich man is as innocent as the parcellaire workman, consigned by his position to all sorts of poverty.

But how happens it that this inevitable inequality is converted into a title of nobility for some, of abjection for others? How happens it, if man is good, that he has not succeeded in levelling by his goodness this wholly metaphysical obstacle, and that, instead of strengthening the fraternal tie that binds men, pitiless necessity breaks it? Here man cannot be excused on the ground of his economic inexperience or legislative shortsightedness; it was enough that he had a heart. Since the martyrs of the division of labor should have been helped and honored by the rich, why have they been rejected as impure? Why is it an unheard-of thing for masters to occasionally relieve their slaves, for princes, magistrates, and priests to change places with mechanics, and for nobles to assume the task of the peasants on the land? What is the reason of this brutal pride of the powerful?

And note that such conduct on their part would have been not only charitable and fraternal, but in accord with the sternest justice. By virtue of the principle of collective force, laborers are the equals and associates of their leaders; so that in the system of monopoly itself, community of action restoring the equilibrium which parcellaire individualism has disturbed, justice and charity blend. On the hypothesis of the essential goodness of man, how then is to be explained the monstrous attempt to change the authority of some into nobility and the obedience of others into plebeianism? Labor, between the serf and the free man, like color between the black and the white, has always drawn an impassable line; and we ourselves, who glory so in our philanthropy, at the bottom of our hearts are of the same opinion as our predecessors. The sympathy which we feel for the proletaire is like that with which animals inspire us; delicacy of organs, dread of misery, pride in separating ourselves from all suffering, — it is these shifts of egoism that prompt our charity.

For in fact — and I desire only this fact to confound us — is it not true that spontaneous benevolence, so pure in its primitive conception (eleemosyna, sympathy, tenderness), alms, in fine, has become for the unfortunate a sign of degradation, a public stigma? And socialists, rebuking Christianity, dare to talk to us of love! The Christian thought, the conscience of humanity, hit the mark precisely, when it founded so many institutions for the relief of misfortune. To grasp the evangelical precept in its depth and render legal charity as honorable to those who had been its objects as to those who had exercised it, there was needed — what? Less pride, less greed, less egoism. If man is good, will any one tell me how the right to alms has become the first link in the long chain of infractions, misdemeanors, and crimes? Will any one still dare to blame the misdeeds of man upon the antagonisms of social economy, when these antagonisms offered him so beautiful an opportunity of manifesting the charity of his heart, I do not say by self-sacrifice, but by the simple doing of justice?

I know — and this objection is the only one that can be offered against my position — that charity is covered with shame and dishonor because the individual who asks it is too often, alas! suspected of misconduct and rarely to be recommended on the score of dignity of morals and of labor. And statistics prove that those who are poor through cowardice and negligence outnumber ten times those who are poor through accident or mischance.

Far be it from me to challenge this observation, the truth of which is demonstrated by too many facts, and which, moreover, has received the sanction of the people. The people are the first to accuse the poor of laziness; and there is nothing more common than to meet in the lower classes men who boast, as if it were a title of nobility, that they have never been in the hospital and in their greatest distress have never been recipients of public charity. Thus, just as opulence avows its robberies, misery confesses its shame. Man is a tyrant or a slave by will before becoming so by fortune; the heart of the proletaire is like that of the rich man, — a sewer of boiling sensuality, the home of crapulence and imposture.

Upon this unexpected revelation I ask how it happens, if man is good and charitable, that the rich calumniate charity while the poor defile it? It is perversion of judgment on the part of the rich, say some; it is degradation of faculties on the part of the poor, say others. But how is it that judgment is perverted on the one hand, and on the other that faculties are degraded? How comes it that a true and cordial fraternity has not arrested on the one side and on the other the effects of pride and labor? Let my questions be answered by reasons, not by phrases.

Labor, in inventing processes and machines which infinitely multiply its power, and then in stimulating industrial genius by rivalry and assuring its conquests by means of the profits of capital and privileges of exploitation, has rendered the hierarchical constitution of society more profound and more inevitable; I repeat that no blame attaches to any one for this. But I call the holy law of the Gospel to witness that it was within our power to draw wholly different consequences from this subordination of man to man, or, better, of laborer to laborer.

The traditions of feudal life and of that of the patriarchs set the example for the manufacturers. The division of labor and the other accidents of production were only calls to the great family life, indications of the preparatory system in accordance with which fraternity was to appear and be developed. Masterships, corporations, and rights of primogeniture were conceived under the influence of this idea; many communists even are not hostile to this form of association; is it surprising that the ideal is so tenacious among those who, conquered but not converted, still appear as its representatives? What, then, prevented charity, union, sacrifice from maintaining themselves in the hierarchy, when the hierarchy might have been only a condition of labor? To this end it would have sufficed if men having machines, valiant knights fighting with equal weapons, had not made a mystery of their secrets or withheld them from others; if barons had set to work, not to monopolize their products, but to cheapen them; and if vassals, assured that war would result only in increasing their wealth, had always shown themselves enterprising, industrious, and faithful. The chief of the workshop would then have been simply a captain putting his men through manoeuvres in their interest as well as in his own, and maintaining them, not with his perquisites, but with their own services.

Instead of these fraternal relations, we have had pride, jealousy, and perjury; the employer, like the vampire of the fable, exploiting the degraded wage-worker, and the wage-worker conspiring against the employer; the idler devouring the substance of the laborer, and the serf, squatting in filth, having no strength left but for hatred.

Called on to furnish for the work of production, these tools, those labor, capitalists and laborers are today in a struggle: why? Because absolutism presides over all their relations; because the capitalist speculates on the need which the laborer feels of procuring tools, while the laborer, in turn, seeks to derive advantage from the need which the capitalist feels of fertilizing his capital. — L. Blanc: Organization of Labor.

And why this absolutism in the relations of capitalist and laborer? Why this hostility of interests? Why this reciprocal enmity? Instead of eternally explaining the fact by the fact itself, go to the bottom, and you will find everywhere, as original motive, a passion for enjoyment which neither law nor justice nor charity restrain; you will see egoism continually discounting the future, and sacrificing to its monstrous caprices labor, capital, life, and the security of all.

The theologians have given the name concupiscence or concupiscible appetite to the passionate greed for sensual things, the effect, according to them, of original sin. I trouble myself little, for the present, as to the nature of the original sin; I simply observe that the concupiscible appetite of the theologians is no other than that need of luxury pointed out by the Academy of Moral Sciences as the ruling motive of our epoch. Now, the theory of proportionality of values demonstrates that luxury is naturally measured by production; that every consumption in advance is recovered by an equivalent later privation; and that the exaggeration of luxury in a society necessarily has an increase of misery as its correlative. Now, were man to sacrifice his personal welfare for luxurious and advance enjoyments, perhaps I should accuse him only of imprudence; but, when he injures the welfare of his neighbor, — a welfare which he should regard as inviolable, both from charity and on the ground of justice, — I say then that man is wicked, inexcusably wicked.

When God, according to Bossuet, formed the bowels of man, he originally placed goodness there. Thus love is our first law; the prescriptions of pure reason, as well as the promptings of the senses, take second and third rank only. Such is the hierarchy of our faculties, — a principle of love forming the foundation of our conscience and served by an intelligence and organs. Hence of two things one: either the man who violates charity to obey his cupidity is guilty; or else, if this psychology is false, and the need of luxury in man must hold a place beside charity and reason, man is a disorderly animal, utterly wicked, and the most execrable of beings.

Thus the organic contradictions of society cannot cover the responsibility of man; viewed in themselves, moreover, these contradictions are only the theory of the hierarchical regime, the first form and consequently an irreproachable form of society. By the antinomy of their development labor and capital have been continually led back to equality at the same time as to subordination, to solidarity as well as to dependence; one was the agent, the other the stimulator and guardian of the common wealth. This indication has been indistinctly seen by the theorists of the feudal system; Christianity came in time to cement the compact; and it is still the sentiment of this misunderstood and broken, but in itself innocent and legitimate, organization which causes regrets among us and sustains the hope of a party. As this system was written in the book of destiny, it cannot be said to be bad in itself, just as the embryonic state cannot be called bad because it precedes adult age in physiological development.

I insist, therefore, on my accusation:

Under the regime abolished by Luther and the French Revolution man could be happy in proportion to the progress of his industry; he did not choose to be; on the contrary, he forbade himself to be.

Labor has been regarded as dishonorable; the clergy and the nobility have made themselves the devourers of the poor; to satisfy their animal passions, they have extinguished charity in their hearts; they have ruined, oppressed, assassinated the laborer. And thus it is that we see capital still hunting the proletariat. Instead of tempering the subversive tendency of economic principles by association and mutuality, the capitalist exaggerates it unnecessarily and with evil design; he abuses the senses and the conscience of the workman; he makes him a valet in his intrigues, a purveyor of his debaucheries, an accomplice in his robberies; he makes him in all respects like himself, and then it is that he can defy the justice of revolutions to touch him. Monstrous thing! the man who lives in misery, and whose soul therefore seems a nearer neighbor of charity and honor, shares his master's corruption; like him, he gives everything to pride and luxury, and if he sometimes cries out against the inequality from which he suffers, it is still less from zeal for justice than from rivalry in desire. The greatest obstacle which equality has to overcome is not the aristocratic pride of the rich man, but the ungovernable egoism of the poor man. And you rely on his native goodness to reform at once both the spontaneity and the premeditation of his malice!

"As the false and anti-social education given to the present generation," says Louis Blanc, "permits no search for any other motive for emulation and encouragement than an increase of reward, the difference of wages should be graduated according to the hierarchy of functions, an entirely new education having to change ideas and morals in this matter."

Dismissing the hierarchy of functions and the inequality of wages for what they are worth, let us consider here only the motive assigned by the author. Is it not strange to see M. Blanc affirm the goodness of our nature, and at the same time address himself to the most ignoble of our propensities, — avarice? Truly, evil must seem to you very deeply rooted, if you deem it necessary to begin the restoration of charity by a violation of charity. Jesus Christ broke openly with pride and greed; apparently the libertines whom he catechised were holy personages compared with the herd infected with socialism. But tell us then, in short, how our ideas have been warped, why our education is anti-social, since it is now demonstrated that society has followed the route traced by destiny and can no longer be charged with the crimes of man.

Really, the logic of socialism is marvellous.

Man is good, they say; but it is necessary to detach his interests from evil to secure his abstinence from it. Man is good; but he must be interested in the good, else he will not do it. For, if the interest of his passions leads him to evil, he will do evil; and, if this same interest leaves him indifferent to good, he will not do good. And society will have no right to reproach him for having listened to his passions, because it was for society to conduct him by his passions. What a rich and precious nature was that of Nero, who killed his mother because she wearied him, and who caused Rome to be burned in order to have a representation of the pillage of Troy! What an artist's soul was that of Heliogabalus, who organized prostitution! What a potent character was Tiberius! But what an abominable society was that which perverted those divine souls, and produced, moreover, Tacitus and Marcus Aurelius!

This, then, is what is called the harmlessness of man, — the holiness of his passions! An aged Sappho, abandoned by her lovers, goes back under the conjugal law; her interest detached from love, she returns to marriage, and is holy. What a pity that this word holy (saint) has not in French the double meaning which it possesses in the Hebrew language! All would be in accord regarding the holiness of Sappho.

I read in a report upon the railways of Belgium that, the Belgian administration having allowed its engineers a premium of two and one-half cents for every bushel of coke saved out of an average consumption of two hundred and ten pounds for a given distance traversed, this premium bore such fruits that the consumption fell from two hundred and ten pounds to one hundred and six. This fact sums up the whole socialistic philosophy: to gradually train the workingman to justice, encourage him to labor, lift him to the sublimity of devotion, by increase of wages, profit-sharing, distinctions, and rewards. Certainly I do not mean to blame this method, which is as old as the world: whatever way you take to tame serpents and tigers and render them useful, I applaud it. But do not say that your beasts are doves; for then, as sole reply, I shall point you to their claws and teeth. Before the Belgian engineers became interested in the economy of fuel, they burned double the quantity. Therefore on their part there was carelessness, negligence, prodigality, waste, perhaps theft, although they were bound to the administration by a contract which obliged them to practise all the contrasted virtues. It is good, you say, to interest the laborer. I say further that it is just. But I maintain that this interest, more powerful over man than voluntarily accepted obligation, more powerful, in a word, than DUTY, accuses man. Socialism goes backward in morality, and it turns up its nose at Christianity. It does not understand charity, and yet, to hear it, one would suppose that it invented charity.

See, moreover, observe the socialists, what fortunate fruits the perfecting of our social order has already borne! The present generation is undeniably better than its predecessors: are we wrong in concluding that a perfect society will produce perfect citizens? Say rather, reply the conservative believers in the dogma of the fall, that, religion having purified hearts, it is not astonishing that institutions have felt the effects. Now let religion finish its work, and have no fears about society.

So speak and retort in an endless wandering from the question the theorists of the two schools. Neither understand that humanity, to use a Biblical expression, is one and constant in its generations, — that is, that everything in it, at every period of its development, in the individual as in the mass, proceeds from the same principle, which is, not being, but becoming. They do not see, on the one hand, that progress in morality is a continual conquest of mind over animality, just as progress in wealth is the fruit of the war waged by labor upon the parsimony of nature; consequently that the idea of native goodness lost through society is as absurd as the idea of native wealth lost through labor, and that a compromise with the passions should be viewed in the same light as a compromise with rest. On the other hand, they refuse to understand that, if there is progress in humanity, whether through religion or from some other cause, the hypothesis of constitutional corruption is nonsense, a contradiction.

But I anticipate the conclusions at which I must arrive: let us, for the present, establish simply that the moral perfection of humanity, like material welfare, is realized by a series of oscillations between vice and virtue, merit and demerit.

Yes, humanity grows in justice, but this growth of our liberty, due entirely to the growth of our intelligence, surely gives no proof of the goodness of our nature; and, far from authorizing us to glorify our passions, it really destroys their sway. The fashion and style of our malice change with time: the barons of the middle ages plundered the traveller on the highway, and then offered him hospitality in their castles; mercantile feudality, less brutal, exploits the proletaire and builds hospitals for him: who would dare to say which of the two has deserved the palm of virtue?

Of all the economic contradictions value is that which, dominating the others and summing them up, holds in a sense the sceptre of society, I had almost said of the moral world. Until value, oscillating between its two poles, — useful value and value in exchange, — arrives at its constitution, thine and mine remain fixed arbitrarily; the conditions of fortune are the effect of chance; property rests on a precarious title; everything in social economy is provisional. What should social, intelligent, and free beings have learned from this uncertainty of value? To make amicable regulations that should protect labor and guarantee exchange and cheapness. What a happy opportunity for all to make up, by honesty, disinterestedness, and tenderness of heart, for the ignorance of the objective laws of the just and the unjust! Instead of that, commerce has everywhere become, by spontaneous effort and unanimous consent, an uncertain operation, a venturesome enterprise, a lottery, and often a deceitful and fraudulent speculation.

What obliges the holder of provisions, the storekeeper of society, to pretend that there is a scarcity, sound the alarm, and provoke a rise of prices? Public short-sightedness places the consumer at his mercy; some change of temperature furnishes him a pretext; the assured prospect of gain finally corrupts him, and fear, skilfully spread abroad, throws the population into his toils. Certainly the motive which actuates the swindler, the thief, the assassin, those natures warped, it is said, by the social order, is the same which animates the monopolist who is not in need. How, then, does this passion for gain, abandoned to itself, turn to the prejudice of society? Why has preventive, repressive, and coercive legislation always been necessary to set a limit to liberty? For that is the accusing fact, which it is impossible to deny: everywhere the law has grown out of abuse; everywhere the legislator has found himself forced to make man powerless to harm, which is synonymous with muzzling a lion or infibulating a boar. And socialism itself, ever imitating the past, makes no other pretence: what is, indeed, the organization which it claims, if not a stronger guarantee of justice, a more complete limitation of liberty?

The characteristic trait of the merchant is to make everything either an object or an instrument of traffic. Disassociated from his fellows, his interests separated from those of others, he is for and against all deeds, all opinions, all parties. A discovery, a science, is in his eyes an instrument of war, out of the way of which he tries to keep, and which he would like to annihilate, unless he can make use of it himself to kill his competitors. An artist, an educated person, is an artilleryman who knows how to handle the weapon, and whom he tries to corrupt, if he cannot win him. The merchant is convinced that logic is the art of proving at will the true and the false; he was the inventor of political venality, traffic in consciences, prostitution of talents, corruption of the press. He knows how to find arguments and advocates for all lies, all iniquities. He alone has never deceived himself as to the value of political parties: he deems them all equally exploitable, — that is, equally absurd.

Without respect for his avowed opinions, which he abandons and resumes by turns; sharply pursuing in others those violations of faith of which he is himself guilty, — he lies in his claims, he lies in his representations, he lies in his inventories; he exaggerates, he extenuates, he over-rates; he regards himself as the centre of the world, and everything outside of him has only a relative existence, value, and truth. Subtle and shrewd in his transactions, he stipulates, he reserves, trembling always lest he may say too much or not enough; abusing words with the simple, generalizing in order not to compromise himself, specifying in order to allow nothing, he turns three times upon himself and thinks seven times under his chin before saying his last word. Has he at last concluded? He rereads himself, he interprets himself, he comments on himself; he tortures himself to find a deep meaning in every part of his contract, and in the clearest phrases the opposite of what they say.

What infinite art, what hypocrisy, in his relations with the manual laborer! From the simple shopkeeper to the big contractor, how skilful they are in exploiting his arms! How well they know how to contend with labor, in order to obtain it at a low price! In the first place, it is a hope for which the master receives a slight service; then it is a promise which he discounts by requiring some duty; then a trial, a sacrifice, — for he needs nobody, — which the unfortunate man must recognize by contenting himself with the lowest wages; there are endless exactions and overcharges, compensated by settlements on pay-days effected in the most rapacious and deceitful spirit. And the workman must keep silent and bend the knee, and clench his fist under his frock: for the employer has the work, and only too happy is he who can obtain the favor of his swindles. And because society has not yet found a way to prevent, repress, and punish this odious grinding process, so spontaneous, so ingenuous, so disengaged from all superior impulse, it is attributed to social constraint. What folly!

The commission-merchant is the type, the highest expression, of monopoly, the embodiment of commerce, that is, of civilization. Every function depends upon his, participates in it, or is assimilated to it: for, as from the standpoint of the distribution of wealth the relations of men with each other are all reducible to exchanges, — that is, to transfers of values, — it may be said that civilization is personified in the commission-merchant.

Now, question the commission-merchants as to the morality of their trade; they will be frank with you; all will tell you that the commission business is extortion. Complaints are made of the frauds and adulterations which disgrace manufactures: commerce — I refer especially to the commission business — is only a gigantic and permanent conspiracy of monopolists, by turns competing or joined in pools; it is not a function performed with a view to a legitimate profit, but a vast organization of speculation in all articles of consumption, as well as on the circulation of persons and products. Already swindling is tolerated in this profession: how many way-bills overcharged, erased, altered! how many stamps counterfeited! how much damage concealed or fraudulently compounded! how many lies as to quality! how many promises given and retracted! how many documents suppressed! what intrigues and combinations! and then what treasons!

The commission-merchant — that is, the merchant — that is, the man -is a gambler, a slanderer, a charlatan, a mercenary, a thief, a forger . . .

This is the effect of our antagonistic society, observe the neo-mystics. So say the commercial people, the first under all circumstances to accuse the corruption of the century. They act as they do, if we may believe them, simply to indemnify themselves and wholly against their inclination: they follow necessity; theirs is a case of legitimate defence.

Does it require an effort of genius to see that these mutual recriminations strike at the very nature of man, that the pretended perversion of society is nothing but the perversion of man, and that the opposition of principles and interests is only an external accident, so to speak, which brings into relief, but without exerting a necessitating influence, both the blackness of our egoism and the rare virtues with which our race is honored?

I understand inharmonious competition and its irresistible eliminating effects: this is inevitable. Competition, in its higher expression, is the gearing by means of which laborers reciprocally stimulate and sustain each other. But, pending the realization of that organization which must elevate competition to its veritable nature, it remains a civil war in which producers, instead of aiding each other in labor, grind and crush each other by labor. The danger here was imminent; man, to avert it, had this supreme law of love; and nothing was easier, while pushing competition to its extreme limits in the interest of production, than to then repair its murderous effects by an equitable distribution. Far from that, this anarchical competition has become, as it were, the soul and spirit of the laborer. Political economy placed in the hands of man this weapon of death, and he has struck; he has used competition, as the lion uses his paws and jaws, to kill and devour. How is it, then, I repeat, that a wholly external accident has changed the nature of man, which is supposed to be good and gentle and social?

The wine merchant calls to his aid jelly, magnin, insects, water, and poisons; by combinations of his own he adds to the destructive effects of competition. Whence comes this mania? From the fact, you say, that his competitor sets him the example! And this competitor, who incites him? Some other competitor. So that, if we make the tour of society, we shall find that it is the mass, and in the mass each particular individual, who, by a tacit agreement of their passions, — pride, indolence, greed, distrust, jealousy, — have organized this detestable war.

After having gathered about him tools, material, and workmen, the contractor must recover in the product, besides the amount of his outlay, first the interest of his capital, and then a profit. It is in consequence of this principle that lending at interest has finally become established, and that gain, considered in itself, has always passed for legitimate. Under this system, the police of nations not having seen at first the essential contradiction of loans at interest, the wage-worker, instead of depending directly upon himself, had to depend upon an employer, as the soldier belonged to the count, or the tribe to the patriarch. This order of things was necessary, and, pending the establishment of complete equality, it was not impossible that the welfare of all should be secured by it. But when the master, in his disorderly egoism, has said to the servant: "You shall not share with me," and robbed him at one stroke of labor and wages, where is the necessity, where the excuse? Will it be necessary further, in order to justify the concupiscible appetite, to fall back on the irascible appetite? Take care: in drawing back in order to justify the human being in the series of his lusts, instead of saving his morality, you abandon it. For my part, I prefer the guilty man to the wild-beast man.

Nature has made man sociable: the spontaneous development of his instincts now makes him an angel of charity, now robs him even of the sentiment of fraternity and the idea of devotion. Did any one ever see a capitalist, weary of gain, conspiring for the general good and making the emancipation of the proletariat his last speculation? There are many people, favorites of fortune, to whom nothing is lacking but the crown of beneficence: now, where is the grocer who, having grown rich, begins to sell at cost? Where the baker who, retiring from business, leaves his customers and his establishment to his assistants? Where the apothecary who, under the pretence of winding up his affairs, surrenders his drugs at their true value? When charity has its martyrs, why has it not its amateurs? If there should suddenly be formed a congress of bondholders, capitalists, and men of business, retired but still fit for service, with a view to carrying on a certain number of industries gratuitously, in a short time society would be reformed from top to bottom. But work for nothing! That is for the Vincent de Pauls, the Fenelons, all those whose souls have always been weaned and whose hearts have been pure. The man enriched by gain will be a municipal councillor, a member of the committee on charities, an officer of the infant schools: he will perform all the honorary functions, barring exactly that which would be efficacious, but which is repugnant to his habits. Work without hope of profits! That cannot be, for it would be self-destruction. He would like to, perhaps; he has not the courage. Video meliora proboque, deteriora sequor. The retired proprietor is really the owl of the fable gathering beech-nuts for its mutilated mice until it is ready to devour them. Is society also to be blamed for these effects of a passion so long, so freely, so fully gratified?

Who, then, will explain this mystery of a manifold and discordant being, capable at once of the highest virtues and the most frightful crimes? The dog licks his master who strikes him, because the dog's nature is fidelity and this nature never leaves him. The lamb takes refuge in the arms of the shepherd who fleeces and eats him, because the sheep's inseparable characteristics are gentleness and peace. The horse dashes through flame and grape-shot without touching with his swiftly-moving feet the wounded and dead lying in his path, because the horse's soul is unalterable in its generosity. These animals are martyrs for our sakes through the constancy and devotion of their natures. The servant who defends his master at the peril of his life, for a little gold betrays and murders him; the chaste wife pollutes her bed because of some disgust or absence, and in Lucrece we find Messalina; the proprietor, by turns father and tyrant, refits and restores his ruined farmer and drives from his lands the farmer's too numerous family, which has increased on the strength of the feudal contract; the warrior, mirror and paragon of chivalry, makes the corpses of his companions a stepping-stone to advancement. Epaminondas and Regulus traffic in the blood of their soldiers, — how many instances have my own eyes witnessed! — and by a horrible contrast the profession of sacrifice is the most fruitful in cowardice. Humanity has its martyrs and its apostates: to what, I ask again, must this division be attributed?

To the antagonism of society, you always say; to the state of separation, isolation, hostility to his fellows, in which man has hitherto lived; in a word, to that alienation of his heart which has led him to mistake enjoyment for love, property for possession, pain for labor, intoxication for joy; to that warped conscience, in short, which remorse has not ceased to pursue under the name of original sin.

When man, reconciled with himself, shall cease to look upon his neighbor and nature as hostile powers, then will he love and produce simply by the spontaneity of his energy; then it will be his passion to give, as it is today to acquire; and then will he seek in labor and devotion his only happiness, his supreme delight. Then, love becoming really and indivisibly the law of man, justice will thereafter be but an empty name, painful souvenir of a period of violence and tears.

Certainly I do not overlook the fact of antagonism, or, as it will please you to call it, of religious alienation, any more than the necessity of reconciling man with himself; my whole philosophy is but a perpetuity of reconciliations. You admit that the divergence of our nature is the preliminary of society, or, let us rather say, the material of civilization. This is precisely the fact, but, remember well, the indestructible fact of which I seek the meaning. Certainly we should be very near an understanding, if, instead of considering the dissidence and harmony of the human faculties as two distinct periods, clean-cut and consecutive in history, you would consent to view them with me simply as the two faces of our nature, ever adverse, ever in course of reconciliation, but never entirely reconciled. In a word, as individualism is the primordial fact of humanity, so association is its complementary term; but both are in incessant manifestation, and on earth justice is eternally the condition of love.

Thus the dogma of the fall is not simply the expression of a special and transitory state of human reason and morality: it is the spontaneous confession, in symbolic phrase, of this fact as astonishing as it is indestructible, the culpability, the inclination to evil, of our race. Curse upon me a sinner! cries on every hand and in every tongue the conscience of the human race. Voe nobis quia peccavimus! Religion, in giving this idea concrete and dramatic form, has indeed gone back of history and beyond the limits of the world for that which is essential and immanent in our soul; this, on its part, was but an intellectual mirage; it was not mistaken as to the essentiality and permanence of the fact. Now, it is this fact for which we have to account, and it is also from this point of view that we are to interpret the dogma of original sin.

All peoples have had their expiatory customs, their penitential sacrifices, their repressive and penal institutions, born of the horror and regret of sin. Catholicism, which built a theory wherever social spontaneity had expressed an idea or deposited a hope, converted into a sacrament the at once symbolic and effective ceremony by which the sinner expressed his repentance, asked pardon of God and men for his fault, and prepared himself for a better life. Consequently I do not hesitate to say that the Reformation, in rejecting contrition, cavilling over the word metanoia, attributing to faith alone the virtue of justification, deconsecrating repentance in short, took a step backward and utterly failed to recognize the law of progress. To deny was not to reply. On this point as on so many others the abuses of the Church called for reform; the theories of repentance, of damnation, of the remission of sin, and of grace contained, if I may venture to say so, in a latent state, the entire system of humanity's education; these theories needed to be developed and grown into rationalism; Luther knew nothing but their destruction. Auricular confession was a degradation of repentance, an equivocal demonstration substituted for a great act of humility; Luther surpassed papist hypocrisy by reducing the primitive confession before God and men (exomologoumai to theo. . . kai humin, adelphoi) to a soliloquy. The Christian meaning then was lost, and not until three centuries later was it restored by philosophy.

Since, then, Christianity — that is, religious humanity — has not been in error as to the REALITY of a fact essential in human nature, — a fact which it has designated by the words original prevarication, let us further interrogate Christianity, humanity, as to the MEANING of this fact. Let us not be astonished either by metaphor or by allegory: truth is independent of figures. And besides, what is truth to us but the continuous progress of our mind from poetry to prose?

And first let us inquire whether this at least singular idea of original prevarication had not, somewhere in the Christian theology, its correlative. For the true idea, the generic idea, cannot result from an isolated conception; there must be a series.

Christianity, after having posited the dogma of the fall as the first term, followed up its thought by affirming, for all who should die in this state of pollution, an irrevocable separation from God, an eternity of punishment. Then it completed its theory by reconciling these two opposites by the dogma of rehabilitation or of grace, according to which every creature born in the hatred of God is reconciled by the merits of Jesus Christ, which faith and repentance render efficacious. Thus, essential corruption of our nature and perpetuity of punishment, except in the case of redemption through voluntary participation in Christ's sacrifice, — such is, in brief, the evolution of the theological idea. The second affirmation is a consequence of the first; the third is a negation and transformation of the two others: in fact, a constitutional vice being necessarily indestructible, the expiation which it involves is as eternal as itself, unless a superior power comes to break destiny and lift the anathema by an integral renovation.

The human mind, in its religious caprices as well as in its most positive theories, has always but one method; the same metaphysics produced the Christian mysteries and the contradictions of political economy; faith, without knowing it, hangs upon reason; and we, explorers of divine and human manifestations, are entitled to verify, in the name of reason, the hypotheses of theology.

What was it, then, that the universal reason, formulated in religious dogmas, saw in human nature, when, by so regular a metaphysical construction, it declared successively the ingenuousness of the offence, the eternity of the penalty, the necessity of grace? The veils of theology are becoming so transparent that it quite resembles natural history.

If we conceive the operation by which the supreme being is supposed to have produced all beings, no longer as an emanation, an exertion of the creative force and infinite substance, but as a division or differentiation of this substantial force, each being, organized or unorganized, will appear to us the special representative of one of the innumerable potentialities of the infinite being, as a section of the absolute; and the collection of all these individualities (fluids, minerals, plants, insects, fish, birds, and quadrupeds) will be the creation, the universe.

Man, an abridgment of the universe, sums up and syncretizes in his person all the potentialities of being, all the sections of the absolute; he is the summit at which these potentialities, which exist only by their divergence, meet in a group, but without penetrating or becoming confounded with each other. Man, therefore, by this aggregation, is at once spirit and matter, spontaneity and reflection, mechanism and life, angel and brute. He is venomous like the viper, sanguinary like the tiger, gluttonous like the hog, obscene like the ape; and devoted like the dog, generous like the horse, industrious like the bee, monogamic like the dove, sociable like the beaver and sheep. And in addition he is man, — that is, reasonable and free, susceptible of education and improvement. Man enjoys as many names as Jupiter; all these names he carries written on his face; and, in the varied mirror of nature, his infallible instinct is able to recognize them. A serpent is beautiful to the reason; it is the conscience that finds it odious and ugly. The ancients as well as the moderns grasped this idea of the constitution of man by agglomeration of all terrestrial potentialities: the labors of Gall and Lavater were, if I may say so, only attempts at disintegration of the human syncretism, and their classification of our faculties a miniature picture of nature. Man, in short, like the prophet in the lions' den, is veritably given over to the beasts; and if anything is destined to exhibit to posterity the infamous hypocrisy of our epoch, it is the fact that educated persons, spiritualistic bigots, have thought to serve religion and morality by altering the nature of our race and giving the lie to anatomy.

Therefore the only question left to decide is whether it depends upon man, notwithstanding the contradictions which the progressive emission of his ideas multiplies around him, to give more or less scope to the potentialities placed under his control, or, as the moralists say, to his passions; in other words, whether, like Hercules of old, he can conquer the animality which besets him, the infernal legion which seems ever ready to devour him.

Now, the universal consent of peoples bears witness — and we have shown it in the third and fourth chapters — that man, all his animal impulses set aside, is summed up in intelligence and liberty, — that is, first, a faculty of appreciation and choice, and, second, a power of action indifferently applicable to good and evil. We have shown further that these two faculties, which exercise a necessary influence over each other, are susceptible of indefinite development and improvement.

Social destiny, the solution of the human enigma, is found, then, in these words: EDUCATION, PROGRESS.

The education of liberty, the taming of our instincts, the enfranchisement or redemption of our soul, — this, then, as Lessing has proved, is the meaning of the Christian mystery. This education will last throughout our life and that of humanity: the contradictions of political economy may be solved; the essential contradiction of our being never will be. That is why the great teachers of humanity, Moses, Buddha, Jesus Christ, Zoroaster, were all apostles of expiation, living symbols of repentance. Man is by nature a sinner, -that is, not essentially ill-doing, but rather ill-done, — and it is his destiny to perpetually re-create his ideal in himself. That is what the greatest of painters, Raphael, felt profoundly, when he said that art consists in rendering things, not as nature made them, but as it should have made them.

Henceforth, then, it is ours to teach the theologians, for we alone continue the tradition of the Church, we alone possess the meaning of the Scriptures, of the Councils, and of the Fathers. Our interpretation rests on the most certain and most authentic grounds, on the greatest authority to which men can appeal, the metaphysical construction of ideas and facts. Yes, the human being is vicious because he is illogical, because his constitution is but an eclecticism which holds in perpetual struggle the potentialities of his being, independently of the contradictions of society. The life of man is only a continual compromise between labor and pain, love and enjoyment, justice and egoism; and the voluntary sacrifice which man makes in obedience to his inferior attractions is the baptism which prepares the way for his reconciliation with God and renders him worthy of that beatific union and eternal happiness.

The object of social economy, in incessantly securing order in labor and favoring the education of the race, is then to render charity — that charity which knows not how to rule its slaves — superfluous as far as possible by equality, or better, to make charity develop from justice, as a flower from its stem. Ah! if charity had had the power to create happiness among men, it would have proved it long ago; and socialism, instead of seeking the organization of labor, would have had but to say: "Take care, you are lacking in charity."

But, alas! charity in man is stunted, sly, sluggish, and lukewarm; in order to act, it needs elixirs and aromas. That is why I have clung to the triple dogma of prevarication, damnation, and redemption, — that is, perfectibility through justice. Liberty here below is always in need of assistance, and the Catholic theory of celestial favors comes to complete this too real demonstration of the miseries of our nature.

Grace, say the theologians, is, in the order of salvation, every help or means which can conduct us to eternal life. That is to say, man perfects himself, civilizes himself, humanizes himself only by the incessant aid of experience, by industry, science, and art, by pleasure and pain, in a word, by all bodily and mental exercises.

There is an habitual grace, called also justifying and sanctifying, which is conceived as a quality residing in the soul, containing the innate virtues and gifts of the Holy Spirit, and inseparable from charity. In other words, habitual grace is the symbol of the predominance of good impulses, which lead man to order and love, and by means of which he succeeds in subduing his evil tendencies and remaining master in his own domain. As for actual grace, that indicates the external means which give scope to the orderly passions and serve to combat the subversive passions.

Grace, according to Saint Augustine, is essentially gratuitous, and precedes sin in man. Bossuet expressed the same thought in his style so full of poesy and tenderness: When God formed the bowels of man, he originally placed goodness there. In fact, the first determination of free will is in this natural goodness, by which man is continually incited to order, to labor, to study, to modesty, to charity, and to sacrifice. Therefore Saint Paul could say, without attacking free will, that, in everything concerning the accomplishment of good, God worketh in us both to will and to do. For all the holy aspirations of man are in him before he begins to think and feel; and the pangs of heart which he experiences when he violates them, the delight with which he is filled when he obeys them, all the invitations, in short, which come to him from society and his education, do not belong to him.

When grace is such that the will chooses the good with joy and love, without hesitation and without recall, it is styled efficacious. Every one has witnessed those transports of soul which suddenly decide a vocation, an act of heroism. Liberty does not perish therein; but from its predeterminations it may be said that it was inevitable that it should so decide. And the Pelagians, Lutherans, and others have been mistaken in saying that grace compromised free choice and killed the creative force of the will; since all determinations of the will come necessarily either from society which sustains it, or from nature which opens its career and points out its destiny.

But, on the other hand, the Augustinians, the Thomists, the congruists, Jansen, Thomassin, Molina, etc., were strangely mistaken when, sustaining at once free will and grace, they failed to see that between these two terms the same relation exists as between substance and form, and that they have confessed an opposition which does not exist. Liberty, like intelligence, like all substance and all force, is necessarily determined, — that is, it has its forms and its attributes. Now, while in matter the form and the attribute are inherent in and contemporary with substance, in liberty the form is given by three external agents, as it were, — the human essence, the laws of thought, exercise or education. Grace, in fine, like its opposite, temptation, indicates precisely the fact of the determination of liberty.

To sum up, all modern ideas regarding the education of humanity are only an interpretation, a philosophy of the Catholic doctrine of grace, a doctrine which seemed obscure to its authors only because of their ideas upon free will, which they supposed to be threatened as soon as grace or the source of its determinations was spoken of. We affirm, on the contrary, that liberty, indifferent in itself to all modality, but destined to act and to take shape according to a preestablished order, receives its first impulse from the Creator who inspires it with love, intelligence, courage, resolution, and all the gifts of the Holy Spirit, and then delivers it to the labor of experience. It follows from this that grace is necessarily pre-moving, that without it man is capable of no sort of good, and that nevertheless free will accomplishes its own destiny spontaneously, with reflection and choice. In all this there is neither contradiction nor mystery. Man, in so far as he is man, is good; but, like the tyrant described by Plato, who was, he too, a teacher of grace, man carries in his bosom a thousand monsters, which the worship of justice and science, music and gymnastics, all the graces of opportunity and condition, must cause him to overcome. Correct one definition in Saint Augustine, and all that doctrine of grace, famous because of the disputes which it excited and which disconcerted the Reformation, will seem to you brilliant with clearness and harmony.

And now is man God?

God, according to the theological hypothesis, being the sovereign, absolute, highly synthetic being, the infinitely wise and free, and therefore indefectible and holy, Me, it is plain that man, the syncretism of the creation, the point of union of all the potentialities manifested by the creation, physical, organic, mental, and moral; man, perfectible and fallible, does not satisfy the conditions of Divinity as he, from the nature of his mind, must conceive them. Neither is he God, nor can he, living, become God.

All the more, then, the oak, the lion, the sun, the universe itself, sections of the absolute, are not God. At the same stroke the worship of man and the worship of nature are overthrown.

Now we have to present the counter-proof of this theory.

From the standpoint of social contradictions we have judged of the morality of man. We are to judge, in its turn and from the same standpoint, the morality of Providence. In other words, is God possible, as speculation and faith offer him for the adoration of mortals?

2. — Exposition of the myth of Providence. — Retrogression of God.

Among the proofs, to the number of three, which theologians and philosophers are accustomed to bring forward to show the existence of a God, they give the foremost position to universal consent.

This argument I considered when, without rejecting or admitting it, I promptly asked myself: What does universal consent affirm in affirming a God? And in this connection I should recall the fact that the difference of religions is not a proof that the human race has fallen into error in affirming a supreme Me outside of itself, any more than the diversity of languages is a proof of the non-reality of reason. The hypothesis of God, far from being weakened, is strengthened and established by the very divergence and opposition of faiths.

An argument of another sort is that which is drawn from the order of the world. In regard to this I have observed that, nature affirming spontaneously, by the voice of man, its own distinction into mind and matter, it remained to find out whether an infinite mind, a soul of the world, governs and moves the universe, as conscience, in its obscure intuition, tells us that a mind animates man. If, then, I added, order were an infallible sign of the presence of mind, the presence of a God in the universe could not be overlooked.

Unfortunately this if is not demonstrated and cannot be. For, on the one hand, pure mind, conceived as the opposite of matter, is a contradictory entity, the reality of which, consequently, nothing can attest. On the other hand, certain beings ordered in themselves — such as crystals, plants, and the planetary system, which, in the sensations that they make us feel, do not return us sentiment for sentiment, as the animals do — seeming to us utterly destitute of conscience, there is no more reason for supposing a mind in the centre of the world than for placing one in a stick of sulphur; and it may be that, if mind, conscience, exists anywhere, it is only in man.

Nevertheless, if the order of the world can tell us nothing as to the existence of God, it reveals a thing no less precious perhaps, and which will serve us as a landmark in our inquiries, — namely, that all beings, all essences, all phenomena are bound together by a totality of laws resulting from their properties, a totality which in the third chapter I have named fatality or necessity. Whether or not there exists then an infinite intelligence, embracing the whole system of these laws, the whole field of fatalism; whether or not to this infinite intelligence is united in profound penetration a superior will, eternally determined by the totality of the cosmic laws and consequently infinitely powerful and free; whether or not, finally, these three things, fatality, intelligence, will, are contemporary in the universe, adequate to each other and identical, — it is clear that so far we find nothing repugnant to these positions; but it is precisely this hypothesis, this anthropomorphism, which is yet to be demonstrated.

Thus, while the testimony of the human race reveals to us a God, without saying what this God may be, the order of the world reveals to us a fatality, — that is, an absolute and peremptory totality of causes and effects, — in short, a system of laws, — which would be, if God exists, like the sight and knowledge of this God.

The third and last proof of the existence of God proposed by the theists and called by them the metaphysical proof is nothing but a tautological construction of categories, which proves absolutely nothing.

Something exists; therefore there is something in existence.

Something is multiple; therefore something is one.

Something comes after something; therefore something is prior to something.

Something is smaller of greater than something; therefore something is greater than all things.

Something is moved; therefore something is mover, etc., ad infinitum.

That is what is called even today, in the faculties and the seminaries, by the minister of public education and by Messeigneurs the bishops, proving the existence of God by metaphysics. That is what the elite of the French youth are condemned to bleat after their professors, for a year, or else forfeit their diplomas and the privilege of studying law, medicine, polytechnics, and the sciences. Certainly, if anything is calculated to surprise, it is that with such philosophy Europe is not yet atheistic. The persistence of the theistic idea by the side of the jargon of the schools is the greatest of miracles; it constitutes the strongest prejudice that can be cited in favor of Divinity.

I do not know what humanity calls God.

I cannot say whether it is man, the universe, or some invisible reality that we are to understand by that name; or indeed whether the word stands for anything more than an ideal, a creature of the mind.

Nevertheless, to give body to my hypothesis and influence to my inquiries, I shall consider God in accordance with the common opinion, as a being apart, omnipresent, distinct from creation, endowed with imperishable life as well as infinite knowledge and activity, but above all foreseeing and just, punishing vice and rewarding virtue. I shall put aside the pantheistic hypothesis as hypocritical and lacking courage. God is personal, or he does not exist: this alternative is the axiom from which I shall deduce my entire theodicy.

Not concerning myself therefore for the present with questions which the idea of God may raise later, the problem before me now is to decide, in view of the facts the evolution of which in society I have established, what I should think of the conduct of God, as it is held up for my faith and relatively to humanity. In short, it is from the standpoint of the demonstrated existence of evil that I, with the aid of a new dialectical process, mean to fathom the Supreme Being.

Evil exists: upon this point everybody seems to agree.

Now, have asked the stoics, the Epicureans, the manicheans, and the atheists, how harmonize the presence of evil with the idea of a sovereignly good, wise, and powerful God? How can God, after allowing the introduction of evil into the world, whether through weakness or negligence or malice, render responsible for their acts creatures which he himself has created imperfect, and which he thus delivers to all the dangers of their attractions? Why, finally, since he promises the just a never-ending bliss after death, or, in other words, gives us the idea and desire of happiness, does he not cause us to enjoy this life by stripping us of the temptation of evil, instead of exposing us to an eternity of torture?

Such used to be the purport of the protest of the atheists.

Today this is scarcely discussed: the theists are no longer troubled by the logical impossibilities of their system. They want a God, especially a Providence: there is competition for this article between the radicals and the Jesuits. The socialists preach happiness and virtue in the name of God; in the schools those who talk the loudest against the Church are the first of mystics.

The old theists were more anxious about their faith. They tried, if not to demonstrate it, at least to render it reasonable, feeling sure, unlike their successors, that there is neither dignity nor rest for the believer except in certainty.

The Fathers of the Church then answered the incredulous that evil is only deprivation of a greater good, and that those who always reason about the better lack a point of support upon which to establish themselves, which leads straight to absurdity. In fact, every creature being necessarily confined and imperfect, God, by his infinite power, can continually add to his perfections: in this respect there is always, in some degree, a deprivation of good in the creature. Reciprocally, however imperfect and confined the creature is supposed to be, from the moment that it exists it enjoys a certain degree of good, better for it than annihilation. Therefore, though it is a rule that man is considered good only so far as he accomplishes all the good that he can, it is not the same with God, since the obligation to do good infinitely is contradictory to the very faculty of creation, perfection and creature being two terms that necessarily exclude each other. God, then, was sole judge of the degree of perfection which it was proper to give to each creature: to prefer a charge against him under this head is to slander his justice.

As for sin, — that is, moral evil, — the Fathers, to reply to the objections of the atheists, had the theories of free will, redemption, justification, and grace, to the discussion of which we need not return.

I have no knowledge that the atheists have replied categorically to this theory of the essential imperfection of the creature, a theory reproduced with brilliancy by M. de Lamennais in his "Esquisse." It was impossible, indeed, for them to reply to it; for, reasoning from a false conception of evil and of free will, and in profound ignorance of the laws of humanity, they were equally without reasons by which either to triumph over their own doubts or to refute the believers.

Let us leave the sphere of the finite and infinite, and place ourselves in the conception of order. Can God make a round circle, a right-angled square? Certainly.

Would God be guilty if, after having created the world according to the laws of geometry, he had put it into our minds, or even allowed us to believe without fault of our own, that a circle may be square or a square circular, though, in consequence of this false opinion, we should have to suffer an incalculable series of evils? Again, undoubtedly.

Well! that is exactly what God, the God of Providence, has done in the government of humanity; it is of that that I accuse him. He knew from all eternity — inasmuch as we mortals have discovered it after six thousand years of painful experience — that order in society — that is, liberty, wealth, science — is realized by the reconciliation of opposite ideas which, were each to be taken as absolute in itself, would precipitate us into an abyss of misery: why did he not warn us? Why did he not correct our judgment at the start? Why did he abandon us to our imperfect logic, especially when our egoism must find a pretext in his acts of injustice and perfidy? He knew, this jealous God, that, if he exposed us to the hazards of experience, we should not find until very late that security of life which constitutes our entire happiness: why did he not abridge this long apprenticeship by a revelation of our own laws? Why, instead of fascinating us with contradictory opinions, did he not reverse experience by causing us to reach the antinomies by the path of analysis of synthetic ideas, instead of leaving us to painfully clamber up the steeps of antinomy to synthesis?

If, as was formerly thought, the evil from which humanity suffers arose solely from the imperfection inevitable in every creature, or better, if this evil were caused only by the antagonism of the potentialities and inclinations which constitute our being, and which reason should teach us to master and guide, we should have no right to complain. Our condition being all that it could be, God would be justified.

But, in view of this wilful delusion of our minds, a delusion which it was so easy to dissipate and the effects of which must be so terrible, where is the excuse of Providence? Is it not true that grace failed man here? God, whom faith represents as a tender father and a prudent master, abandons us to the fatality of our incomplete conceptions; he digs the ditch under our feet; he causes us to move blindly: and then, at every fall, he punishes us as rascals. What do I say? It seems as if it were in spite of him that at last, covered with bruises from our journey, we recognize our road; as if we offended his glory in becoming more intelligent and free through the trials which he imposes upon us. What need, then, have we to continually invoke Divinity, and what have we to do with those satellites of a Providence which for sixty centuries, by the aid of a thousand religions, has deceived and misled us?

What! God, through his gospel-bearers and by the law which he has put in our hearts, commands us to love our neighbor as ourselves, to do to others as we wish to be done by, to render each his due, not to keep back anything from the laborer's hire, and not to lend at usury; he knows, moreover, that in us charity is lukewarm and conscience vacillating, and that the slightest pretext always seems to us a sufficient reason for exemption from the law: and yet he involves us, with such dispositions, in the contradictions of commerce and property, in which, by the necessity of the theory, charity and justice are bound to perish! Instead of enlightening our reason concerning the bearing of principles which impose themselves upon it with all the power of necessity, but whose consequences, adopted by egoism, are fatal to human fraternity, he places this abused reason at the service of our passion; by seduction of the mind, he destroys our equilibrium of conscience; he justifies in our own eyes our usurpations and our avarice; he makes the separation of man from his fellow inevitable and legitimate; he creates division and hatred among us in rendering equality by labor and by right impossible; he makes us believe that this equality, the law of the world, is unjust among men; and then he proscribes us en masse for not having known how to practise his incomprehensible precepts! I believe I have proved, to be sure, that our abandonment by Providence does not justify us; but, whatever our crime, toward it we are not guilty; and if there is a being who, before ourselves and more than ourselves, is deserving of hell, — I am bound to name him, — it is God.

When the theists, in order to establish their dogma of Providence, cite the order of nature as a proof, although this argument is only a begging of the question, at least it cannot be said that it involves a contradiction, and that the fact cited bears witness against the hypothesis. In the system of the world, for instance, nothing betrays the smallest anomaly, the slightest lack of foresight, from which any prejudice whatever can be drawn against the idea of a supreme, intelligent, personal motor. In short, though the order of nature does not prove the reality of a Providence, it does not contradict it.

It is a very different thing with the government of humanity. Here order does not appear at the same time as matter; it was not created, as in the system of the world, once and for eternity. It is gradually developed according to an inevitable series of principles and consequences which the human being himself, the being to be ordered, must disengage spontaneously, by his own energy and at the solicitation of experience. No revelation regarding this is given him. Man is submitted at his origin to a preestablished necessity, to an absolute and irresistible order. That this order may be realized, man must discover it; that it may exist, he must have divined it. This labor of invention might be abridged; no one, either in heaven or on earth, will come to man's aid; no one will instruct him. Humanity, for hundreds of centuries, will devour its generations; it will exhaust itself in blood and mire, without the God whom it worships coming once to illuminate its reason and abridge its time of trial. Where is divine action here? Where is Providence?

"If God did not exist," — it is Voltaire, the enemy of religions, who says so, — "it would be necessary to invent him. " Why? "Because," adds the same Voltaire, "if I were dealing with an atheist prince whose interest it might be to have me pounded in a mortar, I am very sure that I should be pounded." Strange aberration of a great mind! And if you were dealing with a pious prince, whose confessor, speaking in the name of God, should command that you be burned alive, would you not be very sure of being burned also? Do you forget, then, anti-Christ, the Inquisition, and the Saint Bartholomew, and the stakes of Vanini and Bruno, and the tortures of Galileo, and the martyrdom of so many free thinkers? Do not try to distinguish here between use and abuse: for I should reply to you that from a mystical and supernatural principle, from a principle which embraces everything, which explains everything, which justifies everything, such as the idea of God, all consequences are legitimate, and that the zeal of the believer is the sole judge of their propriety.

"I once believed," says Rousseau, "that it was possible to be an honest man and dispense with God; but I have recovered from that error." Fundamentally the same argument as that of Voltaire, the same justification of intolerance: Man does good and abstains from evil only through consideration of a Providence which watches over him; a curse on those who deny its existence! And, to cap the climax of absurdity, the man who thus seeks for our virtue the sanction of a Divinity who rewards and punishes is the same man who teaches the native goodness of man as a religious dogma.

And for my part I say: The first duty of man, on becoming intelligent and free, is to continually hunt the idea of God out of his mind and conscience. For God, if he exists, is essentially hostile to our nature, and we do not depend at all upon his authority. We arrive at knowledge in spite of him, at comfort in spite of him, at society in spite of him; every step we take in advance is a victory in which we crush Divinity.

Let it no longer be said that the ways of God are impenetrable. We have penetrated these ways, and there we have read in letters of blood the proofs of God's impotence, if not of his malevolence. My reason, long humiliated, is gradually rising to a level with the infinite; with time it will discover all that its inexperience hides from it; with time I shall be less and less a worker of misfortune, and by the light that I shall have acquired, by the perfection of my liberty, I shall purify myself, idealize my being, and become the chief of creation, the equal of God. A single moment of disorder which the Omnipotent might have prevented and did not prevent accuses his Providence and shows him lacking in wisdom; the slightest progress which man, ignorant, abandoned, and betrayed, makes towards good honors him immeasurably. By what right should God still say to me: Be holy, for I am holy? Lying spirit, I will answer him, imbecile God, your reign is over; look to the beasts for other victims. I know that I am not holy and never can become so; and how could you be holy, if I resemble you? Eternal father, Jupiter or Jehovah, we have learned to know you; you are, you were, you ever will be, the jealous rival of Adam, the tyrant of Prometheus.

So I do not fall into the sophism refuted by St. Paul, when he forbids the vase to say to the potter: Why hast thou made me thus? I do not blame the author of things for having made me an inharmonious creature, an incoherent assemblage; I could exist only in such a condition. I content myself with crying out to him: Why do you deceive me? Why, by your silence, have you unchained egoism within me? Why have you submitted me to the torture of universal doubt by the bitter illusion of the antagonistic ideas which you have put in my mind? Doubt of truth, doubt of justice, doubt of my conscience and my liberty, doubt of yourself, O God! and, as a result of this doubt, necessity of war with myself and with my neighbor! That, supreme Father, is what you have done for our happiness and your glory; such, from the beginning, have been your will and your government; such the bread, kneaded in blood and tears, upon which you have fed us. The sins which we ask you to forgive, you caused us to commit; the traps from which we implore you to deliver us, you set for us; and the Satan who besets us is yourself.

You triumphed, and no one dared to contradict you, when, after having tormented in his body and in his soul the righteous Job, a type of our humanity, you insulted his candid piety, his prudent and respectful ignorance. We were as naught before your invisible majesty, to whom we gave the sky for a canopy and the earth for a footstool. And now here you are dethroned and broken. Your name, so long the last word of the savant, the sanction of the judge, the force of the prince, the hope of the poor, the refuge of the repentant sinner, — this incommunicable name, I say, henceforth an object of contempt and curses, shall be a hissing among men. For God is stupidity and cowardice; God is hypocrisy and falsehood; God is tyranny and misery; God is evil. As long as humanity shall bend before an altar, humanity, the slave of kings and priests, will be condemned; as long as one man, in the name of God, shall receive the oath of another man, society will be founded on perjury; peace and love will be banished from among mortals. God, take yourself away! for, from this day forth, cured of your fear and become wise, I swear, with hand extended to heaven, that you are only the tormentor of my reason, the spectre of my conscience.

I deny, therefore, the supremacy of God over humanity; I reject his providential government, the non-existence of which is sufficiently established by the metaphysical and economical hallucinations of humanity, — in a word, by the martyrdom of our race; I decline the jurisdiction of the Supreme Being over man; I take away his titles of father, king, judge, good, merciful, pitiful, helpful, rewarding, and avenging. All these attributes, of which the idea of Providence is made up, are but a caricature of humanity, irreconcilable with the autonomy of civilization, and contradicted, moreover, by the history of its aberrations and catastrophes. Does it follow, because God can no longer be conceived as Providence, because we take from him that attribute so important to man that he has not hesitated to make it the synonym of God, that God does not exist, and that the theological dogma from this moment is shown to be false in its content?

Alas! no. A prejudice relative to the divine essence has been destroyed; by the same stroke the independence of man is established: that is all. The reality of the divine Being is left intact, and our hypothesis still exists. In demonstrating that it was impossible for God to be Providence, we have taken a first step in the determination of the idea of God; the question now is to find out whether this first datum accords with the rest of the hypothesis, and consequently to determine, from the same standpoint of intelligence, what God is, if he is.

For just as, after having established the guilt of man under the influence of the economical contradictions, we have had to account for this guilt, if we would not leave man wounded after having made him a contemptible satire, likewise, after having admitted the chimerical nature of the doctrine of a Providence in God, we must inquire how this lack of Providence harmonizes with the idea of sovereign intelligence and liberty, if we would not sacrifice the proposed hypothesis, which nothing yet shows to be false.

I affirm, then, that God, if there is a God, does not resemble the effigies which philosophers and priests have made of him; that he neither thinks nor acts according to the law of analysis, foresight, and progress, which is the distinctive characteristic of man; that, on the contrary, he seems rather to follow an inverse and retrogressive course; that intelligence, liberty, personality in God are constituted not as in us; and that this originality of nature, perfectly accounted for, makes God an essentially anti-civilizing, anti-liberal, anti-human being.

I prove my proposition by going from the negative to the positive, — that is, by deducing the truth of my thesis from the progress of the objections to it.

1. God, say the believers, can be conceived only as infinitely good, infinitely wise, infinitely powerful, etc., — the whole litany of the infinites. Now, infinite

perfection cannot be reconciled with the datum of a will holding an indifferent or even reactionary attitude toward progress: therefore, either God does not exist, or the objection drawn from the development of the antinomies proves only our ignorance of the mysteries of infinity.

I answer these reasoners that, if, to give legitimacy to a wholly arbitrary opinion, it suffices to fall back on the unfathomability of mysteries, I am as well satisfied with the mystery of a God without providence as with that of a Providence without efficacy. But, in view of the facts, there is no occasion to invoke such a consideration of probability; we must confine ourselves to the positive declaration of experience. Now, experience and facts prove that humanity, in its development, obeys an inflexible necessity, whose laws are made clear and whose system is realized as fast as the collective reason reveals it, without anything in society to give evidence of an external instigation, either from a providential command or from any superhuman thought. The basis of the belief in Providence is this necessity itself, which is, as it were, the foundation and essence of collective humanity. But this necessity, thoroughly systematic and progressive as it may appear, does not on that account constitute providence either in humanity or in God; to become convinced thereof it is enough to recall the endless oscillations and painful gropings by which social order is made manifest.

2. Other arguers come unexpectedly across our path, and cry: What is the use of these abstruse researches? There is no more an infinite intelligence than a Providence; there is neither me nor will in the universe outside of man. All that happens, evil as well as good, happens necessarily. An irresistible ensemble of causes and effects embraces man and nature in the same fatality; and those faculties in ourselves which we call conscience, will, judgment, etc., are only particular accidents of the eternal, immutable, and inevitable whole.

This argument is the preceding one inverted. It consists in substituting for the idea of an omnipotent and omniscient author that of a necessary and eternal, but unconscious and blind, coordination. From this opposition we can already form a presentiment that the reasoning of the materialists is no firmer than that of the believers.

Whoever says necessity or fatality says absolute and inviolable order; whoever, on the contrary, says disturbance and disorder affirms that which is most repugnant to fatality. Now, there is disorder in the world, disorder produced by the play of spontaneous forces which no power enchains: how can that be, if everything is the result of fate?

But who does not see that this old quarrel between theism and materialism proceeds from a false notion of liberty and fatality, two terms which have been considered contradictory, though really they are not. If man is free, says the one party, all the more surely is God free too, and fatality is but a word; if everything is enchained in nature, answers the other party, there is neither liberty nor Providence: and so each party argues in its own direction till out of sight, never able to understand that this pretended opposition of liberty and fatality is only the natural, but not antithetical, distinction between the facts of activity and those of intelligence.

Fatality is the absolute order, the law, the code, fatum, of the constitution of the universe. But this code, very far from being exclusive in itself of the idea of a sovereign legislator, supposes it so naturally that all antiquity has not hesitated to admit it; and today the whole question is to find out whether, as the founders of religions have believed, the legislator preceded the law in the universe, — that is, whether intelligence is prior to fatality, — or whether, as the moderns claim, the law preceded the legislator, — in other words, whether mind is born of nature. BEFORE or AFTER, this alternative sums up all philosophy. To dispute over the posteriority or priority of mind is all very well, but to deny mind in the name of fatality is an exclusion which nothing justifies. To refute it, it is sufficient to recall the very fact on which it is based, — the existence of evil.

Given matter and attraction, the system of the world is their product: that is fatal. Given two correlative and contradictory ideas, a composition must follow: that also is fatal. Fatality clashes, not with liberty, whose destiny, on the contrary, is to secure the accomplishment of fatality within a certain sphere, but with disorder, with everything that acts as a barrier to the execution of the law. Is there disorder in the world, yes or no? The fatalists do not deny it, for, by the strangest blunder, it is the presence of evil which has made them fatalists. Now, I say that the presence of evil, far from giving evidence of fatality, breaks fatality, does violence to destiny, and supposes a cause whose erroneous but voluntary initiative is in discordance with the law. This cause I call liberty; and I have proved, in the fourth chapter, that liberty, like reason which serves man as a torch, is as much greater and more perfect as it harmonizes more completely with the order of nature, which is fatality.

Therefore to oppose fatality to the testimony of the conscience which feels itself free, and vice versa, is to prove that one misconstrues ideas and has not the slightest appreciation of the question. The progress of humanity may be defined as the education of reason and human liberty by fatality: it is absurd to regard these three terms as exclusive of each other and irreconcilable, when in reality they sustain each other, fatality serving as the base, reason coming after, and liberty crowning the edifice. It is to know and penetrate fatality that human reason tends; it is to conform to it that liberty aspires; and the criticism in which we are now engaged of the spontaneous development and instinctive beliefs of the human race is at bottom only a study of fatality. Let us explain this.

Man, endowed with activity and intelligence, has the power to disturb the order of the world, of which he forms a part. But all his digressions have been foreseen, and are effected within certain limits, which, after a certain number of goings and comings, lead man back to order. From these oscillations of liberty may be determined the role of humanity in the world; and, since the destiny of man is bound up with that of creatures, it is possible to go back from him to the supreme law of things and even to the sources of being.

Accordingly I will no longer ask: How is it that man has the power to violate the providential order, and how is it that Providence allows him to do so? I state the question in other terms: How is it that man, an integrant part of the universe, a product of fatality, is able to break fatality? How is it that a fatal organization, the organization of humanity, is adventitious, contradictory, full of tumult and catastrophes? Fatality is not confined to an hour, to a century, to a thousand years: if science and liberty must inevitably be ours, why do they not come sooner? For, the moment we suffer from the delay, fatality contradicts itself; evil is as exclusive of fatality as of Providence.

What sort of a fatality, in short, is that which is contradicted every instant by the facts which take place within its bosom? This the fatalists are bound to explain, quite as much as the theists are bound to explain what sort of an infinite intelligence that can be which is unable either to foresee or prevent the misery of its creatures.

But that is not all. Liberty, intelligence, fatality, are at bottom three adequate expressions, serving to designate three different faces of being. In man reason is only a defined liberty conscious of its limit. But within the circle of its limitations this liberty is also fatality, a living and personal fatality. When, therefore, the conscience of the human race proclaims that the fatality of the universe — that is, the highest, the supreme fatality — is adequate to an infinite reason as well as to an infinite liberty, it simply puts forth an hypothesis in every way legitimate, the verification of which is incumbent upon all parties.

3. Now come the humanists, the new atheists, and say:

Humanity in its ensemble is the reality sought by the social genius under the mystical name of God. This phenomenon of the collective reason, — a sort of mirage in which humanity, contemplating itself, takes itself for an external and transcendent being who considers its destinies and presides over them, — this illusion of the conscience, we say, has been analyzed and explained; and henceforth to reproduce the theological hypothesis is to take a step backward in science. We must confine ourselves strictly to society, to man. God in religion, the State in politics, property in economy, such is the triple form under which humanity, become foreign to itself, has not ceased to rend itself with its own hands, and which today it must reject.

I admit that every affirmation or hypothesis of Divinity proceeds from anthropomorphism, and that God in the first place is only the ideal, or rather, the spectre of man. I admit further that the idea of God is the type and foundation of the principle of authority and absolutism, which it is our task to destroy or at least to subordinate wherever it manifests itself, in science, industry, public affairs. Consequently I do not contradict humanism; I continue it. Taking up its criticism of the divine being and applying it to man, I observe:

That man, in adoring himself as God, has posited of himself an ideal contrary to his own essence, and has declared himself an antagonist of the being supposed to be sovereignly perfect, — in short, of the infinite;

That man consequently is, in his own judgment, only a false divinity, since in setting up God he denies himself; and that humanism is a religion as detestable as any of the theisms of ancient origin;

That this phenomenon of humanity taking itself for God is not explainable in the terms of humanism, and requires a further interpretation.

God, according to the theological conception, is not only sovereign master of the universe, the infallible and irresponsible king of creatures, the intelligible type of man; he is the eternal, immutable, omnipresent, infinitely wise, infinitely free being. Now, I say that these attributes of God contain more than an ideal, more than an elevation — to whatever power you will — of the corresponding attributes of humanity; I say that they are a contradiction of them. God is contradictory of man, just as charity is contradictory of justice; as sanctity, the ideal of perfection, is contradictory of perfectibility; as royalty, the ideal of legislative power, is contradictory of law, etc. So that the divine hypothesis is reborn from its resolution into human reality, and the problem of a complete, harmonious, and absolute existence, ever put aside, ever comes back.

To demonstrate this radical antinomy it suffices to put facts in juxtaposition with definitions.

Of all facts the most certain, most constant, most indubitable, is certainly that in man knowledge is progressive, methodical, the result of reflection, — in short, experimental; so much so that every theory not having the sanction of experience — that is, of constancy and concatenation in its representations — thereby lacks a scientific character. In regard to this not the slightest doubt can be raised. Mathematics themselves, though called pure, are subject to the CONCATENATION of propositions, and hence depend upon experience and acknowledge its law.

Man's knowledge, starting with acquired observation, then progresses and advances in an unlimited sphere. The goal which it has in view, the ideal which it tends to realize without ever being able to attain it, — placing it on the contrary farther and farther ahead of it, — is the infinite, the absolute.

Now, what would be an infinite knowledge, an absolute knowledge, determining an equally infinite liberty, such as speculation supposes in God? It would be a knowledge not only universal, but intuitive, spontaneous, as thoroughly free from hesitation as from objectivity, although embracing at once the real and the possible; a knowledge sure, but not demonstrative; complete, not sequential; a knowledge, in short, which, being eternal in its formation, would be destitute of any progressive character in the relation of its parts.

Psychology has collected numerous examples of this mode of knowing in the instinctive and divinatory faculties of animals; in the spontaneous talent of certain men born mathematicians and artists, independent of all education; finally, in most of the primitive human institutions and monuments, products of unconscious genius independent of theories. And the regular and complex movements of the heavenly bodies; the marvellous combinations of matter, — could it not be said that these too are the effects of a special instinct, inherent in the elements?

If, then, God exists, something of him appears to us in the universe and in ourselves: but this something is in flagrant opposition with our most authentic tendencies, with our most certain destiny; this something is continually being effaced from our soul by education, and to make it disappear is the object of our care. God and man are two natures which shun each other as soon as they know each other; in the absence of a transformation of one or the other or both, how could they ever be reconciled? If the progress of reason tends to separate us from Divinity, how could God and man be identical in point of reason? How, consequently, could humanity become God by education?

Let us take another example.

The essential characteristic of religion is feeling. Hence, by religion, man attributes feeling to God, as he attributes reason to him; moreover, he affirms, following the ordinary course of his ideas, that feeling in God, like knowledge, is infinite.

Now, that alone is sufficient to change the quality of feeling in God, and make it an attribute totally distinct from that of man. In man sentiment flows, so to speak, from a thousand different sources: it contradicts itself, it confuses itself, it rends itself; otherwise, it would not feel itself. In God, on the contrary, sentiment is infinite, — that is, one, complete, fixed, clear, above all storms, and not needing irritation as a contrast in order to arrive at happiness. We ourselves experience this divine mode of feeling when a single sentiment, absorbing all our faculties, as in the case of ecstasy, temporarily imposes silence upon the other affections. But this rapture exists always only by the aid of contrast and by a sort of provocation from without; it is never perfect, or, if it reaches fulness, it is like the star which attains its apogee, for an indivisible instant.

Thus we do not live, we do not feel, we do not think, except by a series of oppositions and shocks, by an internal warfare; our ideal, then, is not infinity, but equilibrium; infinity expresses something other than ourselves.

It is said: God has no attributes peculiar to himself; his attributes are those of man; then man and God are one and the same thing.

On the contrary, the attributes of man, being infinite in God, are for that very reason peculiar and specific: it is the nature of the infinite to become speciality, essence, from the fact that the finite exists. Deny then, if you will, the reality of God, as one denies the reality of a contradictory idea; reject from science and morality this inconceivable and bloody phantom which seems to pursue us the more, the farther it gets from us; up to a certain point that may be justified, and at any rate can do no harm. But do not make God into humanity, for that would be slander of both.

Will it be said that the opposition between man and the divine being is illusory, and that it arises from the opposition that exists between the individual man and the essence of entire humanity? Then it must be maintained that humanity, since it is humanity that they deify, is neither progressive, nor contrasted in reason and feeling; in short, that it is infinite in everything, — which is denied not only by history, but by psychology.

This is not a correct understanding, cry the humanists. To have the right ideal of humanity, it must be considered, not in its historic development, but in the totality of its manifestations, as if all human generations, gathered into one moment, formed a single man, an infinite and immortal man.

That is to say, they abandon the reality to seize a projection; the true man is not the real man; to find the veritable man, the human ideal, we must leave time and enter eternity, — what do I say? — desert the finite for infinity, man for God! Humanity, in the shape we know it, in the shape in which it is developed, in the only shape in fact in which it can exist, is erect; they show us its reversed image, as in a mirror, and then say to us: That is man! And I answer: It is no longer man, it is God. Humanism is the most perfect theism.

What, then, is this providence which the theists suppose in God? An essentially human faculty, an anthropomorphic attribute, by which God is thought to look into the future according to the progress of events, in the same way that we men look into the past, following the perspective of chronology and history.

Now, it is plain that, just as infinity — that is, spontaneous and universal intuition in knowledge — is incompatible with humanity, so providence is incompatible with the hypothesis of the divine being. God, to whom all ideas are equal and simultaneous; God, whose reason does not separate synthesis from antinomy; God, to whom eternity renders all things present and contemporary, — was unable, when creating us, to reveal to us the mystery of our contradictions; and that precisely because he is God, because he does not see contradiction, because his intelligence does not fall under the category of time and the law of progress, because his reason is intuitive and his knowledge infinite. Providence in God is a contradiction within a contradiction; it was through providence that God was actually made in the image of man; take away this providence, and God ceases to be man, and man in turn must abandon all his pretensions to divinity.

Perhaps it will be asked of what use it is to God to have infinite knowledge, if he is ignorant of what takes place in humanity.

Let us distinguish. God has a perception of order, the sentiment of good. But this order, this good, he sees as eternal and absolute; he does not see it in its successive and imperfect aspects; he does not grasp its defects. We alone are capable of seeing, feeling, and appreciating evil, as well as of measuring duration, because we alone are capable of producing evil, and because our life is temporary. God sees and feels only order; God does not grasp what happens, because what happens is beneath him, beneath his horizon. We, on the contrary, see at once the good and the evil, the temporal and the eternal, order and disorder, the finite and the infinite; we see within us and outside of us; and our reason, because it is finite, surpasses our horizon.

Thus, by the creation of man and the development of society, a finite and providential reason, our own, has been posited in contradiction of the intuitive and infinite reason, God; so that God, without losing anything of his infinity in any direction, seems diminished by the very fact of the existence of humanity. Progressive reason resulting from the projection of eternal ideas upon the movable and inclined plane of time, man can understand the language of God, because he comes from God and his reason at the start is like that of God; but God cannot understand us or come to us, because he is infinite and cannot re-clothe himself in finite attributes without ceasing to be God, without destroying himself. The dogma of providence in God is shown to be false, both in fact and in right.

It is easy now to see how the same reasoning turns against the system of the deification of man.

Man necessarily positing God as absolute and infinite in his attributes, whereas he himself develops in a direction the inverse of this ideal, there is discord between the progress of man and what man conceives as God. On the one hand, it appears that man, by the syncretism of his constitution and the perfectibility of his nature, is not God and cannot become God; on the other, it is plain that God, the supreme Being, is the antipode of humanity, the ontological summit from which it indefinitely separates itself. God and man, having divided between them the antagonistic faculties of being, seem to be playing a game in which the control of the universe is the stake, the one having spontaneity, directness, infallibility, eternity, the other having foresight, deduction, mobility, time. God and man hold each other in perpetual check and continually avoid each other; while the latter goes ahead in reflection and theory without ever resting, the former, by his providential incapacity, seems to withdraw into the spontaneity of his nature. There is a contradiction, therefore, between humanity and its ideal, an opposition between man and God, an opposition which Christian theology has allegorized and personified under the name of Devil or Satan, — that is, contradictor, enemy of God and man.

Such is the fundamental antinomy which I find that modern critics have not taken into account, and which, if neglected, having sooner or later to end in the negation of the man-God and consequently in the negation of this whole philosophical exegesis, reopens the door to religion and fanaticism.

God, according to the humanists, is nothing but humanity itself, the collective me to which the individual me is subjected as to an invisible master. But why this singular vision, if the portrait is a faithful copy of the original? Why has man, who from his birth has known directly and with out a telescope his body, his soul, his chief, his priest, his country, his condition, been obliged to see himself as in a mirror, and without recognizing himself, under the fantastic image of God? Where is the necessity of this hallucination? What is this dim and ambiguous consciousness which, after a certain time, becomes purified, rectified, and, instead of taking itself for another, definitively apprehends itself as such? Why on the part of man this transcendental confession of society, when society itself was there, present, visible, palpable, willing, and acting, — when, in short, it was known as society and named as such?

No, it is said, society did not exist; men were agglomerated, but not associated; the arbitrary constitution of property and the State, as well as the intolerant dogmatism of religion, prove it.

Pure rhetoric: society exists from the day that individuals, communicating by labor and speech, assume reciprocal obligations and give birth to laws and customs. Undoubtedly society becomes perfect in proportion to the advances of science and economy, but at no epoch of civilization does progress imply any such metamorphosis as those dreamed of by the builders of utopia; and however excellent the future condition of humanity is to be, it will be none the less the natural continuation, the necessary consequence, of its previous positions.

For the rest, no system of association being exclusive in itself, as I have shown, of fraternity and justice, it has never been possible to confound the political ideal with God, and we see in fact that all peoples have distinguished society from religion. The first was taken as end, the second regarded only as means; the prince was the minister of the collective will, while God reigned over consciences, awaiting beyond the grave the guilty who escaped the justice of men. Even the idea of progress and reform has never been anywhere absent; nothing, in short, of that which constitutes social life has been entirely ignored or misconceived by any religious nation. Why, then, once more, this tautology of Society-Divinity, if it is true, as is pretended, that the theological hypothesis contains nothing other than the ideal of human society, the preconceived type of humanity transfigured by equality, solidarity, labor, and love?

Certainly, if there is a prejudice, a mysticism, which now seems to me deceptive in a high degree, it is no longer Catholicism, which is disappearing, but rather this humanitary philosophy, making man a holy and sacred being on the strength of a speculation too learned not to have something of the arbitrary in its composition; proclaiming him God, — that is, essentially good and orderly in all his powers, in spite of the disheartening evidence which he continually gives of his doubtful morality; attributing his vices to the constraint in which he has lived, and promising from him in complete liberty acts of the purest devotion, because in the myths in which humanity, according to this philosophy, has painted itself, we find described and opposed to each other, under the names of hell and paradise, a time of constraint and penalty and an era of happiness and independence! With such a doctrine it would suffice — and moreover it would be inevitable — for man to recognize that he is neither God, nor good, nor holy, nor wise, in order to fall back immediately into the arms of religion; so that in the last analysis all that the world will have gained by the denial of God will be the resurrection of God.

Such is not my view of the meaning of the religious fables. Humanity, in recognizing God as its author, its master, its alter ego, has simply determined its own essence by an antithesis, — an eclectic essence, full of contrasts, emanated from the infinite and contradictory of the infinite, developed in time and aspiring to eternity, and for all these reasons fallible, although guided by the sentiment of beauty and order. Humanity is the daughter of God, as every opposition is the daughter of a previous position: that is why humanity has formed God like itself, has lent him its own attributes, but always by giving them a specific character, — that is, by defining God in contradiction of itself. Humanity is a spectre to God, just as God is a spectre to humanity; each of the two is the other's cause, reason, and end of existence.

It was not enough, then, to have demonstrated, by criticism of religious ideas, that the conception of the divine me leads back to the perception of the human me; it was also necessary to verify this deduction by a criticism of humanity itself, and to see whether this humanity satisfies the conditions that its apparent divinity supposes. Now, such is the task that we solemnly inaugurated when, starting at once with human reality and the divine hypothesis, we began to unroll the history of society in its economic institutions and speculative thoughts.

We have shown, on the one hand, that man, although incited by the antagonism of his ideas, and although up to a certain point excusable, does evil gratuitously and by the bestial impulse of his passions, which are repugnant to the character of a free, intelligent, and holy being. We have shown, on the other hand, that the nature of man is not harmoniously and synthetically constituted, but formed by an agglomeration of the potentialities specialized in each creature, — a circumstance which, in revealing to us the principle of the disorders committed by human liberty, has finished the demonstration of the non-divinity of our race. Finally, after having proved that in God providence not only does not exist, but is impossible; after having, in other words, separated the divine attributes of the infinite Being from the anthropomorphic attributes, — we have concluded, contrary to the affirmations of the old theodicy, that, relatively to the destiny of man, a destiny essentially progressive, intelligence and liberty in God suffered a contrast, a sort of limitation and diminution, resulting from his eternal, immutable, and infinite nature; so that man, instead of adoring in God his sovereign and his guide, could and should look on him only as his antagonist. And this last consideration will suffice to make us reject humanism also, as tending invincibly, by the deification of humanity, to a religious restoration. The true remedy for fanaticism, in our view, is not to identify humanity with God, which amounts to affirming, in social economy communism, in philosophy mysticism and the statu quo; it is to prove to humanity that God, in case there is a God, is its enemy.

What solution will result later from these data? Will God, in the end, be found to be a reality?

I do not know whether I shall ever know. If it is true, on the one hand, that I have today no more reason for affirming the reality of man, an illogical and contradictory being, than the reality of God, an inconceivable and unmanifested being, I know at least, from the radical opposition of these two natures, that I have nothing to hope or to fear from the mysterious author whom my consciousness involuntarily supposes; I know that my most authentic tendencies separate me daily from the contemplation of this idea; that practical atheism must be hence-forth the law of my heart and my reason; that from observable necessity I must continually learn the rule of my conduct; that any mystical commandment, any divine right, which should be proposed to me, must be rejected and combatted by me; that a return to God through religion, idleness, ignorance, or submission, is an outrage upon myself; and that if I must sometime be reconciled with God, this reconciliation, impossible as long as I live and in which I should have everything to gain and nothing to lose, can be accomplished only by my destruction.

Let us then conclude, and inscribe upon the column which must serve as a landmark in our later researches:

The legislator distrusts man, an abridgment of nature and a syncretism of all beings. He does not rely on Providence, an inadmissible faculty in the infinite mind.

But, attentive to the succession of phenomena, submissive to the lessons of destiny, he seeks in necessity the law of humanity, the perpetual prophecy of his future.

He remembers also, sometimes, that, if the sentiment of Divinity is growing weaker among men; if inspiration from above is gradually withdrawing to give place to the deductions of experience; if there is a more and more flagrant separation of man and God; if this progress, the form and condition of our life, escapes the perceptions of an infinite and consequently non-historic intelligence; if, to say it all, appeal to Providence on the part of a government is at once a cowardly hypocrisy and a threat against liberty, — nevertheless the universal consent of the peoples, manifested by the establishment of so many different faiths, and the forever insoluble contradiction which strikes humanity in its ideas, its manifestations, and its tendencies indicate a secret relation of our soul, and through it of entire nature, with the infinite, — a relation the determination of which would express at the same time the meaning of the universe and the reason of our existence.

Pierre-Joseph Proudhon
System of Economical Contradictions: or, The Philosophy of Poverty
1847

Pierre-Joseph Proudhon
System of Economical Contradictions: or, The Philosophy of Poverty
Written: 1847
Source: Rod Hay's Archive for the History of Economic Thought, McMaster University, Canada
Translated from the French by Benjamin R. Tucker. 1888
HTML Markup: Andy Blunden
Retrieved on March 25, 2011 from **www.marxists.org**

LargePrintLiberty.com

Dedicated to offering books on libertarian thought and economics in Large Print paperback.

Titles include:

For a New Liberty, by Murray N. Rothbard (Philosophy)
"A classic that for over two decades has been hailed as the best general work on libertarianism available. Rothbard begins with a quick overview of its historical roots, and then goes on to define libertarianism as resting 'upon one single axiom: that no man or group of men shall aggress upon the person or property of anyone else.' He writes a withering critique of the chief violator of liberty: the State. Rothbard then provides penetrating libertarian solutions for many of today's most pressing problems, including poverty, war, threats to civil liberties, the education crisis, and more."

Principles of Economics, by Carl Menger (Economics)
"In the beginning, there was Menger. It was this book that reformulated, and really rescued, economic science. It kicked off the Marginalist Revolution, which corrected theoretical errors of the old classical school. These errors concerned value theory, and they had sown enough confusion to make the dangerous ideology of Marxism seem more plausible than it really was. Menger set out to elucidate the precise nature of economic value, and root economics firmly in the real-world actions of individual human beings."

Great Wars and Great Leaders, by Ralph Raico (History)
"In the backdrop of this blistering and deeply insightful and scholarly history is the whitewashing of 'great leaders' like Woodrow Wilson, Winston Churchill, FDR, Truman, Stalin, Trotsky, and other collectivists. They are highly regarded because they were on the 'right side' of the rise of the state. But do they deserve adulation? Raico says no: these great leaders were main agents in the decline of civilization in the 20th century, all of them anti-liberals who used their power to celebrate and enhance state power."